Rob,
I hope you enjoy
This scientific and non-scientific
book about the Arctic —

- Erik

ARCTIC DREAMS

Barry Lopez

ARCTIC

DREAMS

Imagination and Desire
in a Northern Landscape

CHARLES SCRIBNER'S SONS · *NEW YORK*

Copyright © 1986 Barry Holstun Lopez

Library of Congress Cataloging-in-Publication Data

Lopez, Barry Holstun, 1945–
Arctic dreams.

Bibliography: p.
Includes index.
1. Natural history—Arctic regions. 2. Arctic
regions—Description and travel. 3. Arctic regions—
Discovery and exploration. I. Title.
QH84.1.L67 1986   508.98   85–24979
ISBN 0–684–18578–4

Published simultaneously in Canada
by Collier Macmillan Canada, Inc.
Copyright under the Berne Convention.

1 3 5 7 9 11 13 15 17 19 F/C 20 18 16 14 12 10 8 6 4 2

Printed in the United States of America.

Book design by Joel Schick
Maps by David Lindroth

Grateful acknowledgment is made to quote from "The Field of the Caribou,"
copyright © 1966 by John Haines, reprinted from Winter News *by*
permission of Wesleyan University Press.

For
Sandra

The landscape conveys an impression of absolute permanence. It is not hostile. It is simply there—untouched, silent and complete. It is very lonely, yet the absence of all human traces gives you the feeling you understand this land and can take your place in it.

EDMUND CARPENTER

Once in his life a man ought to concentrate his mind upon the remembered earth. He ought to give himself up to a particular landscape in his experience; to look at it from as many angles as he can, to wonder upon it, to dwell upon it.

He ought to imagine that he touches it with his hands at every season and listens to the sounds that are made upon it.

He ought to imagine the creatures there and all the faintest motions of the wind. He ought to recollect the glare of the moon and the colors of the dawn and dusk.

N. SCOTT MOMADAY

CONTENTS

ACKNOWLEDGMENTS   xiii

AUTHOR'S NOTE   xvii

PREFACE   xix

Prologue: Pond's Bay, Baffin Island   1

1. Arktikós   15

2. Banks Island: *Ovibos moschatus*   42

3. Tôrnârssuk: *Ursus maritimus*   76

4. Lancaster Sound: *Monodon monoceros*   119

5. Migration: The Corridors of Breath   152

6. Ice and Light   204

7. The Country of the Mind   252

8. The Intent of Monks   302

9. A Northern Passage   355

Epilogue: Saint Lawrence Island, Bering Sea   407

NOTES   417

MAPS   421

APPENDICES   427

BIBLIOGRAPHY   445

INDEX   449

ACKNOWLEDGMENTS

MY DEBTS are great. And my sense of gratitude, especially to those with whom I traveled in the Arctic, is very deep. First to Lloyd Lowry, Bob Nelson, and Kathy Frost, knowledgeable and sterling companions, whom I accompanied on coastal surveys in the Beaufort, Chukchi, and Bering seas. To Bob Stephenson, with whom I traveled extensively in Alaska: in the Brooks Range, in Nelchina Basin, on the upper Yukon, and to Saint Lawrence Island. To Kerry Finley, for his companionship and assistance in northern Baffin Island. To Don Ljungblad, who introduced me to the spring ice in Bering Sea and to bowhead whales. To Ray Schweinsburg, who introduced me to polar bears in the Canadian Archipelago. To Rick Will, Becky Cole, Shirleen Smith, and Bill Abercrombie, my companions on Banks Island; and Bruce Dinneford, my companion at Pingok Island.

I am indebted as well to the officers and men of the MV *Soodoc*, especially Master Pitt Schroter, Ice Master Niels Jorgensen, third mate Jean-Luc Bédard, and second engineer Andre Gill, for their accommodation and patience with my questions. I also wish to thank the officers and crew of the NOAA ship *Oceanographer* and the men working on the Panarctic Oils drill rigs "Cape Mamen" and "Whitefish," and at the Panarctic base camp at Rae Point, Melville Island, for their assistance and cordiality.

Several institutions provided extensive logistical support during periods of field research—the Alaska Department of Fish and

Game in the United States and, in Canada, Polar Continental Shelf Project, Department of Energy, Mines and Resources Canada; Wildlife Management Division, Department of Renewable Resources, Government of the Northwest Territories; and Atmospheric Environment Service, Department of Environment Canada. I would also like to thank the public relations staffs at Panarctic Oils, Sohio Alaska Petroleum Company, and Cominco for their help.

Without the support of Colin Crosbie of Crosbie Shipping I would not have been able to retrace the sea route of John Davis and William Parry. Without the assistance of George Hobson, Director of Polar Continental Shelf, and the willingness of pilot Duncan Grant to seemingly always make room, I could not have traveled as extensively as I was able to in the Canadian Archipelago. I thank each of them sincerely.

Many scientists gave unstintingly of their time in lengthy interviews. I would especially like to thank, in addition to those already mentioned, Anne Gunn, Kent Jingfors, Thor Larsen, Dennis Andriashek, John Burns, Mitch Taylor, Martha Robus, Cliff Hickey, Peter Schledermann, and Bob Janes. Christian Vibe, Frank Miller, Murray Newman, Rick Davis, James Helmer, Diane Lyons, Harriet Critchley, Poul Henrichsen, Greg Galik, Sam Luciani, and Guy Palmer also provided critical interviews.

I feel inadequate in trying to convey my sense of appreciation to the people of various native villages, for their deference and understanding in the face of my intrusion. Among those who were generous with their time I especially wish to pay my respects to George Noongwook, Vernon Slwooko, Alex Akeya, Bob Ahgook, Oolaiuk Nakitavak, and David Kalluk for invaluable interviews and experiences. Qujannamiik.

Often during my travels I was in need of a meal and a place to sleep. I would like to offer private words of gratitude to all who opened their homes to me.

Peter Schledermann generously provided library privileges and working space at the Arctic Institute of North America in

Calgary; Colleen Cabot provided a place to work at the Teton Science School, Kelly, Wyoming, during a critical period. Martin Antonetti and Kerry Finley helped with Latin and Inuktitut translation, respectively. Many individuals graciously answered requests for documents. I would especially like to acknowledge Arthur Credland of Kingston Upon Hull's Town Docks Museum for records of the whaling ship *Cumbrian*; Steve Amstrup, Malcolm Ramsay, and Gordon Stenhouse for material on polar bears; David Gray for material on muskoxen; Jim Levison for information about loons; Bud Fay for material on walrus; Anthony Higgins for data on Oodaaq Island; and Marty Grossman for information on Edward Israel.

I would like to express my personal and professional gratitude to Lewis Lapham at *Harper's*, Robley Wilson at *North American Review*, John Rasmus at *Outside*, and Paul Perry at *Running* for their support while I was at work on the manuscript.

Several people with whom I spoke only briefly were nevertheless instrumental in helping me clarify my ideas and intentions. I would like to express my appreciation for that reason to Ted Muraro, Maurice Haycock, Jørn Thomassen, Martin Luce, and Keith Quinlan.

Some of the ideas in this book grew out of conversations with friends little concerned, directly, with the Arctic. It is difficult to be precise about such debts, but they are no less real than those to a traveling companion. I would like to thank in this capacity Dick Showalter, Tony Beasley, and China Galland.

I owe a special debt of gratitude to Isabel Stirling, who helped me greatly as a research assistant and typist.

Finally, I wish to thank my editor, Laurie Schieffelin, and my agent, Peter Schults, for their faith during a long period of work and for their discerning reading of the manuscript at various stages.

And my wife, Sandra, whose mind and character and support, as always, were like shelter.

My deep and humble gratitude.

Author's Note

The scientific names of northern animals and plants, and geographic coordinates for named places in the North, are listed in the appendices. Bibliographic information is in the text itself, in footnotes, in the Notes section beginning on page 417, and in a selected bibliography on page 445, depending on where its appearance is most appropriate. Maps in the Maps section are cartographically accurate. Maps in the text are mostly simplified sketches and not drawn to scale. Eskimo terms, unless otherwise noted, are from the Inuktitut dialects of the eastern Canadian Arctic. Eskimo words in common English usage, such as "iglu" (house), "kayak," and "qamutiik" (sledge) are not italicized.

PREFACE

BEYOND A REGARD for the landscape itself, this book finds its origin in two moments.

One summer evening I was camped in the western Brooks Range of Alaska with a friend. From the ridge where we had pitched our tent we looked out over tens of square miles of rolling tundra along the southern edge of the calving grounds of the Western Arctic caribou herd. During those days we observed not only caribou and wolves, which we'd come to study, but wolverine and red fox, ground squirrels, delicate-legged whimbrels and aggressive jaegers, all in the unfoldings of their obscure lives. One night we watched in awe as a young grizzly bear tried repeatedly to force its way past a yearling wolf standing guard alone before a den of young pups. The bear eventually gave up and went on its way. We watched snowy owls and rough-legged hawks hunt and caribou drift like smoke through the valley.

On the evening I am thinking about—it was breezy there on Ilingnorak Ridge, and cold; but the late-night sun, small as a kite in the northern sky, poured forth an energy that burned against my cheekbones—it was on that evening that I went on a walk for the first time among the tundra birds. They all build their nests on the ground, so their vulnerability is extreme. I gazed down at a single horned lark no bigger than my fist. She stared back resolute as iron. As I approached, golden plovers abandoned their nests in hysterical ploys, artfully feigning a broken wing to distract me from the woven grass cups that couched their pale, darkly speckled eggs. Their eggs glowed with a soft, pure light, like the window light in a Vermeer painting. I marveled at this intense and concentrated beauty on the vast table of the plain. I walked on to find Lapland longspurs as still on their nests as stones, their dark eyes gleaming. At the nest of two snowy owls I stopped. These are more formidable animals than plovers. I stood motionless. The wild glare in their eyes receded. One owl settled back slowly over its three eggs, with an aura of primitive alertness. The other watched me, and immediately sought a bond with my eyes if I started to move.

I took to bowing on these evening walks. I would bow slightly with my hands in my pockets, toward the birds and the evidence of life in their nests—because of their fecundity, unexpected in this remote region, and because of the serene arctic light that came down over the land like breath, like breathing.

I remember the wild, dedicated lives of the birds that night and also the abandon with which a small herd of caribou crossed the Kokolik River to the northwest, the incident of only a few moments. They pranced through like wild mares, kicking up sheets of water across the evening sun and shaking it off on the far side like huge dogs, a bloom of spray that glittered in the air around them like grains of mica.

I remember the press of light against my face. The explosive skitter of calves among grazing caribou. And the warm intensity of the eggs beneath these resolute birds. Until then, perhaps because the sun was shining in the very middle of the night, so out of tune with my own customary perception, I had never known how benign sunlight could be. How forgiving. How run through with compassion in a land that bore so eloquently the evidence of centuries of winter.

During those summer days on Ilingnorak Ridge there was no dark night. Darkness never came. The birds were born. They flourished, and then flew south in the wake of the caribou.

The second incident is more fleeting. It occurred one night

when I was being driven past a graveyard in Kalamazoo, Michigan. Among the gravestones was one marking the burial place of Edward Israel, a shy young man who sailed north in 1881 with Lieutenant Adolphus Greely. Greely and his men established a base camp on Ellesmere Island, 450 miles from the North Pole, and explored the surrounding territory in the spring of 1882. A planned relief expedition failed to reach them that summer, and also failed again the next year. Desperate, Greely's party of twenty-five retreated south, hopeful of being met by a rescue party in 1884. They wintered at Cape Sabine, Ellesmere Island, where sixteen of them died of starvation and scurvy, another committed suicide, and one man was executed for stealing food. Israel, the expedition's astronomer, died on May 27, 1884, three weeks before the others were rescued. The survivors remembered him as the most congenial person among them.

I remember looking out the back window of the car that evening and seeing Israel's grave in the falling light. What had this man hoped to find? What sort of place did he think lay out there before him on that bright June morning in 1881 when the *Proteus* slipped its moorings at Saint John's, Newfoundland?

No one is able to say, of course. He was drawn on by the fixations of his own imagination, as were John Davis and William Baffin before him and as Robert Peary and Vilhjalmur Stefansson would be after him. Perhaps he intended to make his mark as a scientist, to set his teeth in that high arctic landscape and come home like Darwin to a sedate and contemplative life, in the farmlands of southern Michigan. Perhaps he merely hungered after the unusual. We can only imagine that he desired something, the fulfillment of some personal and private dream, to which he pinned his life.

Israel was buried with great public feeling and patriotic rhetoric. His gravestone reads

IN LIFE A TRUE CHILD OF GOD
IN DEATH A HERO

These two incidents came back to me often in the four or five years that I traveled in the Arctic. The one, timeless and full of light, reminded me of sublime innocence, of the innate beauty of undisturbed relationships. The other, a dream gone awry, reminded me of the long human struggle, mental and physical, to come to terms with the Far North. As I traveled, I came to believe that people's desires and aspirations were as much a part of the land as the wind, solitary animals, and the bright fields of stone and tundra. And, too, that the land itself existed quite apart from these.

The physical landscape is baffling in its ability to transcend whatever we would make if it. It is as subtle in its expression as turns of the mind, and larger than our grasp; and yet it is still knowable. The mind, full of curiosity and analysis, disassembles a landscape and then reassembles the pieces—the nod of a flower, the color of the night sky, the murmur of an animal—trying to fathom its geography. At the same time the mind is trying to find its place within the land, to discover a way to dispel its own sense of estrangement.

The particular section of the Arctic I became concerned with extends from Bering Strait in the west to Davis Strait in the east. It includes great, unrelieved stretches of snow and ice that in summer become plains of open water and an ocean that is the tundra, a tawny island beneath the sky. But there are, too, surprising and riveting sights: Wilberforce Falls on the Hood River suddenly tumbles 160 feet into a wild canyon in the midst of the Canadian tundra, and its roar can be heard for miles. Humboldt Glacier, a towering, 50-mile-long sea margin of the Greenland ice sheet, calves icebergs into Kane Basin with gargantuan and implacable force. The badlands of east-central Melville Island, an eroded country of desert oranges, of muted yellows and reds, reminds a traveler of canyons and arroyos in southern Utah. And there are places more exotic, like the Ruggles River, which flows out of Lake Hazen on Ellesmere Island in winter and runs 2000 feet through the Stygian darkness, wreathed in frost smoke, before it disappears underneath its own ice. South of Cape Bathurst and west of the Horton River in the Northwest Territories, bituminous shale fires that have been burning underground for hundreds of years make those coastal hills seem like a vast, smoldering heap of industrial slag. South of the central Kobuk River, one hundred foot dunes rise above hundreds of square miles of shifting sand. In East Greenland lies an arctic oasis called Queen Louisa Land, a valley of wild grasses and summer wildflowers surrounded by the walls of the Greenland ice cap.

The Arctic, overall, has the classic lines of a desert landscape: spare, balanced, extended, and quiet. In the Queen Elizabeth Islands the well-drained tundra plains and low-lying bogs more familiar in the south give way to expanses of weathered rock and gravel, and the illusion of a desert is even more complete. On Baffin and Ellesmere islands and in northern Alaska, sharply pitched arctic mountain ranges, which retain their remoteness even as you stand within them, complete a pervasive suggestion of austerity. The apparent monotony of the land is relieved, however, by weather systems moving through, and by the activities of animals, particularly of birds and caribou. And because so much of the country stands revealed, and because sunlight passing through the dustless air renders its edges with such unusual sharpness, animals linger before the eye. And their presence is vivid.

Like other landscapes that initially appear barren, arctic tundra can open suddenly, like the corolla of a flower, when any intimacy with it is sought. One begins to notice spots of brilliant red, orange, and green, for example, among the monotonic browns of a tundra tussock. A wolf spider lunges at a glistening beetle. A shred of muskox wool lies inert in the lavender blooms of a saxifrage. When Alwin Pederson, a Danish naturalist, first arrived on the northeast coast of Greenland, he wrote, "I must admit to strange feelings at the sight of this godforsaken desert of stone." Before he left, however, he was writing of muskoxen grazing in lush grass that grew higher than the animals' heads in Jameson Land, and of the stark beauty of nunataks, the ice-free spires of rock that pierce the Pleistocene stillness of the Greenland ice cap. I, like Pederson, when stooping to pick up the gracile rib bone of an arctic hare, would catch sudden and unexpected sight of the silken cocoon of an arctic caterpillar.

The wealth of biological detail on the tundra dispels any feeling that the land is empty; and its likeness to a stage suggests impending events. On a summer walk, the wind-washed air proves depthlessly clear. Time and again you come upon the isolated and succinct evidence of life—animal tracks, the undigested remains of a ptarmigan in an owl's casting, a patch of barren-ground willow nibbled nearly leafless by arctic hares. You are afforded the companionship of birds, which follow after you. (They know you are an animal; sooner or later you will turn up something to eat.) Sandpipers scatter before you, screaming *tuituek*, an Eskimo name for them. Coming awkwardly down a scree slope of frost-riven limestone you make a glass-tinkling clatter—and at a distance a tundra grizzly rises on its hind legs to study you; the dish-shaped paws of its front legs deathly still, the stance so human it is unnerving.

Along creek washouts, in the western Arctic especially, you might stumble upon a mammoth tusk. Or in the eastern Arctic find undisturbed the ring of stones used by a hunter 1500 years ago to hold down the edge of his skin tent. These old Dorset camps, located along the coasts where arctic people have been traveling for four millennia, are poignant with their suggestion of the timeless determination of mankind. On rare occasions a traveler might come upon the more imposing stone foundations of a large house abandoned by Thule-culture people in the twelfth century. (The cold, dry arctic air might have preserved, even down to its odor, the remains of a ringed seal killed and eaten by them 800 years ago.) More often, one comes upon the remains of a twentieth-century camp, artifacts far less engaging than a scrap of worked caribou bone, or carved wood, or skewered hide at a Dorset or Thule site. But these artifacts disintegrate just as slowly—red tins of Prince Albert brand crimp-cut tobacco, cans of Pet evaporated milk and Log Cabin maple syrup. In the most recent camps one finds used flashlight batteries in clusters like animal droppings, and a bewildering variety of spent rifle and shotgun ammunition.

You raise your eyes from these remains, from whatever century, to look away. The land as far as you can see is rung with a harmonious authority, the enduring force of its natural history, of which these camps are so much a part. But the most recent evidence is vaguely disturbing. It does not derive in any clear way from the land. Its claim to being part of the natural history of the region seems, somehow, false.

It is hard to travel in the Arctic today and not be struck by the evidence of recent change. What is found at modern campsites along the coast points to the sudden arrival of a foreign technology —new tools and a new way of life for the local people. The initial adjustments to this were fairly simple; the rate of change, however, has continued to accelerate. Now the adjustments required are bewildering. And the new tools bring with them ever more complicated sets of beliefs. The native culture, from Saint Lawrence Island to Greenland, is today in a state of rapid economic reorganization and of internally disruptive social readjustment. In a recent article about the residents of Nunivak Island, for example, a scientist wrote that the dietary shift from wild to store-bought foods (with the many nutritional and social complications involved) is proceeding so quickly it is impossible to pin down. "By the time this paper appears in print," he wrote, "much of the information in it will be of historical value only."

Industrial changes have also come to the Arctic, following the discovery of oil at Prudhoe Bay, Alaska, in 1968: the 800-mile-long trans-Alaska pipeline itself, with its recent Kuparuk extension; base camps for oil exploration on Canada's Melville Island and Tuktoyaktuk Peninsula; huge lead-zinc mining operations on northern Baffin and Little Cornwallis islands; hundreds of miles of new roads; and increased ship, air, and truck traffic. The region's normally violent and unpredictable weather, its extreme cold and long periods of darkness, the great distance to supply depots, and the problem of stabilizing permanent structures over permafrost (which melts and shifts in erratic ways) have made the cost of these operations astronomical—indeed, in Canada they could not even be contemplated without massive assistance from the federal government.

Seen as widely separated dots and lines on a map, these recent, radical changes do not appear to amount to very much. But their rippling effect in the settlements and villages of the North— their economic, psychological, and social impact—is acute. And their success, though marginal and in some instances artificial, encourages additional schemes for development.* Of special concern to local residents is a growing concentration of power in the

---

* For a summary of specific arctic problems, see note 1.

hands of people with enormous economic resources but a poorly developed geographic sense of the region. A man from Tuktoyaktuk, a village near the mouth of the Mackenzie River, told me a pointed story. In the 1950s he traveled regularly up and down the coast by dogsled. When a distant early warning (DEW) line radar station went up along his accustomed route, he decided to stop to see what it was. The military men welcomed him not as a resident of the region but as a figure of arctic fable. They enthusiastically fed his dogs a stack of raw steaks. Each time the man came, they pounded him on the back and fed his dogs piles of steak. Their largess seemed so odd and his rapport with them so unrealistic he stopped coming. For months afterward, however, he had tremendous difficulty controlling the dogs anytime they passed near the place.

Passing through the villages, even traveling across the uninhabited land, one cannot miss the evidence of upheaval, nor avoid being wrenched by it. The depression it engenders, because so much of it seems a heedless imposition on the land and on the people, a rude invasion, can lead one to despair. I brooded, like any traveler, over these things; but the presence of the land, the sheer weight of it before the senses, more often drew me away from the contemporary issues. What, I wondered, had compelled me to bow to a horned lark? How do people imagine the landscapes they find themselves in? How does the land shape the imaginations of the people who dwell in it? How does desire itself, the desire to comprehend, shape knowledge? These questions seemed to me to go deeper than the topical issues, to underlie any consideration of them.

In pursuit of answers I traveled with people of differing dispositions. With Eskimos hunting narwhals off northern Baffin Island and walruses in Bering Sea. With marine ecologists on hundreds of miles of coastal and near-shore surveys. With landscape painters in the Canadian Archipelago. In the company of roughnecks, drilling for oil on the winter ice in high winds at −30°F; and with the cosmopolitan crew of a freighter, sailing up the west coast of Greenland and into the Northwest Passage. They each assessed the land differently—the apparent emptiness of the tundra, which ran out like a shimmering mirage in the Northern Ocean; the blue-black vault of the winter sky, a cold beauty alive with scintillating stars; a herd of muskoxen, pivoting together on a hilltop to make a defensive stand, their long guard hairs swirling around them like a single, huge wave of dark water; a vein of lead-zinc ore glinting like tiny mirrors in a damp, Mesozoic wall beneath the surface of Little Cornwallis Island; the moaning and wailing in the winter sea ice as the ocean's crust warped and shattered in the crystalline air. All of it, all that the land is and evokes, its actual meaning as well as its metaphorical reverberation, was and is understood differently.

These different views make a human future in that northern landscape a matter of conjecture, and it is here that one encounters dreams, projections of hope. The individual's dream, whether it be so private a wish as that the joyful determination of nesting arctic birds might infuse a distant friend weary of life, or a magnanimous wish, that a piece of scientific information wrested from the landscape might serve one's community—in individual dreams is the hope that one's own life will not have been lived for nothing. The very much larger dream, that of a people, is a story we have been carrying with us for millennia. It is a narrative of determination and hope that follows a question: What will we do as the wisdom of our past bears down on our future? It is a story of ageless conversation, not only conversation among ourselves about what we mean and wish to do, but a conversation held with the land—our contemplation and wonder at a prairie thunderstorm, or before the jagged line of a young mountain, or at the sudden rise of ducks from an isolated lake. We have been telling ourselves the story of what *we* represent in the land for 40,000 years. At the heart of this story, I think, is a simple, abiding belief: it is possible to live wisely on the land, and to live well. And in behaving respectfully toward all that the land contains, it is possible to imagine a stifling ignorance falling away from us.

Crossing the tree line to the Far North, one leaves behind the boreal owl clutching its frozen prey to its chest feathers to thaw it. Ahead lies an open, wild landscape, pointed off on the maps with arresting and anomalous names: Brother John Glacier and Cape White Handkerchief. Navy Board Inlet, Teddy Bear Island, and the Zebra Cliffs. Dexterity Fiord, Saint Patrick Canyon, Starvation Cove. Eskimos hunt the ringed seal, still, in the broad bays of the Sons of the Clergy and Royal Astronomical Society islands.

This is a land where airplanes track icebergs the size of Cleveland and polar bears fly down out of the stars. It is a region, like the desert, rich with metaphor, with adumbration. In a simple bow from the waist before the nest of the horned lark, you are able to stake your life, again, in what you dream.

ARCTIC DREAMS

PROLOGUE
Pond's Bay, Baffin Island

O<small>N A WARM</small> summer day in 1823, the *Cumbrian*, a 360-
ton British whaler, sailed into the waters off Pond's
Bay (now Pond Inlet), northern Baffin Island, after
a short excursion to the north. The waters of Lancaster Sound,
where she had been, were supposed to be a promising "new water,"
but the *Cumbrian* hadn't struck a whale in two weeks of cruising.
Worse, in her captain's view, the forty-odd ships that had chosen
instead to dally at the mouth of Pond's Bay had met with spectacular
success in her absence. "Several ships," lamented Captain Johnson
in his log, "had captured upwards of 12, one or two [ships] 15
apiece, and one had got full. . . ."

But the *Cumbrian* did not have long to wait. The newly discovered waters of western Baffin Bay, the West Water, teemed
with the men's special prey, the Greenland whale. On the very
next day, July 28, they killed three. In the days that followed they
took another twelve, for a total of twenty-three for the season. On
August 20 the *Cumbrian* sailed for ice-free waters off the coast of
Greenland and then doubled Cape Farewell for England. The
whale blubber she carried would render 236 tons of oil to light the
street lamps of Great Britain and process the coarse wool of its
textile mills. Also in her hold were more than four and a half tons
of whalebone (baleen), to be turned into umbrella staves and
venetian blinds, portable sheep pens, window gratings, and furni-
ture springing.

The *Cumbrian* made port at Hull on September 26, to dock-
side cheers. Young boys from town swarmed her rigging in quest of
the traditional garland of sun-bleached ribbons, halfway up the
main-topgallant mast. The ship's owners beamed with pleasure.
The year before the *Cumbrian* had taken but half this many whales,
for no ship that year had been able to breach the ice in Davis
Strait. And in 1821 the *Cumbrian* had returned with grim news—
three ships from Hull, and at least four others from British ports,
were lost, crushed in the ice.

The season of 1823 eased these awful memories. The West
Water off Pond's Bay seemed most promising. And the *Cumbrian*
had also brought back walrus hides and ivory, traded from the
Eskimos of West Greenland and northern Baffin Island. And also
several narwhal tusks. If the prices for oil and whalebone held, if
there were a few good ice-years back to back, and if London didn't
rescind the industry's price supports or abolish the protective trade
tariffs. . . .

None of this had been much on the minds of the men of the
Cumbrian. In the West Water, they had worked the odd hours of
men who knew no night, who jumped for the whaleboat davits
whenever a "fish" was sighted. They slept sprawled on the decks

and ate irregularly. Their days in the ice were heady, the weather splendid. The distant landscapes of Bylot and Baffin islands at Pond's Bay were etched brilliantly before them by a high-tempered light in air clear as gin—an unearthly sight that filled them with a mixture of disbelief and pleasure. They felt exhilaration in the constant light; and a sense of satisfaction and worth, which came partly from their arduous work.

The summer of 1823 marked a high point in the halcyon days of British arctic whaling, which followed the close of the Napoleonic Wars. The discovery of the West Water came at a time when the market for whale products was resurgent, and it made the merchants and investors of Hull and Peterhead, of Dundee and Aberdeen and Whitby, a rich bounty between 1818 and 1824. In 1825 it would begin to unravel—technological advances and British economic policy would weaken the home and foreign markets for oil and whalebone, and the too-frequent and expensive loss of uninsured ships would dry up investment capital. With 2000 whales killed in 1823 alone, overfishing, too, would begin to be a problem.

The object of all this attention was a creature the British had been hunting commercially for 212 years, first in the bays of Spitsbergen and in the loose pack ice of the Greenland Sea, then in the southern reaches of Davis Strait, and finally in the North Water and West Water of Baffin Bay. Long slats of blue-black, plankton-straining baleen hung from the roof of its mouth in a U-shaped curtain, some of the blades nearly 15 feet long. The stout body, with a massive head one-third the animal's length, was wrapped in blubber as much as 20 inches thick—a higher ratio of blubber to weight than that for any other whale. The blubber of a good-size animal might yield 25 tons of oil; its 300 or more baleen plates might mean more than a ton of whalebone. The 45-foot carcass—minus baleen and its flukes (taken to make glue) and flensed of its blubber—was cut adrift as a "crang" underneath ever-present, mobbing clouds of seabirds.

Because it was a slow swimmer, because it floated when it was

killed, and because of the unusual quantity of bone and oil it
yielded, it was the right whale to take—the Greenland right. The
polar whale. *The* whale. Later, in the western Arctic, it would be
called "bowhead," after the outline of its jaw.

The skin of this animal is slightly furrowed to the touch, like
coarse-laid paper, and is a velvet-black color softened by gray.
Under the chin and on the belly the skin turns white. Its dark
brown eyes, the size of an ox's, are nearly lost in the huge head.
Its blowhole rises prominently, with the shape of a volcano, allowing the whale to surface in narrow cracks in the sea ice to breathe.
It is so sensitive to touch that at a bird's footfall a whale asleep at
the surface will start wildly. The fiery pain of a harpoon strike can
hardly be imagined. (In 1856 a harpooner aboard the *Truelove*
reported striking a whale that dived so furiously it took out 1200
yards of line in three and a half minutes before crashing into the
ocean floor, breaking its neck and burying its head eight feet deep
in blue-black mud.)

Its strength is prodigious. A bowhead harpooned in the Greenland Sea took out 10,440 yards (7000 pounds) of line, snapping
two 2¼-inch hemp lines (one of 1560 yards, the other 3360 yards)
and pulling an entangled 28-foot whaleboat down with it before it
was subdued. On May 27, 1817, thirty hours after it had been
harpooned, another Greenland right whale was still towing a fully
rigged ship at two knots into a "moderate brisk breeze."

The pursuit of this animal was without restraint. A month
before she entered Lancaster Sound in 1823, the *Cumbrian* killed a
huge Greenland right, a 57-foot female, in Davis Strait. They came
upon her while she was asleep in light ice. Awakened by their
approach, she swam slowly once around the ship and then put her
head calmly to its bow and began to push. She pushed the ship
backward for two minutes before the transfixed crew reacted with
harpoons. The incident left the men unsettled. They flinched
against such occasional eeriness in their work.

Precisely where they then stood in Davis Strait, off the northern west coast of Greenland, an odd whistling sound was sometimes heard by whalers in calm weather like this—a high note that eventually faded away to a very low note. It was the sign of a gale coming, from the direction most feared in that quarter, the south-west. The louder the whistle, the harder the winds would blow. They heard no whistling that year as they worked their way through the ice streams—but they had not liked the whale pushing against them, as though urging them to go back.

Many were ill at ease with arctic whaling, because of the threat to their lives presented by the unpredictable sea ice; but also in the regions where they hunted they found a beauty more penetrating and sublime than any they had ever known—so they said in their journals. Glaciers collapsed into the dark green sea before them like cliffs of marble as high as the Cliffs of Dover. Winds tore water from melt ponds atop icebergs, to trail off in sheets of rain-bowing mists. Pods of white belukha whales glided ghostlike beneath their keels. A thousand auklets roared through the ship's rigging in a wildshower of sound. Walruses with their gleaming tusks and luminous whiskers swam slowly across calm bays in water burning like manganese in the evening sun. Men wrote in earnest, humble prose that they were overwhelmed by the "loveliness and grandeur."

What they saw made the killing seem inappropriate; but it was work, too, security for their families, and they could quickly put compassion and regret aside. "The object of the adventure," wrote one captain, "the value of the prize, the joy of the capture, cannot be sacrificed to feelings of compassion."

On the 27th of July, still lamenting the wasted days cruising in Lancaster Sound, the *Cumbrian* was bearing south along landfast ice east of Bylot Island, past the gruesome evidence of other ships' successes. "Here and there," the log reads, "along the floe edge lay the dead bodies of hundreds of flenched whales . . . the air for miles around was tainted with the foetor which arose from such masses of putridity. Towards evening, the numbers come across were ever increasing, and the effluvia which then assailed our olfactories became almost intolerable."

The northern fulmars and glaucous gulls wheeled and screeched over the crangs. It was the carnage of wealth.

AT the southeast tip of Bylot Island that year the local Eskimo, the Tununirmiut, had established a narwhal hunting camp. They traded informally with the British whalers, whom they called *upirnaagiit*, "the men of springtime"—offering polar bear skins, walrus hides and ivory, and sealskin mitts for tin pots, needles, steel knives, and other useful or decorative items. In later years this trading would become a hedge for shipowners, a commercial necessity when the whaling alone no longer paid. Ships' captains would turn to furs, hides, ivory, and the collection of zoo animals to make ends meet. But those years, years of exploitation and social change for the Eskimo, lay ahead. For the moment the Tununirmiut were still aboriginal hunters, their habits largely unchanged by an availability of trade goods. They moved nomadically over the sea ice and the land, according to the itineraries of the animals they pursued for food, clothing, tools, and utensils.

If one were to generalize about this early trading relationship, it would be to say that the Eskimo were trying to accommodate themselves—in carefully limited ways—to an unfamiliar culture that could produce whale meat with ease, in astonishing quantities in little time, and that also made available a number of extremely useful items, such as canvas and saws. The Europeans, looking largely to their own ends, enjoyed the primitive and exotic aspects of these encounters. They were eager for souvenirs and sexual contact with the women, and hoped to trade for a profit. On those salubrious summer afternoons off Pond's Bay, then, young native women returned from the whaling ships to tell their husbands that the white men lived in tiers of hammocks like *appaliarsuit*— dovekies on a sea cliff. The husband wiped seal grease from his fingers with a ptarmigan wing and waited to see if she had brought, perhaps, some tobacco. The Eskimo put a great value on the basic fact of their own long survival. They were not nearly as taken with the men and their ships as Europeans liked to believe.

The sophistication the whalers felt next to the Eskimo was a false sophistication, and presumptuous. The European didn't value the Eskimo's grasp of the world. And, however clever Eskimos might be with ivory implements and waterproof garments, he thought their techniques dated or simply quaint next to his own. A ship's officer of the time wrote summarily that the Eskimo was "dwindled in his form, his intellect, and his passions." They were people to be taken mild but harmless advantage of, to be chastised like children, but not to be taken seriously. The Europeans called them yaks.

As for the Eskimo, they thought the whalers strange for trying to get on without the skills and companionship of women. They gave them full credit for producing "valuable and convenient articles and implements," but laughed at their inability to clothe, feed, and protect themselves. They regarded the whalers with a mixture of *ilira* and *kappia*, the same emotions a visitor to the modern village of Pond Inlet encounters today. *Ilira* is the fear that accompanies awe; *kappia* is fear in the face of unpredictable violence. Watching a polar bear—*ilira*. Having to cross thin sea ice—*kappia*.

By the summer of 1832, after only a few years of commerce in the region, the whalers were already beginning to find the silent villages of spring—places where everyone had died during the winter of European diphtheria and smallpox. The apparently timeless Arctic, they saw, was in fact changeable. And the vast and particular knowledge of the Eskimo, garnered from hundreds of years of their patient interrogation of the landscape, was starting to slip away.

FAR to the northeast of Pond's Bay, west of Cape York on the Greenland coast, was a remarkable phenomenon whalers at the time called the Crimson Cliffs, red-tinged snow they variously explained as due to fungal growth or to the red mute of guillemots feeding on shrimp.* At an unknown spot to the east of those cliffs, a place the local Eskimos called Savissivik, was a collection of meteorites that the British heard about for the first time in 1818. (The Polar Eskimo chipped bits of iron-nickel from them for harpoon tips and knife blades, and for use in trade with other Eskimos. Among them *savik* meant both "knife" and "iron.") In 1823 even officers of the British whaling fleet had little idea where a meteorite might come from. They couldn't say, either, whether Greenland was actually an island. Nor at that time had anyone been within 500 miles of the North Pole. For all they knew, it was what Henry Hudson believed it was when he sailed for it in 1607, a massive boulder of black basalt sitting in the middle of a warm, calm sea. They were unaware that the Greenland right actually "sang," like the humpback whales they heard in the North Atlantic en route to the arctic fishery. The life history of the Greenland shark, an "unwholesome and lethargic brute" upon which the Danes would build Greenland's first commercial fishery (for the oil from its liver), was unknown to them. The existence of a culture that had preceded the Eskimo's in the Arctic was unsuspected, though they traded, unawares, for its artifacts.

In 1823 the North American Arctic was still as distant as fable, inhabited by remarkable animals and uncontacted peoples, the last undiscovered complex ecosystem on the planet. A landscape of numinous events, of a forgiving benediction of light, and a darkness so dunning it precipitated madness; of a cold that froze vinegar, that fractured whatever it penetrated, including the stones. It was uncharted, unclaimed territory, and Europeans had perished miserably in it since the time of the Norse—gangrenous with frostbite, poisoned by polar bear liver, rotted by scurvy, dead of exposure on the ice beside the wreckage of a ship burned to the water line for the last bit of its warmth.

---

* The tint is from blood-red pigments in the cell walls of species of freshwater algae present on the snow.

The confidence and élan of the whalemen at Pond's Bay was tempered with this macabre knowledge; and they suspected that their own ignorance of the place, even the ignorance of those among them who made such erudite notes about the biology of whales or the colors of plankton in the current, was extensive. They were overcome, however, by neither fear nor ignorance. Their vessels, for the moment, were "safe as a life boat and tight as a bottle." In two months they would be home to their families, with a year's pay and perhaps a pair of polar bear trousers to show, or a flint-blade knife for a son. And with stories to hold a neighbor enthralled, stories of a breathtaking escape from drowning, or of having collected 6000 eider eggs on a coastal flat one morning. Or of sleeping with an Eskimo woman.

It is easy to imagine their sense of wild adventure, that on one of those July afternoons off Pond's Bay, on a Sunday when a strict Christian captain would permit no whaling, that the crew might be lounging on the sunlit decks comparing exotic arctic souvenirs: the perplexing skull of a muskox, with its massive horn bosses and protruding eye orbitals—"from a kind of polar cattle," as they understood it from the Eskimo, which lived way off to the west and the north. Or a bit of chain mail, which, someone argued, was certain proof that Viking explorers had sailed far north of the Greenland settlements, hundreds of years before. Or a small ivory carving of a human face, twisted in psychotic anguish, an artifact from the vanished Dorset culture. They likely felt a tension between the unfamiliar quality of these objects and the commonplaces of their own daily lives—the boot-worn deck on which they sat, or the intricate but familiar rigging of sails and spars overhead.

Perhaps someone recalled having seen a polar bear once, far offshore in a storm, swimming with measured strokes through great dark seas—and, with that, introduced yet another tension peculiar to the place, that between beauty and violence. Or perhaps they spoke of the Eskimos, how astonishing they were to be able to survive here, how energetic and friendly; and yet how unnerving with their primitive habits: a mother wiping away a child's feces with her hair, a man pinching the heart of a snared bird to kill it, so as not to ruin the feathers.

In their own separate, spare quarters, the ship's officers might have been reading William Scoresby's *Account of the Arctic Regions* or the recently published discovery narrative of William Parry, who had opened the way to the West Water in 1818 with John Ross. They admired Parry; overall, however, they viewed the British discovery expeditions—in ships that were ice-strengthened to a fare-thee-well, manned by inexperienced crews and commanded by officers seeking "imperishable renown"—as a pompous exercise in state politics, of little or no practical value.

Men and officers alike would have mused more on the blubber and bone below decks, for *that* was tangible wealth. These two parts of just a single whale would sell on the docks at Hull for ten to fifteen times what a man could expect to make in a year's work ashore.

The men on the decks, dozing in the sun on their day off, likely had no thought at all of how utterly devastating their way of life would prove to the Eskimo and the bowhead. They felt, instead, a sense of fortune. And they yearned for home.

THE Canadian historian W. Gillies Ross cautiously suggests that as many as 38,000 Greenland right whales may have been killed in the Davis Strait fishery, largely by the British fleet. A sound estimate of the size of that population today is 200. There are no similar figures for the number of native people in the region who fell to diphtheria, smallpox, tuberculosis, poliomyelitis, and other diseases—historians have suggested that 90 percent of the indigenous population of North America is not an unreasonable figure. The Eskimos are still trying, as it were, to recover.*

---

* "Eskimo" is an inclusive term, referring to descendants of the Thule cultural tradition in present-day Canada and the Punuk and Birnirk cultural traditions in modern-day Alaska. See note 2.

What happened around Pond's Bay in the heyday of arctic whaling represents in microcosm the large-scale advance of Western culture into the Arctic. It is a disquieting reminder that the modern industries—oil, gas, and mineral extraction—might be embarked on a course as disastrously short-lived as was that of the whaling industry. And as naive—our natural histories of this region 150 years later are still cursory and unintegrated. This time around, however, the element in the ecosystem at greatest risk is not the bowhead but the coherent vision of an indigenous people. We have no alternative, long-lived narrative to theirs, no story of human relationships with that landscape independent of Western science and any desire to control or possess. Our intimacy lacks historical depth, and is still largely innocent of what is obscure and subtle there.

And our conceptions of its ultimate value vary markedly. The future disposition of the Arctic is not viewed in the same way by a Montreal attorney working on the settlement of Inuit land claims and by a naval architect in Sweden designing an ice-breaking tanker capable of plying the polar route from Rotterdam to Yokahama. And the life history of the Arctic—the pollination of its flowers by the bumblebee, the origins and thoughts of the Dorset people, the habits of the wolverine—means one thing to an *inuk* pulling on his fishnets at the mouth of the Hayes River, another to a biologist watching a caribou herd encounter the trans-Alaska pipeline, and yet something else to the modern tourist, bound for a caviar-and-champagne luncheon at the North Pole.

Such a variety of human views and interests in an emerging land is not new; what is new for us, and troubling, is a difference in the land itself, which changes the very nature of these considerations. In the Temperate Zone, we are accustomed to dealing with landscapes that can easily accommodate opposing views. Their long growing seasons, mild temperatures, great variety of creatures, and moderate rainfall make up for much human abuse. The biological nature of arctic ecosystems is different—they are far more vulnerable ecologically to attempts to "accommodate both sides." Of concern in the North, then, is the impatience with which reconciliation and compromise are now being sought.

Our conceptual problems with these things, with commercial and industrial development in the North and with the proprieties of an imposed economics there, can be traced to a fundamental strangeness in the landscape itself, to something as subtle as our own temperate-zone predilection toward a certain duration and kind of light. Or for the particular shape that time takes in a temperate land, where the sun actually sets on a summer evening, where cicadas give way in the twilight to crickets, and people sit on porches—none of which happens in the Arctic.

Difficulty in evaluating, or even discerning, a particular landscape is related to the distance a culture has traveled from its own ancestral landscape. As temperate-zone people, we have long been ill-disposed toward deserts and expanses of tundra and ice. They have been wastelands for us; historically we have not cared at all what happened in them or to them. I am inclined to think, however, that their value will one day prove to be inestimable to us. It is precisely because the regimes of light and time in the Arctic are so different that this landscape is able to expose in startling ways the complacency of our thoughts about land in general. Its unfamiliar rhythms point up the narrow impetuosity of Western schedules, by simply changing the basis of the length of the day. And the periodically frozen Arctic Ocean is at present an insurmountable impediment to timely shipping. This land, for some, is irritatingly and uncharacteristically uncooperative.

If we are to devise an enlightened plan for human activity in the Arctic, we need a more particularized understanding of the land itself—not a more refined mathematical knowledge but a deeper understanding of its nature, as if it were, itself, another sort of civilization we had to reach some agreement with. I would draw you, therefore, back to the concrete dimensions of the land and to what they precipitate; simply to walk across the tundra; to watch the wind stirring a little in the leaves of dwarf birch and willows; to hear the hoof-clacket of migrating caribou. Imagine your ear against the loom of a kayak paddle in the Beaufort Sea, hearing the long, quivering tremolo voice of the bearded seal. Or feeling the surgical sharpness of an Eskimo's obsidian tool under the stroke of your finger.

Once in winter I was far out on the sea ice north of Melville Island in the high Arctic with a drilling crew. I saw a seal surface at some hourless moment in the day in a moon pool, the open water directly underneath the drilling platform that lets the drill string pass through the ice on its way to the ocean floor. The seal and I regarded each other in absolute stillness, I in my parka, arrested in the middle of an errand, the seal in the motionless water, its dark brown eyes glistening in its gray, catlike head. Curiosity held it. What held me was: how far out on the edge of the world I am. A movement of my head shifted the hood of my parka slightly, and the seal was gone in an explosion of water. Its eyes had been enormous. I walked to the edge of the moon pool and stared into the dark ocean. I could not have been more surprised by the seal's appearance if it had fallen out of the winter sky overhead, into the spheres of light that embraced the drill rig and our isolated camp.

To contemplate what people are doing out here and ignore the universe of the seal, to consider human quest and plight and not know the land, I thought, to not listen to it, seemed fatal. Not perhaps for tomorrow, or next year, but fatal if you looked down the long road of our determined evolution and wondered at the considerations that had got us this far.

At the heart of this narrative, then, are three themes: the influence of the arctic landscape on the human imagination. How a desire to put a landscape to use shapes our evaluation of it. And, confronted by an unknown landscape, what happens to our sense of wealth. What does it mean to grow rich? Is it to have red-blooded adventures and to make a fortune, which is what brought the whalers and other entrepreneurs north? Or is it, rather, to have a good family life and to be imbued with a far-reaching and intimate knowledge of one's homeland, which is what the Tununirmiut told the whalers at Pond's Bay wealth was? Is it to retain a capacity for awe and astonishment in our lives, to continue to hunger after what is genuine and worthy? Is it to live at moral peace with the universe?

It is impossible to know, clearly, the answer to this question; but by coming to know a place where the common elements of life are understood differently one has the advantage of an altered perspective. With that shift, it is possible to imagine afresh the way to a lasting security of the soul and heart, and toward an accommodation in the flow of time we call history, ours and the world's.

That dream, as it unfolds in the following chapters, is the dream of great and common people alike.

One
ARKTIKÓS

O N A WINTER AFTERNOON—a day without a sunrise, under a moon that had not set for six days—I stand on the frozen ocean 20 miles off Cape Mamen, Mackenzie King Island. The sea ice of Hazen Strait is not completely featureless, but its surface does not show, either, any evidence of severe torture, such as one would find, for example, in the Lincoln Sea. The currents are relatively calm here. During the nine or ten months the water is frozen, this platform hardly moves.

To the south I can see a thin streak of violet and cobalt sky stretching across 80° of the horizon. But the ice and snow barely reflect these colors. The pervasive light here is the milky blue of the reflected moon. It is possible to see two or three miles in the moonlight; but the pale light gives nothing an edge. Except for the horizon to the south, the color of a bruise, the world is only moonlit ice and black sky.

The sky has no depth because of the fullness of the moon, but stars shine brightly. The stars have caused me to pause in the middle of my walk. Polaris, the North Star, is directly overhead. Whenever before I have located the Big Dipper in the sky and followed the imaginary line through its indicator stars to find Polaris, I have been looking to the north, into a northern sky. This afternoon I look straight up.

It is a celestial accident that Polaris is located over the earth's Geographic North Pole (there is no comparable South Pole star). It seems to sit precisely on an extension of the earth's axis; and it has shifted its position so little in our time we think of it as a constant. It nearly is; it has been steady enough to anchor routes of navigation for people in the Northern Hemisphere for as long as history records. Astronomers call the mathematical point in the sky above the North Pole the North Celestial Pole, and Polaris is within a degree of it.

I look straight up at that anchor now, a yellowish star one hundred times the size of the sun, *alpha Ursae Minoris*, the only one that never seems to move. Pivoting around it are the seven bright stars and seven fainter ones that can be joined to create the familiar cup with its handle, or to form the hips and tail of Ursa Major, the Great Bear. In the early history of Western civilization the parts of the world that lay to the far north were understood to lie beneath these stars. The Greeks called the whole of the region Arktikós, the country of the great bear.

The Old World regarded the Arctic as an inaccessible place. Beyond a certain gloomy and hostile border country, however, they did not imagine it as inhospitable. Indeed, in Greek myth this most distant part of the Arctic was a country of rich lacustrine soils, soft azure skies, gentle breezes (zephyrs), fecund animals, and trees that bore fruit even in winter, a region farther north than the birthplace of the North Wind (Boreas). The inhabitants of Hyperborea, as it was called, were thought to be the oldest of the human races, and to be comparable themselves with the land—compassionate in temperament, knowing no want, of a contemplative bent. In some legends of Hyperborea there are striking images of this blessed atmosphere—white feathers falling from the sky, for example. (The allusion is probably to a gentle lamellation of snow; but the reference is not entirely metaphorical. On the coast of Alaska one summer day, an immense flock of molting ducks flew over my head, and hundreds of their feathers rocked quietly to earth as they passed. In histories of nineteenth-century arctic exploration, too, one finds a correspondence, with descriptions of a kind of hoarfrost that built up like a vaning of feathers on a ship's rigging.)

Perhaps some traveler's story of irenic northern summers reached the Greeks and convinced them of the Hyperboreans' salutary existence. A darker side of this distant landscape, however, was more frequently evoked. The indigenous southern cultures regarded it as a wasteland of frozen mountains, of violent winds and incipient evil. For theological writers in the seventh century it was a place of spiritual havoc, the abode of the Antichrist. During the time when the southern cultures in Europe were threatened by Goths, Vandals, and other northern tribes (including, later, the Vikings), two quintessentially malevolent figures from the Old Testament, Gog and Magog, emerged as the figurative leaders of a mythic horde poised above the civilized nations. These were the forces of darkness, arrayed against the forces of light. In English legend the northern armies are defeated and Gog and Magog captured and taken to London in chains. (Their effigies stood outside Guildhall in the central city for 500 years before being destroyed in an air raid in World War II.)

A gentler ending than this is found with a hill outside Cambridge called Gogmagog. One of the northern giants in that barbaric army, the story goes, fell in love with one of the young women of the South. She spurned him because of his brutish nature. He lay down in remorse, never to move again. His body became the hills.

In a more prosaic attempt to define the Arctic we have arranged it around several poles.* The precise location of the most exact of these northern poles, the North Pole itself, varies (on a small scale). Tectonic activity, the gravitational pull of the moon, and the continuous transport of sediments from one place to another by rivers cause the earth to wobble slightly, and its axis to shift as it does so. If the North Pole were a scribing stylus, it would trace a line every 428 days in the shape of an irregular circle, with a diameter varying from 25 to 30 feet. Over the years, these irregular circles would all fall within an area some 65 feet across, called the Chandler Circle. The average position of the center of this circle is the Geographic North Pole.

Other northern poles are as hard to locate precisely. In 1985 the North Magnetic Pole, around which the earth's magnetic field and its magnetosphere (far above the earth's atmosphere) are organized, lay at 77°N 120°W, some 30 miles east of Edmund Walker Island, at the southern end of the Findlay Group. This is 400 miles farther north and somewhat west of where it was when James Clark Ross discovered it in 1831, on the west side of Boothia Peninsula.

The North Geomagnetic Pole, around which the earth's magnetic field and its magnetosphere are theoretically (mathematically) arranged, lies about 500 miles east of the North Magnetic Pole, in the vicinity of Inglefield Land in northern Greenland.

---

* There is no generally accepted definition for a southern limit to the Arctic. The Arctic Circle, for example, would enclose a part of Scandinavia so warmed by a remnant of the Gulf Stream that it harbors a lizard, *Lacerta vivipera*, an adder, *Vivipera berus*, and a frog, *Rana temporaria*. It would also exclude the James Bay region of Canada, prime polar bear habitat. The southern extent of permafrost, the northern tree line, the geographical distribution of certain animals, the southern extent of the 50°F isotherm in July—all have been proposed and argued away by scientists.

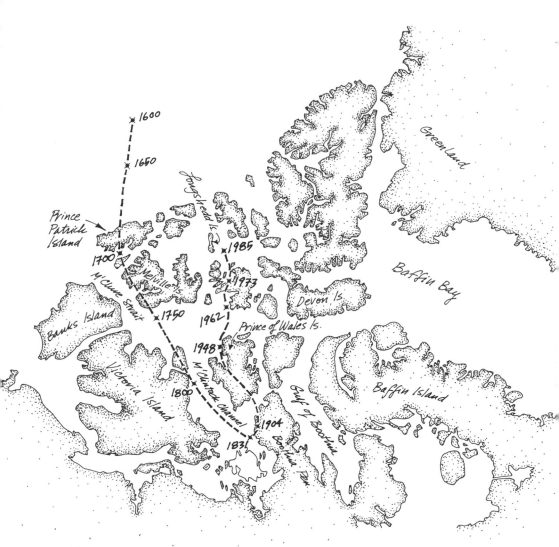

Movement of the North Magnetic Pole, A.D. 1600 to the present. Locations prior to 1831 are approximate.

A fifth northern pole, hardly noted anymore, has been made obsolete. In the nineteenth century people believed no point on earth was more difficult to attain than a place in the sea ice north of Alaska, at about 84°N 160°W. The pack ice of the Arctic Ocean was thought to pivot slowly around this spot, making an approach by ship impossible and a journey on foot or by dog sledge too perilous. No more evident to the eye than the Geographic North Pole, this Pole of Inaccessibility has now been "seen" numerous times from the air and even "visited," probably, by Russian icebreakers.*

More useful, perhaps, than any set of lines in developing an understanding of the arctic regions is an image of the annual movement of the sun across the arctic sky. To the temperate-zone eye the movement is irregular and unorthodox. The borders that divide periods of light (days) from periods of darkness (nights) seem too vague and the duration of both too prolonged or too short, depending.

It is difficult to imagine the sun's arctic movement because our thought about it has been fixed for tens of thousands of years, ever since we moved into the North Temperate Zone. We also have trouble here because as terrestrial, rather than aerial or aquatic, creatures we don't often think in three dimensions. I remember the first time these things were impressed on me, on a winter flight to Barrow on the north coast of Alaska. It was around noon and we were flying north. By craning my neck and pressing my face against the cabin window, I was able to see the sun low on the southern horizon. It seemed to move not at all from that spot during the two-hour flight. When we landed at Barrow, it seemed to have set in the same spot. As I walked through the village, I realized I had never understood this before: in a far northern winter, the sun surfaces slowly in the south and then disappears at nearly the same spot, like a whale rolling over. The idea that the sun "rises in the east and sets in the west" simply does not apply. The thought that a "day" consists of a morning and a forenoon, an afternoon and an evening, is a convention, one so imbedded in us we hardly think about it, a convention of our literature and arts. The pattern is not the same here.†

---

* The Soviet icebreaker *Arktika*, of 23,400 tons displacement and 75,000 shaft horsepower, reached the Geographic North Pole in August 1977.

† Northern peoples everywhere—Eskimos in Canada, Yakuts in Russia, Samis (Lapps) in Scandinavia—have rearranged their lives in recent

To grasp the movement of the sun in the Arctic is no simple task. Imagine standing precisely at the North Pole on June 21, the summer solstice. Your feet rest on a crust of snow and windblown ice. If you chip the snow away you find the sea ice, grayish white and opaque. Six or seven feet underneath is the Arctic Ocean, dark, about 29°F and about 13,000 feet deep. You are standing 440 miles from the nearest piece of land, the tiny island of Oodaaq off the coast of northern Greenland. You stand in each of the world's twenty-four time zones and north of every point on earth. On this day the sun is making a flat 360° orbit exactly 23½° above the horizon.

If we could stay within the limits of this twenty-four-hour day and if you could walk down the 100th meridian, toward Mexico City, you would notice at first very little change in the sun's path around the sky. Soon, however, you would begin to sense that the sun's orbit was tilted, its arc higher in the southern sky and lower in the northern sky. The tilt of the sun's arc would become more and more pronounced as you walked south. When you reached the vicinity of Garry Lake in the Northwest Territories, where the 100th meridian crosses a line of latitude at 66°33′N (the Arctic Circle), the sun would have dropped low enough to touch the northern horizon behind you for the first time. You would be far enough into a time zone now for it to make a difference, and that moment when the sun touched the horizon would be "midnight." At the same spot twelve hours later, the sun would stand 47° above the southern horizon; it would be "noon," local time. You would say, now, that the sun seemed more to move *across* the sky than *around* in it. It has begun to slip below the northern horizon; from here, still walking south on June 21, you would start to experience "night." Short nights, only prolonged

years to synchronize themselves with the day/night rhythm of the southern countries, a source of schedules and of patterns of information organization on which they are increasingly dependent.

periods of twilight really, at first. But slowly the twilight would start to deepen during the evening hours and to wax in the morning hours. Somewhere on the plains of Manitoba you would finally sense "the middle of the night"—enough of real darkness so you couldn't continue walking without fear of stumbling.

If you carried on, as you could if we held June 21 in suspension like this, you would begin to notice three things: the nights would get noticeably longer; the sun would stand higher and higher in the southern sky at noon (and more clearly seem to "rise in the east" and "set in the west"); and periods of twilight at dawn and dusk would shorten, until twilight would be only a passing phenomenon. The sun rises and sets sharply in Mexico City. Sunshine is a daily, not a seasonal, phenomenon, as it is in the North.

If you stood at the North Pole six months later, on December 21, the winter solstice, the middle of the polar night, you would not see a single star set—they would all pass before you from left to right. If they left behind the light-streak traces they do on time-exposed film, you would see the varicolored rings stacked one atop another, parallel to the horizon, shrinking in diameter, until the last ring, less than 2° across and traced by Polaris, circled the dark spot of empty space that lies over the North Pole.

If you walked south from the Pole on December 21, you would find the phenomena of six months earlier reversed. It would be utterly dark at the Pole on that day. On the plains of Manitoba the balance of day and night would feel right to you if you were familiar with the short days of winter in the Temperate Zone. In the tropics there would again be days and nights of equal length, with very little twilight.*

You would have to walk a very long way south on December 21, 1611 statute miles, all the way to the Arctic Circle, to actually

---

* This uneven pattern of illumination in the Arctic is caused by the earth's rotation on its tilted axis and its annual revolution around the sun. See note 3.

set eyes on the sun. The winter darkness, however, would not be complete. Prolonged periods of twilight penetrate the long arctic night, and the strength of even scant illumination from the stars is enhanced all winter by the reflective surfaces of ice and snow. Too, there is no forest canopy to dim the land and, save in a few places, no night shadow of a mountain range to contend with. The Arctic is like the desert in this way—open, unobstructed country, lit well enough by a full moon to permit travel at night.

It makes little sense in more southerly latitudes to dwell on a consideration of twilight, but it is meaningful in the Arctic, where this soft light lingers for such long periods of time that astronomers distinguish several types.* In the Temperate Zone, periods of twilight are a daily phenomenon, morning and evening. In the Far North they are (also) a seasonal phenomenon, continuous through a day, day after day, as the sun wanes in the fall and waxes in the spring. In the Temperate Zone each day is noticeably shorter in winter and longer in summer but, still, each day has a discernible dawn, a protracted "first light" that suggests new beginnings. In the Far North the day does not start over again every day.

In 1597 the icebound and shipwrecked Dutch explorer Willem Barents was forced to overwinter with his crew in wretched circumstances at the northern tip of Novaya Zemlya. They awaited the return of the sun in a state of deep anxiety. More than the cold they hated the darkness; no amount of prolonged twilight could make up for the unobstructed view of that beaming star. They quoted Solomon to each other: "The light is sweet; and it is delightful for the eyes to see the sun." When the sun finally did appear it came twelve days earlier than they expected. They acknowledged

---

* *Civilian twilight* lasts from the moment after sunset until the sun is 6° below the horizon. The period when it is between 6° and 12° below the horizon is called *nautical twilight*. When the sun is between 12° and 18° below the horizon, the period of *astronomical twilight*, it is getting dark enough, finally, for astronomers to begin their work, which begins with true night, with the sun more than 18° below the horizon.

a divine intervention. They gestured toward it with joy and disbelief, and took courage against their difficulties from its appearance.

What they saw that January day, we now know, was not the sun but only a solar mirage—the sun was still 5° below the horizon, its rays bent toward them by a refractive condition in the atmosphere. Such images, now called Novaya Zemlya images, are common in the Arctic. They serve as a caution against precise description and expectation, a reminder that the universe is oddly hinged.

If, at the termination of this imaginary southward journey through the realms of winter and summer light, you were to turn around and come back, you would notice many changes in the biological life around you. The total number of species of animals and plants (biological diversity) would diminish—strikingly so by the time you reached the arctic regions. Overall biological productivity (annual number of offspring per species) would also fall off. And the timing of the birth of young would be related increasingly to the cycle of the seasons. The various strategies animals use to survive, to procreate, feed, and protect themselves from the climate, would also change. The long-term biological stability of the ecosystems would decrease. You would travel from a land in which the four seasons are phantoms; from jungles of towering hardwood species where water is always a liquid, trickling somewhere; and where the list of animals is voluminous but unfinished. You would arrive, finally, in a land of seasonal hibernation, of periodically frozen water and low, ground-hugging trees, where the list of mammalian denizens is short enough to memorize in a few moments.

The overall impression, coming from the South, would be of movement from a very complex world to a quite simplified one— there would come a moment when you passed from the mixed forests of the South, where no one kind of tree stood out, into the coniferous forests where trees of only one or two kinds existed, imparting a single shade of green to a hillside. But this sensation of simplicity would be something of an illusion. Arctic ecosystems have the same elegant and Byzantine complexities, the same wild grace, as tropical ecosystems; there are simply fewer moving parts —and on the flat, open tundra the parts are much more visible, accessible, and countable. The complexities in arctic ecosystems lie not with, say, esoteric dietary preferences among 100 different kinds of ground beetle making a living on the same tropical acre, but with an intricacy of rhythmic response to extreme ranges of light and temperature. With the seasonal movement of large numbers of migratory animals. And with their adaptation to violent, but natural, fluctuations in their population levels.

In traveling north from the tropics, however, we would still find that broad-scale changes apparent to our eyes suggested an undeveloped country. To the unscientific eye the land would seem to have run out of the stuff of life—running water, light, warmth— to have reached absolute limits. It would seem to offer few niches for animals to occupy. As for the human animal, there would seem to be no such nurturing recesses at all. But there are niches here; and they are filled by animals completely and comfortably at home in them. (The awe one feels in an encounter with a polar bear is, in part, simple admiration for the mechanisms of survival it routinely employs to go on living in an environment that would defeat us in a few days. It is also what impresses someone on an arctic journey with Eskimos. Their resourcefulness, as well as their economy of action, bespeak an intense familiarity with the environment. Of course, they are the people there.)

On our journey north we would notice significant changes in the soil under our feet. Soil is a living system, a combination of dirt (particles of sand, clay, and silt) and decaying and processed organic matter. It is created by erosion, fracture, and the secretion of organic acids; by animals and plants like beetles (saprophages) and mushrooms (saprophytes) that break down dead matter; and by the excretions of earthworms. It draws in oxygen like an animal, through myriad tunnels built by ants, rodents, and worms. And it is inhabited throughout by hundreds of creatures—nematodes, mites, springtails, and soil bacteria and fungi.

In the tropics, saprophages and saprophytes break down organic matter quickly. The recycling of nutrients (phosphorus, sodium, and potassium) is so swift that little soil remains behind. In the Temperate Zone, the turnover in organic matter and the recycling of nutrients are much slower, especially in winter, when cold-blooded soil organisms are lethargic or inactive. As a result, rich, deep layers of humus build up over a reddish, sterile clay base familiar from the tropics. To the north these fertile layers of humus give way to firmer, less fertile brown soils, because of a reduction both in the numbers and kinds of saprophages and saprophytes and in aerating and soil-building organisms that can adapt to the loss of solar energy. These acidic podzols of the boreal forests and prairies reach their northern limit at the tree line, where one first encounters the inhospitable soils of the tundra.

Almost everywhere you wander on the open tundra you find whole dead leaves, preserved flower parts, and bits of twig, years of undisturbed organic accumulation. Decomposition in the Arctic is exceedingly slow, work that must be accomplished by even fewer organisms operating for even shorter periods of time—but since overall biological production is not nearly what it is in the Temperate Zone, little humus builds up. Arctic soils are thin, acidic, poorly drained, and poorly aerated. They are rich in neither the nitrogen nor the phosphorus essential for plant growth. (The soil at fox dens and at the slight rises on the tundra that snowy owls and jaegers routinely use as perches while eating their prey is an exception. The concentration of nutrients at these "organic dumps" accounts for the sometimes luxuriant growth of grasses and the bright display of summer wildflowers at these spots.)

So: the soils would change in depth and quality beneath our feet as we came north. And the different kinds of animals and plants living within and upon the soil, less and less able to adapt to the reduction of solar energy, would dwindle. And the ones that remained would work slowly or not at all in the dark and cold. If we kept walking, we would eventually stand in a country without the earthworm or the carrion beetle, a place where earth and decay are almost unknown, on the lifeless gravels of the polar desert.

Traveling north from the equator you could not help but notice, too, the emergence of recognizable seasons, periods of time characterized by conditions of rising, falling, or relatively stable light, in association with certain ranges of temperature. By the time you entered the Temperate Zone you would find a set of seasons distinct enough to be named and easily separated. Farther north, "spring" and "fall" would seem increasingly transitory, until each became a matter of only a few weeks. Winter, you would eventually find, lasted appreciably longer than summer. And together the two would define the final landscape.

The seasons are associated in our minds with the growth of vegetation. Outside of the four primary seasons (a constant referent with us, a ready and seemingly natural way to organize our ideas), we speak of a growing season and of a fallow season, when we picture the earth lying dormant. In the middle of an arctic winter, however, there is such a feeling of a stone crushed beneath iron that it is hard to imagine any organism, even a seed, living, let alone lying fallow. In summer, in the sometimes extravagant light of a July day, one's thoughts are not of growth, of heading wheat and yellowing peaches, but of suspension, as if life had escaped the bounds of earth. In this country, which lacks the prolonged moderations between winter and summer that we anticipate as balmy April mornings and dry Indian summer afternoons, in this two-season country, things grow and die as they do elsewhere, but they are, more deeply than living things anywhere else, seasonal creatures.

The trees are no exception. The northern limit of the continental forests in North America seems anomalous if you try to make sense of the tree line. The boundary sweeps southwest from Labrador to pass beneath James Bay, then turns northwest, crossing Canada's Precambrian Shield and paralleling the Mackenzie River Valley nearly to the Arctic Ocean before zigzagging west through the valleys of the Brooks Range and the Kobuk River to Norton Sound. The explanation for the irregularity of the line lies with the seasonal climate—it marks the average southward extension of arctic air masses in summer.

The far northern trees, like the animals, constitute a very few species—willows growing in valleys where they are protected from the wind and a dwarf form of birch. Along the tree line itself, the only successful strategists are species in the pine and birch families. Their numbers thin out over a span of several miles, with trees persisting farther north in isolated patches where there is a fortuitous conjunction of perennially calm air, moisture, and soil nutrients. Islands of trees in the tundra ocean.

The growth of trees in the Arctic is constrained by several factors. Lack of light for photosynthesis of course is one; but warmth is another. A tree, like an animal, needs heat to carry on its life processes. Solar radiation provides this warmth, but in the Arctic there is a strong correlation between this warmth and closeness to the ground. In summer there may be a difference of as much as 15°F in the first foot or so of air, because of the cooling effect of the wind above and the ability of dark soils to intensify solar radiation. To balance their heat budgets for growth and survival, trees must hug the ground—so they are short. Willows, a resourceful family to begin with, sometimes grow tall, but it is only where some feature of the land stills the drying and cooling wind.

Lack of water is another factor constraining the development of trees. No more moisture falls on the arctic tundra in a year than falls on the Mojave Desert; and it is available to arctic plants in the single form in which they can use it—liquid water—only during the summer.

Permafrost, the permanently frozen soil that underlies the tundra, presents arctic trees with still other difficulties. Though they can penetrate this rocklike substance with their roots, deep roots, which let trees stand tall in a windy landscape, and which can draw water from deep aquifers, serve no purpose in the Arctic. It's too cold to stand tall, and liquid water is to be found only in the first few inches of soil, for only this upper layer of the ground melts in the summer. (Ironically, since the permafrost beneath remains impervious, in those few weeks when water *is* available to them, arctic trees must sometimes cope with boglike conditions.)

Trees in the Arctic have an aura of implacable endurance about them. A cross-section of the bole of a Richardson willow no thicker than your finger may reveal 200 annual growth rings beneath the magnifying glass. Much of the tundra, of course, appears to be treeless when, in many places, it is actually covered with trees—a thick matting of short, ancient willows and birches. You realize suddenly that you are wandering around on *top* of a forest.

VIRTUALLY all of the earth's biological systems are driven by solar radiation. As the light falls, so must the animals and plants arrange their growth and daily activities. The Arctic receives, strangely, the same amount of sunshine in a year as the tropics, but it comes all at once, and at a low angle of incidence—without critical vigor. The regular rhythm of light-fall in the tropics, that predictable daily infusion of energy, together with its high angle of incidence, are the primary reasons for the natural stability of these ecosystems. The rainy season aside, temperature and humidity on a day in May are not so different from temperature and humidity on a day in December. The animals and plants have evolved breeding and feeding strategies, of course, that depend on this almost uninterrupted flow of light.

In the Temperate Zone, periods of daily light-fall are not equal during the year. The animals and plants must adjust to a seasonal way of life. In the Arctic this situation becomes much more extreme. Periods of light-fall can't readily be divided into days. The average temperature fluctuates over a period of 365 days, not twenty-four hours; sources of water are frozen; and the dim light puts a special burden on animals that must use their eyes to search. The very rhythm of light itself creates a difficulty. Most animals live lives in biological keeping with the earth's twenty-four-hour period of rotation. They have neither the stamina nor the flexibility, apparently, to adapt to the variable periods of light they encounter in the Arctic's nightless summer and dayless winter.*

The adaptive strategies of arctic animals to failing light and low temperatures are varied. In general, they must either develop insulation against the cold or slow down, or halt, their metabolic processes to survive. Warm-blooded animals and flowering plants aside (these must bloom and fruit rapidly in the summer), the most salient, overall adaptive strategy of arctic organisms is their ability to enter a frozen state or a state of very low metabolic activity whenever temperatures drop, and then to resume full metabolic activity whenever it warms sufficiently. Many arctic spiders and insects, along with lichens, ferns, and mosses, lie frozen for the duration of winter. Trees, along with grizzly bears and ground squirrels, carry on their life processes but at a very low metabolic rate. Fish and various beetles use cellular antifreeze agents (glycoproteins) to extend their periods of activity during freezing weather. Other adaptive strategies show parallels with those of desert plants. The leathery leaves of saxifrages and the hairy leaves of Labrador tea, for example, both reduce the transpiration of precious water in the short summer.

Slowing down their rate of growth is another strategy cold-blooded animals use. The scant solar energy available to them in the summer is often not enough to complete their development from larval to adult stages, so they must "plan" not to be at a vulnerable point of transition just as winter is coming on. Other strategies to take advantage of short periods of light for growth

---

* A few arctic animals, possibly auks and other nonpasserine birds, for example, might be "free-running." The rest maintain a twenty-four-hour rhythm, which they synchronize without the benefit of a sunrise or a sunset. Some, apparently, regularly mark the position of the sun over a certain landmark, or respond to fluctuations in the spectral composition (color temperature) of sunlight, which in the Arctic is different at midnight from what it is at noon.

and sustenance include the winter carryover of evergreen leaves by the dwarf birch (so it does not have to grow leaves again in the spring to begin photosynthesis); and the very large yolks of arctic cod eggs, which give these embryos a nutritional head start before the return of light in the spring triggers a bloom of plankton, their principal food when they hatch. With this head start they are larger and stronger and better able to survive when the ocean begins to freeze over in the fall.

Scientists believe tropical ecosystems are the oldest ones on earth. Compared with northern ecosystems, where development has been periodically halted or destroyed by the advance of glaciers, they have had many more thousands of years of undisturbed biological evolution. They are also characterized by a special kind of biological stability not found in the North—the finite number of individuals in any given tropical species hardly varies through time. This biological stability is linked to the stability of the climate and is perpetuated by highly intricate food webs and high rates of biological production. Many species, producing many young, exploit a very large number of biological niches. The system is practically invulnerable to most natural disturbances, such as a disease that might wipe out every one of a certain kind of tree. It is too diversified to be affected.

Some biologists believe all ecosystems tend to develop in the direction of stability, that is, toward many types of animals (great species diversity) and very small population surges and declines. Temperate-zone and arctic ecosystems, according to this view, are slowly evolving toward the kind of diversity and stability one sees in the tropics. But they are not liable to develop the complex food webs of the tropics, that kind of resilient diversity, on any scale of time in which we are used to thinking. The northerly ecosystems must contend with significant fluctuations in the amount of solar energy received; their rate of biological evolution, therefore, is much slower. In addition, the northerly ecosystems regularly experience severe biological disturbances related to normal weather patterns (the "unseasonable weather" blamed for the loss of a citrus crop in Florida or the early emergence of hibernating bears in Montana). Arctic climatic patterns are further characterized by unpredictable and violent weather.

The communal alliances of far northern plants and animals we call ecosystems are distinguished from more southerly ecosystems by larger biomasses and lower overall productivity. Instead of many species, each with relatively few individuals in it, we find relatively few species, each with many individuals—large herds of caribou, for example, or vast swarms of mosquitoes. But, generally speaking, these large populations do not include enough surviving young each year to keep their populations stable. The size of the population often changes, dramatically, as a matter of course; the violent weather typical of early and late summer routinely wreaks havoc on some arctic populations, particularly those of warm-blooded animals. On Wrangel Island in the Siberian Arctic, for example, an unbroken, ten-year series of late spring snowstorms prevented lesser snow geese from ever laying their eggs. Between 1965 and 1975 the population fell from 400,000 to fewer than 50,000 birds. In different years in the Greenland Sea where harp seals pup on the ice floes, spring storms have swept hundreds of thousands of infant harp seals into the sea, where they have drowned. In the fall of 1973, an October rainstorm created a layer of ground ice that, later, musk-oxen could not break through to feed. Nearly 75 percent of the muskox population in the Canadian Archipelago perished that winter.

Biologists, for these mostly climatological reasons, characterize arctic ecosystems as "stressed" or "accident-prone," underscoring the difference between them and temperate and tropical ecosystems. With their milder climates and longer growing seasons the latter are more forgiving. In the South, the prolongation of spring permits birds to lay two or even three clutches of eggs if the first is destoryed by predation or adverse weather. An arctic nester, by comparison, has only a short period of solar energy available, which it must take swift and efficient advantage of for rearing its young, laying on reserves of fat for its southward journey, and accomplishing its own molt, a fatiguing process that its southern relatives can spread out over several months. (The solar energy upon which it is dependent, of course, is producing more than warmth and light. It is melting water to drink, fueling photosynthesis in the bird's food plants, and bringing to life the insects upon which it depends for protein.)

Because arctic nesters must face unpredictable weather along with an abbreviated period of solar energy, the timing of their arrival on the nesting ground and of their egg-laying and departure is critical. When a June sleet storm or a sudden August freeze destroys an entire generation of young birds, or 10,000 seals, or hundreds of caribou calves, it comes home in the starkest way that this is an environment marked by natural catastrophe, an inherently vulnerable ecosystem. The stress apparent to us, however, is not a sign of any weakness or fragility in arctic ecosystems. In fact, they show a remarkable resiliency. The Canadian muskox population increased dramatically after the winter of 1973–74. The harp seal thrives today in the Greenland Sea. The population of snow geese on Wrangel Island was back to about 300,000 by 1982.*

If we finally stood, then, at the end of our journey, looking over the tundra with that short list of arctic creatures to hand, wondering why it had dwindled so, we would need to look no further than that yellow star burning so benignly in the blue summer sky. It is the sunlight, always the streaming sunlight, that matters most. It is more critical even than temperature as a limiting factor on life. The salient reason there are so few species here

---

* The operation of the biological mechanisms responsible for the recovery of arctic species remains largely mysterious. Current research, however, indicates that, unlike their temperate-zone counterparts, arctic animals are apparently unable to tolerate both the inherent stress to which, in an evolutionary sense, they are accustomed and new stresses of man-made origin—oil blowouts, pollution from mine tailings, noise from arctic shipping, and the unnatural patterns of sea-ice disruption associated with icebreakers. They are therefore probably more vulnerable to man-made intrusions than the populations of any animals we have ever dealt with.

is that so few have metabolic processes or patterns of growth that can adapt to so little light. (Secondarily, many warm-blooded creatures can't conserve enough heat to survive in the extreme cold.) Of the roughly 3200 species of mammal we could possibly have encountered on the way north, we would find only 23 or so living beyond the tree line in this cold, light-poor desert.* Of some 8600 species of birds, only six or seven—common raven, snowy owl, rock ptarmigan, hoary redpoll, gyrfalcon, Ross's gull, and ivory gull—overwinter in the high Arctic, and only about 70 come north to breed. Of the boundless species of insect, only about 600 are to be found in the Arctic.† Of perhaps 30,000 species of fish, fewer than 50 have found a way to live here.

In certain parts of the Arctic—Lancaster Sound, the shores of Queen Maud Gulf, the Mackenzie River Delta, northern Bering Sea, the Yukon-Kuskokwin Delta—great concentrations of wild-life seem to belie violent fluctuations in this ecosystem. The Arctic seems resplendent with life. But these are summer concentrations, at well-known oases, widely separated over the land; and they consist largely of migratory creatures—geese, alcids, and marine mammals. When the rivers and seas freeze over in September they will all be gone. The winter visitor will find only caribou and muskoxen, and occasionally arctic hares, concentrated in any number, and again only in a few places.

All life, of course, cannot fly or swim or walk away to a warmer climate. When winter arrives, these animals must dis-

---

* Grizzly bear, polar bear, short-tailed weasel (ermine), least weasel, mink, wolverine, coyote, wolf, red fox, arctic fox, hoary marmot, arctic ground squirrel, collared lemming, brown lemming, tundra redback vole, tundra vole, Alaska vole, porcupine, arctic hare, tundra hare, moose, caribou, muskox.

† They include about 175 species of parasitic wasp, 25 species of sawfly, 40 species of moth, 100 species of root maggot, and 150 species of midge, as well as smaller numbers of species of black and crane flies, blowflies, hover flies, bumblebees, mosquitoes, springtails, fleas, butterflies, and about 60 species of beetle.

perse to areas where they will have a good chance to find food and where there is some protection from the weather. A few hibernate for seven or eight months. Voles and lemmings go to ground too, but remain active all winter. Wolves shift their home ranges to places where caribou and moose are concentrated. Arctic foxes follow polar bears out onto the sea ice, where they scavenge the bear's winter kills. Arctic hares seek out windblown slopes where vegetation is exposed. All these resident animals have a measure of endurance about them. They expect to see you, as unlikely as it may seem, in the spring.

In my seasonal travels the collared lemming became prominent in my mind as a creature representative of winter endurance and resiliency. When you encounter it on the summer tundra, harvesting lichen or the roots of cotton grass, it rises on its back feet and strikes a posture of hostile alertness that urges you not to trifle. Its small size is not compromising; it displays a quality of heart, all the more striking in the spare terrain.

Lemmings are ordinarily sedentary, year-round residents of local tundra communities. They came into the central Arctic at the end of the Pleistocene some 8000 years ago, crossing great stretches of open water and extensive rubble fields of barren sea ice to reach the places they live in today. In winter lemmings live under an insulating blanket of snow in a subnivean landscape, a dark, cool, humid world of quiet tunnels and windless corridors. They emerge in spring to a much brighter, warmer, and infinitely more open landscape—where they are spotted by hungry snowy owls and parasitic jaegers and are hunted adroitly by foxes and short-tailed weasels. In most years, in most places, there is not much perplexing about this single link in several arctic food chains. In some places, every three or four years, however, the lemming population explodes. Lemmings emerge from their subnivean haunts in extraordinary numbers and strike out—blindly is the guess—across the tundra.

The periodic boom in lemming populations—there are comparable, though more vaguely defined, cycles affecting the periodic rise and fall of snowshoe hare and lynx populations, and caribou and wolf populations—is apparently connected with the failure of the lemmings' food base. The supply of available forage reaches a peak and then collapses, and the lemmings move off smartly in all directions as soon as traveling conditions permit in the spring. Occasionally many thousands of them reach sea cliffs or a swift-moving river; those pushing in the rear force the vanguard into the water to perish.

Arctic scientist Laurence Irving, camped once on a gravel bar off the Alaska coast, wrote: "In the spring of a year of climaxing abundance, a lively and pugnacious lemming came into my camp . . . [more] tracks and a dead lemming were seen on the ice several kilometers from shore. The seaward direction of this mad movement was pointless, but it illustrates stamina that could lead to a far dispersal." Irving's regard, of course, is a regard for the animal itself, not for the abstract mechanisms of population biology of which it seems to merely be a part. Its apparently simple life on the tundra suggests it can be grasped, while its frantic migrations make it seem foolish. In the end, it is complex in its behavior, intricately fitted into its world, and mysterious.

Whenever I met a collared lemming on a summer day and took its stare I would think: Here is a tough animal. Here is a valuable life. In a heedless moment, years from now, will I remember more machinery here than mind? If it could tell me of its will to survive, would I think of biochemistry, or would I think of the analogous human desire? If it could speak of the time since the retreat of the ice, would I have the patience to listen?

One time I fell asleep on the tundra, a few miles from our camp. I was drowsy with sun and the weight of languid air. I nestled in the tussock heath, in the warm envelope of my down parka, and was asleep in a few moments. When I awoke I did not rise, but slowly craned my head around to see what was going on. At a distance I saw a ground squirrel crouched behind a limestone slab that rose six or eight inches out of the ground like a wall. From its attitude I thought it was listening, confirming the presence of some threat on the other side of the rock, in a shallow draw. After a while it put its paws delicately to the stone and slowly rose up to peer over, breaking the outline of the rock with the crown of its head. Then, with its paws still flat at the rim, it lowered itself and rested its forehead on the rock between its forelegs. The feeling that it was waiting for something deadly to go away was even stronger. I thought: Well, there is a fox over there, or a wolverine. Maybe a bear. He'd better be careful.

I continued to stare at him from the warm crevice in the earth that concealed me. If it is a bear, I thought, I should be careful too, not move from here until the ground squirrel loses that tension in its body. Until it relaxes, and walks away.

I lay there knowing something eerie ties us to the world of animals. Sometimes the animals pull you backward into it. You share hunger and fear with them like salt in blood.

The ground squirrel left. I went over to the draw beyond the rock but could find no tracks. No sign. I went back to camp mulling the arrangements animals manage in space and in time—their migrations, their patience, their lairs. Did they have intentions as well as courage and caution?

Few things provoke like the presence of wild animals. They pull at us like tidal currents with questions of volition, of ethical involvement, of ancestry.

For some reason I brooded often about animal behavior and the threads of evolution in the Arctic. I do not know whether it was the reserves of space, the simplicity of the region's biology, its short biological history, striking encounters with lone animals, or the realization of my own capacity to annihilate life here. I wondered where the animals had come from; and where we had come from; and where each of us was going. The ecosystem itself is only 10,000 years old, the time since the retreat of the Wisconsin ice. The fact that it is the youngest ecosystem on earth gives it a certain freshness and urgency. (Curiously, historians refer to these same ten millennia as the time of civilized man, from his humble beginnings in northern Mesopotamia to the present. Arctic eco-

systems and civilized man belong, therefore, to the same, short
epoch, the Holocene. Mankind is, in fact, even older than the
Arctic, if you consider his history to have begun with the emergence
of Cro-Magnon people in Europe 40,000 years ago.)

Human beings dwell in the same biological systems that contain
the other creatures but, to put the thought bluntly, they are not
governed by the same laws of evolution. With the development of
various technologies—hunting weapons, protective clothing, and
fire-making tools; and then agriculture and herding—mankind has
not only been able to take over the specific niches of other animals
but has been able to move into regions that were formerly un-
available to him. The animals he found already occupying niches in
these other areas he, again, either displaced or eliminated. The other
creatures have had no choice. They are confined to certain niches—
places of food (stored solar energy), water, and shelter—which
they cannot leave without either speciating or developing tools. To
finish the thought, the same technological advances and the enormous increase in his food base have largely exempted man from the
effect of natural controls on the size of his population. Outside
of some virulent disease, another ice age, or his own weapons
technology, the only thing that promises to stem the continued
increase in his population and the expansion of his food base (which
now includes oil, exotic minerals, fossil ground water, huge tracts of
forest, and so on, and entails the continuing, concomitant loss of
species) is human wisdom.

Walking across the tundra, meeting the stare of a lemming, or
coming on the tracks of a wolverine, it would be the frailty of our
wisdom that would confound me. The pattern of our exploitation
of the Arctic, our increasing utilization of its natural resources, our
very desire to "put it to use," is clear. What is it that is missing, or
tentative, in us, I would wonder, to make me so uncomfortable
walking out here in a region of chirping birds, distant caribou, and
redoubtable lemmings? It is restraint.

Because mankind can circumvent evolutionary law, it is in-
cumbent upon him, say evolutionary biologists, to develop another

law to abide by if he wishes to survive, to not outstrip his food base. He must learn restraint. He must derive some other, wiser way of behaving toward the land. He must be more attentive to the biological imperatives of the system of sun-driven protoplasm upon which he, too, is still dependent. Not because he must, because he lacks inventiveness, but because herein is the accomplishment of the wisdom that for centuries he has aspired to. Having taken on his own destiny, he must now think with critical intelligence about where to defer.

A Yup'ik hunter on Saint Lawrence Island once told me that what traditional Eskimos fear most about us is the extent of our power to alter the land, the scale of that power, and the fact that we can easily effect some of these changes electronically, from a distant city. Eskimos, who sometimes see themselves as still not quite separate from the animal world, regard us as a kind of people whose separation may have become too complete. They call us, with a mixture of incredulity and apprehension, "the people who change nature."

I remember one summer evening on the sea ice at the mouth of Admiralty Inlet, lying on caribou skins in my tent, nursing a slight wound I had suffered during the butchering of a narwhal. I was one of two white men in the group of eight and the only one who did not speak Inuktitut, which, far out on the sea ice, increased my feelings of isolation. As I lay there, however, I recalled vaguely some words of Wilfred Thesiger, who traveled among the Bedouin, which I later looked up: "I was happy in the company of these men who had chosen to come with me. I felt affection for them personally and sympathy with their way of life. But though the easy quality of our relationship satisfied me, I did not delude myself that I could be one of them. They were Bedu and I was not; they were Muslims and I was a Christian. Nevertheless I was their companion and an inviolable bond united us."

Lying there in the tent, I knew, as does everyone I think who spends some time hunting with Eskimos, that they are not idyllic people, errorless in the eyes of God. But they are a people, some of them, still close to the earth, maintaining the rudiments of an ancient philosophy of accommodation with it that we have abandoned. Our first wisdom as a species, that unique metaphorical knowledge that distinguishes us, grew out of such an intimacy with the earth; and, however far we may have come since that time, it did not seem impossible to me that night to go back and find it. I wanted to enquire among these people, for what we now decide to do in the North has a certain frightening irrevocability about it.

I wanted to enquire, as well, among thoughtful visitors, people who were taken with the land. Each culture, it seemed to me, is a repository of some good thought about the universe; we are valuable to each other for that. Lying there, I thought of my own culture, of the assembly of books in the library at Alexandria; of the deliberations of Darwin and Mendel in their respective gardens; of the architectural conception of the cathedral at Chartres; of Bach's cello suites, the philosophy of Schweitzer, the insights of Planck and Dirac. Have we come all this way, I wondered, only to be dismantled by our own technologies, to be betrayed by political connivance or the impersonal avarice of a corporation?

I had no idea as I lay on those caribou skins that evening precisely where wisdom might lie. I knew enough of quantum mechanics to understand that the world is ever so slightly but uncorrectably out of focus, there are no absolutely precise answers. Whatever wisdom I would find, I knew, would grow out of the land. I trusted that, and that it would reveal itself in the presence of well-chosen companions.

I looked out of the tent. It was after one in the morning. A south wind blew, but so slightly. The kind of wind nineteenth-century sailors called "inclinable to calm." Nakitavak lay stretched out on caribou skins and a cotton sleeping bag on his big sled, his qamutiik, watching the still black water between two massive ice floes, the open lead into which narwhals would come, sooner or later. His brother David, both hands wrapped around a mug of tea, was looking to the west, the direction from which he thought they would come. His lips stretched to the steaming, hot surface of the tea, and in the chill air I heard the susurrations of his sipping.

These Tununiarusirmiut men, relatives of the Tununirmiut to the east who had met the whalers 160 years ago, knew beyond a shadow of a doubt, beyond any hesitation, what made them happy, what gave them a sense of satisfaction, of wealth. An abundance of animals.

And so, we waited.

Two

BANKS ISLAND
Ovibos moschatus

I T IS THE MIDDLE OF JUNE, so it is apparent, as it would never
be on a dark and frozen day in December, that the Thomsen
River is actually a river. It rises among unnamed creeks in
east-central Banks Island and flows black and sparkling under the
summer light, north to Castel Bay on M'Clure Strait. It is a highway of nutrients, and northwest Banks Island is an arctic oasis
because of it, a kind of refuge for plants and animals.

The verdant, fertile valley of the Thomsen River is striking
country in part because so much of the rest of the island is a desert
of gravel, of bare soils and single, far-flung plants—a patch of
yellow cinquefoil blooms, say, or a bright green cushion of moss

campion. On the west bank of the Thomsen, where I am camped between Able and Baker creeks, the landscape is stark: gully erosion has cut deeply into a high-rising plateau to the west. But even here is a suggestion of the refugelike character of the Thomsen River Valley, for these desert-colored shores were never touched by Pleistocene glaciers. Like most of western and interior Alaska, much of Banks Island went unscathed during the glacial epoch. These, in fact, might have been the shores of an ice-free Arctic Ocean 20,000 years ago.

I have come here to watch muskoxen. The muskox, along with the American bison, is one of the few large animals to have survived the ice ages in North America. Most all of its companions—the mammoth, the dire wolf, the North American camel, the short-faced bear—are extinct. The muskox abides, conspicuously alone and entirely at ease on the tundra, completely adapted to a polar existence.

I am sitting at the edge of a precipitous bluff, several hundred feet above the Thomsen, with a pair of high-powered binoculars. At this point the river curves across a broad plain of seepage meadows and tundra in a sweeping oxbow to my left; on my right Baker Creek has cut a steep-banked gash into the badlands to the west. Far to the south, in front of me, are clusters of black dots; at a distance of more than two miles they arrest even the naked eye with a strange, faint reflection. The mind knows by that slow drift of dark points over a field of tan grasses on an open hillside that there is life out there. But an older, deeper mind is also alerted by the flash of light from those distant, long-haired flanks. The predatory eye is riveted.

The broad valley in which the muskoxen graze has the color and line of a valley in Tibet. I raise my field glasses to draw it nearer. Beyond the resolution of the ground glass the animals look darker, the tans of the hills more deeply pigmented, and the sky at the end of the distant valley is a denser blue. The light shimmers on them. I recall the observation of a Canadian muskox biologist: "They are so crisp in the landscape. They stand out like no other animal, against the whites of winter or the colors of the summer tundra."

I put the glasses back in my lap. A timeless afternoon. Off to my left, in that vast bowl of stillness that contains the meandering river, tens of square miles of tundra browns and sedge meadow greens seem to snap before me, as immediate as the pages of my notebook, because of unscattered light in the dustless air. The land seems guileless. Creatures down there take a few steps, then pause and gaze about. Two sandhill cranes stand still by the river. Three Peary caribou, slightly built and the silver color of the moon, browse a cutbank in that restive way of deer. Tundra melt ponds, their bright dark blue waters oblique to the sun, stand out boldly in the plain. In the center of the large ponds, beneath the surface of the water, gleam cores of aquamarine ice, like the constricted heart of winter.

On the far side of the Thomsen other herds of muskoxen graze below a range of hills in clusters of three or four. In groups of ten and twelve. I sketch the arrangements in my notebook. Most remarkable to me, and clear even at a distance of two or three miles because of the contrast between their spirited, bucking gambols and the placid ambling of the others, is the number of calves. Among forty-nine animals, I count twelve calves. The mind doesn't easily register the sustenance of the sedge meadows, not against the broad testimony of the barren hills and eroded plateaus. It balks at the evidence of fecundity, and romping calves. The muskoxen on the far side of the river graze, nevertheless, on sweet coltsfoot, on mountain sorrel, lousewort, and pendant grass, on water sedge. The sun gleams on them. On the melt ponds. The indifferent sky towers. There is something of the original creation here.

I bring my glasses up to study again the muskoxen in the far valley to the south. Among fifty or sixty animals are ten or fifteen calves. I regard them for a while, until I hear the clattering alarm call of a sandhill crane. To the southwest an arctic hare rises up immediately, smartly alert. To the southeast a snowy owl sitting on a tussock, as conspicuous in its whiteness as the hare, pivots its head far around, right then left. The hare, as intent as if someone had whistled, has found me and fixed me with his stare. In that moment I feel the earth bent like a bow and sense the volume of space between us, as though the hare, the owl, and I stood on a dry lakebed. The moment lasts until the hare drops, becomes absorbed again in the leaves of a willow. The owl returns its gaze to the river valley below.

The indictment of the sandhill cranes continues; I shift my perch so they cannot see me, and their calls cease.

Behind me to the north my four companions, dressed in patterns of color unmistakably human, are at work on a hillside: archaeologists, meticulously mapping the placement of debris at a nineteenth-century Copper Eskimo campsite called PjRa-18, or, informally, the Kuptana site. Like others in the region, this campsite sits near the top of a windswept hill and looks down on well-developed sedge meadows, exceptional muskox pasturage. Scattered over 20,000 square yards at the campsite are more than 27,000 pieces of bone, representing the skeletal debris of about 250 muskoxen. The archaeologists call it a "death assemblage." There are also rings of river stones there, which once anchored caribou-skin tents against wind and rain; and the remnants of meat caches built of shale and ironstone slabs, and of charcoal fires of willow twigs and arctic white heather. The lower jaw of an arctic char, eaten a hundred years ago, still glistens with fish oil. A sense of timelessness is encouraged by this primordial evidence of human hunger.

The muskoxen grazing so placidly in the hills to the south and in the sedge meadows to the east, so resplendent with life, are perhaps descendants of these, whose white, dark-horned skulls now lie awry on the land.

The story of this camp begins in the previous century.

In September 1851, Captain Robert M'Clure was guiding HMS *Investigator* along the north coast of Banks Island, desperate for relief from the press of heavy ice in the strait later named for him. Toward the island's eastern cape M'Clure found a shallow,

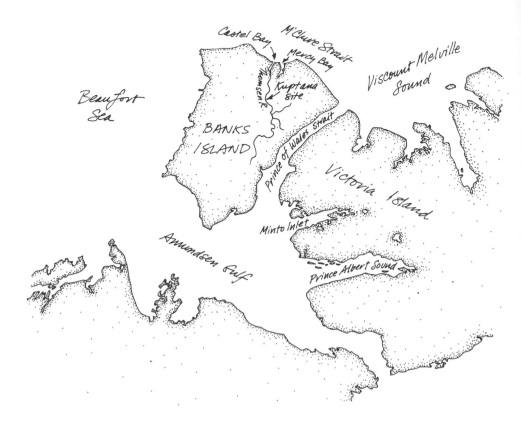

protected embayment, which he called the Bay of God's Mercy. He and his men overwintered there. The following summer the ice did not go out of the bay, and they were forced to overwinter again in the same spot. In the spring of 1853 a rescue party reached them from HMS *Resolute*, a sister ship in winter quarters at Melville Island. (Both ships were part of a British search force looking for the lost Franklin Expedition.) M'Clure, reluctantly accepting the fact that *Investigator* was inextricably trapped, abandoned the 450-ton, copper-sheathed vessel and followed the rescue party back to Melville Island.

Copper Eskimos living more than 200 miles away on Victoria Island somehow learned of the abandoned ship. (These Kanghiryuakmiut and Kanghiryuachiakmiut people, from around Minto

Inlet and Prince Albert Sound, had never seen white people. They would not be contacted by whites until American whalers visited them in 1906. Shortly thereafter they would be named Copper Eskimos, identifying them with the tools they made from local copper deposits.) When the Victoria Island people first crossed over the spring ice of Prince of Wales Strait to Banks Island is not known, but they left a clear trail up the Thomsen River Valley to Mercy Bay.

It was ironic that such wealth should fall into the hands of the Victoria Island people. Until that moment they had found themselves at the far end of not one but two arctic trade routes. The first came from the west, from Siberia across the north coast of Alaska; the other came from the south, up the Mackenzie River from the interior of Canada. Now they could reverse the flow of trade goods.* Rarely had they seen the likes of the materials they found at Mercy Bay, and never in such abundance. The shore cache and the ship itself were as marvelous to them as the discovery of a well-provisioned vehicle from space.

The Eskimos likely traveled lightly on their annual excursions to Mercy Bay, saving space on their small sleds and inside dog panniers for salvaged materials. Most prized were strips of iron and sheets of canvas, and softwood boards, which were easier to carve than caribou antler. Also cooper sheathing, woven cloth, hemp lines, wool yarn, and leather boots (for the leather alone—they were completely unsuitable as arctic footwear, a point the British were slow to learn).

On their journeys north, except for small amounts of seal meat and blubber carried with them from Victoria Island, the Eskimos ate what they killed en route—an occasional caribou,

---

* The reversal in the flow of trade goods initially confused anthropologists trying to figure out the development of trading patterns in the Far North. Others, unaware of the effect the *Investigator* had had on the lives of Victoria Island Eskimos, mistakenly assumed for years that these tribal groups were part of a pristine aboriginal culture.

molting geese (which, flightless, could not escape), fish, and a great many muskoxen. They drove the muskoxen out of the sedge meadows along the river and up onto hilltops where, predictably, they turned to make a stand and Eskimo dogs held them at bay. The hunters shot them with copper- and iron-tipped arrows, the shafts carefully assembled from willow twigs bound together with bits of sinew. (Today, shoulder blade after shoulder blade bears the small, round arrow hole, at an angle that would have carried the arrow straight to the heart. Their knowledge of the animal's anatomy was precise.)

The muskoxen were butchered where they fell, and a camp was set up. From such camps, presumably, small parties traveled back and forth to the *Investigator* and its cache all summer. In early fall, when the first snows provided a traveling surface for the sleds, the people returned south to country where seal hunting would hold them in good stead through the coming winter. The same camps were used year after year, apparently, and the skeletons of hundreds of muskoxen piled up at some of them, like PjRa-18. By 1981, scientists had found 150 such campsites, large and small, along the Thomsen River, along with the dismembered skeletons of about 3000 muskoxen.

The muskox population, some think, collapsed under this heavy hunting pressure before the ship and its cache were fully exploited. (Remnants of the cache remain. The ship either sank in the bay or floated away—it has never been found.) After about 1890, no people from Victoria Island traveled the route anymore.

Between 1914 and 1918 the explorer Vilhjalmur Stefansson crossed Banks Island several times, but he never once saw muskoxen. None, in fact, was seen thereafter anywhere on the island until the summer of 1952, when a Canadian biologist spotted a lone bull in the Thomsen River drainage. The bull could have been part of a small, remnant population, previously undetected, or from a group that crossed over from Victoria Island and followed the same route the Eskimo had taken to the north. During the 1950s and 1960s muskoxen were seen sporadically on northern

Banks Island, and surveys conducted in the early 1970s confirmed
the presence of between 1200 and 1800 animals. A 1975 survey
indicated further increases, and surveys in the early 1980s revealed the population had reached an astonishing size—16,000 to
18,000 animals.

The phenomenal recovery of muskoxen on Banks Island is
something biologists cannot adequately explain. They do not have
enough information about muskox reproductive biology and nutrition or about the play of other factors, such as prolonged periods
of favorable weather or the absence of caribou competing for some
of the same food. Informally, however, there is agreement that the
lush sedge meadows and grasslands of the Thomsen River Valley
have played a critical role in the recovery at the northern end of
the island, and in the extension of the animals' range toward the
south.

A modern visitor to the Thomsen River district feels the
resilience of the country right away, in the rich and diverse bird
life, the numbers of arctic fox, the many lemming burrows, and
in the aggregations of arctic hare and caribou grazing on the hillsides. And in seeing how many calves there are in the muskoxen
herds. The valley is robust and serene with its life.

To leave the story here, with the herds recovered and the
hunting excesses of the Copper Eskimo a part of the past, would
serve a sense of restitution. We could imagine that the muskoxen
had been killed out by rough and thoughtless people, preoccupied
with retrieving the wealth at Mercy Bay. An isolated incident.
But a parallel with incidents at Pond's Bay suggests itself; and
something else about man and nature and extinction, much older,
flows here.

Fatal human involvement with wild animals is biologically and
economically complicated. In the 1940s and 1950s, Banks Island
Eskimos all but wiped out the wolf population at the southern end
of the island in an effort to protect their arctic fox trap lines from
scavenging. In 1981 and 1982, they brought heavy hunting pressure
to bear against muskoxen in the southern portion of the island, to

protect the caribou herds upon which they are dependent for food, which, in their view, compete poorly with muskoxen for the same forage. (The northeastern end of the island, the Thomsen River country, the Eskimos regard as an oasis, an endlessly productive landscape from which animals pour forth to satisfy the many needs of mankind for flesh and hides, bones, sinews, and furs. They neither hunt nor trap there.)

Hunting wild animals to the point of extinction is a very old story. Aleut hunters, for example, apparently wiped out populations of sea otter in the vicinity of Amchitka Island in the Aleutians 2500 years ago. New Zealand's moas were killed off by Maori hunters about 800 years ago. And zoogeographers working in the Hawaiian Islands discovered recently that more than half of the indigenous bird life there was killed off by native residents before the arrival of the first Europeans in 1778. (The motivations of the hunters involved are unknown to us. Nor do we know whether they understood the consequences of their acts. Nor, if they did, whether they would have behaved differently. Some anthropologists caution, too, that the apparent incidents of slaughter of bison at buffalo jumps in North America and of caribou at river crossings in historic and prehistoric times were ethical in context and consistent with a native understanding of natural history and principles of conservation.)

Man's ability to destroy whole wildlife populations goes back even farther than this, however. Arthur Jelinek, a vertebrate paleontologist, has referred to early man in North America in very harsh terms, calling him a predator "against whom no [naturally] evolved defense systems were available" and "a source of profound changes" in the ecosystems of North America at the beginning of the Holocene. This was "an extremely efficient and rapidly expanding predator group," Jelinek writes, with "a formidable potential for disruption."

The specific events on which Jelinek bases these judgments are the catastrophic die-offs of large mammals that began about

18,000 years ago in North America and in which he believes man played the crucial role. Collectively the events are known as the Pleistocene extinction.

We are used to thinking of the North American plains as a place that teemed with life before the arrival of Europeans—60 million buffalo and millions of pronghorn antelope, elk, and deer, and grizzly bears and wolves. Oddly, however, this was only the remnant of an aggregation of animals the likes and numbers of which were truly staggering. By comparison with the late Pleistocene, eighteenth-century North America was an impoverished world, one "from which all the hugest, the fiercest, and strangest forms had recently disapepared." Giant armadillo, ground sloths that stood as tall on their hind legs as modern giraffes, the North American cheetah, saber-toothed cats, mammoths, fleet horses and camels, and close relatives of the muskox as well—all were gone, both species and populations. And the land itself had changed radically. Where the eighteenth-century traveler saw deserts there had once been lush grasslands, and great herds of browsers and grazers and their attendant predators and scavengers.

There are sharply differing explanations of why all these animals died out at or near the end of the Pleistocene, but there is some general agreement that it was for one of two reasons. Either the climate changed swiftly and radically and the animals couldn't adapt, or they were hunted to extinction by man. Some scientists are quick to discount human hunting as a factor. They find the idea that this "intelligent" predator was a waster of meat untenable (though evidence to the contrary is overwhelming in early as well as modern times). And they are skeptical about the killing efficiency of the weapons and hunting techniques involved. They also believe there were too few human beings by far to account for the sheer numbers of animals killed. A climatic explanation alone, they suggest, might suffice. The land, according to this argument, dried up, and the composition and distribution of plant life changed radically. The large herbivorous mammals most dependent on these plants died out, along with their predators and scavengers. In this model the predatory efficiency of man is sometimes regarded as the final blow to the ecosystem at a time of extreme environmental stress.

Intricate, cogent, and forceful arguments have been made in support of both explanations. That man played a significant, if not decisive, role, however, seems inescapable. His capacity to do so is clear and, to judge from the fate of the plains buffalo, the passenger pigeon, the great auk, and the bowhead whale, he can be lethally and extensively efficient. The pattern, some would argue, is still with us, and the extinctions are about to increase again, because of the exponential destruction of natural habitat attendant upon the expansion of human numbers.

We lament the passing of the Eskimo curlew, the sea mink, the Labrador duck, Pallas' cormorant, and Steller's sea cow. Their lives are now beyond our inquiry. Our reluctance to accept direct responsibility for these losses, however, is sound if somewhat complicated biological thinking, rooted in a belief that there is nothing innately wrong with us as a species and in our belief that we are not solely responsible for every extinction. (The California condor, for example, is perhaps doomed on its own ecological account.) Our recent biological heritage has been exactly this, to sharply reduce the populations of other species or eliminate them entirely and occupy their niches in the food web whenever we had need or desire. It is not denigrating, not even criticizing from a certain point of view, to so understand ourselves. The cold view to take of our future is that we are therefore headed for extinction in a universe of impersonal chemical, physical, and biological laws. A more productive, certainly more engaging view, is that we have the intelligence to grasp what is happening, the composure not to be intimidated by its complexity, and the courage to take steps that may bear no fruit in our lifetimes.

Squatting over the detritus at the Kuptana site on a June evening, picking at the earth between two willow runners with a muskox rib, one cannot blame the Copper Eskimo who killed the muskoxen here. Perhaps they even understood, at some level in the human makeup now irretrievable to us, that the muskoxen would come back, even if it seemed they had killed them all. Nor can one blame the modern Eskimo hunters on the island for wanting to get rid of wolves to protect the cash income from their trap lines, or to get rid of muskoxen to ensure a good supply of caribou meat. They are trying to adapt to an unorthodox, for them, economics. But we could help each other. Their traditional philosophy is insistent on the issue of ethical behavior toward animals. Within the spirit of this tradition and within the European concept of compassionate regard may lie the threads of a modern realignment with animals. We need an attitude of enlightened respect which will make both races feel more ethically at ease with animals, more certain of following a dignified course in the years ahead, when the animals will still be without a defense against us.

Here in the dirt, pushing past the desiccated winter pellets of muskoxen with my rib bone, past the fresher pellets of arctic hare, past windblown tufts of shed caribou hair, and a layer of dry, curled leaves from willows and saxifrage, I find a damp and precious mud. A foundation. Whatever their moral predilections may have been, the Kanghiryuakmiut and Kanghiryuachiakmiut ate the flesh of the muskoxen who browsed these willows. They made ladles from their horns, tools from their bones, and slept through the first, freezing storms of autumn on the thick insulation of their hides. And they survived. In the long history of man, before and after the coming of the glaciers, this counts for more than one can properly say.

When I stand up and look out over the valley I can feel the tremendous depth of time: myself at this 100-year-old campsite, before a valley the scientists say was never touched by glacial ice, and which the modern Eskimo say is and has been a sacred precinct. The muskoxen graze out there as though I were of no more importance than a stone. The skulls of their ancestors lie in the sun at my feet, and cool winds come down the Kuptana slope and ride up over my bare head.

THE first muskoxen I ever saw were on a research farm outside Fairbanks, Alaska. It was summer, a pleasant day when the light air, the cleared fields beyond, and the surrounding hills seemed innocent. A lone animal emerged from tall, dry grasses at the foot of a slope below me. The grasses rolled in his wake, until he stood stolid on open ground, his long flank hair falling still with the stilling grass. In that moment I was struck by qualities of the animal that have stayed with me the longest: the movement was Oriental, and the pose one of meditation. The animal seemed to quiver with attention before he lowered his massive head and moved on, with the most deliberate step I have ever seen a large animal take. The shaft of a dark horn came into view, forward of the high shoulders and the full collar of his distinctive mane. The muskox settled then in my mind as a Buddhist monk, a samurai warrior. In the months after, these characterizations proved impetuous; but like many unbidden insights they served, and I retain them.

I entered that six-acre enclosure with the animals' caretaker, a Danish student at the University of Alaska named Poul Henrichsen. The animals had moved into a patch of spruce trees, and Henrichsen warned me to be alert, to stay near the fence and be ready to climb it. We came upon them from below the crest of a hill, with only their backs visible, and I was struck by how easily in this view the animal, with its shoulder hump and the tawny saddle behind its withers, could be confused with a grizzly bear. We came closer. I was surprised by how small they were. And, as we drew nearer still, by how adroitly they moved in the trees, and, as they moved, how close to each other they remained, hip to flank, flank to flank, even in that confining picket of spruce trees.

We did not press them further, but retreated toward the fence and watched in silence. Occasionally I would ask a question in low tones, and Henrichsen would reply. The animals regarded us warily, testing the cool air in the trees with the flared nostrils of their broad black noses, rolling their large, golden-brown eyes as though we were two figures caught in a light they could not quite fathom.

Later, walking across a pasture in which caribou grazed (in comparison with the muskoxen they seemed high-strung and confused in their movements), I told Henrichsen of my Oriental impression of the muskox.

"But you know where they come from?"

"Yes," I said, smiling, "but I had forgotten."

They came from the high plains of northern China, where their evolutionary ancestors adapted in sheeplike and cattlelike ways to alpine and tundra life. Richard Harington, a Canadian vertebrate paleontologist, believes the genus *Ovibos* itself emerged about 2 million years ago on the steppes of central Siberia, finding its expression in several species. One, *Ovibos pallantis*, a Eurasian muskox hunted by Cro-Magnon people, may have survived into modern times on the Taimyr Peninsula in Russia. *Ovibos moschatus*, the modern North American animal, migrated across the Bering land bridge about 125,000 years ago, at the end of the Illinoian ice advance, or perhaps earlier. It was probably preceded by its own ancestors and relatives, including *Symbos cavifrons*, a taller, more slender animal and the dominant muskox in North America during the Pleistocene; *Praeovibus*, also larger, longer-legged, and more slender; *Bootherium*, a small woodland muskox; and *Euceratherium*, an alpine-adapted muskox. All these animals died out at the end of the Pleistocene, along with several species of *Ovibos* itself—*O. yukonensis* and *O. proximus*. Remains of the only one of this group to survive, *O. moschatus*, the modern animal, have been found as far south as New Jersey and Nebraska, where they lived during the height of the last, or Wisconsin, ice age.

When the Wisconsin ice began to retreat about 18,000 years ago, a current theory goes, muskoxen living in what is now the central and eastern United States began moving north. Their very

distant offspring—the animals found today south of Queen Maud
Gulf, north of Great Bear Lake, and along the Thelon River—are
called barren ground or mainland Canadian muskoxen. A second
group of muskoxen, which moved south from high arctic refugia
after the retreat of the ice, down the east coast of Greenland and
onto Ellesmere, Devon, and Melville islands, are called high arctic
or Greenland muskoxen.*

The muskox has a single living relative, the takin of northern
Tibet, a calflike animal of ponderous build with a bulging snout
like a saiga antelope's, short, stout legs, and small, swept-back
horns, showing the same montane sheep/goat ancestry in its con-
formation and movements as the modern muskox. (The thick
golden fleece Jason sailed in quest of was that of the takin.)

Early observers were confused about the muskox's heredity.
Because of its heavy head and shoulders, Ernest Thompson Seton
thought it was related to the buffalo. Stefansson thought it was
related to the highland cattle of Europe, and Otto Sverdrup, a
Norwegian explorer, called the animals "polar oxen." Distant relatives all. The muskox's nearest relatives after the takin include
the Japanese serow, the chamois, the Rocky Mountain goat, and
the Barbary sheep.

In the end its scientific name, O. moschatus, the "sheeplike
cow with a musky smell," as well as its popular name, is ill-fitting.
The animal has no musk glands. During their rut muskoxen bulls
secrete a substance in their urine that is evident on their breath
and even in the flesh of a carefully butchered animal. The late
John Teal, an American muskox researcher, characterized the
smell as "pungent and faintly sweetish." Another biologist has
called it "a muskily sweet scent, resembling that of a gorilla."
Because the odor, in Teal's judgment, is less rank than that of other
ruminants, it is odd that the name "muskox" stuck. One explana-

---

* The successful transplants of muskoxen to several ranges in Alaska,
where the muskox was wiped out in the nineteenth century, have been
made with animals from this population.

tion is that in the seventeenth century, when the animals were first seen by Europeans on the western shores of Hudson Bay, their exotic appearance and the smells of bulls in rut led entrepreneurs to believe an association with musk deer of the Orient might exist. The wishful confusion of the riches of the Orient with those of North America was common at the time, and the illusion of a trade base was not discouraged by seventeenth-century traders.

THE long, glossy skirt of its guard hair is, initially, the muskox's most striking feature, particularly if the animal is moving. (The Eskimo word for the animal, *oomingmaq*, means "the animal with skin like a beard.") It is not so wild an affair as Nicolas Jérémie maintained in *Relation de détroit de la baye de Hudson* (1720), when he wrote that one could not tell "at a short distance which end the head was on." The pelage is an orderly arrangement of several sorts of hair, which appeared in disarray to Jérémie and others because they saw the animals only in the summer, when they are shedding. An extremely dense underfur of fine, woolly hairs, about two inches long, lies close to the skin and covers all of the animal but its hooves and horns and a patch of skin between its nostrils and lips. Its rump, belly, flanks, and throat are covered as well by a dense layer of long, coarse guard hair that hangs down skirtlike and that melds across the shoulders with a layer of thick but less coarse hairs which come up over the shoulders from low on the neck to form a mane. Behind the withers these hairs fade into an area of woolly underfur without guard hairs called the saddle.

The longest guard hairs—25 inches or more—grow down from the throat. The hairs of the skirt, which are replaced continuously, become more prominent with age and are most lustrous in rutting bulls. The underfur is shed in patches and streamers from late May to mid-July, though this strong, extremely light fleece continues to work its way out through the guard hairs until August, giving the animal a primordial appearance. This inelastic underfur, eight times warmer than sheep's wool by weight, is as soft as the pashm of Kashmir goats or the wool of the vicuña. A single muskox might carry ten pounds of it, enough, in the estimation of one diligent observer, to make a single forty-strand thread 150 miles long.

Calves are born with a short coat of natal underfur and a fine layer of cinnamon-colored overfur. These are replaced toward the end of the first summer by thicker underfur and longer overfur. Coarse guard hairs don't begin to appear until the second year.

The underfur in the saddle area is white to tawny yellow, and elsewhere light brown, with shadings of cinnamon. The overlying guard hairs are black on the rump and flanks, shading to blackish browns with auburn highlights on the forequarters. The legs below the "knee" (the heel, actually) are white. Among certain populations (and with some individuals) white hairs are prominent on the face, muzzle, and back of the head, behind the horn boss, and between the horns of females. An unusual strain of muskoxen with cream-colored guard hairs is known to Eskimos living in the Queen Maud Gulf region and has recently been described for the first time by scientists. (British sailors reported seeing an albino muskox cow with a dark calf near Cape Smyth, Melville Island, in June 1853.)

The great thickness of their hair—short, roundly pointed ears are almost hidden in the ruff of hair forward of the neck, as is a short tail at the other end—makes muskoxen seem larger than they are. Their weights vary widely, depending on sex, the season, and their diets. An "average" mature male might weigh 650 pounds, a female 400 pounds. An adult male might stand 55 inches at the shoulder and measure 90 inches from nose to rump, with a female measuring 48 inches and 75 inches, respectively.

Both sexes grow slowly. Males reach maturity in size in their sixth or seventh year and females at five or six. According to Canadian zoologist Ben Hubert, muskoxen weights vary so much because, in the case of males, the animals are in a "positive nutritional state" (i.e., gaining weight) for only two months out of the year, July and August. He found them to be in a "neutral balance" for four months, and to be slowly losing weight the other six months, during rut in the fall and for much of the winter. Females gain weight during about five months of the year, and lose it in winter and during calving and lactation (the calves are nursed for about fifteen months).

The muskox's unique, characteristic horns suggest a cape buffalo's, but they curve down close to the cheeks before hooking out and up in a recurved point. The female's horns are shorter and more slender. They also taper more sharply than the male's and do not grow together, helmetlike, in a boss over the skull. The horns, which turn a darker brown with light tips in older animals, continue to grow slowly throughout an animal's life. The female's attain the finished line of the adult shape in about four years, the male's in six. The horns are primarily defensive weapons, wielded against predators, but they also serve to uproot vegetation and in an important and complex way for social display and in fighting during the males' rut.

The large eyes, which protrude from the skull to clear the thick pelt and permit a wider field of lateral vision, are superbly well adapted. A double retina serves to intensify images in the darkness and the low light of winter, and the pupil, a horizontal slit, can close completely to prevent snowblindness. (Traditional Eskimo snow goggles imitate this design.) The pupil is also heavily lined with corpora nigra, which shield the retina against glare from the sky above and from snow and ice on the ground.

For its size, the muskox is surprisingly nimble and surefooted. In part this is due to the shape and structure of its hooves, which are broadly round and sharp-edged with concave bottoms. A broad heel pad gives the animal excellent traction on rock and hard ground and on various snow surfaces. The front hooves, which are larger, are used in winter to break and paw through wind-slabbed snow and groundfast ice. The muskox also uses its chin for this purpose.

Muskoxen appear to have only two gaits, a walk and a gallop. The gallop is swift and energetic, in contrast to the slow, almost drifting walk. The animals can gallop for several miles without breaking stride, stop short in perfect balance, and run up steep talus slopes with remarkable speed, revelations of their mountain-climbing heritage. They have a curious habit of occasionally pausing to sit on their haunches when rising from a resting position, an action that gives them an air of being preoccupied with thought. Adults also roll over on their backs and loll, with their legs suspended in the air.

Adults maintain a generally stolid demeanor, even when calves cavort wildly among them or when arctic foxes scamper and feint back and forth through a herd. In summer, however, adults are just as apt to romp in creeks and rivers, which they seem to delight in splashing and whirling through. (An American archaeologist working on Banks Island told me about a herd of seventeen or eighteen he watched slide down a gravel hill into a creek on their rumps and then go bucking off like horses in various directions.) Moving water is a short-lived summer phenomenon, and Anne Gunn, a Scottish biologist, remembers watching new-born calves encountering it for the first time. "The calves were spell-bound. There were seven or eight of them, about two months old. They jostled each other at the edge, shocked to get their feet wet, then ran off into the herd, stomping and bucking to get away from it." Young calves chase each other regularly through a grazing herd and play "king of the mountain," perching their oddly tapirlike bodies on tussocks, their small feet pressed together like a mountain goat's.

Muskoxen are unique among ruminants in the amount of body contact they make. Even when they are fleeing, they gallop away shoulder to shoulder, flank to flank. One of the most dazzling displays of this I ever witnessed occurred on Seward Peninsula when a herd of muskoxen spun around on a hill in confusion at the approach of a low-flying aircraft. They moved as a single animal, rising in a tight turn to change direction. The wild, synchronous sweep of their long skirts was like a dark wave of water climbing a sea cliff before falling back on itself. Long-term muskoxen researchers frequently comment on these synchronous aspects of their behavior, noting, for example, that a herd feeds and rests on a rough cycle of 150-minute periods, winter and summer.

At the approach of a threatening animal, including men and their dogs, muskoxen begin to draw near to each other, sometimes quickly, and occasionally in response to the sudden bellow of a herd bull. (The herd bull is more often distinguished, however, by being the last to respond, and the first to relax, in these situations.) The animals may initially press together in a line abreast, with the herd bull toward the center and slightly forward, and younger bulls at the flanks. If the approaching animal changes direction, or if more than one animal is approaching, the muskoxen may back around into a rosette, rump to rump, with calves and yearlings wedged between adults.

This defensive formation is not always symmetrical, nor do muskoxen always take this position when challenged—sometimes they just run off. But in evolutionary terms it has been exceedingly effective against their major predator, the wolf. Bulls and cows rush out from this formation to make short, hooking charges with lowered heads. Wolves are only successful if they can get behind a charging animal and cut it off from the herd, or if they dash into a momentary opening and snatch a calf. Wolves are patient and opportunistic in these situations, or they wouldn't still be around either.

This close-contact, defensive formation is found in no other species, and it is interesting to speculate about its origin. Some researchers have suggested that muskoxen prefer hilly country to open plains, noting that they often run to a hilltop before assuming their defensive formation. When caught out alone by wolves, a muskoxen will try to back itself into a snowbank or a landform of some sort, even backing slowly into a fast-moving river, to protect its hindquarters. In the defensive rosette, of course, each animal creates a back and a side wall for the others. This suggests that somewhere in their evolutionary history muskoxen lived a long while in open country, where they discovered a way to

create, cooperatively, the spatial relief necessary to protect themselves.

Muskoxen herds change size and composition over the year.
Summer groups tend to be small, from two to ten animals, while
winter herds may consist of sixty or more animals. In summer, too,
one is especially likely to see lone animals, almost always bulls,
and single-sex herds—bulls or cows accompanied by younger animals and calves. As bulls come into rut the presence of a mature
breeding bull within a herd may become apparent, though it is
taking a step in the wrong direction to call such aggregations
"bulls with their harems." (Bulls are selecting themselves out as
suitable male parents in their violent rutting encounters; what
females are doing at this time is more obscure, but chances are
they are not as passive in this drama as they appear.)*

The makeup of a particular herd, to take the extreme examples, can change frequently or remain stable for months on end.
A large herd grazing in a sedge meadow may, after longer scrutiny,
be seen actually to consist of multiple, discrete herds. Two herds
may merge to become one; a day later three herds may emerge.
Herds are neither disorganized nor rigidly organized. They are
cohesive social arrangements existing in time. Biologists posit that
they give some animals advantages in their feeding, breeding, and
survival strategies, but they are not certain what these are.

Changes in the composition of muskox herds suggest that both
individual animals and the aggregations themselves have "personalities." Mixed herds do not always consist of retiring females
and younger animals being led by domineering males. Cows as

---

* In trying to generalize about herd behavior, one is always confronted
with knowledge of variation and inconsistency; for example, the ratio
of one age class in a herd to another, as well as its sexual makeup, may
result in two herds behaving differently under apparently similar
circumstances. It is a simple truth of field biology that it is easy to
miss and hard to figure out what, exactly, an animal is doing. And what
animals do may be more complex than the descriptions we apply or the
measurements we devise.

well as bulls influence herd movement and behavior, though the activity of herd bulls is frequently more evident. Herd leaders emerge not only at the approach of predators but whenever obstacles present themselves—a formidable river, a steep escarpment, or a crumbling cutbank. A knowledge of the other animals' personalities, some actual experience with each other, may come into play in these situations and may be especially apparent in the creation of a defensive formation. Perhaps animals somewhat unknown to each other are the ones that panic, running off to leave calves and their mothers behind; while other groups, better known to each other, are the ones that move with efficient precision, the older animals butting and kicking momentarily confused or obstinate calves to the protective interior of the formation.

We are sometimes at a loss in trying to describe such events because we unthinkingly imagine the animals as instinctual. We are suspicious of motive and invention among them. The lesson of evolution with the muskox, an animal that has changed little in 2 million years, is that whether it is witty or dull in its deliberation, a significant number have consistently chosen correctly.

The muscular, restless behavior of rutting bulls is so charged with energy that humans experience nervous amusement as well as exhilaration in watching it. The same interactions—head-butting, horn display, charging—go on all year, but they increase in frequency and intensity during the rut. The bulls' otherwise placid and presumably subtle relationships with each other take on a raw edge of intolerance.

David Gray, a Canadian muskox biologist who observed bulls' behavior closely for a number of years in the Polar Bear Pass region of Bathurst Island, was the first to fully describe these male encounters, using the categories that follow (from least to most intense).

First is the (usually) passive displacement of one bull by another at a feeding spot. As one bull approaches, the other simply moves on, often to displace another animal. A bull might raise its head to regard another bull, ordinarily a sign of attentiveness or alarm as well as a mild threat display (or, to be perfectly candid, a sign he is only urinating). A more serious threat display, one unique to muskoxen, is lowering the head to rub one or the other of two pear-shaped glands below the eye on the inside of a foreleg. This is often done with great vigor, suggesting a "whetting of the horns." More agitation still is expressed by an animal raking the ground with the tips of his horns, or escalating his irritation to head tilting. In head tilting, bulls move toward each other with averted eyes, leading with a shoulder and a prominent display of the horn boss. In doing so alone, one bull appears to be circling sideways around the other animal; when two bulls are head tilting simultaneously, they are said to be "parallel walking."

The most serious confrontations are actual head butts and charges, which vary in their intensity. Two bulls may place their horn bosses together and push mild-manneredly at each other for a few moments—or push off their forequarters with driving strength and quick, ferocious thrusts of the head. A loss of advantage here opens an animal to sideways, jabbing hooks with the horns, or goring. When two bulls engage each other like this —head tilting, parallel walking, butting and charging—their movements become stylized. They select flat terrain for these meetings, heightening the aura of ritual. The usual deliberate walking gait becomes stiff-legged, slow, and exaggerated. A charge is preceded by side-to-side head swinging and a backing away from each other, as though the air between them had suddenly expanded. They charge from 20 to 30 feet apart, furious head-to-head crashes that can knock one animal back on its haunches or carry both animals up on their hind legs. The sound of their meeting is like the fracturing of sea ice.

Bulls may charge each other repeatedly. When they back away, bristling with energy, the image is primordial. The mane is erect. The neck is swollen, exaggerating the size of the forequarters. Their eyes, their long guard hairs, glisten with light. Should a wind be blowing and tatters of underfur be whipping about their flanks in streamers, their appearance is apocalyptic, savage with intent. The encounters are sometimes fatal.

Mating is a less violent affair. The males, again in the human view, seem fulsome in their attentions to receptive females. They approach them repeatedly, overwrought and obsequious, sniffing the vaginal opening, drawing close along the female's flanks and resting a chin on her buttocks, nosing her neck, sometimes scraping her flanks with a foreleg. Bulls also engage in a mating display of sorts by twisting their heads over to look up at a female. And they bellow. David Gray describes the sound as "similar to the roar of a caged African lion."

Mating occurs when a female, repeatedly tested in these ways, remains stationary. The bull, rising on his hind legs, mounts her. The act lasts but a moment.

Mating takes place from mid-August to mid-September. Calves are born 240 to 250 days later, in mid-April to mid-May. Like most prey species, muskox calves are born precocious, able to stand up almost immediately and very soon able to run. Mid-April is still winter, but as long as they do not get wet, calves seem to survive very well. They are well insulated and born with ample adipose (brown) fat reserves from which they can draw heat. They spend much of their first few days resting and nursing. Their mothers call after them softly. In cool weather they take advantage of their mother's body as a shield, curling between her legs to sleep while she turns her back to the wind.

Herds are stationary during calving, which might go on for a month; but they rarely travel far at any time. Their summer ranges, where succulent sedges and other forbs emerge in June, and their winter ranges, where sun-cured grasses are exposed by winds, are often within only a few miles of each other. The infrequency of large-scale movement underscores a salient aspect of muskox ecology: only a relatively few, widely scattered feeding areas in this severe arctic environment will support muskoxen.

Researchers speculate that migration to a new area may occur as a result of the rut, when a single male forces other mature males to leave the area and these bulls depart with a few cows to establish a herd of their own. One theory about how whole herds locate new range to move to is that solitary bulls, wandering great distances in summer, find areas of suitable, year-round forage, then return to a herd in the vicinity of the one they left. Come fall, they lead the herd across sparsely vegetated range (including sea ice) to the new pasture. Pheromones (biochemical substances an animal produces and which its olfactory system can later detect) might make such movements possible. Bulls scent-mark by dribbling their urine on grasses and other elevated spots, especially during the rut. They also mark tussocks with secretions from their preorbital glands. These scent posts very likely play a role in mating but may also be important in regulating the spatial arrangement of muskoxen in a given landscape. Over time, such scent-making might well prevent over-grazing in those areas where muskoxen thrive, by "forcing" animals to spread out.

How muskoxen navigate over their native landscapes in darkness and snow, how they conceive of the space around them, is unknown.

Muskoxen maintain a constant body temperature of about 101°F, no matter what the air temperature. Because they routinely endure extremes of −40°F for prolonged periods of time, conditions that would drive polar bears and perhaps even arctic fox to shelter, the ability to maintain a constant temperature is striking. The heat they depend upon is generated by normal cell metabolism and the burning of stored fats and by other complex biochemical processes connected with nutrition. Their thick coats provide such excellent insulation that little of this heat escapes, the reason why snow that accumulates on their backs in a storm doesn't melt.

Ecologists are reasonably certain that arctic animals do not increase their basal rate of metabolism until the temperature reaches a certain critical level, different for each animal but around −50°F. (Birds are an exception.) The climate, in other words, does not force arctic animals to eat more. Heat retention, not increased heat production, is an animal's principal defense against cold. In 1847 Karl Bergmann suggested that since heat production is a three-dimensional process (heat radiates in all directions) and heat loss is a two-dimensional phenomenon (it occurs only at the surface of the skin), it would stand to reason that animals living in cold environments would evolve larger body sizes, with a greater ratio of mass (heat production) to surface (heat loss).

Bergmann's Rule, as it is called, is a somewhat archaic concept, as is a companion, Allen's Rule, set out in 1877. Allen believed that in cold environments there is a tendency toward the evolution of shorter extremities—ears, limbs, tails, and snouts. Both rules have a firm empirical basis in spite of many exceptions. What makes them archaic is that other adaptations for heat retention are comparatively more effective. The insulation provided by hair and underfur, exceptional in the case of the arctic fox and the muskox, is one source of warmth in severe cold. Polar bears are heavily insulated with fat, and den up in the worst weather. Other animals, particularly birds, warm cold venous blood from exposed extremities by running it through a coil of warm arterial blood before it reaches the body core. Animals also use differential heating (arctic fox, for example, can reduce the temperature of their footpads to near $32\,°F$), and changes in the electrical conductivity of their nervous systems to stay warm. No single one of these adaptations, however, is effective by itself; and physiological and biochemical research continues to reveal a more complicated picture of how arctic animals function in severe cold (e.g., how they control the loss of water from their bodies, or replenish what they do lose).

Muskoxen and other animals also conserve heat in winter by a conspicuous economy of action. In very cold weather, when any movement at all requires the burning of limited fat reserves, animals will just stand still for long periods of time, so long that someone has suggested the term "standing hibernation." When muskoxen do travel in cold weather, they move in single file through any appreciable accumulation of snow, stepping carefully in the track cleared by the animal ahead of them. During blizzards they might even bed down for several days. (An explorer in Greenland once terrified himself by seeking refuge from a storm in the lee of what he first took to be mounds of snow-covered earth. They were muskoxen, and they began to stand up as he walked over them.) Alwin Pederson believed that in the severest storms muskoxen choose an open area where the wind blows in a single direction and form a wedge into it, the herd bull at the apex, calves and yearlings to the rear. David Gray, for one, doubts that this occurs. He once observed a herd of muskoxen in a storm with 24-knot winds, blowing snow, and a temperature of −27°F (wind chill about −90°F). The animals "continued to feed in the usual manner or remained lying down" with their backs and sides to the wind.*

Kent Jingfors, a Swedish muskox biologist, once camped out in the drainage of the Sadlerochit River in Alaska in winter, in an effort to learn how muskoxen survived there. He recalls "days" of brutal cold and darkness when it took nearly all his will to carry out the simple tasks he set for himself. The animals moved slowly through the willows, wary of him. He followed behind with a flashlight, peering closely to see which plants they were browsing. He came to look on them with awe. Anyone who has tried to work effectively in −40°F weather, to contend with darkness in winter for long periods of time or the knife slash of windblown snow at these temperatures, wonders that any creature can endure like this for weeks on end, let alone seem to be at peace.

*   *   *

---

* Annual snowfall over most of the Arctic is light, often no more than four to six inches, and actual snowstorms are rare. Ground blizzards frequently occur in coastal areas, however, where most settlements are located. High winds and a furious swirling of dry snow already on the ground might persist for days, the condition commonly referred to in the Far North as a "blizzard."

WHAT muskoxen eat in their "marginal existence" in the Arctic, as well as when and how often, vitally affects their survival, but precisely how it does remains a mystery. Their year-long metabolic rhythms are as complex as their uptake of nutrients. There are some clues. They synthesize B-complex vitamins in their rumens. In winter they might draw vitamin A from storage in the liver. In the months without sunshine they may also draw on stores of vitamin D (needed for the uptake of calcium and phosphorus). They consume about 10 pounds of browse and fodder a day, more in July and August, when they are laying on adipose fat reserves for the winter. If biologists could determine what an optimal muskox diet is (how much of what when), and how animals use the plants available to them in breeding and nonbreeding years, and what their preference for such things as lousewort and oxytrope means—if they knew this, they would be close to answering one of the most perplexing questions about muskoxen: in response to what variables do these animals breed and bear young? And a corollary: how can we recognize excellent muskox habitat in areas where the animals no longer live?

The phenomenal recovery of the Banks Island muskox population is not an isolated event. In 1973–74, when an early winter rainstorm created a layer of groundfast ice that kept muskoxen from feeding in many places in the high Arctic, 48 percent of the herds on eastern Melville Island perished, including most of the animals in an area called Dundas Peninsula. When, several years later D. C. Thomas of the Canadian Wildlife Service found the Dundas Peninsula population thriving again, he suggested that the area had been repopulated from a nearby muskox refuge, an arctic oasis on Melville Island called Bailey Point.

Bailey Point represents perhaps the best muskox habitat in the high Arctic. Total precipitation (snow accumulation) is low. Ground ice rarely forms. It is protected from winter storms. And its lowlands and stream valleys are fertile and productive. There are at least three other such areas in the high Arctic: at Mokka

Fiord on the east coast of Axel Heiberg Island; on Fosheim Peninsula, northern Ellesmere Island; and at Truelove and adjacent lowlands on the northeast coast of Devon Island. Thomsen River is likely a fifth place. Peary Land on the north coast of Greenland and Hochstetter Peninsula on its east coast are very likely other refuges.

Research does not yet exist to compare the nutrition available to muskoxen in each of these areas (or to compare what is in these areas with what is in other areas where muskoxen are occasionally found), but Martha Robus, an American botanist, believes nutrition plays a critical role in how quickly muskoxen repopulate an area. Her studies were focused on a remarkable area of the Sadlerochit River in northeastern Alaska, where Kent Jingfors also pursued his graduate studies. (The muskoxen living along the Sadlerochit arrived there around June 1969, after fifty-one of them were transplanted by the U.S. Fish and Wildlife Service to Barter Island, 40 miles away on the Alaska coast. Others of these animals have since taken up life in adjacent drainages of the Jago River and, from a 1970 transplant, the Canning River.)

The conventional wisdom about sexual maturity in muskoxen, before Jingfors began his study of the Sadlerochit herd, was that females bred only every other year beginning in their fourth year and rarely twinned. Although Jingfors saw no twins on the Sadlerochit, he noticed cows were calving in their second year, and some cows were even calving in successive years. The population was expanding at a tremendous rate.

The Sadlerochit drainage is obviously lush, but it takes a tutored eye to make the connection between the kinds and abundance of plants here and large numbers of muskoxen. Start on a ridge west of the river. The soil is mostly barren, a rubble of talus, scree, and frost boils with very few plants—mountain avens, veiny-leafed willow, woodrush, and oxytrope. During spring melt in May and June, when the river valley floods, muskoxen climb up to this ridge and begin to feed here and in the dry tundra beyond, a tussock meadow of tea-leaf willow, dwarf birch, and cottongrass.

At the foot of the ridge a snowbank waters a meadow of sedges and tundra grass. Beyond, toward the river, is a plain of heathlike tundra with dwarf birch, mountain cranberry, diamond-leaf willow, and cottongrass. Near a small creek is yet another sort of willow muskoxen favor, Richardson willow. Muskoxen feed heavily here in the summer.

Beyond this plain lies the Sadlerochit River itself, with riparian thickets of blue, feltleaf, and barren-ground willows, fields of grasses, and leguminous forbs rich in nitrogen, including sweet-broom, blue-spike lupine, alpine milkvetch, and dwarf fireweed.

If you were a muskox, you would look on the abundance and variety of edible plants here as boon and bounty. It is on the willows that the Sadlerochit muskoxen browse most heavily, and Robus believes the high nutritional value of these plants puts Sadlerochit muskoxen in a favorable energy balance for longer periods of time than might be the case in more marginal areas. This makes it possible for the herd to sustain its high rate of productivity.

In other parts of their arctic range, where willows are not as plentiful, muskoxen depend more on sedges and grasses. For a long time it was thought that the muskox diet was simple. Now it is known that they consume a great variety of flowering plants, grasses, sedges, mosses, and forbs—bluegrass and willow herb, bladder campion and foxtail, cowberry, mountain sorrel, and Labrador tea. Their diet varies with the season, according to where they are, and according to their idiosyncratic needs and tastes. They favor some of the same forage that attracts caribou, but can subsist on a coarser diet than perhaps any other ruminant.

We do not often think of animals in relation to the other animals in their communities much beyond the way they serve each other as food. Observers who have followed muskoxen on foot over the tundra, however, and who have had memorable if not always pleasant encounters with them, often remark on the muskox's relationships with birds. Snow buntings and Lapland longspurs line their tundra nests with muskox wool. These and other ground-nesters such as plovers and jaegers are seen flying up in displays of indignant irritation when the big animals threaten to step on their nests. In their winter pawing, muskoxen expose food for arctic hares and willow buds for ptarmigan. Arctic fox derive some unknown delight in their company. And in their wandering they stir up insects, which the birds feed upon.

At death their carcasses feed the scavengers, and the insects that break down their flesh under the short summer sun are, again, the food of the snow bunting.

An old muskox is one approaching twenty, though some live longer. They die of their environment, as victims of predation, and by drowning in rivers, especially during breakup in the spring. They die of starvation and exposure, or from broken necks in falling from ridges. They are fatally gored in the rut, or die of infections from their broken horns. They are remarkably free of external parasites, which is why one so rarely sees them grooming. They are occasionally bothered by mosquitoes and flies about their eyes and ears.

They are tranquil animals, but their equipoise should not be confused with docility. John Teal once observed a rutting bull leap clear of the ground in an apparent attempt to snag the pontoons of a low-flying aircraft. Martha Robus watched a muskox rout a grizzly bear that had stumbled into its willow patch. And Anne Gunn once found herself confronting an irritated bull on Prince of Wales Island, an animal that had been bested in a bout with another bull. Though she was armed, she permitted the bull to force her into a river at her back, gun, notebook, and camera held high over her head. She recalls whimpering with pain in the cold water, waiting for the animal to back off.

Gunn's forebearance, and the patience and unobtrusive attitude of muskox researchers in general, make up in some way for inanities of the past. One arctic traveler, curious about the resilience of a bull's horn boss, shot a muskox in the head with a 9.3-mm armor-piercing bullet to see what would happen. Another curious fellow bound a month-old calf up in a sled dog harness (after shooting its mother) to study "the instinctive mode of defense against a wolf hanging to the flanks." He then tied a dead wolf to the calf to record the methods by which it attempted to free itself. Such witless amusement once passed for science, and, with a strong enough statistical basis, might still pass in some quarters.

THE two most disastrous periods in history for muskoxen came in the nineteenth century, when they were exterminated in the eastern subarctic by Indians and Eskimos to feed American whalers and to be used in trade to the Hudson's Bay Company; and in the early twentieth century, when entire herds were shot to provide a calf or two for zoos, or to provision fur trappers and their dogs in Greenland. While the former story, like the exploitation of beaver in eastern North America or the havoc wreaked on American bison, is familiar, the latter events are relatively obscure.

At the turn of the century, muskoxen lived in fairly large numbers (perhaps as many as 2000) along the northeast coast of Greenland, at places like Hold With Hope and Hochstetter peninsulas, Clavering Island, and in Jameson Land on Scoresby Sound. Whalers and sealers working along these coasts were wont to put ashore to hunt muskoxen for fresh meat. They easily put the animals to bay with dogs and shot them to the last animal. "After an invasion like ours," noted one ship's naturalist, "when every animal obtainable is slain for food, it must take some years to restock the ground."

After the turn of the century, Norwegian fur trappers living in these same areas shot muskoxen for trap bait and to feed both their sled dogs and the wild animals they were collecting for zoos. They shot hundreds of muskoxen; in a short time their depredations seriously threatened the animal's future in northeast Greenland. Under sharp criticism for these practices the Norwegians

were testy enough to charge that, actually, the Danish trappers, of
which there were a few, were more to blame because they were
not as "racially adept" as the Norwegians on cross-country skis
and therefore traveled more slowly and had to kill more animals
along the way to survive until they got back to their trapping
camps.

Worse in its effect on the animals was what happened when
zoos became interested in muskoxen. Entrepreneurs found the
only practical way to secure a calf was to kill all the adults in a
defensive formation. The hooking charges of the last animal among
its dead companions must have been one of the most pathetic
sights ever engineered by civilized people. Ejnar Mikkelsen, a
Danish historian working with an American, Elisabeth Hone,
estimated in 1932 that five adults were killed for every calf secured.
Hone arrived at a figure of some 2000 animals killed this way
between 1899 and 1926. Zoos finally signed an agreement that put
an end to the business. And the fur trappers, who had done most
of this work, finally moved out as Denmark began to exercise a
protective hegemony over the east coast of Greenland.

Today the muskox survives in Alaska, where, at this writing,
there are about 1000 animals, the progeny of successful transplants; in Canada, where as many as 40,000 live along the northern
rim of the continent and in the Canadian Archipelago; and in
North and East Greenland, where P. C. Lent estimates there are
1500. In the face of an ice storm, or with human disruption of
their refugia, none of which is fully protected, these numbers could
change radically tomorrow.

In the eroded hills south of the Copper Eskimo site called PjRa-18,
I wrote a note to myself. It was not the sort of thought I would
forget, but I am too much a creature of such habits, or, perhaps, was
too encouraged by the earnest note-taking of my scientific companions, to be able to let it go. On pages crowded with crude field
drawings of the snow bunting and the pattern of a bone scatter
along Baker Creek, I wrote: "the innocence."

The words came at the end of a long afternoon in which I had wandered with and sat at the perimeter of a small herd of seven adults, a yearling, and four calves. It was a reaction to something I could not have located on a muskox farm: they were so intensely good at being precisely what they were. The longer you watched, the more intricately they seemed a part of where they were living, of what they were doing. Their color, their proportions against the contours of the land, were exquisite.

They were, in evolution's terms, innocent of us and of our plans.

On the long trek back to PjRa-18, and as the five of us crossed the tundra from there to our tent camp on the river, I thought of their vulnerability. At PjRa-18 the idea of innocence founders in the evidence of an encounter between two non-Socratic societies, the cunning hunters and these most obvious and least retiring of arctic mammals.

Over our meal, Cliff Hickey, the senior anthropologist in the group, said of the Copper Eskimo, "You ignore at your peril the variety in human culture."

After dinner I went down by the water to wash my hair and to sit. Two silver-gray caribou were grazing on the far side of the river. It was so warm I was barefoot. In the hills beyond were the black dots of muskoxen and the white dots of browsing arctic hare. The sound of the river was in my head, and its cold drops ran down my chest. A Chipewyan guide named Saltatha once asked a French priest what lay beyond the present life. "You have told me heaven is very beautiful," he said. "Now tell me one more thing. Is it more beautiful than the country of the muskoxen in the summer, when sometimes the mist blows over the lakes, and sometimes the water is blue, and the loons cry very often? That is beautiful. If heaven is still more beautiful, I will be glad. I will be content to rest there until I am very old."

In the reprieve at the end of a day, in the stillness of a summer evening, the world sheds its categories, the insistence of its future, and is suspended solely in the lilt of its desire.

Three

TÔRNÂRSSUK
Ursus maritimus

THE SEASCAPE WAS almost without color beneath a low gray sky. Scattered ice floes damped any motion of large waves, and fogs and thin snow showers came and went in the still air. The surface of the water was the lacquered black of Japanese wooden boxes.

Three of us stood in the small open boat, about a hundred miles off the northwest coast of Alaska, at the southern edge of the polar pack in the Chukchi Sea. I and two marine scientists were hunting ringed seals that cold September day. In the seal stomachs we found what fish they had been eating; from bottom trawls we learned what the fish they were eating had eaten; and from plankton samplings we learned what the creatures the fish ate were eating.*

We had been working at this study of marine food chains for several weeks, moving west in our boat across the north coast of Alaska, from the west end of the Jones Islands to Point Barrow. At Barrow we boarded a 300-foot oceanographic research vessel, the *Oceanographer*, and headed out into the Chukchi Sea. Each morning for the next two weeks our boat was lowered from the deck of this mother vessel and we worked in the sea ice until evening.

We had been hunting seals intensively for three days without success. Twice we had seen a seal, each time for only a split second. We moved slowly, steadily, through the ice floes, without conversation, occasionally raising a pair of field glasses to study a small, dark dot on the water—a piece of ice? A bird? A seal breaking the surface of the water to breathe? It is not so difficult to learn to distinguish among these things, to match a "search image" in the mind after a few days of tutoring with the shading, shape, and movement that mean *seal*. Waiting in silence, intently attentive, was harder to learn.

We were three good sets of eyes, hunting hard. Nothing. A fog would clear. A snow squall drift through. In the most promising areas of the ice we shut off the engines and drifted with the currents. The ice, despite its occasional vertical relief, only compounded a sense of emptiness in the landscape, a feeling of directionlessness. The floes were like random, silent pieces of the earth. Our compass, turning serenely in its liquid dome, promised, if called upon to do so, to render points on a horizon obliterated in slanting snow and fog.

---

* This project was part of a Bureau of Land Management/Outer Continental Shelf study of Alaskan coastal marine life, results of which were to lead offshore oil development in the least harmful direction.

We drifted and sipped hot liquids, and stared into the quilt-work of gray-white ice and ink-black water. If one of us tensed, the others felt it and were alert. Always we were *hunting*. This particular habitat, the number of cod in the water, the time of the year —everything said ringed seals should be here. But for us they weren't.

Late summer in the sea ice. Eventually the cold, damp air finds its way through insulated boots and wool clothing to your bones. The conscious mind, the mind that knows how long you have been out here, importunes for some measure of comfort. We made a slow, wide turn in the boat, a turn that meant the end of the day. Though we still watched intently, thoughts of the ship were now upon us. Before this, we had camped on the beach in tents; now a hot shower, an evening meal in light clothing at a table, and a way to dry clothes awaited us. In the back of your mind at the end of the day you are very glad for these things.

My friend Bob saw the bear first: an ivory-white head gliding in glassy black water 300 feet ahead, at the apex of a V-wake. We slowed the boat and drew up cautiously to within 30 feet. A male. The great seal hunter himself. About three years old, said Bob.

The bear turned in the water and regarded us with irritation, and then, wary, he veered toward a floe. In a single motion of graceful power he rose from the water to the ice, his back feet catching the ice edge at the end of the movement. Then he stepped forward and shook. Seawater whirled off in flat sheets and a halo of spray. His head lowered, he glared at us with small, dark eyes. Then he crossed the floe and, going down on his forelegs, sliding headfirst, he entered the water on the other side without a splash and swam off.

We found our way to him again through the ice. We were magnetically drawn, in a fundamental but perhaps callow way. Our presence was interference. We approached as slowly as before, and he turned to glower, treading water, opening his mouth—the gray tongue, the pale violet mouth, the white teeth—to hiss. He paddled away abruptly to a large floe and again catapulted from the water, shook his fur out, and started across the ice to open water on the far side.

We let him go. We watched him, that undeterred walk of authority. "The farmer," the whalers had called him, for his "very agricultural appearance as he stalks leisurely over the furrowed fields of ice." John Muir, on a visit to these same waters in 1899, said bears move "as if the country had belonged to them always."

The polar bear is a creature of arctic edges: he hunts the ice margins, the surface of the water, and the continental shore. The ice bear, he is called. His world forms beneath him in the days of shortening light, and then falls away in the spring. He dives to the ocean floor for mussels and kelp, and soundlessly breaks the water's glassy surface on his return, to study a sleeping seal. Twenty miles from shore he treads water amid schooling fish. The sea bear. In winter, while the grizzly hibernates, the polar bear is out on the sea ice, hunting. In summer his tracks turn up a hundred miles inland, where he has feasted on crowberries and blueberries.

Until a few years ago this resourceful hunter was in a genus by himself: *Thalarctos*. Now he is back where he started, with the grizzly and black bear in the genus *Ursus*, where his genes, if not his behavior, say he belongs.

What was so impressive about the bear we saw that day in the Chukchi was how robust he seemed. At three years of age a bear in this part of the Arctic is likely spending its first summer alone. To feed itself, it has had to learn to hunt, and open pack ice is among the toughest of environments for bears to hunt in. This was September, when most bears are thin, waiting for the formation of sea ice, their hunting platform. In our three days of diligent searching, in this gray and almost featureless landscape of ice remnants so far off the coast, we had seen but two seals. We were transfixed by the young bear. We watched him move off across the ice, into a confusing plane of grays and whites. We were shivering a little and opened a thermos of coffee. A snow shower moved quickly through, and when it cleared we could barely make

him out in the black water with field glasses from the rocking boat.
A young and successful hunter, at home in his home.

He had found the seals.

THE polar bear is only lately known to science, and not yet well.
What has been learned, especially about the size and movements of
its different geographic populations, has been difficult and expensive to determine, and it has come on the heels of fears that the
bear was threatened with extinction.

The Russians were the first to raise an alarm. They banned
polar bear hunting in 1956; in 1961 Savva Uspenskii speculated
that the world population of polar bears was only about 5000.
American biologists thought it was more like 17,000 to 19,000—
but no one had any reliable information; nor did the technology
to find out exist. At the time, Americans in Alaska and Norwegians
in Svalbard were exerting a tremendous hunting pressure on polar
bears, as were hunters in Canada.* In Alaska in the mid-sixties a
combination of hunting by native people and airborne sportsmen
was accounting for a kill of about 300 bears a year. Canadian
hunters were taking more than 400 a year. Greenlanders were killing about 200 a year, and more than 400 polar bears were being
killed every year in Svalbard by commercial trappers and European sport hunters. The reported kill (smaller than the actual kill),
then, was about 1300 bears a year, nearly 25 percent of the population if Uspenskii was right.

Uspenskii, fortunately, was wrong; but indications of the
bear's vulnerability, and the fact that there was no scientific ground
on which to base any decisions, precipitated an international meeting in Fairbanks in 1965, sponsored by the United States. This
meeting produced an international agreement for polar bear man-

---

* Svalbard is the Norwegian name for an arctic archipelago whose
largest island is Spitsbergen, a name sometimes used in English to refer
to the entire archipelago.

agement under the auspices of the International Union for the Conservation of Nature and Natural Resources (IUCN). By 1968 an IUCN Polar Bear Specialist Group had been established, to share information and coordinate management programs for an animal that drifts between countries and occupies the high seas in its wanderings.*

What emerged from the research initiated by this group of polar bear biologists was both new information, some of it startling, and the end for some old theories. It had been previously thought, for example, that polar bears followed the roughly clockwise movement of ice around the Pole, bearing their young in Canada, say, with those bears then growing up in the Russian Arctic and breeding in Svalbard and in northern Greenland the next year. This notion was early laid to rest. Polar bears do wander, sometimes very far over the sea ice; but populations in the Arctic are fairly discrete. Polar bears show a high degree of fidelity to winter seal-hunting areas, summer retreats, and ancestral denning areas such as those along the Owl River in Manitoba, in Bogen Valley on Kongsøya Island in Svalbard, or in the Drem-Head Mountains on Wrangel Island.

Within these major populations—one of them seems to wander back and forth between Svalbard, Franz Josef Land, and the east coast of Greenland; another to stay around the north and northwest coasts of Alaska; a third in the Canadian Arctic—there are smaller, somewhat less discrete populations. For example, the bears of southern Hudson Bay and of James Bay appear to be a self-contained group. (They also have a unique summer diet, denning habits different from those of other bears, and different population dynamics—they raise more cubs, who strike off on their own at an earlier age than the young of other bear populations.) Polar

---

* The IUCN Polar Bear Agreement, signed by Russia, Norway, Denmark, Canada, and the United States in 1973, became effective on May 26, 1976. It is the only treaty of general agreement between the five polar nations.

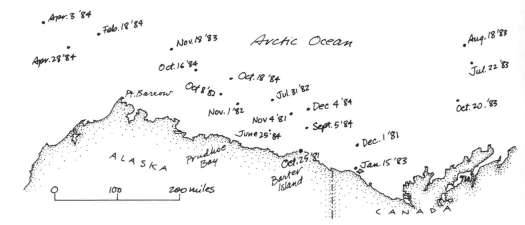

Locations of a radio-collared polar bear off the north coast of Alaska
between October 25, 1981 and December 4, 1984. Adapted from S. C.
Amstrup, 1985, unpublished data, U.S. Fish and Wildlife Service,
Anchorage, Alaska.

bears are rather retiring and unaggressive, especially in comparison
with grizzly bears. Robert Brown, an English traveler writing in
1868 and reacting to the popular stories of his day, said he would
far rather meet a polar bear than a grizzly. "I cannot help thinking," he wrote, ". . . the impressions which we have imbibed
regarding the polar bear's ferocity are due more to old notions of
what it *ought to be* rather than what it *is*. . . ."

Polar bears vary in size, and their weights can change dramatically during the year. (Very large polar bears may stand 12
feet on their hind legs and weigh 2000 pounds. The number of
12- and 13-foot bears weighing 2200 or 2400 pounds that have been
reported, however, says more about unadjusted scales, stretched
hides, and wishful exaggeration than about polar bears.) Bears eat
prodigiously in the spring, lightly in late summer, and lightly or
not at all (in the case of denning females) during the winter. An
adult male might weigh between 550 and 1700 pounds and measure

75 to 100 inches from tip of nose to tip of tail. Females weigh between 350 and 750 pounds and measure from 70 to 75 inches in length.

In addition to being smaller and lighter, females have narrower skulls and lower foreheads. Young adult males are longer in the leg and are generally rangier-looking than young adult females. Some longtime observers say females have longer hair on their backs, while males have longer hair in the feathering at the back of the forelegs. The hair of older animals is often shorter, with more dark skin showing through on the snout. Eskimos make a fine distinction between male and female tracks, not merely on the basis of size—a male's paw may be 13 inches long and 9 wide— but because of faint marks left by longer hairs around a male's foot and because of the female's slightly more pigeon-toed track.

A polar bear walks in a way all its own. Coming toward you, the front legs appear to swing out to the side and the huge paws to fold toward the body like paddles, until they flick forward and are set down. The back feet appear actually to kick the front feet forward, they come so close to meeting. From the rear the walk appears bandy-legged, a trait most evident in mature males. The front legs seem long because the chest is shallow, the cleft between the legs extending into the neck. The rear legs, in fact, are longer. Viewed head-on, its hips stick out past its shoulders. From the side, from above, or from the front the bear is wedge-shaped, a form that emphasizes the sinuous movements of its long neck.

A bear walks at about 2.5 miles per hour. When it trots, it paces, moving both legs on one side of its body forward in the same motion. Over short distances—charging a resting seal—it moves in a quick bound at nearly 25 miles per hour. Over any distance, females and cubs tend to outdistance males.

Bears move with a supple agility, seeming to flow over steep, complex obstacles like sea-ice pressure ridges. They also have tremendous strength and dexterity. The same bear that pries tiny thalia from a kelp strand with a single claw can knock a belukha whale senseless with a blow from its foreleg. Deft and quick enough to snatch a lemming from the grass, it can also flip a 400-pound bearded seal into the air.

The ivory and pearl shading we see in a polar bear's fur is caused by the refraction of sunlight (the same phenomenon that makes clouds appear white) in its guard hairs. The hair itself is optically transparent, or colorless. The brightest whites show up at the spring molt, the purest of these being those of young cubs. With exposure to sunlight, the hairs take on a subtle coloring; soft yellowish tones appear on the hips, along the flanks, and down the legs—a pale lemon wash, apricot yellows, cream buffs, straw whites. The tones deepen each year as the animal ages. In the low sunlight of a fall afternoon an older male's fur might suggest the yellow golds of ripe wheat.

A polar bear's fur is like that of no other mammal. An early mystery about it was that it seemed a relatively poor insulator compared with wolf or caribou hair; too, unlike beaver fur, which traps a layer of air between skin and water, polar bear fur loses 90 percent of its insulative value in water. Polar bears, it turned out, depend instead on a layer of blubber to keep them warm in the water (which conducts heat away from the body at about twenty times the rate of still air). On land, the bear is protected by a thick underlayer of dense wool and a relatively open layer of guard hairs about six inches long. These guard hairs are so hard and shiny they appear synthetic. They are also hollow, which means that a polar bear's fur stays erect and doesn't mat when it is wet. Also, because of the open spacing and smoothness of its guard hairs, a bear can easily shake free of water before it freezes. (He also rolls in snow, an excellent blotter, to daub off moisture— as do people who accidently fall through the ice.)

A second function of the bear's hollow hair, a key to understanding how it might stay warm on land, was discovered by accident. White bears show up poorly when photographed from the air against white snow and ice. In the late 1960s, an American scientist, reasoning that a mammal should give off more heat than sea ice, tried infrared photography, but polar bears proved too well insulated to appear on the film. The only bit of black the film recorded was in the polar bear's tracks, which were warm for several minutes after an animal passed. (Polar bears get rid of excess body heat through their claws and footpads.) He next tried ultraviolet-sensitive film. Bears absorbed light in those wavelengths and finally appeared black on the white ice, and this led to the second discovery: polar bear guard hairs work like light pipes. They funnel short-wavelength energy from the sun to the bear's black skin, where it plays an as yet incompletely understood role in the bear's complex system of heat regulation.*

POLAR bears apparently moved into the Arctic only very recently, sometime in the middle or late Pleistocene. A population of brown bears, the prevailing theory goes, became isolated in Siberia and quickly evolved into polar bears. (The rate of evolution here is apparently astonishing. Polar bears now even show consistent variation in size within their own populations, being typically very slightly larger as one moves westward from the east coast of Greenland, reaching their largest size in the Bering/Chukchi Sea region.) The genetic distance between polar bears and brown bears, however, is not so great that they can't produce fertile young together (offspring capable themselves of reproducing).

---

* As commonly experienced in zoos, a polar bear's color, as well as its bulk, can be misleading—and the bear's hollow guard hairs can play a strange part in the overall distortion. Blue-green algae living in freshwater pools in zoo enclosures can migrate through a polar bear's damaged guard hairs and bloom in the hollow spaces within. Bears afflicted in this way, as they have been recently in zoos in San Diego and elsewhere, appear green to visitors. The disinfectants and cleaners used by zoos and circuses and the chemicals used to tan polar bear furs for rugs take much of the delicate shading out of the fur. The bears' true appearance is further compromised when they are kept in climates where they produce neither a substantial layer of blubber nor heavy winter coats. With so much of their dark skin showing through, they seem barbered and gaunt.

And their blood chemistries are still quite similar. But they are markedly different animals.

Brown bears, including the grizzly bear, are terrestrial creatures. They live largely on vegetable matter and have clear enough spatial images of their territories to defend them. The polar bear lives almost exclusively on meat. Its "territory" is something it carries with it over the ice. The difference in diets is evident in an examination of the teeth. The polar bear's are those of an ambusher and a flesh eater—long canines, smaller, shearing molars, vestigial premolars, and incisors that angle forward, enabling the bear to use them like a pair of delicate clippers. The brown bear's canines are shorter, and its molars and premolars are broader and flatter, adapted to the grinding of vegetation.

The difference evolution has made is also evident in the overall shape of their bodies. Where the brown bear is broad-shouldered and dish-faced, the polar bear is narrow-shouldered and Roman-nosed. His neck is longer, his head smaller. He stands taller than the brown bear but is less robust in the chest and generally of lighter build. The polar bear's feet are larger and thickly furred between the pads. The toes are partially webbed, the blackish-brown claws sharper and smaller than the brown bear's. It lacks the brown bear's shoulder hump and more expressive face, with its prehensile lips, well suited to stripping bushes of their berries.

The remarkable thing, again, is that they have become so different in such a short time. We call them both "bears," but when you see a polar bear surface quietly in a lead, focus its small brown eyes on a sleeping bearded seal, draw breath soundlessly, and submerge without a ripple, you wonder at the insouciance with which we name things.*

*   *   *

---

* A "lead" (pron. leed) is a passage through sea ice navigable by a surface vessel such as a kayak. Smaller fractures are called cracks.

When the five polar bear nations embarked on the IUCN's program of cooperative research, each nation, by mutual agreement, went in a slightly different direction. The Americans and Norwegians pioneered techniques of marking bears and then later relocating them, establishing the broad boundaries of discrete populations. The Americans also began developing a technology for electronic tracking. The Canadians looked at general hunting behavior and at the bear's relationship with the animal it is most dependent on for food, the ringed seal. The Norwegians, with Canadian help, also began investigating the bear's physiology. The latter work, conducted at a laboratory at Churchill, Manitoba, was carried out by Nils Øritsland with live-trapped bears from the southern Hudson Bay population.

Øritsland quickly uncovered a number of fascinating things. Because bears climb in and out of the water regularly, they have special heating and cooling problems. Eventually, Øritsland discovered that the bear's basal metabolism was adequate to keep it warm in all seasons under a variety of conditions. He also determined that their winter pelage provided adequate protection in temperatures as low as −40°F with a 15-mile-per-hour wind. (Laboratory results are always somewhat problematic because they oversimplify. In the field bears tend to lie down in the leeward protection of drifts and pressure ridges or to dig temporary dens in −15°F to −20°F weather with 15-mile-per-hour winds.)

The bears' only "problem," Øritsland found out, was getting rid of the heat produced by working muscles. They do so, Øritsland learned, by increasing blood flow to their footpads and claws, to their snouts and legs (the least insulated parts of their bodies), and, most remarkably, to two unique sheets of thin muscle that lie across the bear's back behind its shoulder blades, between the skin and a layer of blubber. Blood shunted to all these areas either radiates heat off into space or comes into contact with previously cooled blood, which it warms in countercurrent or heat-exchange systems. When the core temperatures of bears in Øritsland's experiments began to climb above 101.6°F, their heartbeat increased from a resting pulse of about 45 per minute to as high as 148 per minute, and they switched from a pattern of regular breathing to rapid, shallow breathing (panting) to bring cool air to the lungs.

Bears do not overheat when they are swimming, so they will also jump in the water to cool off. And eat snow.

It is its layer of blubber that causes a polar bear to overheat so easily. The blubber is heaviest on the outside of the back legs and over the buttocks and lower back, where it may be as much as 4.3 inches thick. Lesser amounts are on the upper body, front legs, and neck. Polar bears depend on their blubber for warmth, especially in the water, and for nourishment. During the five months a female is hibernating, giving birth, and nursing her cubs, she lives entirely on her fat reserves. Bears waiting out storms in temporary dens and bears ashore waiting for sea ice to form in the fall do the same. This regimen is such that in southern Hudson Bay denning females may come ashore weighing 750 pounds in early August and emerge from their dens in April weighing only 350 pounds. Similarly, males coming ashore in late summer may lose 30 percent or more of their body weight in the three months that pass before ice forms and they are able to hunt on the sea ice again.

During the summer, especially on the tundra of the Hudson Bay coast, bears dig summer sleeping pits to get out of direct sunlight, sometimes digging down to the layer of permafrost to cool off. When trying to sleep in warm weather, they often roll on their backs in order to expose their bellies and feet. In cold weather they hug their back legs to their stomachs with their forelegs, curling tight to bury their heads in their chests, where they breathe warm air with their backs against the wind.

Øritsland's experimental findings have a certain attractiveness because they simplify and provide numbers. To watch polar bears in the wild, however, is to marvel at the intricacy of their physiology and behavior. The animals alternately seek shelter or exposure, sleep and travel, hunt down certain foods, and mate and hibernate. The interplay here among rest, exertion, and nutrition that carries them comfortably through life is something that cannot be broken down into pieces. Like the skater's long, graceful arc, it is a statement about life, the full exercise of which is beautiful.

THE bears that are successful, that respond with insight to new circumstances, that do the right thing at the right time, season after season, may live to be thirty. Beyond learning how to secure food, the most intriguing aspects of their behavior are the steps female bears take to ensure that there will be more bears.

Before she dens, usually in late October or early November, a female bear must put on a heavy layer of fat to sustain herself (and her cubs) until she emerges to hunt again in the spring. If the weather doesn't turn stormy and food is abundant, a female might den late. If little food is available, she may decide not to den at all that year. In the face of early storms that keep her from feeding, she may make a temporary den, wait out the weather, and then decide what to do. Polar bears conceive during the female's three-week estrus in April and May, but the fertilized eggs do not implant in the uterine wall until much later—some speculate at the moment the female commits herself to a long denning period, which only females carrying fertilized eggs do.

Bears are as particular about the type of snow they select for a maternity den as Eskimos are in constructing an iglu, and the two structures have many features in common. The female usually chooses a site where snowdrifts develop in early autumn, often close to the top of the leeward side of a ridge. Midwinter storms are not likely to expose a den built there, nor is the den likely to be buried in an avalanche. The variety of structures denning females build is great, but they share a certain architecture: an entrance tunnel 5 to 10 feet long and 24 to 28 inches wide and high; a small room at the end of the upward-sloping tunnel, just big enough for the bear to turn around in; and a ventilation hole.

By designing for the flow of air and controlling the thickness of snow, an excellent insulator, a female can keep fresh air moving through her den all winter and maintain the temperature at about 32°F, no matter how cold it gets outside. She does this by radiating a small amount of heat, about as much as a 200-watt bulb, and by trapping that heat in the den chamber with a sloping entrance tunnel and an air dike, or sill, where the tunnel enters the den. She also adjusts the thickness of the roof. (Eskimos put the same techniques to use.)

The female is not actually hibernating during the winter. Her heartbeat and rate of respiration are greatly reduced, but her temperature falls only very slightly. She can awaken and become alert in moments. If her den gets too warm, ice will form on the walls, cooling the chamber and inhibiting the exchange of carbon dioxide and oxygen through the snow walls. The bear may then scrape off the ice and adjust the ventilation, or dig a new chamber adjacent to the old one. Jørn Thomassen, who has watched denning bears in Svalbard for several years, speculates that some females are more successful than others at designing and maintaining these structures, and that older bears, learning from their own mistakes, subsequently build dens where the exchange of gases, the conservation of heat, and, later, the expansion of the den to allow the cubs to exercise before they emerge, are accomplished with more economy.

Dens are very clean. By metabolizing fat instead of protein, the female produces very little body waste. Except for a mouthful of snow now and again, she also draws all the water she needs from her fat reserves.

Cubs, usually two but sometimes one or three, and very rarely four, are born sometime in December or early January. They are blind, deaf, poorly insulated, and unable to walk or smell. In their first weeks they are dependent on three things for survival: the protection of the den, the warm crevices of their mother's body, and her rich milk. (Polar bear milk has the consistency of cream. Those who have tasted it say it tastes like cod liver oil and smells of seals or fish. It is richer than whale milk and higher in protein than seal milk.) Again, it is only with the protection of a well-made den that a female can conserve and direct her metabolism to produce the heat and milk that her cubs need.

The cubs are so small at birth, barely a pound, that the female can hide one in the rolled toes of her front paw. At about twenty-four days they can hear, and a week later they are able to see. It is several more weeks before they can walk and smell. By late March or early April the cubs weigh about 25 pounds, and the female, depending on the weather and the cubs' condition, breaks out of her den. For the first days she might just sit drowsily in the sun at the den entrance. Or roll in the snow to revive her coat. Or nose about in a desultory way, looking for grasses and lichens to nibble.

A well-placed den entrance will be protected from the wind and directed in some measure to the south and west to take advantage of the sun's afternoon warmth. Cubs venture forth onto this sheltered sun porch a few days after their mother and for the next few weeks do not travel far at all. Their mother often nurses them here in a sitting position in the sunshine, with her back against a snowbank. The cubs lie on her belly. While they nurse she may put her head back and stare at the sky, or roll her head slowly from side to side, or rock her cubs gently in the cradle of her forelegs.

These first few weeks are a critical time for all three animals. The female balances her desire to leave in order to hunt to feed herself against an investment in the cubs' learning, exercise, and preparation for travel. For most bears the sea is no more than a day away. For others, like those denning on the southern coast of Hudson Bay, the journey is much longer and requires making temporary dens along the way.

Rasmus Hansson and Jørn Thomassen, who have watched more bears emerge from their dens than probably anyone else, studied bears for several years at a traditional denning area called Bogen Valley, in Svalbard. Most of the bears there den in a long line just below the ridge of Retzius Mountain. (In spite of this density it is very rare to see two families outside their dens at the same time. How the females manage periods of exercise so as not to interfere with each other is not known.)

Since portions of the southwest face of Retzius Mountain slope at an angle of 70°, the first problem cubs face there is getting down to the floor of Bogen Valley. They learn to imitate their mothers, who slide down rump first, looking over their shoulders and breaking with their claws; or on their sides, leading with all four feet; or headfirst on their bellies. Mothers at the bottom catch cubs veering out of control.

In those first few days outside together, say Hansson and Thomassen, the females tend to rest while the cubs exercise vigorously. The cubs pick up blocks of ice or snow, which they then throw and chase or wrestle with violently, biting and chewing like cats. Cubs also stand up to swat at each other and roll over thrashing and neck-biting in the snow. In analyzing the cubs' behavior, the two Norwegian scientists concluded that the cubs were developing in three areas: strength and coordination; social habits and communication skills, which would permit the female and her cubs to live and hunt together efficiently during the next two years; and fighting techniques. In the future the latter would serve males in their battles with each other during the breeding season, and females in the defense of their own cubs. (Male bears, according to some researchers, will try to kill any cub they encounter, especially if the female offers a weak defense.)

When cubs reach some threshold level of strength and coordination, when they are able to walk well and are responsive to their mother's instructions to "stay" and "come," the bears depart from the den. The time of all three having to live solely on the stored fat of the female is nearly over.

THE Polar Eskimos of northwest Greenland call the polar bear *pisugtooq*, the great wanderer. On the basis of mark-and-recapture studies and radio-tracking information, scientists have determined that individual bears wander largely within a local area; but some, indeed, are long-distance travelers. A polar bear tagged in Svalbard, for example, showed up a year later near Nanortalik, Greenland, 2000 miles to the southwest. Another bear, a female, traveled a straight-line distance of 205 miles in two days. Polar bears have also been found far afield in unlikely places, at the crest of Mount Newton in Svalbard, for example, 6600 feet above sea level, or 30 miles inland on the Greenland ice cap. An American crew on the ice island Alpha saw a female and her cub at 84°N in December 1957. (She had become entangled in runway lighting, which she tore out moments before a plane attempted a landing.) A Russian ice-island crew spotted a female and her cubs a little more than a hundred miles from the Pole in the summer of 1937.

Because we think of polar bears as northern animals, and of "the North" as an area that doesn't extend very far south, it is somewhat surprising to discover that bears den at only 53°N, on Akimiski Island at the southern end of Hudson Bay. Or that bears still turn up occasionally on the east coast of Newfoundland as far south as Saint John's. Some stories of their wandering have an esoteric perseverance and loneliness about them. In 1938, for example, an aging female was shot far inland in the province of Quebec, near Peribonka on Lac Saint-Jean. She had apparently ascended the Saguenay River from the Gulf of Saint Lawrence and was headed for James Bay, some 360 miles farther north.

Once, looking up from the sea ice at the coastal cliffs of Devon Island, Ray Schweinsburg, a Canadian polar bear biologist, said to me, "I used to think the land would stop them. But I think they can cross nearly any terrain. The only thing that stops them is a place where there is no food."

The bear is a great wanderer not solely because it travels far, but because it travels with curiosity, and tirelessly. The Eskimo hunters in Greenland mean that it covers the ground successfully and intelligently when they pronounce the word *pisugtooq*.

Eskimos, long-time, keen observers of the polar bear, have advanced other thoughts about polar bears that science has treated with skepticism, and in some quarters with cynical disdain. Eskimos widely assert, for example, that most polar bears are left-pawed, that if one must leap in desperation from a charging bear it should always be to the bear's right.* Eskimos have also asserted that polar bears push blocks of ice ahead of them as shields when they are stalking seals; that a wounded bear will staunch the flow of its blood with snow; that they will hurl ice and rocks at walrus to wound and distract them, hoping to snatch an unprotected calf; and that females use anal plugs when they den.

Refuting any of these things is a complicated business. It becomes not only a denial of the integrity of the person telling the story, but a denial of the resourcefulness of the polar bear. Too, because of poor translations, you might end up refuting something that was never meant. The best field biologists, with a fundamental grasp of the animal's behavior, take the attitude that these things could happen, though they themselves have not seen them. The anthropologist Richard Nelson has offered succinct advice on this issue. "Eskimos," he writes, "are highly reliable observers of animal behavior, and many of their least believable statements have been proved to me by personal observation." Some scientists strongly resisted the notion that bears might use tools until a Canadian biologist found evidence in 1972, on the north coast of Devon Island, that a female with two cubs had smashed in the roof of a ringed-seal lair with a 45-pound piece of ice. Scientists have also found that bears intentionally stalk small prey like lemmings, which Eskimos have long claimed they do. And that a polar bear will hunt sea ducks by coming up underneath a flock of them in the water like a killer whale.

One of the most persistent of bear legends—that they cover their dark noses with a paw or a piece of snow when they are stalking a seal—may have originated with Eskimos, but the thought

---

* On the basis of this, Greenland Eskimos object to the depiction of a polar bear extending its right paw on the official seal of the Royal Greenland Trading Company as inaccurate.

has the flavor of invention about it. At a distance of 1000 yards, the argument goes, you can barely distinguish a polar bear on the sea ice, but you can clearly see its black nose. How could a seal not notice it? It's possible that it does—and that that is exactly what the bear intends. To a seal, a polar bear approaching in a straight line over flat ice, its lowered forequarters sliding along ahead of its hindquarters, would show very little body movement—the pushing motion of the rear legs does not break the outline of the hips. If the seal focuses on the dark nose, the bear's shape falls into vague relief against the surrounding ice. And at that distance the nose looks like another seal resting on the ice. Because of an optical phenomenon, the size of the bear's nose does not begin to fill more of the seal's image of that part of the sea ice until the bear is almost on top of the seal. And at that point the bear rises and bounds toward it.

It is possible the bear goes down on its forequarters only to keep the horizon from showing up between its legs; but it is also possible it wants its dark nose down there on the ice where it looks like a seal. Without direct evidence, without setting up an experiment, one can only speculate.

The desire to verify conjecture, to witness spontaneous, unstructured events in the wild, is of course very sharp among field biologists. Nothing—no laboratory result or field-camp speculation—can replace the rich, complex texture, the credibility, of something that takes place "out there." And scientists working in the field know that what they see in the field always has the potential to contradict what they have read or been told.* Onetime events, like seeing a polar bear stalk and kill a seal in open

---

* In a recent laboratory experiment, polar bears were declared "inefficient walkers" because they overheated on a treadmill. An experienced polar bear biologist smiled when I asked him about this. "The bear can't walk properly on a treadmill. . . . Walking into the wind, making that great pendulum swing of his legs, opening and closing his body to the cool air, you don't see that on a treadmill. Out on the sea ice you see he can walk a long way without overheating."

water (some biologists doubted this ever occurred, until one of
them, Donald Furnell, and an Eskimo companion, David Oolooyuk,
saw a bear do so in 1978), may be of no *statistical* importance. It
may not be possible, in other words, to generalize about all bears
from these incidents. But such events emphasize the resourcefulness of the individual bear and the range of capability in the
species; or they may reveal an unusual technique widespread only
in a certain population. These events underscore something critical
in the biology of large predators: the range of capability in the
species. No matter how long you watch, you will not see all it
can do.

Once, in a helicopter flying along Barrow Strait, Ray
Schweinsburg and I saw a lone bear headed south across the ice.
"I'd like to follow him," Schweinsburg shouted over the engine
noise. "I'd like to go down there and just follow him." And he
rolled his eyes and smiled at the impossibility of it.

I looked out the window, at the hundreds of square miles of
ice that lay ahead of the bear. Even if it were possible to follow,
I thought, how well could we put together what we saw? What
would we miss out there? I remembered again the desert writing
of Wilfred Thesiger, wandering in the Empty Quarter with his
Bedouin companions. The Arctic reminds one of the desert not
only because of the lack of moisture and the barren topography,
but because it puts a like strain on human life. It favors tough and
practical people, people aware of the vaguest flutter of life in an
environment that seems featureless and interminable to the un-
trained eye. People with a predator's alertness for minutiae, for
revealing detail. The loss of "a native eye" among civilized cultures
has been commented on by people as diverse as Vladimir Arseniev,
writing about the Manchurian native Dersu Uzala, and Laurens
van der Post, writing about Kalahari Desert people.

It not only takes a long time of watching the animal before
you can say what it is doing; it takes a long time to learn how to
watch. This point is raised, deferentially but repeatedly, in encounters with Eskimos. They are uneasy, they manage to say, about

the irrevocability of decisions made by people who are not sensually perceptive, not discriminating in these northern landscapes, not enthusiastic about long-term observations. When I hear these points made, my instinct is to nod yes; but it always causes me to reflect on something else—how dependent we are on Western field biologists to tell us fully and accurately what the animals did while they were there. How we hope they regain some approximation of "the native eye" in their studies.

The bear I was watching disappeared, cut off by the door frame of the helicopter.

To follow a bear, or simply follow in its tracks, is to "*reeeally* learn something," as the Eskimos say, smiling. Not only about where a bear went, but how it dealt with what happened along the way. A set of tracks might show where a bear had leaped into the air and come down headed in another direction—and you would look around for evidence of what surprised it. The trail of a cub alongside its mother disappears where it has crawled up onto its mother's back for a ride on a cold day. Bear tracks on the sea ice might follow the line of a pressure ridge (where seal lairs are likely to be) at a distance of 100 feet or so on the downwind side. Fresh tracks turning into a fiord might make no sense until you saw a bird rookery, beneath which the bear had scavenged dead birds. A male's tracks might cross a female's and turn to follow. Another set of tracks might turn suddenly and continue in an unerring line, and an aglu, a seal's breathing hole, would be there at the end, with signs of the bear's patient waiting. Tracks below a high bluff would show where a bear had hunted on a July morning, out of the sun.

The wide walk of a fat bear in June, you would see, differs from the walk of a thin bear in October. Bear tracks would show a consistent avoidance of deep snow; in spring they would not cross melt pools, where needle ice can puncture a bear's foot. On a sheet of sea ice so thin it would not support a human step, you would see traces where a bear had crossed with skating steps like a water strider, sprawled nearly on its chest.

These signs reveal that the polar bear lives in an olfactory and a visual landscape, and that it is attentive, especially in summer, to a thermal landscape. It looks for cool places.

From following hundreds of such tracks, polar bear biologists have developed certain impressions. Males keep largely to the coasts in summer, while females with cubs and subadults are more apt to travel overland from place to place. Bears make use of mountain passes, ravines, and other features of the land in such a way as to suggest that these are traditional routes across isthmuses as well as occasional one-time shortcuts around an area of bad ice or open water. (To take a shortcut, a creature must have a map in its head of where it is—memory is no help. How bears create and use such maps is one of the most intriguing of all the questions about them.)

Beyond using celestial clues and a knowledge of prevailing winds and currents, which reliably guide Eskimos across the angular topography of shifting sea ice, no one knows how bears find their way. But they consistently travel directly to aggregations of seals; they return to core denning and breeding areas every year; and they find their way unerringly to the coast from hundreds of miles offshore. This would be astonishing enough if they only did it on land, where there are perennial landmarks, but they also do it at sea, where a frozen landscape is created anew each year, where it can change from one day to the next with the sudden rise of a new pressure ridge or the opening of a lead, with a shift of pack ice in the currents. In some areas of stable ice, bears may travel for weeks without seeing a break in the continuity of the sharp blue line of the horizon, with only "the infinite expanse of the frozen plain, the infinite dome of the cold blue sky, and the cold, white sun" before them.

Gathering ground to themselves. Navigating. Wandering with purpose.

THE large black nose pulls cool air continuously across the nasal membranes, straining it for scent. The female bear climbs on top of an old piece of multiyear ice and rises on her hind legs to scan the ice fields beyond. She shields her eyes against the brilliant March light with her paw. She goes on. Partway across a refrozen lead the bear pauses motionless, one paw off the ground. Her head tilts and the small ears pivot independently. She puts the paw down. She sniffs the air at several levels, then the head is still, the attention fixed. She has found *netsik*. And *netsik*, somewhere beneath the snow and ice of Viscount Melville Sound, knows, perhaps, that *nanuq* has come.

The relationship between the hunted animal and the hunter has only recently come to be studied with the same intensity that biologists have brought to the study of the isolated life histories of the individual species. A Canadian polar bear biologist, Ian Stirling, has added greatly to a Western understanding of the polar bear by combining his study of bears hunting seals with a study of ringed seals and ice dynamics. In the spring of 1974, Stirling, with the help of ringed-seal biologist Tom Smith, was able to explain a peculiar sudden decline of the polar bear population in Amundsen Gulf. In the winter of 1973–74, he said, little snow fell in the area —too little to permit seals to excavate their snow lairs on the ice except in a few isolated places. Also, the ice itself remained stable and unbroken in areas where there were usually leads in winter. Perhaps the solid ice also affected concentrations of the seals' food. At any rate, a number of seals moved out (one of Smith's tagged seals moved all the way to Cape Dezhnev, Siberia), very few seals made birth lairs, and many bears either starved or moved on. Because, in essence, it didn't snow enough that year.

The ringed seal that the polar bear habitually hunts is a small marine mammal completely at home in the sea ice. Its short snout and large eyes suggest a cat's face, though its sleek head is earless. Its short-necked, broad-shouldered, barrel-chested, tapered body is like that of its relatives, the harp, ribbon, and spotted seals. Like them, too, the ringed seal is awkward out of water because its hind flippers don't pivot forward like a walrus's or a sea lion's to help it walk.

Ringed seals are the most abundant large mammal in the Arctic

—the Russians estimate a minimal population of 2.5 million—but they are relatively unsocial, rarely gathering in dense numbers. The young are born in snow-covered lairs on top of the ice in early April. Eight to ten weeks later they are on their own. Adults breed in late April and early May, at about six years of age. They feed, interestingly, at two levels of arctic marine food chains, consuming both fish in the cod family and the zooplankton those fish feed on. Differences in age at weaning—if the ice breaks up early a pup is not nursed as long—partially account for the variety of size in ringed seals. An adult may range from 40 to 60 inches in length and weigh from 80 to 250 pounds. During breeding, nursing, and molting, ringed seals feed lightly and may lose as much as 30 percent of their body weight. They are also territorial at this time, sometimes so aggressively defensive around their breathing holes that young seals who have crawled out on the ice through the wrong hole are kept at bay by another seal in the water until they are frozen out.

Among many questions about the ringed seal are how it finds food beneath the ice in the darkness of winter and how it "remembers" the location of its breathing holes, particularly after a deep dive in ocean currents.

A ringed seal is most vulnerable to the polar bear when it surfaces to breathe. When it is hauled out on the ice it is unusually vigilant, looking up for six or eight seconds every twenty to thirty seconds, and napping so close to its breathing hole that it can usually escape. Seals in birth lairs and males and nonbreeding females in haul-out lairs under the snow present another set of circumstances, to be considered in a moment.*

From the polar bear's perspective, the seal is a swift, alert animal that can be taken advantage of only at that moment of vulnerability—when it breaks the surface of the water to draw

---

* Marine mammals that have crawled up onto the sea ice or come ashore are said to be "hauled out." A snow cave dug out by a seal above its aglu as a concealed place of rest is called a haul-out lair.

breath, or when it is hauled out. Bears stalk seals over the ice or
approach by swimming quietly toward them. The patience and
judgment evident in these stalks can rivet a human observer's
attention.

The bear we left hunting on Viscount Melville Sound had
heard a seal surfacing in its snow cave, a muffled tinkle of water at
its aglu as it pulled itself out. The bear's footfalls are nearly sound-
less as it approaches—the hair between its footpads muffles the
crunch and squeak of snow. The bear pinpoints in her mind the spot
where the seal now rests. When she is 20 feet away—she pauses
ten seconds at one step, fifteen seconds with another step, ears
twitching to detect the seal's movement—she lunges, comes slam-
ming through the snow roof with all four feet centered precisely
over the aglu. The seal is cut off, finished.

Sometimes all it takes to break in the roof of a seal's lair is a
single calculated blow of the 40-pound paw. But these are stout
structures, and the bear may be forced to dig. Perhaps once in five
times, overall, it is successful. It understands precisely, however,
where in the chamber the aglu is, and its explosive entries into seal
lairs of all kinds are almost invariably centered at that spot.

Probably no other predator employs as many hunting strategies with one animal as the polar bear does with the ringed seal.
It may take a half hour to patiently approach a seal resting on
the edge of an ice floe, surfacing quietly to reconnoiter, then
submerging again. A bear may drift toward a seal like an innoc-
uous piece of ice; when it reaches the floe edge it explodes from
the water and smacks the seal dead all in one motion. When it
stalks seals over the ice, it flattens itself on its forequarters and
slides along slowly on chest and forelegs, taking advantage of
every piece of cover. It will scrape away the sea ice at a breathing
hole until there is just a thin layer left, and then cover the ice with
its body to cut off sunlight, so it looks to the seal below as if the
thick crust of ice and snow are still present. It will build a snow
wall to hide behind while it waits at an aglu. And it will rise up
suddenly in a resting seal's own aglu.

Stirling, who has watched them hunting for more than 2000 hours in the field, emphasizes several points about bears. First, the bear is only occasionally successful. The overall hunting success in any particular situation, considering the variety of ice cover, the number of seals present, the time of year, the age and sex of the bear, and the age of the seal, might range from 2 to 25 percent. The highest rate of success for a technique that is persistently applied, in Stirling's view, is the patient wait at an aglu for a seal to show up. (The bear can tell from small details of ice accumulation and sometimes by catching a whiff of seal odor whether the aglu has been used recently enough to make waiting worthwhile.)

Older bears, especially, have exceptional patience. They will wait for three or four hours at an aglu, lying downwind of the hole on their chests, out of the seal's line of sight. To stretch its muscles a bear will sometimes rise to sit or stand up quietly, ready to drop again soundlessly if it hears a seal.

Just before it surfaces, the seal exhales, and the sight or sound of the bubbles alerts the bear. The seal rises headfirst up a cone-shaped tunnel to its breathing hole, which, on smooth ice, appears as a low mound. A small amount of water forced up ahead of the seal splashes out on the ice and freezes. (The seal keeps the tunnel open and the aglu from freezing over completely by scouring with its claws.) The bear must time its strike perfectly and move with exceptional speed. It usually strikes with one or both paws and follows so quickly with its snout that if the smashing blow of its paws doesn't kill the seal, the impact of its snout will. "Everything cooperates," writes Frans Van de Velde, "—paws, claws, snout, and teeth—to give a blow that is so rapid that the seal has hardly a chance of getting away."

When it charges a basking seal, the bear does not seem so much to run as to pounce. Thor Larsen, a biologist who has observed polar bears in Svalbard for more than fifteen years, when I asked him about their hunting behavior, said, "Cats. They are like big cats." Fast? "It is absolutely unbelievable how fast they are—oh, do they come fast." Shrewd? "Yes. They are making judgments at every point about what to do. And they are patient."

Larsen, Stirling, Dennis Andriashek, Schweinsburg, and other polar bear biologists with long field experience often comment on the bear's seeming ability to analyze an unfamiliar situation and attempt a practical solution; on its ability to learn quickly when confronted with something new; and the novel approaches bears take to commonplace situations. "They are smart," says Larsen, "and precisely because they are, they sustain all the legends about them doing these extraordinary things, like using tools and moving blinds along ahead of them."

Bears prey on an impressive range of animals, each of which requires something different of the bear. They hunt spotted and ribbon seals in the western Arctic and harp seals in the eastern Arctic. The large bearded seal and hooded seals off the coast of Greenland are much stronger quarry. In leads and at savssats, bears prey on belukha and narwhals.* Bears prey heavily on bearded seal pups and kill an occasional muskox, walrus, dozing hare, or goose caught flightless during its molt. They eat bird eggs, seaweed, varieties of tundra berries. And carrion. (A bear can live for months on a bowhead whale carcass or beach-cast walrus.) The bear also leaves carrion in its wake; and here lies an interesting aspect of its ecology. An adult bear in good health will usually eat only a ringed seal's blubber, leaving the rest behind for a retinue that never seems far off—the arctic fox, glaucous and Thayer's gulls, the shier ivory gull, and the ubiquitous raven. (In winter arctic foxes live far out on the sea ice, entirely dependent on scavenging polar bear kills for their survival.)

---

* Savssats occur most often in fiords, where a band of sea ice too wide for marine mammals to swim under on a single breath cuts them off from the open sea. As the fiord continues to freeze over, the animals, often hundreds of narwhals and belukha, are restricted to a smaller and smaller opening in the ice for breathing. If the ice doesn't break up or recede, the trap is fatal.

When a female with cubs makes a kill, on the other hand, the family normally consumes the whole seal carcass. But they also scavenge carcasses left behind by the adult males. While it is not clear how, it is evident that sharing these kills is critically important to a healthy polar bear population.

Polar bears are neither gregarious nor social, in the sense that, say, wolves or cheetahs are social. Their repertoire of body language and vocalizations seems limited, used largely to communicate a desire to avoid each other. When they are seen, they are usually seen alone—a single male or female, or a female with her cubs. They gather together in special circumstances, however, and some of these assemblies are memorable.

In 1874 two American observers saw between 250 and 300 polar bears together on Saint Matthew Island in Bering Sea, placidly "grazing and rooting about like hogs in a common." (A ship's captain who saw polar bears ranging together in a lush coastal valley in eastern Greenland likened them to sheep pastured in an English meadow.) At Cape Churchill, Manitoba, in September and October great numbers of bears are milling about waiting, like the Saint Matthew bears, for the formation of sea ice, so they can quit the coast and a life of sleeping and browsing in these summer retreats.

Food draws bears together in at least two ways. When a single bear finds a good seal-hunting ground, ten or fifteen other bears are likely to show up at the same place within half a day or so. Somehow they know. Savssats and beached carrion also draw bears. In 1980, scientists counted fifty-six of them at a bowhead whale carcass on the Svalbard coast. Larsen says scientists don't have an explanation for how bears get wind of these things. Odor likely plays a role, but bears come in from all directions and some from very far away. "They just get to a place where something is happening," says Larsen, "and they get there quickly."

Bears seem to pay each other very little mind under these circumstances. They feed, interact very little with each other, and go on their way. It is a different situation entirely when a female with cubs encounters a lone male. She runs away immediately. Or when two males meet each other on the track of a female in estrus. The ensuing fights can be violent and protracted. (Fighting among males is so common that it is a rare male past the age of six that doesn't carry facial scars from these encounters.) On the other hand, a little-understood pairing apparently occasionally occurs with young male bears who become hunting and traveling companions.

The enduring social unit is a female and her cubs. They are usually together for two years, during which time the female teaches the cubs to hunt. Their social interaction is constant and intense. Older bears infrequently make sounds—they hiss loudly, growl, and champ their teeth when they are irritated; and when they are very agitated they make a soft chuffing sound. Cubs, on the other hand, have an impressive vocal repertoire. When they are around human observers they hiss, squall, and whimper, make a wet, popping sound by smacking their lips, and emit throaty rumblings. Scientists guess that their mothers communicate with them vocally—perhaps using only a few simple sounds. One could be a version of the adult's chuff, a quiet, repetitive call "easily located in space but not traveling far," used to warn her cubs away from danger—an approaching male, rotten ice, a rabid fox.

Somehow the female must control her cubs until they can feed themselves, if for no other reason than that they can so easily disrupt her own hunting, on which they all depend. (One scientist suggested to me that females solve this problem by walking the cubs until they are so tired they curl up together to sleep. While they rest, she hunts.)

Young bears apparently understand the basic skills of stalking and still-hunting, but require practice. Perhaps their mothers also provide some instruction by creating opportunities for them; and perhaps they learn a good deal by watching and imitating. Their initial attempts to catch seals are frantic and impatient. A young bear may give up its watch at an aglu after only ten minutes. Or charge wildly across an ice floe and dive headfirst into a lead in pursuit of a seal. As with other predators, an acute sense of need plays a crucial role in the determination to succeed. For cubs-of-the-year (coys) and yearlings, mother will provide.

Polar bears have relatively few young, but they put a great deal of time and energy into raising and protecting them, which ensures that most of them will survive. When they are between twenty-four and twenty-eight months old, usually, the family breaks up and the cubs are on their own. The female often mates again. The cubs may stay together for a while, but then they, too, separate. At this point, the survival of *Ursus maritimus* hinges on learning to live alone. And among all age classes of bears, it is those in this transitional stage that suffer the greatest mortality.

Charles Jonkel, a biologist, summarizes the situation that faces a young bear in its first summer alone. First, it lacks experience, an indispensable attribute for a successful hunter. Second, it is somewhat limited in its ability to secure food because of its small size (a large bearded or hooded seal could get away); and it might not have strength enough to break through a seal lair before the seal escapes. Third, it has a pressing need for food, not only for its continued growth, but to build up a layer of blubber on which to draw during lean periods. Fourth, it has to learn to find its way, to comprehend and then remember the relationships between currents, prevailing winds, the position of certain land masses, the trend of coastlines. Last, it must face competition from and conflict with older bears, who may take its seals away.

A female's unique competence lies in figuring out something new and difficult—den construction—in the middle of her life; and in teaching her cubs to survive. What makes the males impressive is their year-round success as hunters (for they are more often abroad in the winter than the female) and their assertive curiosity. Males investigate almost anything they spot on the sea ice. In evolutionary terms this might only be simple resourcefulness. Curious bears may in the end eat more often. The darker side of this is that, today, with the spread of oil camps and the abandonment of military installations, curious bears are sometimes killed by the things they test.

THERE is a famous object of Dorset art—the Dorset culture flourished in the Arctic between about 500 B.C. and A.D. 1000—which archaeologists refer to as a "floating" or "flying" bear. The best-known example was found at a site called Alernerk, near the present village of Igloolik on Melville Peninsula in the eastern Canadian Arctic. It is carved from ivory, about six inches long, and dates from about A.D. 500. The bear's head and body are streamlined, the forelegs sweeping back along the sides and the rear legs trailing. The bear appears to be gliding or flying. There is something human in the shape of the rear legs, and it is incised with a stylized skeleton, a backbone and ribs, with the cervical vertebrae and limb joints clearly marked. The underside—the chest and abdomen—is longitudinally concave, suggesting the lack of a body; and there is a tiny compartment with a sliding wood cover in the neck, which apparently once held red ocher.

The Dorset culture, particularly toward its close, may have been dominated by influential shamans who made these carvings. Dorset shamans in self-induced trances "flew away," departing their human bodies for a spirit realm at the bottom of the sea or on the moon. Here they consulted, appeased, and cajoled on their own behalf or on behalf of their patients. They were frequently accompanied on these journeys by powerful helping spirits, and among these the polar bear was without peer. The bear helped the *angakoq*, or shaman, get outside his body so he could fly. (The skeleton carved on the bears is thought to emphasize this disembodied form of travel.)

One of the most interesting things about these carvings is how realistic they actually are. At first I thought they were stylized like modern Eskimo soapstone carvings. After I saw polar bears on the ice, I realized it was instead my conceptions that were stylized. Polar bears strike poses in real life that are but slightly exaggerated in Dorset and modern carvings—a reminder of the native eye, the kernels of realism that lie within seemingly exaggerated native ideas.

I once asked Ray Schweinsburg about polar bears that went down into the sea, that swam down to the bottom of the ocean with their *angakoq* companions. "Once," replied Schweinsburg, "I saw a set of bear tracks that led up to the edge of a large hole in the ice, where they disappeared. There were no tracks coming out, and there was nowhere else the bear could have surfaced in that floe ice. You can easily understand the view that there are bears walking around on the bottom of the ocean."

And if you have ever seen a polar bear swimming 30 feet below the surface in clear water, watched it stroke and glide, turn and roll down there like a sea otter, you would not wonder that bears could fly.

The artistic and philosophical evocation of the polar bear by Eskimo and pre-Eskimo cultures leads one to believe that their insight derives from a special affinity with the bear. To an extent, the Eskimo and the polar bear are alike, the lines of their successful adaptation to the Arctic being parallel. The prey of both, though not the principal prey of some Eskimo groups, is the ringed seal. Their hunting methods—waiting patiently at the aglu, various kinds of stalking—are strikingly similar. (Polar bears arrived in the Arctic ahead of the Eskimo, and it is likely Eskimos learned, or at least refined, some of their techniques by watching bears hunt.) Some groups of Eskimos move off the land and onto the sea ice in winter, like bears. And after about two weeks at a place where seal hunting is good, the area seems to be hunted out for both sorts of hunter, and they move on. Both make their living at the edge of the sea ice and along the shore. And both live with the threat of starvation if the seals disappear.

Man and bear are affected as well by the vicissitudes of a harsh climate, which seems to give each of them a discernable aura of successful endurance. Anthropologists and biologists turn to the same words to describe each: "tough," "practical," "tenacious,"

"inventive," "a one-time learner." And they note a difference between the two. Bears seem occasionally to lose their temper when
they are hunting. "I have seen [a polar bear] watch a seal for half a
day," wrote a traveler, and failing to catch it by any stratagem,
"it roared hideously, tossing snow in the air, and trotted off." Other
observers have seen bears smash off projections of ice or smack the
water repeatedly in frustration after just missing a seal. Eskimos
rarely lose their temper, and almost never when they are hunting.
The usual response to failure in these circumstances is laughter.

The Eskimos' affinity for the polar bear is easy to understand
from the parallels in their ecology and the similarity of their dwellings, mentioned earlier; and from knowing the esteem with which
Eskimos regard a successful hunter. And from seeing a polar bear
stripped of its skin, how disquietingly human its appearance is. But
there is something far deeper in their involvement, for each is prey
to the other.

The bear fears both the killer whale and the walrus when it is
in the water, for it has no lethal leverage there. On land, it is wary
of the walrus and of men, too, but it will stalk both. A hungry bear
will test the resistance of either. The image of a strong, determined,
cunning animal stalking them must have entered the minds of all
people who felt their vulnerability out on the sea ice. Over that
uneven topography the bear could draw near without ever being
noticed. The fear of being hunted is vestigial in us, a dim memory
from the open savannas of southern Africa. For a man waiting
alone at an aglu for a seal on a winter afternoon, looking around in
the half-light, alert at a subconscious and primitive level for the
triggering sound of the bear's footfall, the fear must have been
palpable.

Bears approached men as though they were a kind of resting
seal. Some of these encounters must have ended with a pounce, a
single blow, a man dead. But some of them were finished with a seal
harpoon or a knife, a bear dead of a fatal miscalculation. Of the
latter, some were encounters deliberately courted, by men on the
verge of manhood. These were not simply terrifying moments but

moments of awe and apotheosis. These were moments that kept alive within the culture the overarching presence of a being held in fearful esteem. *Tôrnârssuk*, the Polar Eskimo called him, "the one who gives power."

To encounter the bear, to meet it with your whole life, was to grapple with something personal. The confrontation occurred on a serene, deadly, and elevated plain. If you were successful you found something irreducible within yourself, like a seed. To walk away was to be alive, utterly. To be assured of your own life, the life of your kind, in a harsh land where life took insight and patience and humor. It was to touch the bear. It was a gift from the bear.

Knud Rasmussen, an arctic traveler, once asked an Eskimo man about happiness, about exhilaration, and he answered, "To come across fresh bear tracks and be ahead of all the other sledges."

To men who grappled, instead, with abstractions of geography, with dreams of a mother lode of wealth in the New World, the bear was something else. In 1597, during that winter they saw the sun rise early, Barents and his men were frightened often by polar bears. Bears had killed two of the group the previous year, and now they seemed to prowl continuously around Barents' winter quarters. His men watched, unnerved, as the bears dragged huge slabs of meat (from a beached whale) past them in the dusky light. On April 15, 1597, when no bears had been seen for weeks, one of the men volunteered to crawl into a den—"but not to farre," wrote Gerrit de Veer, "for it was fearfull to behold" with hoar-frosted hairs dangling from its ceiling and its ice-covered, claw-scraped walls.

De Veer's chronicle—and a later one by Jacob van der Brugge, about a 1634 expedition to Svalbard that also suffered predation by bears—projected an image of the polar bear as a ghostly marauder. The image persisted throughout the period of arctic exploration, and was one the polar bear lent itself to. Bears loomed together suddenly in numbers on a foggy beach, like white wolves. They tore open graves and strewed the bodies about, which men found more ominous than if the bears had eaten the corpses. They entered camps boldly on their large, silent feet and, accustomed as they were to the crack and explosion of sea ice, were not startled by gunfire. Explorers who arrived at their caches to find them torn apart by bears—sacks of flour dragged off in one direction, sleeping bags in another, equipment crates smashed to kindling, food tins surgically opened with the rake of a single claw—felt violated. Those who ate bear meat indiscriminately thought they had been tricked by their victims—poisoned—when they suffered the nauseous lethargy, the crushing headaches and loss of skin and hair that came from eating the bear's liver. Or when they developed trichinosis from eating the bear's flesh.*

Thousands of miles from familiar surroundings, genuinely frightened, and perhaps strained by the grim conditions of shipboard life, Europeans took to killing any polar bear they saw. They shot them out of pettiness and a sense of rectitude. In time, killing polar bears became the sort of amusement people expected on an arctic journey. Travelers regularly shot them from the ship's deck, for target practice. One idle summer afternoon in 1896, a whaling captain in Amundsen Gulf with nothing else to do shot thirty-five, for sport. The curious and unaggressive bear, so easily attracted to a ship, an object cruising so oddly in the ice, time and again stepped into its own death. In 1875 the crew of a whaler was playing football on a shelf of landfast ice in thick fog next to the ship. In the middle of the game a polar bear appeared and began chasing the ball in and out among the men. The whalers fled. Such stories only confirmed some in their sense of being offended, of being trifled with in this difficult place. They shot the animals with colonial indifference.

The most disturbing and deplorable aspect of nineteenth-century encounters with polar bears was a perverse manipulation of the bond between a female and her cubs, a common amusement of

---

* Vitamin A is found in toxic concentrations in polar bear liver. Eating it causes hypervitaminosis-A. And about 60 percent of the present polar bear population carries species of *Trichinella*.

sailors aboard whaling and sealing ships. William Scoresby tells of an incident involving walrus hunters who had set fire to a pile of blubber to attract bears. A female and two cubs drew near. The female settled her cubs at a short distance and then started trying to hook pieces of blubber out of the fire. The men watched from the safety of the deck as she fought with the flames. They threw her small bits of blubber, which she took to the cubs. As she approached them with the last piece, the men shot the two cubs dead. For the next half hour she "laid her paws first upon one, and then the other, and endeavored to raise them up." She walked off and called to them, she licked their wounds. She went off again and "stood for some time moaning" before returning to paw them "with signs of inexpressible fondness." Bored, or perhaps mortified, the men shot the female and left her on the ice with her cubs.

Sometimes a cub was taken alive, for a zoo or as a present for someone. In November 1876, a Sir Allen Young shot a female and one of her cubs from the deck of a steamship. The other cub he lassoed as a gift for the Prince of Wales.* The cub fought wildly until it was secured with chains to ringbolts in the deck. The female was butchered and the cub wrapped in her skin in the hope of appeasing him. Three or four days later the cub succeeded in tearing free of the ringbolts. He was then placed in a small cage, where he remained for the duration of the voyage. The cub roared for hours on end and pulled at the length of chain still around his neck. He was tormented by the ship's dog, which stole his food and bit his paws. The origin of the meat he was fed can be imagined. By the time the ship reached England, the cub lay prostrate in his cage, convulsing and panting. He died a week later. "Had he lived,"

---

* European royalty received live polar bears as gifts from explorers and adventurers from the tenth century onward. They, in turn, historically found them "an extremely valued and efficient instrument of diplomacy" in North Africa and the Middle East, where they were sent, along with gyrfalcons, in royal retinues.

wrote Frank Buckland, reflecting the attitudes of the age, "he would, no doubt, have been an honour to his country and his race."

These stories, of course, are from another era; but the craven taunting, the witless insensitivity, and the phony sense of adventure that propelled them are not from another age. They still afflict us. For these men, the bear had no intrinsic worth, no spiritual power of intercession, no ability to elevate human life. The circumstances of its death emphasized the breach with man. During these same years, by contrast, the killing of polar bears by Eskimos occurred in an atmosphere of respect, with implicit spiritual obligations. The dead bear, for example, was propitiated with gifts. Such an act of propitiation is sometimes dismissed as "superstition." "Technique of awareness" would come much closer to the mark, words that remind you of what you are dealing with.

Europeans were ill at ease in the Arctic. The polar bear was for them a symbol of the implacable indifference of an inhospitable landscape. Whatever remorse they suffered over their harsh treatment of the polar bear eventually became admiration, but for a bear that was really a curious image of themselves. De Veer's marauding ghost bear, which became an impediment to Western progress and then an amusement, a nuisance, finally became a vaguely noble creature, wandering in a desolate landscape, saddled with melancholy thoughts. A romantic, estranged, self-absorbed creature.

In the stories Eskimos tell, down to the present, the polar bear is most often cast as a helper or companion of one sort or another, like *Tôrnârssuk*. But he is known as *Kokogiaq*, too, the ten-legged or many-legged bear. *One time, one winter, it seemed people who went off hunting in a certain direction never came back. What happened to them was that there was a ten-legged bear down there. When people looked over there, Kokogiaq moved his legs around a little. It looked like people walking around on the ice. So other people went down there to see them. That's how Kokogiaq got people. Finally a man got the bear to come after him. He got him to chase him into a place in the ice where Kokogiaq couldn't turn*

*around. Then that man ran around and killed him from behind with
his spear. When people go hunting down there now, they always
come back.*

The stories go like that.

Often in a story about *Kokogiaq* or *Tôrnârssuk* there is some
hint not only of the bear's biology (how that wedge-shaped body
could get caught in ice where a man could slip through) but of its
personality. The bear's melancholy wandering, for example, is
underscored in a Polar Eskimo story about a bear who falls in love
with a young married woman. He cautions her never to tell her
husband of their meetings because her husband will surely try to
kill him. But she takes pity on her husband's failures in hunting
bears and tells him where her lover lives. Far away, the bear hears
her whispering to her husband in the night, and he leaves his home
before the husband arrives. He goes straight to the woman's snow
house. He raises his paws to smash it in—and then he lowers his
paws to his side. Feeling betrayed, overcome with grief, he sets off
on a long and solitary journey.

To the European mind the story is poignant. For the Eskimo
it is charged with danger. For the bear to go off preoccupied with
such a subject means it will not be paying attention to where it is
going, that it may fall through bad ice or miss signs that will lead it
to an aglu and sustenance.

A bear's long, solitary journeys across the frozen ocean, science tells
us, are not precisely what the imagination once conjectured. And
now, too often, wherever they go someone is in the way. Between
1978 and 1981, eight-four polar bears were killed in the Canadian
Arctic as threats to human life. The threat is real. In 1973, a bear
killed a tractor operator near Kendall Island in the Beaufort Sea. In
1975, also in the Beaufort, a bear killed a construction worker on the
deck of a barge. In August 1975, a polar bear severely mauled a man
in a scientific camp on Somerset Island. And at Churchill, Manitoba,
bears mauled people in 1966 and 1967, and killed a boy in 1968 and
a man in 1983.

The former deaths are associated with industrial development in the Arctic; the attacks at Churchill derive from a more peculiar set of circumstances. For many years, polar bears at the southern end of Hudson Bay have come ashore in late July and early August with southward-drifting ice. Females commonly den for the winter in country between the Nelson and Churchill rivers, while adult males and subadults of both sexes drift northward up the coast to the vicinity of Cape Churchill, 25 miles east of the village, where coastal ice is likely to form earliest. They remain in this vicinity, "temporarily removed from their specialized predatory niche," as one scientist put it, throughout September and October.

This unusual staging was not discovered until the 1960s, when bears began turning up at the village of Churchill. Scientists theorize that when a Hudson's Bay Company post at the mouth of the Nelson River closed, an American Strategic Air Command base closed, and military maneuvers ceased at Fort Churchill, all in 1957, the hunting pressure on polar bears was relieved and the population began to increase. By the mid-sixties, polar bears were turning up in large numbers at garbage fires in Churchill, frightening people. The people, in turn, began tormenting the bears by shooting them with small-caliber weapons and chasing them with cars.

In recent years, though the bear population has continued to grow, a program of warning, local education, deterrence, and management has reduced the numbers of bears killed, and there have been few attacks. Residents of Churchill now regard the bears, somewhat fondly, as a tourist attraction. Others who have visited the area find the sight of bears ominous and peculiar—some with huge dark numerals painted on their sides, some rooting in the smoke and flames of the smoldering dump, where a bear once died from trying to eat an automobile battery.

The parade of amateur and professional photographers, film-makers, and television personnel, baiting bears with jars of mayonnaise and importuning Churchill people to assist them in staging various scenes, is unending. More than anything, Churchill represents a moment in time when an animal in a comparatively accelerated state of evolutionary development has encountered another creature evolving at a very much higher rate of change. Churchill, for the moment, is the answer to the question of what industrial development in the Arctic means—along with the thirty or so bears shot each year in northern Canada as "nuisances" and threats. The bears at Churchill, it should be observed, depart the day the ice will support their weight.

Recent research into the size and dynamics of polar bear populations has resulted in a hunting moratorium in Svalbard and a partial ban on hunting in the United States.* Native hunting in Greenland continues, apparently without serious effect on the population. Native hunting in Canada is under a quota system, which has worked well in the past, although quotas are subject to political manipulation and, as one scientist pointed out to me, often regarded not so much as limits but as numbers to strive for.

In 1965, polar bear biologists, meeting at the University of Alaska to pool what they knew, feared that bears might need protection from excessive hunting. The greatest danger to them now, stressed every scientist I spoke with, is not hunting but industrial development and what it brings with it, including summary demands for data on polar bear biology and ecology.† Uppermost in scientists' minds are three areas of concern. First is environmental poisoning. Bears feed at the top of a marine food chain that concentrates PCBs, heavy metals, and chlorinated hydrocarbons like

---

* According to the terms of the Marine Mammal Protection Act, which supersedes the stricter provisions of the IUCN Polar Bear Agreement, there are no seasonal limits and no limits on the number of bears that can be killed by native hunters. Nor are clubs, females with cubs, or denning females protected.

† In the face of such demands some polar bears have been wounded or killed in poorly designed research projects or poorly thought-through experiments. For a description of experiments that killed two bears see N. A. Øritsland et al., *Effect of Crude Oil on Polar Bears*, Environmental Studies No. 24 (Ottawa: Northern Affairs Program, Northern Environmental Protection Branch, 1981).

dieldrin, all of which have been found in polar bears. The waste from drilling and mining operations has also proved lethal to bears. A second concern is the disruption of female bears at their denning sites, the result of intensive overflights and other transportation corridor development and of repeated seismic surveys.* A third area of concern is what effect industrial development will have on the distribution of seals, and therefore bears.

The most pressing problem is finding a way to keep curious bears away from industrial sites. Deterrent systems that do not seriously injure bears—electric fences, rubber batons fired from riot guns—have met with some success, but polar bears are not easily stopped or fooled.

In the light of all these potential problems, IUCN polar bear biologists have asked for "no-activity zones" or what a Russian scientist has called "zones of peace," where bears will simply not be bothered by various human projects.

FAR from all these disturbing concerns, one May afternoon, I accompanied two polar bear biologists searching for breeding females on the sea ice of Lancaster Sound. I knew and trusted and liked these two men. I also sympathized with their ambivalent feelings about their work. One of them had once come upon a female nursing her cubs. Unaware of his presence, she had settled back against a bank of snow with them and was staring calmly out across the empty sea ice. "I saw that, and I said to myself, why in God's name am I bothering theses animals?" They were ambivalent, too, about the drugs they were using to immobilize the bears. What they were using—Ketamine (ketamine hydrochloride) and Rhompun (xylazine hydrochloride)—was an improvement over earlier drugs like Sernylan (phencyclidine hydrochloride, the street drug called "angel dust"), which appeared to induce psychotic reactions and

---

* Seismic surveys employ explosion and vibration to map the earth's crust in search of mineral and petroleum deposits. When improvements are made in seismic technology, the same areas are often surveyed again.

cause breathing difficulties. But immobilizing drugs are still problematic. One bear biologist told me, "Every time I chase an animal to put a dart in it, I am in conflict. How can I justify getting the information like this?"

That afternoon on Lancaster Sound, in the completion of the somewhat somber duties of tagging and recording data and fitting the animals with radio collars to permit satellite tracking, we saw many bears. We landed once to inspect the remains of a walrus that had been killed, perhaps, or possibly only scavenged, by a bear. We saw two-year-old cubs with their mothers striding apprehensively away from the sound of our helicopter, and we saw males and females together, mating pairs, turning beneath us to stare. And females with five-month-old cubs, scrambling over pressure ridges with a boost from their mother's nose.

One of the females we darted went down near a jumble of shattered ice. While the others made measurements, I looked at her feet. I had once been told that polar bear claws show an annual shading, faint rings, which could be used reliably to age a bear, as is the case with ringed seals. But there were none that I could detect. I looked at details of her fur and felt the thickness of her ears, as though examining a museum specimen. Uncomfortable with all this, I walked over to the pressure ridge and sat on a slab of broken sea ice. It was a beautiful day, the skies clear behind a thin layer of very high cirrus, which made the sky a paler blue. About five below zero. No wind.

As I sat there my companions rolled the unconscious bear over on her back and I saw a trace of pink in the white fur between her legs. The lips of her vulva were swollen. Her genitalia were in size and shape like a woman's. I looked away. I felt I had invaded her privacy.

For the remainder of the day I could not rid myself of this image of vulnerability.

Four

LANCASTER SOUND
Monodon monoceros

I AM STANDING at the margin of the sea ice called the floe edge at the mouth of Admiralty Inlet, northern Baffin Island, three or four miles out to sea. The firmness beneath my feet belies the ordinary sense of the phrase "out to sea." Several Eskimo camps stand here along the white and black edge of ice and water. All of us have come from another place—Nuvua, 30 miles to the south at the tip of Uluksan Peninsula. We are here to hunt narwhals. They are out there in the open water of Lancaster Sound somewhere, waiting for this last ice barrier to break up so they can enter their summer feeding grounds in Admiralty Inlet.

As I walk along the floe edge—the light is brilliant, the cease-less light of July; but after so many weeks I am weary of it; I stare at the few shadows on the ice with a kind of hunger—as I walk along here I am aware of both fear and elation, a mix that comes in remote regions with the realization that you are exposed and the weather can be capricious, and fatal. The wind is light and from the north—I can see its corrugation on the surface of the water. Should it swing around and come from the south, the ice behind us would begin to open up. Traverse cracks across the inlet, only a few inches wide yesterday, would begin to widen. We would have difficulty getting back to Nuvua, even if we left at the first sign of a wind shift.

A few days ago one of these men was caught like that. A distant explosion, like dynamite, told him what a compass bearing he quickly took on Borden Peninsula confirmed—that the five-square-mile sheet of floe ice he had camped on was being swept out of Admiralty Inlet toward open water in Lancaster Sound. He and his companion, knowing the set of local currents, struck out immediately to the east. Twelve hours later, near exhaustion, they came to a place where the ice floe was grounded in shallow coastal water, making a huge, slow turn in the current before breaking loose into Lancaster Sound. They leaped and plunged across broken ice cakes for the firm shore.

I am not so much thinking of these things, however, as I am feeling the exuberance of birds around me. Black-legged kittiwakes, northern fulmars, and black guillemots are wheeling and hovering in weightless acrobatics over the streams and lenses of life in the water—zooplankton and arctic cod—into which they plunge repeatedly for their sustenance. Out on the ice, at piles of offal from the narwhal hunt, glaucous and Thayer's gulls stake a rough-tempered claim to some piece of flesh, brash, shouldering birds alongside the more reticent and rarer ivory gulls.

Birds fly across these waters in numbers that encourage you to simply flip your pencil in the air. Certain species end their northward migration here and nest. Others fly on to Devon and Ellesmere islands or to northwest Greenland. From where I now stand I can study some that stay, nesting in an unbroken line for 10 miles on a cliff between Baillarge Bay and Elwin Inlet, a rugged wall of sedimentary and volcanic rock pocked with indentations and ledges, rising at an angle of 80° from the water. More than 50,000 northern fulmars. At other such rookeries around Lancaster Sound, guillemots, murres, and kittiwakes congregate in tens and even hundreds of thousands to nest and feed during the short summer. Gulls, arctic terns, snow geese, eiders, red-breasted mergansers, and dovekies have passed through in droves already. Of the dovekies— a small, stocky seabird with a black head and bright white underside—something on the order of a third of the northwest Greenland population of 30 *million* passes over Lancaster Sound in May and June.

On the white-as-eggshell ice plain where we are camped, with the mottled browns and ochers of Borden Peninsula to the east and the dark cliffs of Brodeur Peninsula obscured in haze to the west, the adroit movements of the birds above the water give the landscape an immediate, vivid dimension: the eye, drawn far out to pale hues on the horizon, comes back smartly to the black water, where, *plunk*, a guillemot disappears in a dive.

The outcry of birds, the bullet-whirr of their passing wings, the splashing of water, is, like the falling light, unending. Lancaster Sound is a rare arctic marine sanctuary, a place where creatures are concentrated in the sort of densities one finds in the Antarctic Ocean, the richest sea waters in the world. Marine ecologists are not certain why Lancaster Sound teems so with life, but local upwelling currents and a supply of nutrients from glacial runoff on Devon Island seem critical.*

---

* Lancaster Sound has been proposed as a world biological reserve by the International Biological Programme and singled out by the United Nations as a Natural Site of World Heritage Quality. The stability of this ecosystem is currently threatened by offshore oil development and increased shipping traffic. David Nettleship, an arctic ornithologist with preeminent experience here, has written that such economic development "should be strictly controlled in order to prevent the destruction of a uniquely rich high arctic oasis. To harm it would go far towards making a desert of arctic waters."

Three million colonial seabirds, mostly northern fulmars, kittiwakes, and guillemots, nest and feed here in the summer. It is no longer the haunt of 10,000 or so bowhead whales, but it remains a summering ground for more than 30 percent of the belukha whale population of North America, and more than three-quarters of the world's population of narwhals. No one is sure how many harp, bearded, and ringed seals are here—probably more than a quarter of a million. In addition there are thousands of Atlantic walrus. The coastal regions are a denning area for polar bear and home to thousands of arctic fox in the summer.

I am concerned, as I walk, however, more with what is immediate to my senses—the ternlike whiffle and spin of birds over the water, the chicken-cackling of northern fulmars, and cool air full of the breath of sea life. This community of creatures, including all those invisible in the water, constitutes a unique overlap of land, water, and air. This is a special meeting ground, like that of a forest's edge with a clearing; or where the fresh waters of an estuary meet the saline tides of the sea; or at a river's riparian edge. The mingling of animals from different ecosystems charges such border zones with evolutionary potential. Flying creatures here at Admiralty Inlet walk on ice. They break the pane of water with their dives to feed. Marine mammals break the pane of water coming the other way to breathe.

The edges of any landscape—horizons, the lip of a valley, the bend of a river around a canyon wall—quicken an observer's expectations. That attraction to borders, to the earth's twilit places, is part of the shape of human curiosity. And the edges that cause excitement are like these where I now walk, sensing the birds toying with gravity; or like those in quantum mechanics, where what is critical straddles a border between being a wave and being a particle, between being what it is and becoming something else, occupying an edge of time that defeats our geometries. In biology these transitional areas between two different communities are called ecotones.

The ecotone at the Admiralty Inlet floe edge extends in two planes. In order to pass under the ice from the open sea, an animal must be free of a need for atmospheric oxygen; the floe edge, therefore, is a barrier to the horizontal migration of whales. In the vertical plane, no bird can penetrate the ice and birds like gulls can't go below water with guillemots to feed on schools of fish. Sunlight, too, is halted at these borders.

To stand at the edge of this four-foot-thick ice platform, however, is to find yourself in a rich biological crease. Species of alga grow on the bottom of the sea ice, turning it golden brown with a patchwork of life. These tiny diatoms feed zooplankton moving through the upper layers of water in vast clouds—underwater galaxies of copepods, amphipods, and mysids. These in turn feed the streaming schools of cod. The cod feed the birds. And the narwhals. And also the ringed seal, which feeds the polar bear, and eventually the fox. The algae at the bottom of this food web are called "epontic" algae, the algae of the sea ice. (Ringed seals, ivory gulls, and other birds and mammals whose lives are ice-oriented are called "pagophylic.") It is the ice, however, that holds this life together. For ice-associated seals, vulnerable on a beach, it is a place offshore to rest, directly over their feeding grounds. It provides algae with a surface to grow on. It shelters arctic cod from hunting seabirds and herds of narwhals, and it shelters the narwhal from the predatory orca. It is the bear's highway over the sea. And it gives me a place to stand on the ocean, and wonder.

I walk here intent on the birds, half aware of the biological mysteries in these placid, depthless waters in which I catch fleeting silver glimpses of cod. I feel blessed. I draw in the salt air and feel the warmth of sunlight on my face. I recall a childhood of summer days on the beaches of California. I feel the wealth to be had in life in an aimless walk like this, through woods or over a prairie or down a beach.

It is not all benign and ethereal at the ice edge, however. You cannot—I cannot—lose completely the sense of how far from land this is. And I am wary of walrus. A male walrus is a huge animal, approaching the size of a small car. At close range in the water its agility and speed are intimidating. Walruses normally eat only bottom-dwelling organisms like clams, worms, and crabs, but there is an unusual sort of walrus—almost always a male, a loner, that deliberately hunts and kills seals. Its ivory tusks are crosshatched with the claw marks of seals fighting for their lives. (It is called *angeyeghaq* by the Eskimos on Saint Lawrence Island, who are familiar with its unusual behavior.) This rare carnivore will charge off an ice floe to attack a small boat, and actively pursue and try to kill people in the water. A friend of mine was once standing with an Eskimo friend at an ice edge when the man cautioned him to step back. They retreated 15 or 20 feet. Less than a minute later a walrus surfaced in an explosion of water where they had been standing. A polar bear trick.

When I walk along the floe edge I think of that story. I have no ear educated as was his companion's to anticipate the arrival of the walrus. A native ear. Experience. I walk here susceptible as any traveler to the unknown.

I stood still occasionally to listen. I heard only the claver of birds. Then there was something else. I had never heard the sound before, but when it came, plosive and gurgling, I knew instinctively what it was, even as everyone in camp jumped. I strained to see them, to spot the vapor of their breath, a warm mist against the soft horizon, or the white tip of a tusk breaking the surface of the water, a dark pattern that retained its shape against the dark, shifting patterns of the water. Somewhere out there in the ice fragments. Gone. Gone now. Others had heard the breathing. Human figures in a camp off to the west, dark lines on the blinding white ice, gesture toward us with upraised arms.

THE first narwhals I ever saw lived far from here, in Bering Strait. The day I saw them I knew that no element of the earth's natural history had ever before brought me so far, so suddenly. It was as though something from a bestiary had taken shape, a creature strange as a giraffe. It was as if the testimony of someone I had no reason to doubt, yet could not quite believe, a story too farfetched, had been verified at a glance.

I was with a bowhead whale biologist named Don Ljungblad, flying search transects over Bering Sea. It was May, and the first bowheads of spring were slowly working their way north through Bering Strait toward their summer feeding grounds in the Chukchi and Beaufort seas. Each day as we flew these transects we would pass over belukha whale and walrus, ringed, spotted, and ribbon seals, bearded seals, and flocks of birds migrating to Siberia. I know of no other region in North America where animals can be met with in such numbers. Bering Sea itself is probably the richest of all the northern seas, as rich as Chesapeake Bay or the Grand Banks at the time of their discovery. Its bounty of crabs, pollock, cod, sole, herring, clams, and salmon is set down in wild numbers, the rambling digits of guesswork. The numbers of birds and marine mammals feeding here, to a person familiar with anything but the Serengeti or life at the Antarctic convergence, are magical. At the height of migration in the spring, the testament of life in Bering Sea is absolutely stilling in its dimensions.

The two weeks I spent flying with Ljungblad, with so many thousands of creatures moving through the water and the air, were a heady experience. Herds of belukha whale glided in silent shoals beneath transparent sheets of young ice. Squadrons of fast-flying sea ducks flashed beneath us as they banked away. We passed ice floes stained red in a hundred places with the afterbirths of walrus. Staring all day into the bright light reflected from the ice and water, however, and the compression in time of these extraordinary events, left me dazed some evenings.

Aspects of the arctic landscape that had become salient for me —its real and temporal borders; a rare, rich oasis of life surrounded by vast stretches of deserted land; the upending of conventional kinds of time; biological vulnerability made poignant by the forgiving light of summer—all of this was evoked over Bering Sea.

The day we saw the narwhals we were flying south, low over Bering Strait. The ice in Chukchi Sea behind us was so close it did not seem possible that bowheads could have penetrated this far; but it is good to check, because they can make headway in ice as heavy as this and they are able to come a long way north undetected in lighter ice on the Russian side. I was daydreaming about two bowheads we had seen that morning. They had been floating side by side in a broad lane of unusually clear water between a shelf of shorefast ice and the pack ice—the flaw lead. As we passed over, they made a single movement together, a slow, rolling turn and graceful glide, like figure skaters pushing off, these 50-ton leviathans. Ljungblad shouted in my earphones: "Waiting." They were waiting for the ice in the strait to open up. Ljungblad saw nearly

300 bowheads waiting calmly like this one year, some on their backs, some with their chins resting on the ice.

The narwhals appeared in the middle of this reverie. Two males, with ivory tusks spiraling out of their foreheads, the image of the unicorn with which history has confused them. They were close to the same size and light-colored, and were lying parallel and motionless in a long, straight lead in the ice. My eye was drawn to them before my conscious mind, let alone my voice, could catch up. I stared dumbfounded while someone else shouted. Not just to see the narwhals, but *here*, a few miles northwest of King Island in Bering Sea. In all the years scientists have kept records for these waters, no one had ever seen a narwhal alive in Bering Sea. Judging from the heaviness of the ice around them, they must have spent the winter here.* They were either residents, a wondrous thought, or they had come from the nearest population centers the previous fall, from waters north of Siberia or from northeastern Canada.

The appearance of these animals was highly provocative. We made circle after circle above them, until they swam away under the ice and were gone. Then we looked at each other. Who could say what this was, really?

Because you have seen something doesn't mean you can explain it. Differing interpretations will always abound, even when good minds come to bear. The kernel of indisputable information is a dot in space; interpretations grow out of the desire to make this point a line, to give it a direction. The directions in which it can be sent, the uses to which it can be put by a culturally, professionally, and geographically diverse society, are almost without limit. The possibilities make good scientists chary. In a region like the Arctic, tense with a hunger for wealth, with fears of plunder, interpretation can quickly get beyond a scientist's control. When asked to assess

---

* The narwhal is not nearly as forceful in the ice as the bowhead. It can break through only about 6 inches of ice with its head. A bowhead, using its brow or on occasion its more formidable chin, can break through as much as 18 inches of sea ice.

the meaning of a biological event—What were those animals doing out there? Where do they belong?—they hedge. They are sometimes reluctant to elaborate on what they saw, because they cannot say what it means, and they are suspicious of those who say they know. Some even distrust the motives behind the questions.

I think along these lines in this instance because of the animal. No large mammal in the Northern Hemisphere comes as close as the narwhal to having its very existence doubted. For some, the possibility that this creature might actually live in the threatened waters of Bering Sea is portentous, a significant apparition on the eve of an era of disruptive oil exploration there. For others, those with the leases to search for oil and gas in Navarin and Norton basins, the possibility that narwhals may live there is a complicating environmental nuisance. Hardly anyone marvels solely at the fact that on the afternoon of April 16, 1982, five people saw two narwhals in a place so unexpected that they were flabbergasted. They remained speechless, circling over the animals in a state of wonder. In those moments the animals did not have to mean anything at all.

WE know more about the rings of Saturn than we know about the narwhal. Where do they go and what do they eat in the winter, when it is too dark and cold for us to find them? The Chilean poet and essayist Pablo Neruda wonders in his memoirs how an animal this large can have remained so obscure and uncelebrated. Its name, he thought, was "the most beautiful of undersea names, the name of a sea chalice that sings, the name of a crystal spur." Why, he wondered, had no one taken Narwhal for a last name, or built "a beautiful Narwhal Building?"

Part of the answer lies with a regrettable connotation of death in the animal's name. The pallid color of the narwhal's skin has been likened to that of a drowned human corpse, and it is widely thought that its name came from the Old Norse for "corpse" and "whale," *nár* + *hvalr*. A medieval belief that the narwhal's flesh was poisonous has been offered in support of this interpretation, as well as the belief that its "horn" was proof at that time against being poisoned.

The eighteenth-century naturalist Buffon characterized the animal for all the generations that would read him as one that "revels in carnage, attacks without provocation, and kills without need." Among its associations with human enterprise in the inhospitable north is the following grim incident. In 1126, Arnhald, first bishop of Iceland, was shipwrecked off the Icelandic coast. Drowned men and part of the contents of the ship's hold washed up in a marsh, a place afterward called the Pool of Corpses. Conspicuous among the items of salvage were a number of narwhal tusks, "with runic letters upon them in an indelible red gum so that each sailor might know his own at the end of the voyage."

W. P. Lehmann, a professor of Germanic languages, believes the association with death is a linguistic accident. The Old Norse *nárhvalr* (whence the English *narwhal*, the French *narval*, the German *Narwal*, etc.), he says, was a vernacular play on the word *nahvalr*—the way *high-bred corn* is used in place of *hybrid corn*, or *sparrowgrass* is used for *asparagus*. According to Lehmann, *nahvalr* is an earlier, West Norse term meaning a "whale distinguished by a long, narrow projection" (the tusk).

Some, nevertheless, still call the narwhal "the corpse whale," and the unfounded belief that it is a cause of human death, or an omen or symbol to be associated with human death, remains intact to this day in some quarters. Animals are often fixed like this in history, bearing an unwarranted association derived from notions or surmise having no connection at all with their real life. The fuller explanations of modern field biology are an antidote, in part, to this tendency to name an animal carelessly. But it is also, as Neruda suggests, a task of literature to take animals regularly from the shelves where we have stored them, like charms or the most intricate of watches, and to bring them to life.

The obscurity of narwhals is not easily breeched by science. To begin with, they live underwater. And they live year-round in the polar ice, where the logistics and expense involved in approaching them are formidable barriers to field research, even in summer. Scientists have largely been limited to watching what takes place at the surface of the water in the open sea adjacent to observation points high on coastal bluffs. And to putting hydrophones in the water with them, and to making comparisons with the belukha whale, a close and better-known relative. About the regular periodic events of their lives, such as migration, breeding, and calving, in relation to climatic changes and fluctuations in the size of the population, we know next to nothing.*

Scientists can speak with precision only about the physical animal, not the ecology or behavior of this social and gregarious small whale. (It is the latter, not the former, unfortunately, that is most crucial to an understanding of how industrial development might affect narwhals.) Adult males, 16 feet long and weighing upwards of 3300 pounds, are about a quarter again as large as adult females. Males are also distinguished by an ivory tusk that pierces the upper lip on the left side and extends forward as much as 10 feet. Rarely, a female is found with a tusk, and, more rarely still, males and females with tusks on both sides of the upper jaw.

From the side, compared with the rest of its body, the narwhal's head seems small and blunt. It is dominated by a high, rounded forehead filled with bioacoustical lipids—special fats that allow the narwhal to use sound waves to communicate with other whales and to locate itself and other objects in its three-dimensional world. Its short front flippers function as little more than diving planes. The cone-shaped body tapers from just behind these flippers —where its girth is greatest, as much as eight feet—to a vertical ellipse at the tail. In place of a dorsal fin, a low dorsal ridge about five feet long extends in an irregular crenulation down the back. The tail flukes are unique. Seen from above, they appear heart-

---

* The knowledge and insight of Eskimos on these points, unfortunately, are of little help. Of all the areas of natural history in which they show expertise, native hunters are weakest in their understanding of the population dynamics of migratory animals. The reason is straight-forward. Too much of the animal's life is lived "outside the community," beyond the geographic and phenomenological landscape the Eskimos share with them.

shaped, like a ginkgo leaf, with a deep-notched center and trailing edges that curve far forward.

Viewed from the front, the head seems somewhat squarish and asymmetrical, and oddly small against the deep chest. The mouth, too, seems small for such a large animal, with the upper lip just covering the edge of a short, wedge-shaped jaw. The eyes are located just above and behind the upturned corners of the mouth, which give the animal a bemused expression. (The evolutionary loss of facial muscles, naturalist Peter Warshall has noted, means no quizzical wrinkling of the forehead, no raised eyebrow of disbelief, no pursed lip of determination). A single, crescent-shaped blowhole on top of the head is in a transverse line with the eyes.

Narwhal calves are almost uniformly gray. Young adults show spreading patches and streaks of white on the belly and marbling on the flanks. Adults are dark gray across the top of the head and down the back. Lighter grays predominate on top of the flippers and flukes, whites and light yellow-whites underneath. The back and flanks are marbled with blackish grays. Older animals, especially males, may be almost entirely white. Females, say some, are always lighter-colored on their flanks.

The marbled quality of the skin, which feels like smooth, oiled stone, is mesmerizing. On the flukes especially, where curvilinear streaks of dark gray overlap whitish-gray tones, the effect could not be more painterly. Elsewhere on the body, spots dominate. "These spots," writes William Scoresby, "are of a roundish or oblong form: on the back, where they seldom exceed two inches in diameter, they are the darkest and most crowded together, yet with intervals of pure white among them. On the side the spots are fainter, smaller, and more open. On the belly, they become extremely faint and few, and in considerable surfaces are not to be seen." These patterns completely penetrate the skin, which is a half-inch thick.

In the water, depending on sunlight and the color of the water itself, narwhals, according to British whaling historian Basil Lubbock, take on "many hues, from deep sea green to even an intense lake [blue] colour."

Narwhals are strong swimmers, with the ability to alter the contours of their body very slightly to reduce turbulence. Their speed and maneuverability are sufficient to hunt down swift prey— arctic cod, Greenland halibut, redfish—and to avoid their enemies, the orca and the Greenland shark.

Narwhals live in close association with ice margins and are sometimes found far inside heavy pack ice, miles from open water. (How they determine whether the lead systems they follow into the ice will stay open behind them, ensuring their safe return, is not known.) They manage to survive in areas of strong currents and wind where the movement of ice on the surface is violent and where leads open and close, or freeze over, very quickly. (Like seabirds, they seem to have an uncanny sense of when a particular lead is going to close in on them, and they leave.) That they are not infallible in anticipating the movement and formation of ice, which seals them off from the open air and oxygen, is attested to by relatively unusual and often fatal event called a savssat.

Savssats are most commonly observed on the west coast of Greenland. Late in the fall, while narwhals are still feeding deep in a coastal fiord, a band of ice may form in calm water across the fiord's mouth. The ice sheet may then expand toward the head of the fiord. At some point the distance from its landward to its seaward edge exceeds the distance a narwhal can travel on a single breath. By this time, too, shorefast ice may have formed at the head of the fiord, and it may grow out to meet the sea ice. The narwhals are thus crowded into a smaller and smaller patch of open water. Their bellowing and gurgling, their bovinelike moans and the plosive screech of their breathing, can sometimes be heard at a great distance.

The Danish scientist Christian Vibe visited a savssat on March 16, 1943, on the west coast of central Greenland. Hundreds of narwhals and belukhas were trapped in an opening less than 20 feet square. The black surface of the water was utterly "calm and still," writes Vibe. "Then the smooth surface was suddenly broken by black shadows and white animals which in elegant curves came up and disappeared—narwhals and white whales by the score. Side by side they emerged so close to each other that some of them would be lifted on the backs of the others and turn a somersault with the handsome tail waving in the air. First rows of narwhal, then white whales and then again narwhals—each species separately. It seethed, bobbed, and splashed in the opening. With a hollow, whistling sound they inhaled the air as if sucking it in through long iron tubes. The water was greatly disturbed . . . and the waves washed far in over the ice." The splashed water froze to the rim of the breathing hole, as did the moisture from their exhalations, further reducing the size of the savssat. In spite of the frenzy, not a single animal that Vibe saw was wounded by the huge tusks of the narwhal.*

The narwhal is classed in the suborder Odontoceti, with toothed whales such as the sperm whale, in the superfamily Delphinoidea, along with porpoises and dolphins, and in the family Monodontidae with a single companion, the belukha. In contrast to the apparently coastally-adapted belukha, biologists believe the narwhal is a pelagic or open-ocean species, that it is more ice-adapted, and that it winters farther to the north. Extrapolating on the basis of what is known of the belukha, it is thought that narwhals breed in April and give birth to a single, five-foot, 170-pound calf about fourteen months later, in June or July. Calves carry an inch-thick layer of blubber at birth to protect them against the cold water. They appear to nurse for about two years and may stay with their mothers for three years, or more. Extrapolating once again

---

* Eskimo hunters killed 340 narwhals and belukhas at this savssat in a week, before the ice fractured and the rest escaped. In the spring of 1915, Eskimos at Disko Bay took more than a thousand narwhals and belukhas at two savssats over a period of several months. Inattentive birds, especially thick-billed murres and dovekies which require a lot of open water to take off, may also suddenly find themselves with insufficient room and may be trapped.

from the belukha, it is thought that females reach sexual maturity between four and seven years of age, males between eight and nine years.

Narwhals are usually seen in small groups of two to eight animals, frequently of the same sex and age. In the summer, female groups, which include calves, are sometimes smaller or more loosely knit than male groups. During spring migration, herds may consist of 300 or more animals.

Narwhals feed largely on arctic and polar cod, Greenland halibut, redfish, sculpins, and other fish, on squid and to some extent on shrimps of several kinds, and on octopus and crustaceans. They have a complex, five-chambered stomach that processes food quickly, leaving undigested the chitonous beaks of squid and octopus, the carapaces of crustaceans, and the ear bones and eye lenses of fish, from which biologists can piece together knowledge of their diets.

Two types of "whale lice" (actually minute crustaceans) cling to their skin, in the cavity where the tusk passes through the lip, in the tail notch in the flukes, and in wounds (all places where they are least likely to be swept off by the flow of water past the narwhal's body). The tracks of the sharp, hooked legs of these tiny creatures are sometimes very clear on a narwhal's skin. Older animals may carry such infestations of these parasites as to cause an observer to wince.

IF you were to stand at the edge of a sea cliff on the north coast of Borden Peninsula, Baffin Island, you could watch narwhals migrating past more or less continuously for several weeks in the twenty-four-hour light of June. You would be struck by their agility and swiftness, by the synchronicity of their movements as they swam and dived in unison, and by a quality of alert composure in them, of capability in the face of whatever might happen. Their attractiveness lies partly with their strong, graceful movements in three dimensions, like gliding birds on an airless day. An impressive form of their synchronous behavior is their ability to deep-dive in groups. They disappear as a single diminishing shape, gray fading to darkness. They reach depths of 1000 feet or more, and their intent, often, is then to drive schools of polar cod toward the surface at such a rate that the fish lose consciousness from the too-rapid expansion of their swim bladders. At the surface, thousands of these stunned fish feed narwhals and harp seals, and rafts of excited northern fulmars and kittiwakes.

Watching from high above, one is also struck by the social interactions of narwhals, which are extensive and appear to be well organized according to hierarchies of age and sex. The socializing of males frequently involves the use of their tusks. They cross them like swords above the water, or one forces another down by pressing his tusk across the other's back, or they face each other head-on, their tusks side by side.

Helen Silverman, whose graduate work included a study of the social organization and behavior of narwhals, describes as typical the following scene, from her observations in Lancaster Sound. "On one occasion a group of five narwhals consisting of two adult males, one adult female, one [calf] and one juvenile were moving west with the males in the lead. The group stopped and remained on the surface for about 30 [seconds]. One male turned, moved under the [calf], and lifted it out of the water twice. There was no apparent reaction from the mother. The male then touched the side of the female with the tip of its tusk and the group continued westward."

Sitting high on a sea cliff in sunny, blustery weather in late June—the familiar sense of expansiveness, of deep exhilaration such weather brings over one, combined with the opportunity to watch animals, is summed up in a single Eskimo word: *quviannikumut*, "to feel deeply happy"—sitting here like this, it is easy to fall into speculation about the obscure narwhal. From the time I first looked into a narwhal's mouth, past the accordian pleats of its tongue, at the soft white interior splashed with Tyrian purple, I have thought of their affinity with sperm whales, whose mouths are similarly colored. Like the sperm whale, the narwhal is a deep diver. No other whales but the narwhal and the sperm whale are known to sleep on the surface for hours at a time. And when the narwhal lies at the surface, it lies like a sperm whale, with the section of its back from blowhole to dorsal ridge exposed, and the rest of its back and tail hanging down in the water. Like the sperm whale, it is renowned for its teeth; and it has been pursued, though briefly, for the fine oils in its forehead.

Like all whales, the narwhal's evolutionary roots are in the Cretaceous, with insect-eating carnivores that we, too, are descended from. Its line of development through the Cretaceous and into the Paleocene follows that of artiodactyls like the hippopotamus and the antelope—and then it takes a radical turn. After some 330 million years on dry land, since it emerged from the sea during the Devonian period 380 million years ago, the line of genetic development that will produce whales returns to the world's oceans. The first proto-whales turn up in the Eocene, 45 million years ago, the first toothed whales 18 million years later, in the Oligocene. By then, the extraordinary adjustments that had to take place to permit air-breathing mammals to live in the sea were largely complete.

Looking down from the sea cliffs at a lone whale floating peacefully in the blue-green water, it is possible to meditate on these evolutionary changes in the mammalian line, to imagine this creature brought forward in time to this moment. What were once its rear legs have disappeared, though the skeleton still shows the trace of a pelvis. Sea water gave it such buoyancy that it required little in the way of a skeletal structure; it therefore has achieved a large size without loss of agility. It left behind it a world of oscillating temperatures (temperatures on the arctic headland from which I gaze may span a range of 120°F over twelve months) for a world where the temperature barely fluctuates. It did not relinquish its warm-blooded way of life, however; it is insulated against the cold with a layer of blubber two to four inches thick.

The two greatest changes in its body have been in the way it now stores and uses oxygen, and in a rearrangement of its senses to suit a world that is largely acoustical, not visual or olfactory, in its stimulations.

When I breathe this arctic air, 34 percent of the oxygen is briefly stored in my lungs, 41 percent in my blood, 13 percent in my muscles, and 12 percent in the tissues of other of my organs. I take a deep breath only when I am winded or in a state of emotion; the narwhal always takes a deep breath—its draft of this same air fills its small lungs completely. And it stores the oxygen differently, so it can draw on it steadily during a fifteen-minute dive. Only about 9 percent stays in its lungs, while 41 percent goes into the blood, another 41 percent into the muscles, and about 9 percent into other tissues. The oxygen is bound to hemoglobin molecules in its blood (no different from my own), and to myoglobin molecules in its muscles. (The high proportion of myoglobin in its muscles makes the narwhal's muscle meat dark maroon, like the flesh of all marine mammals.)

Changes in the narwhal's circulatory system—the evolution of *rete mirabile*, "wonder nets" of blood vessels; an enlargement of its hepatic veins; a reversible flow of blood at certain places—have allowed it to adapt comfortably to the great pressures it experiences during deep dives.

There is too little nitrogen in its blood for "the bends" to occur when it surfaces. Carbon dioxide, the by-product of respiration, is effectively stored until it can be explosively expelled with a rapid flushing of the lungs.

It is only with an elaborate apparatus of scuba gear, decompression tanks, wet suits, weight belts, and swim fins that we can explore these changes. Even then it is hard to appreciate the radical alteration of mammalian development that the narwhal represents. First, ours is largely a two-dimensional world. We are not creatures who look up often. We are used to exploring "the length and breadth" of issues, not their "height." For the narwhal there are very few two-dimensional experiences—the sense of the water it feels at the surface of its skin, and that plane it must break in order to breathe.

The second constraint on our appreciation of the narwhal's world is that it "knows" according to a different hierarchy of senses than the one we are accustomed to. Its chemical senses of taste and smell are all but gone, as far as we know, though narwhals probably retain an ability to determine salinity. Its tactile sense remains acute. Its sensitivity to pressure is elevated—it has a highly discriminating feeling for depth and a hunter's sensitivity to the slight turbulence created by a school of cod cruising ahead of it in its dimly lit world. The sense of sight is atrophied, because of a lack of light. The eye, in fact, has changed in order to accommodate itself to high pressures, the chemical irritation of salt, a constant rush of water past it, and the different angle of refraction of light underwater. (The narwhal sees the world above water with an eye that does not move in its socket, with astigmatic vision and a limited ability to change the distance at which it can focus.)

How different must be "the world" for such a creature, for whom sight is but a peripheral sense, who occupies, instead, a three-dimensional acoustical space. Perhaps only musicians have some inkling of the formal shape of emotions and motivation that might define such a sensibility.

The Arctic Ocean can seem utterly silent on a summer day to an observer standing far above. If you lowered a hydrophone, however, you would discover a sphere of "noise" that only spectrum analyzers and tape recorders could unravel. The tremolo moans of bearded seals. The electric crackling of shrimp. The baritone boom of walrus. The high-pitched bark and yelp of ringed seals. The clicks, pure tones, birdlike trills, and harmonics of belukhas and narwhals. The elephantine trumpeting of bowhead whales. Added to these animal noises would be the sounds of shifting sediments on the sea floor, the whine and fracture of sea ice, and the sound of deep-keeled ice grounding in shallow water.

The narwhal is not only at home in this "cacophony," as

possessed of the sense of a neighborhood as we might conceivably be on an evening stroll, but it manages to appear "asleep," oblivious at the surface of the water on a summer day in Lancaster Sound.

The single most important change that took place in the whale's acoustical system to permit it to live in this world was the isolation of its auditory canals from each other. It could then receive waterborne sound independently on each side of its head and so determine the direction from which a sound was coming. (We can do this only in the open air; underwater, sound vibrates evenly through the bones of our head.) The narwhal, of course, receives many sounds; we can only speculate about what it pays attention to, or what information it may obtain from all that it hears. Conversely, narwhals also emit many sounds important, presumably, to narwhals and to other animals too.

Acoustical scientists divide narwhal sound into two categories. Respiratory sounds are audible to us as wheezes, moans, whistles, and gurgles of various sorts. The second group of sounds, those associated with, presumably, echolocation and communication, scientists divide into three categories: clicking, generated at rates as high as 500 clicks per second; pulsed tones; and pure tones. (Certain of these sounds are audible to someone in a boat in the open air, like an effervescence rising from the surface of the water.)

Narwhals, it is believed, use clicking sounds to locate themselves, their companions, their prey, and such things as floe edges and the trend of leads. Pulsed tones are thought to be social in nature and susceptible to individual modification, so each narwhal has a "signature" tone or call of its own. Pure-tone signals, too, are thought to be social or communicative in function. According to several scientists writing in the *Journal of the Acoustical Society of America*, the narwhal "seems much less noisy [than the belukha], appears to have a smaller variety of sounds, and produces many that are outside the limits of human hearing." A later study, however, found narwhals "extremely loquacious underwater," and noted that tape recordings were "almost saturated with acoustic signals of highly variable duration and frequency composition." The same

study concluded, too, that much of the narwhal's acoustically related behavior "remains a matter of conjecture."

I dwell on all this because of a routine presumption—that the
whale's ability to receive and generate sound indicates it is an
"intelligent" creature—and an opposite presumption, evident in a
Canadian government report, that the continuous racket of a subsea
drilling operation, with the attendant din of ship and air traffic
operations, "would not be expected to be a hazard [to narwhals]
because of . . . the assumed high levels of ambient underwater noise
in Lancaster Sound."

It is hard to believe in an imagination so narrow in its scope,
so calloused toward life, that it could write these last words. Ceta-
ceans may well be less "intelligent," less defined by will, imagination, and forms of logic, than we are. But the *idea* that they are
intelligent, and that they would be affected by such man-made
noise, is not so much presumption as an expression of a possibility,
the taking of a respectful attitude toward a mystery we can do no
better than name "narwhal." Standing at the edge of a cliff, studying the sea-washed back of such a creature far below, as still as a
cenobite in prayer, the urge to communicate, the upwelling desire,
is momentarily sublime.

I stare out into Lancaster Sound. Four or five narwhals sleep
on the flat calm sea, as faint on the surface as the first stars emerging in an evening sky. Birds in the middle and far distance slide
through the air, bits of life that dwindle and vanish. Below, underneath the sleeping narwhal, fish surge and glide in the currents,
and the light dwindles and is quenched.

THE first description of a unicorn, according to British scholar
Odell Shepard, appears in the writings of Ctesias, a Greek physician
living in Persia in the fifth century B.C., who had heard reports of
its existence from India. The existence of such an animal, a fierce,
horselike creature of courageous temperament, with a single horn
on its forehead, gained credibility later through the writings of
Aristotle and Pliny and, later still, in the work of Isidore of Seville,

an encyclopedist. The Bible became an unwitting and ironic authority for the unicorn's existence when Greek translators of the Septuagint rendered the Hebraic term *re'em* (meaning, probably, the now extinct aurochs, *Bos primigenius*) as "the unicorn."

The legend of the unicorn, and the subsequent involvement of the narwhal, is a story intriguing at many levels. Until well into the Middle Ages the legend passed only from one book to another, from one learned individual to another; it was not a part of the folk culture of Europe. During the Renaissance, scientists, scholars, and theologians put forth various learned "explanations" for the unicorn's existence. However farfetched these explanations might have seemed to skeptics, the concrete evidence of a narwhal's tusk to hand seemed irrefutable. Furthermore, no Christian could deny the unicorn's existence without contradicting the Bible.

Scholars argue that the animal in Ctesias' original report from Persia represents the transposed idea of an oryx or a rhinoceros. It went unquestioned, they speculate, because Greeks such as Ctesias took "the grotesque monstrosities of Indian religious art" rendered in the Persian tapestries they saw for real animals. In medieval Europe, trade in rare narwhal and walrus tusks, confusion with the mythical animals of Zoroastrian as well as Christian tradition, and the bucolic practice of making bizarre alterations in the horns of domestic animals, all lent credence to the legend. The interest of the wealthy and learned in this regal animal, moreover, went beyond mere fascination; it was also practical. European royalty was besieged with politically motivated poisonings in the fourteenth and fifteenth centuries, and the unicorn's horn was reputedly the greatest proof against them.

In *The Lore of the Unicorn*, Odell Shepard writes of the great range of appreciation of Renaissance people for the unicorn's horn; it was "their companion on dark nights and in perilous places, and they held it near their hearts, handling it tenderly, as they would a treasure. For indeed it was exactly that. It preserved a man from the arrow that flieth by day and the pestilence that walketh in darkness, from the craft of the poisoner, from epilepsy, and from several less dignified ills of the flesh not to be named in so distinguished a connection. In short it was an amulet, a talisman, a weapon, and a medicine chest all in one."

The narwhal's tusk, traded in bits and pieces as the unicorn's horn, sold for a fortune in the Middle Ages, for twenty times its weight in gold. Shepard estimates that in mid-sixteenth-century Europe there were no more than fifty whole tusks to be seen, each with a detailed provenance. They were gifted upon royalty and the church and sought as booty by expeditionary forces who knew of their existence. Two tusks stolen from Constantinople in 1204 were delivered by Crusaders to the Cathedral of Saint Mark in Venice, where they may be seen to this day.

The presence of these tusks in Europe depended upon Greenlandic and Icelandic trade. The oddity was that they were delivered to Europe by men like those who drowned with the Bishop of Iceland, sailors with no notion of unicorns and no knowledge of the value of the tusk to those who did know. On the other hand, the tusk was frequently bought by people who had not the remotest notion of the existence of such an animal as the narwhal.

The first European to bring these disparate perceptions together, it seems, was the cartographer Gerhard Mercator, who clearly identified the narwhal as the source of the unicorn's horn in 1621. In 1638, Ole Wurm, a Danish professor and a "zoologist and antiquarian of high attainment," delivered a speech in Copenhagen in which he made the same connection. But by then the story of the unicorn was simply too firmly entrenched at too many levels of European society to be easily dispelled, and the horn itself was too dear an item of commerce to be declared suddenly worthless. Besides, it was argued, was not the tusk simply the horn of the unicorn of the sea? Why shouldn't it have the same power as the horn of the land unicorn?

Over time the narwhal's tusk lost its influence in medical circles, trade dwindled, and the legend itself passed out of the hands of ecclesiastics and scholars to the general populace, where it became dear to the hearts of romantics, artists, and poets. It was passed on, however, in a form quite different from the secular tradition in Ctesias. In its secular rendering the unicorn was a creature of nobility and awesome though benign power. It was a creature of compassion, though solitary, and indomitably fierce. It became, as such, the heraldic symbol of knights errant and of kings. It was incorporated into the British coat of arms by James I in 1424, and in 1671 Christian V became the first Danish king to be crowned in a coronation chair made entirely of narwhal tusks.

Under Christian influence, the story of the unicorn became the story of a captured and tamed beast. The animal lost its robust, independent qualities, that aloofness of the wild horse, and was presented as a small, goatlike animal subdued by a maiden in a pastoral garden. The central episode of its fabulous life, its power to turn a poisonous river into pure water so that other creatures might drink, as Moses had done with his staff at the waters of Marah, passed into oblivion. The creature of whom it was once written in Solinus' *Polyhistoria*, "It is an animal never to be taken alive—killed possibly, but not captured," became a symbol of domestic virginity and obeisance.

One winter afternoon in Vancouver, British Columbia, I spoke with the only person ever to have succeeded in putting an adult narwhal, briefly, on display. (The six animals, brought back from northern Canada in 1970, all died of pneumonia within a few months.) Murray Newman, director of the British Columbia Aquarium, explained the great difficulties inherent in capturing such animals and later of maintaining them in captivity, especially the male, with its huge tusk. He doubted any aquarium would ever manage it successfully. The description from Solinus' *Polyhistoria* seemed at that moment, as we gazed across the aquarium's trimmed lawns toward Vancouver's harbor, oddly apt and prophetic.

A narwhal's tusk, hefted in the hands, feels stout but resilient. It is a round, evenly tapered shaft of ivory, hollow for most of its length. (The cavity is filled with dental pulp in the living animal.)

A large tusk might weigh 20 pounds, be eight or nine feet long, and taper from a diameter of four inches at the socket down to a half-inch at the tip. The smooth, polished tip, two to three inches long, is roundly blunt or sometimes wedge-shaped. The rest of the tusk is striated in a regular pattern that spirals from right to left and may make five or six turns around the shaft before fading out. Often a single groove parallel to the spiraling striations is apparent. The tusk also shows a slight, very shallow ripple from end to end in many specimens.

The striated portion is rough to the touch, and its shallow grooves are frequently encrusted with algae. These microorganisms give the tusk a brindled greenish or maroon cast, contrasting with the white tip and with the 10 to 12 inches of yellower ivory normally embedded in the upper left side of the animal's skull.

Well into the nineteenth century there was a question about which of the sexes carried the tusk (or whether it might be both). Although many thought it was only the males, a clear understanding was confounded by authenticated reports of females with tusks (a female skull with *two* large tusks, in fact, was given to a Hamburg museum in 1684 by a German sea captain), and an announcement in 1700 by a German scientist, Solomon Reisel, that some narwhals carried "milk tusks." It did not help matters, either, that there was much conjecture but no agreement on the function of the tusk. (A more prosaic error further confused things— printers sometimes inadvertently reversed drawings, making it seem that the tusk came out of the right side of the head instead of the left, and that it spiraled from left to right.)

Several certainties eventually emerged. The tusk spirals from right to left. In normal development, two incipient tusks form as "teeth" in the upper jaw of both sexes, one on each side. In the female, both teeth usually harden into solid ivory rods with a protuberance at one end, like a meerschaum pipe (these were Reisel's "milk tusks"). In males, the tusk on the right remains undeveloped, "a miniature piece of pig iron," while the one on the

left almost always develops into a living organ, a continually growing, fully vascularized tooth. On very rare occasions, both tusks
develop like this, in both sexes. And both tusks spiral from right
to left (i.e., they are not symmetrical like the tusks of an elephant
or a walrus). Viewed from above, twin tusks diverge slightly from
each other. In some males the left tusk never develops (nor does
the right in these instances). In perhaps 3 percent of females a
single tusk develops on the left.

Solving this problem in sexual systematics and physiology
proved simpler than determining the tusk's purpose. It was proposed as a rake, to stir up fish on the seabed floor; as a spear to
impale prey; and as a defensive weapon. All three speculations
ignored the needs of narwhals without tusks. In addition, Robin
Best, a Canadian biologist with a long-standing interest in the question, has argued that the tusk is too brittle to stand repeated use
as a rake or probe; that attacking the sorts of fish narwhals habitually eat with the tusk would be difficult and unnecessary and
getting large fish off the tusk problematic; and that there are no
records of narwhals attacking other animals or defending themselves with their tusks.

The fact that narwhals frequently cross their tusks out of
water and that the base of the tusk is located in the sound-producing
region of the narwhal's skull led to speculation that it might serve
some role in sound reception or propagation (again ignoring the
female component of the population). Oral surgeons determined
that the tooth's pulp does not contain the bioacoustical lipids necessary for echolocation, but this does not mean that the narwhal
can't in some way direct sound with it and, as some have suggested,
"sound-joust" with other males. (On their own, the oral surgeons
speculated that because the tooth was so highly vascularized, the
narwhal could get rid of a significant amount of body heat this
way, which would presumably allow males to hunt more energetically. The biologists said no.)

William Scoresby, as bright and keen-eyed an observer as ever went to sea, speculated in 1820 that the tusk was only a secondary sexual characteristic, like a beard in humans, and was perhaps used to fracture light ice when narwhals of both sexes needed to breathe. Scientists say narwhals are too careful with their tusks to subject them to such impact, but on the first point Scoresby was correct.

Male narwhals engage in comparative displays of their tusks, like the males of other species, but they also appear to make some kind of violent physical contact with each other occasionally. The heads of many sexually mature males are variously scarred, and scientists have even found the broken tips of tusks in wounded narwhals. (A scientist who made a detailed examination of the narwhal's musculature said the muscles are not there in the neck to allow the animals to parry and thrust with rapierlike movements. Indeed, males appear always to move their tusks with deliberation, and dexterously, as at savssats.) The circumstances under which head scarring might occur—the establishment and continual testing of a male social hierarchy, especially during the breeding season—are known; but how these wounds are suffered or how frequently they are inflicted is still widely debated. One plausible thought is that males align their tusks head-on and that the animal with the shorter tusk is grazed or sometimes severely poked in the process.

A significant number of narwhals, 20 to 30 percent, have broken tusks. Some broken tusks have a curious filling that effectively seals off the exposed pulp cavity. Oral surgeons say this rod-shaped plug is simply a normal deposition of "reparative dentine," but others have long insisted it is actually the tip of another narwhal's tusk, to which it bears an undeniable resemblance. (The broken tips of other narwhals' tusks are filled with stones and sediment.)

Exposed tooth pulp creates a site for infection, not to mention pain. That animals would try to fill the cavity (if "reparative dentine" didn't) makes sense. That one narwhal entices another into this ministration is as intriguing a notion as the thought that males put the tips of their tusks on the opposite male's sound-sensitive melon and generate a "message" in sound-jousting. It would be rash to insist categorically that narwhals don't do *something* odd with the tusk on occasion, like prodding a flatfish off the sea bottom. (Herman Melville drolly suggested they used it as a letter opener.) But it seems clear that its principal, and perhaps only, use is social. Robin Best argues, further, that because of its brittleness, its length, and the high proportion of broken tusks, the organ may have reached an evolutionary end point.

A remaining question is, Why is the tusk twisted? D'Arcy Wentworth Thompson, a renowned English biologist who died in 1948, offered a brilliant and cogent answer. He argued that the thrust of a narwhal's tail applied a very slight torque to its body. The tusk, suspended tightly but not rigidly in its socket in the upper jaw, resisted this force with a very slight degree of success. In effect, throughout its life, the narwhal revolved slowly around its own tusk, and over the years irregularities of the socket gouged the characteristic striations in the surface of the tooth.

Thompson pointed out that the tooth itself is not twisted—it is straight-grained ivory, engraved with a series of low-pitched threads. No one has disproved, proved, or improved upon Thompson's argument since he set it forth in 1942.

BECAUSE the ivory itself dried out and became brittle and hard to work, the greatest virtue of a narwhal tusk to the Eskimos who traditionally hunted the animal was its likeness to a wood timber. Some of the regions where narwhals were most intensively hunted were without either trees or supplies of driftwood. The tusk served in those places as a spear shaft, a tent pole, a sledge thwart, a cross brace—wherever something straight and long was required.

Narwhals were most often hunted by Eskimos during their near-shore migration in spring, and in bays and fiords during the summer. To my knowledge, Eskimos attach no great spiritual importance to the narwhal. Like the caribou, it is a migratory food animal whose spirit (*kirnniq*) is easily propitiated. The narwhal does not have the intercessionary powers or innate authority of the polar bear, the wolf, the walrus, or the raven.

Beyond its tusk, Greenlanders valued the narwhal's skin above all other leathers for dog harnesses, because it remained supple in very cold weather and did not stretch when it became wet. The sinews of the back were prized as thread not only for their durability but also for their great length. The outside layer of the skin was an important source of vitamin C, as rich in this essential vitamin as raw seal liver. The blubber, which burned with a bright, clean yellow flame, gave light and warmth that were utilized to carve a fishhook or sew a mitten inside the iglu in winter. A single narwhal, too, might feed a dog team for a month.

It is different now. The hunter's utilitarian appreciation of this animal is an attitude some now find offensive; and his considerable skills, based on an accurate and detailed understanding of the animal and its environment, no longer arouse the sympathetic admiration of very many people.

In the time I spent watching narwhals along the floe edge at Lancaster Sound in 1982 no whale was butchered for dog food. The dogs have been replaced by snow machines. No sinews were removed for sewing. Only the tusk was taken, to be traded in the village for cash. And muktuk, the skin with a thin layer of blubber attached, which was brought back to the hunting camp at Nuvua. (This delicacy is keenly anticipated each spring and eaten with pleasure. It tastes like hazelnuts.)

The narwhal's fate in Lancaster Sound is clearly linked with plans to develop oil and gas wells there, but current hunting pressure against them is proving to be as important a factor. In recent years Eskimo hunters on northern Baffin Island have exhibited some lack of discipline during the spring narwhal hunt. They have made hasty, long-range, or otherwise poorly considered shots and used calibers of gun and types of bullets that were inadequate to kill, all of which left animals wounded. And they have sometimes exceeded the quotas set by Department of Fisheries and Oceans

Canada and monitored by the International Whaling Commission.*
On the other side, Eskimos have routinely been excluded from
the upper levels of decision-making by the Canadian government
in these matters and have been offered no help in devising a kind
of hunting behavior more consistent with the power and reach of
modern weapons. For the Eskimos, there is a relentless, sometimes
condescending scrutiny of every attempt they make to adjust their
culture, to "catch up" with the other culture brought up from the
south. It is easy to understand why the men sometimes lose their
accustomed composure.

In the view of Kerry Finley, a marine mammal biologist
closely associated with the Baffin Island narwhal hunts, "It is critical [to the survival of narwhals] that Inuit become involved in
meaningful positions in the management of marine resources." The
other problems, he believes, cannot be solved until this obligation
is met.

I would walk along the floe edge, then, in those days, hoping to
hear narwhals, for the wonder of their company; and hoping, too,
that they would not come. The narwhal is a great fighter for its
life, and it is painful to watch its struggle. When they were killed,
I ate their flesh as a guest of the people I was among, out of respect
for distant ancestors, and something older than myself.

I watched closely the ivory gull, a small bird with a high,
whistly voice. It has a remarkable ability to appear suddenly in
the landscape, seemingly from nowhere. I have scanned tens of
square miles of open blue sky, determined it was empty of birds,
and then thrown a scrap of seal meat into a lead, where it would

---

* These charges are detailed in K. J. Finley, R. A. Davis, and H. B.
Silverman, "Aspects of the Narwhal Hunt in the Eastern Canadian
Arctic," *Report of the International Whaling Commission* 30 (1980):
459–464; and K. J. Finley and G. W. Miller, "The 1979 Hunt for
Narwhals (*Monodon monoceros*) and an Examination of Harpoon
Gun Technology Near Pond Inlet, Northern Baffin Island," *Report of
the International Whaling Commission* 32 (1982): 449–460.

float. In a few minutes an ivory gull would be overhead. It is hard to say even from what direction it has come. It is just suddenly there.

So I would watch them in ones and twos. Like any animal seen undisturbed in its own environment, the ivory gull seems wondrously adapted. To conserve heat, its black legs are shorter in proportion to its body than the legs of other gulls, its feet less webbed. Its claws are longer and sharper, to give it a better grip of frozen carrion and on the ice. It uses seaweed in its nest to trap the sun's energy, to help with the incubation of its eggs. To avoid water in winter, which might freeze to its legs, it has become deft at picking things up without landing. In winter it follows the polar bear. When no carrion turns up in the polar bear's wake, it eats the polar bear's droppings. It winters on the pack ice. Of the genus *Pagophila*. Ice lover.

And I would think as I walked of what I had read of a creature of legend in China, an animal similar in its habits to the unicorn but abstemious, like the ivory gull. It is called the *ki-lin*. The *ki-lin* has the compassion of the unicorn but also the air of a spiritual warrior, or monk. Odell Shepard has written that "[u]nlike the western unicorn, the *ki-lin* has never had commercial value; no drug is made of any part of his body; he exists for his own sake and not for the medication, enrichment, entertainment, or even edification of mankind." He embodied all that was admirable and ideal.

With our own Aristotelian and Cartesian sense of animals as objects, our religious sense of them as mere receptacles for human symbology, our single-mindedness in unraveling their workings, we are not the kind of culture to take the *ki-lin* very seriously. We are another culture, and these other times. The *ki-lin*, too, is no longer as highly regarded among modern Chinese as it was in the days of the Sung dynasty. But the idea of the *ki-lin*, the mere fact of its having taken shape, is, well, gratifying. It appeared after men had triumphed over both their fear and distrust of nature and their desire to control it completely for their own ends.

The history of the intermingling of human cultures is a history of trade—in objects like the narwhal's tusk, in ideas, and in great narratives. We appropriate when possible the best we can find in all of this. The *ki-lin*, I think, embodies a fine and pertinent idea—an unpossessible being who serves humans when they have need of its wisdom, a creature who abets dignity and respect in human dealings, who underlines the fundamental mystery with which all life meets analysis.

I do not mean to suggest that the narwhal should be made into some sort of symbolic *ki-lin*. Or that buried in the more primitive appreciation of life that some Eskimos retain is an "answer" to our endless misgivings about the propriety of our invasions of landscapes where we have no history, of our impositions on other cultures. But that in the simple appreciation of a world not our own to define, that poised arctic landscape, we might find some solace by discovering the *ki-lin* hidden within ourselves, like a shaft of light.

Five

MIGRATION
The Corridors of Breath

I
T WAS STILL DARK, and I thought it might be raining lightly. I pushed back the tent flap. A storm-driven sky moving swiftly across the face of a gibbous moon. Perhaps it would clear by dawn. The ticking sound was not rain, only the wind. A storm, bound for somewhere else.

Half awake, I was again aware of the voices. A high-pitched cacophonous barking, like terriers, or the complaint of shoats. The single outcries became a rising cheer, as if in a far-off stadium, that rose and fell away.

Snow geese, their night voices. I saw them flying down the north coast of Alaska once in September, at the end of a working day. The steady intent of their westward passage, that unwavering line, was uplifting. The following year I saw them over Banks Island, migrating north in small flocks of twenty and thirty. And that fall I went to northern California to spend a few days with them on their early wintering ground at Tule Lake in Klamath Basin.

Tule Lake is not widely known in America, but the ducks and geese gather in huge aggregations on this refuge every fall, creating an impression of land in a state of health, of boundless life. On any given day a visitor might look upon a million birds here—pintail, lesser scaup, Barrow's goldeneye, cinnamon teal, mallard, northern shoveler, redhead, and canvasback ducks; Great Basin and cackling varieties of Canada geese, white-fronted geese, Ross's geese, lesser snow geese; and tundra swans. In open fields between the lakes and marshes where these waterfowl feed and rest are red-winged blackbirds and Savannah sparrows, Brewer's sparrows, tree swallows, and meadowlarks. And lone avian hunters —marsh hawks, red-tailed hawks, bald eagles, the diminutive kestrel.

The Klamath Basin, containing four other national wildlife refuges in addition to Tule Lake, is one of the richest habitats for migratory waterfowl in North America. To the west of Tule Lake is another large, shallow lake called Lower Klamath Lake. To the east, out past the tule marshes, is a low escarpment where barn owls nest and the counting marks of a long-gone aboriginal people are still visible, incised in the rock. To the southwest, the incongruous remains of a Japanese internment camp from World War II. In agricultural fields to the north, east, and south, farmers grow malt barley and winter potatoes in dark volcanic soils.

The night I thought I heard rain and fell asleep again to the cries of snow geese, I also heard the sound of their night flying, a great hammering of the air overhead, a wild creaking of wings. These primitive sounds made the Klamath Basin seem oddly un-tenanted, the ancestral ground of animals, reclaimed by them each year. In a few days at the periphery of the flocks of geese, however,

I did not feel like an interloper. I felt a calmness birds can bring to people; and, quieted, I sensed here the outlines of the oldest mysteries: the nature and extent of space, the fall of light from the heavens, the pooling of time in the present, as if it were water.

There were 250,000 lesser snow geese at Tule Lake. At dawn I would find them floating on the water, close together in a raft three-quarters of a mile long and perhaps 500 yards wide. When a flock begins to rise from the surface of the water, the sound is like a storm squall arriving, a great racket of shaken sheets of corrugated tin. (If you try to separate the individual sounds in your head, they are like dry cotton towels snapping on a wind-blown clothesline.) Once airborne, they are dazzling on the wing. Flying against broken sunlight, the opaque whiteness of their bodies, a whiteness of water-polished shells, contrasts with grayer whites in their translucent wings and tail feathers. Up close they show the dense, impeccable whites of arctic fox. Against the bluish grays of a storm-laden sky, their whiteness has a surreal glow, a brilliance without shadow.

When they are feeding in the grain fields around Tule Lake, the geese come and go in flocks of five or ten thousand. Sometimes there are forty or fifty thousand in the air at once. They rise from the fields like smoke in great, swirling currents, rising higher and spreading wider in the sky than one's field of vision can encompass. One fluid, recurved sweep of ten thousand of them passes through the spaces within another, counterflying flock; while beyond them lattice after lattice passes, like sliding Japanese walls, until in the whole sky you lose your depth of field and feel as though you are looking up from the floor of the ocean through shoals of fish.

What absorbs me in these birds, beyond their beautiful white-ness, their astounding numbers, the great vigor of their lives, is how adroitly each bird joins the larger flock or departs from it. And how each bird while it is a part of the flock seems part of something larger than itself. Another animal. Never did I see a single goose move to accommodate one that was landing, nor geese on the water ever disturbed by another taking off, no matter how

closely bunched they seemed to be. I never saw two birds so much
as brush wingtips in the air, though surely they must. They roll
up into a headwind together in a seamless movement that brings
thousands of them gently to the ground like falling leaves in but
a few seconds. Their movements are endlessly attractive to the
eye because of a tension they create between the extended para-
bolic lines of their flight and their abrupt but adroit movements, all
of it in three dimensions.

And there is something else that draws you in. They come
from the ends of the earth and find this small lake every year with
unfailing accuracy. They arrive from breeding grounds on the
northern edge of the continent in Canada, and from the river
valleys of Wrangel Island in the Russian Arctic. Their ancient
corridors of migration, across Bering Strait and down the Pacific
coast, down the east flank of the Rockies, are older than the nations
they fly from. The lives of many animals are constrained by the
schemes of men, but the determination in these lives, their traditional pattern of movement, are a calming reminder of a more
fundamental order. The company of these birds in the field is
guileless. It is easy to feel transcendent when camped among them.

Birds tug at the mind and heart with a strange intensity. Their
ability to flock elegantly as the snow goose does, where individual
birds turn into something larger, and their ability to navigate over
great stretches of what is for us featureless space, are mysterious,
sophisticated skills. Their flight, even a burst of sparrows across a
city plaza, pleases us. In the Arctic, one can see birds in enormous
numbers, and these feelings of awe and elation are enhanced. In
spring in the Gulf of Anadyr, off the Russian coast, the surface of
the water flashes silver with schools of Pacific herring, and flocks
of puffins fly straight into the water after them, like a hail of gravel.
They return with the herring to steep cliffs, where the broken
shells of their offspring fall on gusts of wind into the sea by the
thousands, like snow. On August 6, 1973, the ornithologist David
Nettleship rounded Skruis Point on the north coast of Devon
Island and came face to face with a "lost" breeding colony of

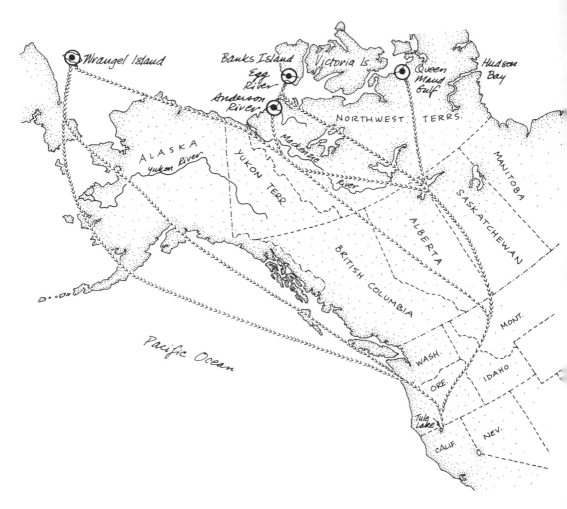

Fall migration of lesser snow geese from nesting areas on Wrangel Island and in northern Canada to Tule Lake, California.

black guillemots. It stretched southeast before him for 14 miles. On the Great Plain of the Koukdjuak on Baffin Island today, a traveler, crossing the rivers and wading through the ponds and braided streams that exhaust and finally defeat the predatory fox, will come on great windrows of feathers from molting geese, feathers that can be taken in handfuls and thrown up in the air to drift downward like chaff. From the cliffs of Digges Island and adjacent Cape Wolstenholme in Hudson Strait, 2 million thick-billed murres will swim away across the water, headed for their winter grounds on the Grand Banks.

Such enormous concentrations of life in the Arctic are, as I have suggested, temporary and misleading. Between these arctic oases stretch hundreds of miles of coastal cliffs, marshes, and riverine valleys where no waterfowl, no seabird, nests. And the flocks of migratory geese and ducks come and go quickly, laying their eggs, molting, and getting their young into the air in five or six weeks. What one witnesses in the great breeding colonies is a kind of paradox. For a time the snow and ice disappear, allowing life to flourish and birds both to find food and retrieve it. Protected from terrestrial predators on their island refuges and on nesting grounds deep within flooded coastal plains, birds can molt all their flight feathers at once, without fearing the fact that this form of escape will be lost to them for a few weeks. And, for a while, food is plentiful enough to more than serve their daily needs; it provides the additional energy needed for the molt, and for a buildup of fat reserves for the southward journey.

For the birds, these fleeting weeks of advantage are crucial. If the weather is fair and their timing has been good, they arrive on their winter grounds with a strange, primal air of achievement. When the snow geese land at Tule Lake in October, it is not necessary in order to appreciate them to picture precisely the line and shading of those few faraway places where every one of them was born—Egg River on Banks Island, the mouth of the Anderson River in the Northwest Territories, the Tundovaya River Valley on Wrangel Island. Merely knowing that each one began its life, took first breath, on those intemperate arctic edges and that it alights here now for the first or fifth or tenth time is enough. Their success urges one to wonder at such a life, stretched out over so many thousands of miles, and moving on every four or five weeks, always moving on. Food and light running out behind in the fall, looming ahead in the spring.

I would watch the geese lift off the lake in the morning, spiral up white into the blue California sky and head for fields of two-row barley to feed, able only to wonder what this kind of nomadic life meant, how their lives fit in the flow of time and made clearer the extent of space between ground and sky, between here and the Far North. They flew beautifully each morning in the directions they intended, movements of desire, arabesques in the long sweep south from Tundovaya Valley and Egg River. At that hour of the day their lives seemed flush with yearning.

ONE is not long in the field before sensing that the scale of time and distance for most animals is different from one's own. Their overall size, their methods of locomotion, the nature of the obstacles they face, the media they move through, and the length of a full life are all different. Formerly, because of the ready analogy with human migration and a tendency to think only on a human scale, biologists treated migratory behavior as a special event in the lives of animals. They stressed the great distances involved or remarkable feats of navigation. The practice today is not to differentiate so sharply between migration and other forms of animal (and plant) movement. The maple seed spiraling down toward the forest floor, the butterfly zigzagging across a summer meadow, and the arctic tern outward bound on its 12,000-mile fall journey are all after the same thing: an environment more conducive to their continued growth and survival. Further, scientists now understand animal movements in terms of navigational senses we are still unfamiliar with, such as an ability to detect an electromagnetic field or to use sound echos or differences in air pressure as guides.

In discussing large-scale migration like that of snow geese, biologists posit a "familiar area" for each animal and then speak of its "home range" within that area, which includes its winter and summer ranges, its breeding range, and any migratory corridors. The familiar area takes in the whole of the landscape an animal has any notion of, an understanding it gains largely through exploration of territory adjacent to its home range during adolescence. Intense adolescent exploration, as far as we know, is common to all animals. Science's speculation is that such exploring ensures the survival of a group of animals by familiarizing them with alternatives to their home ranges, which they can turn to in an emergency.

A question that arises about the utilization of a home range is: how do animals find their way to portions of the home range they have never seen? And how do they know when going there would be beneficial? The answers to these questions still elude us, but the response to them is what we call migration, and we have some idea about how animals manage those journeys. Many animals, even primitive creatures like anemones, possess a spatial memory of some sort and use it to find their way in the world. Part of this memory is apparently genetically based, and part of it is learned during travel with parents and in exploring alone. We know animals use a considerable range of senses to navigate from one place to another, to locate themselves in space, and actually to *learn* an environment, but which senses in which combinations are used, and precisely what information is stored—so far we can only speculate.

The vision most of us have of migration is of movements on a large scale, of birds arriving on their wintering grounds, of spawning salmon moving upstream, or of wildebeest, zebra, and gazelle trekking over the plains of East Africa. The movements of these latter animals coincide with a pattern of rainfall in the Serengeti-Mara ecosystem; and their annual, roughly circular migration in the wake of the rains reveals a marvelous and intricate network of benefits to all the organisms involved—grazers, grasses, and predators. The timing of these events—the heading of grasses in seed, the dropping of manure, the arrival of the rains, the birth of the young—seems perfectly fortuitous, a melding of needs and satisfactions that caused those who first examined the events to speak of a divine plan.

The dependable arrival of swallows at the mission of San Juan Capistrano, the appearance of gray whales off the Oregon coast in March, and the movement of animals like elk from higher to lower ranges in Wyoming in the fall are other examples of migration familiar in North America. I first went into the Arctic with no other ideas than these, somewhat outsize events to guide me. They opened my mind sufficiently, however, to a prodigious and diverse movement of life through the Arctic; they also prompted a realization of how intricate these seemingly simple natural events are. And as I watched the movement of whales and birds and caribou, I thought I discerned the ground from which some people have derived so much of their metaphorical understanding of symmetry, cadence, and harmony in the universe.

Several different kinds of migration are going on in the Arctic at the same time, not all of them keyed to the earth's annual cycle. Animals are still adjusting to the retreat of the Pleistocene glaciers, which began about 20,000 years ago. Some temperate-zone species are moving gradually but steadily northward, altering their behavior or, like the collared lemming and the arctic fox, growing heavier coats of fur as required.

Climatic fluctuations measured over a much shorter period of time—on the order of several hundred years—are responsible for cyclic shifts of some animal populations north and south during these periods. Over the last fifty years, for example, cod and several species of bird have been moving farther north up the west coast of Greenland, while populations of red fox have been establishing themselves farther north on the North American tundra.* As animals long resident in the Arctic respond to certain kinds of short-term ecological disaster, as was the case with muskoxen in the winter of 1973–74, or to violent fluctuations in their population, as with lemmings, they reinhabit, over time, former landscapes and abandon others.

To cope with annual cycles—the drop in temperature, the loss of light, the presence of snow cover, and a reduction in the amount of food available—arctic animals have evolved several

---

* American robins have moved as far north as Baffin Island in recent years. The Eskimos around Pond Inlet and Arctic Bay, who recognized the bird from stories white travelers told them about it, first saw them around 1942. Eskimos say the robin came that far north then because there was "a lot of fighting in the south" at that time.

strategies. Lemmings move under the snow; bumblebees hibernate; and arctic foxes move out onto the sea ice. Many other animals, including caribou, walrus, whales, and birds, migrate over quite significant distances. Arctic terns, for example, fly to the Antarctic Ocean at the end of the arctic summer, an annual circuit on which they see fewer hours of darkness than probably any animal on earth. Other migratory birds that head out to sea change their ecological niche. The long-tailed jaeger, a rodent hunter on the summer tundra, becomes a pelagic scavenger on the high seas in winter.

On a scale smaller yet than these annual cycles are the migrations of animals during a season, like the movement of muskoxen; and the regular patterns of localized movement keyed to an animal's diurnal rhythms, like the habit among some wolf packs of leaving a den each evening to hunt. (Arctic animals, as mentioned earlier, maintain a diurnal pattern in spite of the presence of continuous daylight in summer.)

When one considers all these comings and goings, and that an animal like the muskox might be involved simultaneously in several of these cycles, or that when the lemming population crashes, snowy owls must fly off in the direction of an alternative food supply, and when one adds to it the movement of animals to the floe edges in spring, or the insects that rise in such stupendous numbers on the summer tundra, a vast and complex pattern of animal movement in the Arctic begins to emerge. Also to be considered are the release of fish and primitive arthropods with the melting of lake and ground ice. And the peregrinations of bears. And a final, wondrous image—the great ocean of aerial plankton, that almost separate universe of ballooning spiders and delicate larval creatures that drifts over the land in the summer.

The extent of all this movement is difficult to hold in the mind. Deepening the complications for anyone who would try to fix this order in time is that within the rough outlines of their traditional behaviors, animals are always testing the landscape.

They are always setting off in response to hints and admonitions not evident to us.

The movement of animals in the Arctic is especially compelling because the events are compressed into but a few short months. Migratory animals like the bowhead whale and the snow goose often arrive on the last breath of winter. They feed and rest, bear their young, and prepare for their southward journey in that window of light before freeze-up and the first fall snowstorms. They come north in staggering numbers, travel hundreds or even thousands of miles to be here during those few weeks when life swirls in the water and on the tundra and in the balmy air. Standing there on the ground, you can feel the land filling up, feel something physical rising in it under the influence of the light, an embrace or exaltation. Watching the animals come and go, and feeling the land swell up to meet them and then feeling it grow still at their departure, I came to think of the migrations as breath, as the land breathing. In spring a great inhalation of light and animals. The long-bated breath of summer. And an exhalation that propelled them all south in the fall.

ANIMALS define much of the space one encounters in the Arctic because the land, like the sea, is expansive and there are so few people about. Nowhere is this more apparent than in northern Bering Sea in the spring. Certain regions of the world, sea straits in particular, funnel the movements of migrating animals. This is true at the Bosporus and at Gibraltar, for example, where land birds move north and south and sea creatures east and west, as if through the throat of an hourglass. Bering Strait, however, is unique in the way it concentrates life. The arrangement of the earth's land masses is such that they come close to meeting only in the North; at Bering Strait the Chukchi Peninsula of the Eastern Hemisphere, with its birds and animals, nearly touches the Seward Peninsula of the Western Hemisphere, with its birds and animals. Moreover, the North Pacific coasts converge here, bringing together the offshore migrations of whales and pelagic seabirds, the near-shore migrations of seals and walrus, and the coastal migrations of birds like eiders.*

The Bering Sea itself concentrates life as well because it is an extremely rich feeding ground for marine mammals. Many of the birds, fish, and sea mammals moving within its borders during the height of migratory activity in the spring and fall are local populations. The nearness of the two continents, the convergence of the coasts, and the size and diversity of local bird populations, in fact, have made the Bering Strait region the very image of a remote paradise for European and American bird-watchers.

In the spring, summer, and fall of different years, I have either been on the water in northern Bering Sea or flying transects over it with marine scientists. In the course of that time I have wondered why the concentration of life here in the spring is so little known to North Americans, for the concentrations are astounding. To the southeast, to begin with, some 24 *million* migratory waterfowl and shorebirds nest and feed on the delta of the Yukon and Kuskokwim rivers (the Y-K Delta) between May and September. These include black brant, sandhill cranes, several species of eider and loon, surface-feeding ducks such as the green-winged teal and greater scaup, plovers, phalaropes, and turnstones and the entire North American populations of emperor geese and spectacled eider.†

---

* Sea mammals migrating up the North American coast negotiate the Aleutian barrier at Unimak Pass, providing an observer at Cape Sarichef on Unimak Island with a spectacular view. In the eastern Arctic, the convergence of Greenland and Baffin Island at Davis Strait and the presence of an extensive floe edge in Lancaster Sound concentrate the migrations of sea mammals and birds, similarly, for an observer at Cape Hay on Bylot Island.

† Many of these particular birds—pintail ducks, white-fronted geese, and tundra swans, for example—will fly to Klamath Basin in the fall, together with snow geese that stop briefly to feed on the Y-K Delta en route from Siberia.

In the Bering Sea itself, stocks of herring, pollock, halibut, and yellowfin sole, and what are probably the largest clam beds in the world, put this sea in a class almost by itself. From here, beginning in late May, hundreds of thousands of chinook (king) salmon will start up the rivers of western Alaska, followed quickly by even larger numbers of chum (dog) salmon, which will be followed a week or so later by numbers as large of pink (humpback) salmon. Finally, in July, will come runs of coho (silver) and stupendous runs of sockeye (red) salmon.

Ornithologists believe that, in addition to the 24 million migratory birds nesting on the Y-K Delta in the spring, there are an additional 5 million seabirds living in northern Bering Sea, mostly auklets, murres, and kittiwakes, and smaller numbers of horned and tufted puffins, pelagic cormorants, and pigeon guillemots. And some 500,000 oldsquaw ducks that winter south of Saint Lawrence Island. Around the margins of Bering Sea, in saltwater marshes and lagoons, are yet more birds, flocks of migratory Steller's eider, long-billed dowitchers, dunlins, and whimbrels, all searching the shallows for food; plovers, turnstones, and sandpipers; and many of the species of bay and sea duck already mentioned. An observer in the coastal lagoons might take in 10,000 or even 20,000 birds at a glance, many of them in stunningly colorful nuptial plumages. When numbers fail, as they always do, one thinks of mesmerizing incidents, like the day in May 1982 when sandhill cranes passed in flocks over the village of Nome almost continuously for two hours, on their way to Russia. Or the afternoon 75,000 king eiders flew past Dall Point on the Y-K Delta in two hours.

That is only the birds, and to suggest the uncountable fish. In March, more than three-quarters of a million marine mammals are concentrated at the southern edge of the Bering Sea ice, in an area scientists call the ice front: 300,000 bearded seals, 75,000 ribbon seals, 225,000 spotted seals, 250,000 Pacific walrus, 4400 bowhead whales, and 15,000 belukhas. Living in the fast ice along the Bering Sea coast, deep within the ice pack, are more than one million ringed seals, the most ice-adapted of the seals.

In the spring, all of this animal life is poised to move north, awaiting only the fracturing and melting of the ice. Until then, they are confined to open water to the south. The ranges of the bearded, spotted, and more solitary ribbon seals overlap toward the edge of the ice front (a region 10 to 40 miles wide, depending on prevailing winds and storm conditions in the north Pacific). The walrus winters deeper inside the ice front, where there are intact floes large enough to bear its great weight. (Walrus can surface through as much as eight inches of sea ice, using their massive heads as rams, and if they are trapped out on the ice by a sudden freeze, they can walk to areas where they can break through to feed, which arctic seals can't do.) The whales move throughout the ice front during the winter months. As early as late April, when the ice north of Saint Lawrence Island is still solid, the bowheads may start pressing north, on the Russian side of Bering Sea. If the ice is not heavy, they will be followed or accompanied by herds of belukhas. As the ice begins to open up in late April and May, walrus will head north, followed a few weeks later by the three species of ice seal. Almost as soon as cracks and leads begin to appear, they will be used for feeding by flocks of migrating king and common eiders and oldsquaw ducks.

The surface of the great expanse of ice covering Bering Sea in April and May is infinitely varied. Cracked, rafted up over itself, and refrozen where it has briefly opened, it shows a dozen shades of gray and a dazzling pattern of fractures. Or for tens of square miles it may stretch unbroken beneath a layer of snow, a nearly continuous tone of white, with only the slight irregularities called ice hummocks or the disc rows of rubble where two floes have ground against each other to create shadows. Then a lead half a mile long and 20 feet wide will suddenly appear, revealing water dark as ink, with the facing edges of the ice being mirror images of each other. Most of the longer, broader cracks, it soon becomes apparent, tend to occur along a southwest-northeast axis. Occasionally these expand into areas of open water the size of small lakes. By the middle of May, bowhead whales are moving through these annually recurring lead systems, northeast through Bering Strait and northward to Point Barrow. They leave behind a recognizable trail, where their backs have rubbed the underside of the ice or where they have broken through in refrozen leads or at enlarged seal holes to breathe. (These trails are evidence of the bowhead's remarkable ability to find its way from one system of open leads to the next in heavy ice.) Because of their white chins and belly markings, it is sometimes possible to spot bowheads cruising just below the translucent ice. More often, one notices herds of white belukha accompanied by their gray calves.

If the ice ahead is still solid (somehow they know), bowheads will mill about together in the larger leads, cavorting in small groups, breaching, and even spy-hopping. Mating also occurs at this time. Walrus, bearded seal, and ringed seal may be swimming in these lead systems at the same time. And new ice in the area will show holes with characteristically different shapes where each species of animal has broken through to breathe.

Because the prevailing lead systems encourage marine mammals to swim in certain directions and because they concentrate animals in certain places if the ice ahead is too heavy, memorable sightings occasionally occur in the ice south of Bering Strait. In April 1981, one scientist, flying along a channel three-quarters of a mile wide and about 15 miles long, counted 332 bowhead whales, nearly a tenth of the Pacific population, before he was obliged to turn back at the international date line (the Russian border at sea).

After the bowheads have passed north, along with a large portion of the belukha whale and walrus populations and large numbers of bearded, spotted, and ringed seals, Bering Sea becomes the summer ground of several other species of whale. Gray whales arrive from the North American and Korean coasts, and minke whales and orcas arrive from the Pacific. Sei, humpbacks, and an occasional Pacific right whale may come as far as Saint Lawrence Island. (The same waters rendered idyllic in May by the gentle mating of bowhead whales seem ominous in June, when orcas are hunting walrus and gray whales with chilling precision. The walrus they sometimes abandon uneaten; and they may take no more than the tongue of a gray whale they have drowned. The presence of diverse animals in such abundance here each year, however, testifies to a set of equitable relationships, however ruthless they may seem to us on occasion.)

The breadth of our still incomplete understanding of the Bering Sea ecosystem is exemplified by a current confusion over the identity of some of its larger parts. An unnamed whale, smaller than the bowhead and with a flat rather than a bowed head, and with denser rib and jaw bones and a lighter-colored baleen, swims in Bering Sea. Eskimos, who refer to the bowhead as *ingitivak*, call this other whale *ingutuk*. Its existence has been known to scientists since at least the time of whaling captain and historian Charles Scammon in the 1870s, but it has never been fully described. Another cetacean, even less known, is a large, brown, bowhead-type whale that might be a color phase of *Balaena mysticetus*.

A spring visitor to the village of Nome on Seward Peninsula would stand at the edge of this great seasonal upwelling of life in Bering Sea. From Cape Nome east of the village he could watch whales spouting and see walrus and seals passing, alcid birds diving for fish, and ducks flying up and down the coastline. Salmon would be coming up the Nome River. Near Safety Sound, where swans, ducks, and geese would be feeding, spotted seals might be hauled out on the beaches. Up on the tundra north of the village one might be lucky enough to encounter a remarkable open-country bird called a northern wheatear, a small thrush with as great a claim to making a prodigious migratory journey as the arctic tern. The wheatear arrives from Russia each spring with bluethroats, yellow wagtails, and arctic warblers; certain individuals may have come from as far away as Saudi Arabia, perhaps even the northern edge of the Sahara. They fly as far east in North America as the Mackenzie River.

The northern wheatear is a reminder that all migration is not strictly north and south, and, because it is a newcomer to North America, that animals are experimenters, pushing at the bounds of their familiar areas in response to changes in their environment. Nothing is ever quite fixed for them. One afternoon a man in Nome remarked that the bowhead migration through Bering Strait was "late this year." It was not really "late" of course, but only part of an arrangement that differs slightly from year to year. They are not on our schedules. Their appointments are not solely with us.

AFTER the passage of fish and marine mammals through the Bering Sea region, and the arrival of birds at their accustomed deltas and sea rookeries, there is a third great migratory spectacle to behold in the Arctic: the movement of caribou.

North American caribou are divided into three groups. The woodland caribou, the largest of the three, lives in the taiga forests of the subarctic and migrates over only relatively short distances. Peary caribou, the smallest of the three, occupy parts of the Greenland coast and northern islands in the Canadian Archipelago and also move over relatively short distances each year. Barren-ground caribou are the distant travelers. As many as 2 million of them trek hundreds of miles each year between their winter range near the tree line and well-defined calving grounds on the tundra.*

Caribou biologists recognize more than thirty different arctic herds, each occupying a different region. The ones that migrate the farthest each year are the Western and Central Arctic herds in northern Alaska; the Porcupine herd, which straddles the U.S.-Canada border; and, from west to east in Canada, the Bluenose, Bathurst, Beverly, and Kaminuriak herds.

---

* None of the three caribou is a reindeer. Reindeer, a separate sub-species of *Rangifer tarandus*, are the deer native to northern Europe and Asia. Of the many that have been brought to Alaska as domestic stock, a significant number have joined herds of caribou.

Scientists are uncertain what starts caribou on their northward journey—knowledge that they have stored enough fat to carry them through, perhaps. They endure spring blizzards on their journeys and cross ice-choked rivers with great determination and a sure sense of bearing, but they also choose paths of least resistance over the land, often following in each other's tracks through deep snow. Pregnant cows are normally in the lead; mature bulls may be as much as a month behind the cows, or never arrive at the calving grounds at all. By the end of their arduous journey the females are thin and tattered-looking. Behind them, in places where they have had to cross rivers in a stage of breakup, there may be the carcasses of hundreds of drowned and fatally injured animals. Their calving grounds, writes biologist George Calef, appear "bleak and inhospitable. Meltwater lies in pools on the frozen ground, the land is often shrouded in fog, and the wind whistles unceasingly among the stunted plants and bare rocks." The advantages of these dismal regions, however, are several. The number of predators is low, wolves having dropped away from the herds at more suitable locations for denning to the south. Food plants are plentiful. And these grounds either offer better protection from spring snowstorms or experience fewer storms overall than adjacent regions.

Most calves are born within a few days of each other, and calving occurs at least a month before swarms of emergent mosquitoes, blackflies, warble flies, and botflies embark on a harassment of the caribou that seems merciless to a human observer. If one were to think of events that typify arctic life—the surge of energy one feels with daily gains of ten or fifteen minutes of sunlight in the spring, or waking up one morning to find the ocean frozen—one would also include that feeling of relief that descends over a caribou herd when a wind comes up and puts hordes of weak-flying mosquitoes to the ground.

After calving, cows and their offspring join immature animals, barren cows, and the bulls in "postcalving" aggregations of 75,000 or more animals, their numbers stretching from horizon to horizon.

Distribution of major caribou herds in the North American Arctic.

They trek slowly south, breaking up into smaller herds. The first fall storms catch them in open country, and in the cold, snowy air these "gray shepherds of the tundra," as the Alaskan poet John Haines calls them, "pass like islands of smoke." They take shelter in the short timber of the taiga for the winter.

After the herds have gone, the calving grounds can seem like the most deserted places on earth, even if you can sense strongly that the caribou will be back next year. When they do return, hardly anything will have changed. A pile of caribou droppings

may take thirty years to remineralize on the calving grounds. The carcass of a wolf-killed caribou may lie undisturbed for three or four years. Time pools in the stillness here and then dissipates. The country is emptied of movement.

The coming and going of the animals during the short summer gives the Arctic a unique rhythmic shape, but it is to be felt only in certain places. Mostly, summer and winter, the whole land is still. The arctic explorer George De Long called it "a glorious country to learn patience in." Time here, like light, is a passing animal. Time hovers above the tundra like the rough-legged hawk, or collapses altogether like a bird keeled over with a heart attack, leaving the stillness we call death. In the thin film of moisture that coats a bit of moss on a tundra stone, you can find, with a strong magnifying glass, a world of movement buried within the larger suspended world: ageless pinpoints of life called water bears migrate over the wet plains and canyons of jade-green vegetation. But even here time is on the verge of collapse. The moisture freezes in winter. Or a summer wind may carry the water bear off and drop it among bare stones. Deprived of moisture, it shrivels slowly into a desiccated granule. It can endure like this for thirty or forty years. It waits for its time to come again.

Long, unpunctuated hours pass for all creatures in the Arctic. No wild frenzy of feeding distinguishes the short summer. But for the sudden movements of charging wolves and bolting caribou, the gambols of muskox calves, the scamper of an arctic fox, the swoop of a jaeger, the Arctic is a long, unbroken bow of time. Twilight lingers. There are no summer thunderstorms with bolts of lightning. The ice floes, the caribou, the muskoxen, all drift. To lie on your back somewhere on the light-drowned tundra of an Ellesmere Island valley is to feel that the ice ages might have ended but a few days ago. Without the holler of contemporary life, that constant disturbance, it is possible to feel the slope of time, how very far from Mesopotamia we have come. We move at such a fast clip now. We draw up geological charts at a snap, showing the possibilities for oil in Tertiary rocks in the Sverdrup Basin beneath Ellesmere's tundra. We delineate the life history of the ground squirrel. We list the butterflies: the sulphurs, the arctics, a copper, a blue, the lesser fritillaries. At a snap. We enumerate the plants. We name everything. Then we fold the charts and the catalogs, as if, except for a stray fact or two, we were done with a competent description. But the land is not a painting; the image cannot be completed this way.

Lying flat on your back on Ellesmere Island on rolling tundra without animals, without human trace, you can feel the silence stretching all the way to Asia. The winter face of a muskox, its unperturbed eye glistening in a halo of snow-crusted hair, looks at you over a cataract of time, an image that has endured through all the pulsations of ice.

You can sit for a long time with the history of man like a stone in your hand. The stillness, the pure light, encourage it.

FOR years scientists have been aware of different rhythms of life in the Arctic, though they are not particularly arctic rhythms. Tundra soil cores examined by fossil-pollen experts have shown that changes in the composition of arctic plant communities have occurred periodically with a change in climate. Borings in the Greenland ice cap have revealed rhythmic fluctuations in average temperature over the centuries. A careful examination of arctic refuse middens by archaeologists, paleobotanists, and paleozoologists has revealed a succession of differently equipped early human cultures, whose entries into the Arctic are also related to periods of climatic change. The animal bones found in their camps confirm parallel fluctuations in the populations of the animals they hunted.

A number of scientists feel all this information should mesh, that in some way the rhythms of human migration, climatic change, and animal population cycles should be interrelated. With a precise enough mathematics even the "nine-year lynx–snowshoe hare cycle" and the "seventy-year caribou cycle" should fit neatly into a basic pattern. Few have sought to rigorously integrate this material, and many don't believe the relationships even exist, except in a general way. Since the 1930s, however, the Danish scientist Christian Vibe has taken the possibility very seriously, and no other body of work has been so clearly linked with the attempt to find a basic period of arctic cycling, a tantalizing bit of information of enormous interest to biologists, historians, and arctic developers.

Climatic change—the advance and retreat of glacial ice in the Northern Hemisphere—is the hallmark of the Pleistocene, the epoch of man's emergence.* Vibe, keeping this in mind, and believing whatever he learned could be applied to understanding the climatic future of Europe and America, posed certain questions for himself. Why, he asked, were seals scarce at Ammassalik on the east coast of Greenland at the turn of the century, while at the same time they were plentiful along Greenland's southwest coast? Why did the caribou population of western Greenland crash suddenly at the end of both the eighteenth and nineteenth centuries? And what accounted for the periodic northward movements of Atlantic herring and cod in the North Atlantic?

Vibe scrutinized the records of the Royal Greenland Trading Company, which took in sealskins and fox skins, narwhal ivory, and other indicators, and by comparing these records with annual records of sea-ice movement and annual rainfall and snowfall, Vibe thought he could discern patterns. He checked his findings, to corroborate them further, by going over 232 years of fur-trading records from the Hudson's Bay Company in Canada, and by examining records kept by wool growers in southwest Greenland.

The first pattern to emerge for Vibe was a cycle of sea-ice formation and movement that lasted about 150 years, which records from arctic ships of exploration seemed to support. Vibe regarded as a key insight in this early work the fact that fluctuations in the arctic climate that were responsible for shifts of land and sea animals north and south over prolonged periods were tied to a lunar cycle of 18.6 years (the time it takes the moon to intersect the earth's orbit around the sun again at the same spot). Because the length of this lunar cycle is not a whole number, the maximum and minimum effect it has on the earth's tides (and therefore on ice formation and weather) can occur at different seasons of the

---

* Glacial periods are relatively rare in the earth's history. Scientists have discovered only four in the last 600 million years, the last of which is still going on. The Holocene, as far as we know, is only an interglacial stage, a reprieve, between the retreat of the Wisconsin ice (or Würm ice in Europe) and the next glacial advance.

year, in successive 18.6-year periods. This led Vibe to posit a primary period of 698 years for the Arctic's weather pattern, with secondary periods of 116.3 years, and what Vibe calls a basic "true ecological cycling period" of 11.6 years.

Depending upon your point of view, either Vibe's insights are ingenious and his mathematics elegant, or his system is impossibly broad and complicated and of little help in understanding arctic change. His inquiry might be considered an entirely esoteric and rarefied pursuit, in fact, if it were not for two things. In the Arctic one is constantly aware of sharp oscillation. It is as familiar a pattern of human thought and animal movement to the arctic resident as the pattern of four seasons is to a dweller in the Temperate Zone. In spite of the many manifestations of this rhythm, and the effect of sharp oscillation not only on resident animals but, probably, too, on the cultures that matured in these regions, Vibe's remains the only serious attempt at a description. Second, insofar as Vibe's theories explain oscillation in temperate-zone climate patterns or indicate harbingers of another ice age, they have a significant bearing on our developing patterns of commerce and economics, especially in the Arctic.

It is easy to say that the Arctic is characterized by sharp oscillation, just as it is to say that the airs of a temperate-zone spring are felicitous, but it is difficult to say precisely why. The basal annual rhythm of the North is winter/summer. The weeks during breakup and freeze-up are short, frequently perilous times, when strategies employed by both animals and human hunters to secure food are momentarily disrupted. The long winter and short summer constitute a temporal pattern around which life carefully arranges itself. Preparations for winter show up clearly everywhere in the land. The short-tailed weasel grows its white coat and the collared lemming its long snow claws. Tundra rodents shift from their night-active summer pattern to a day-active winter pattern, with but a few days of irregular rhythm in between. The arctic fox lines lemmings up in neat rows in its winter caches.

A second pattern complements this oscillation—long stillnesses broken by sudden movement. The river you have been traveling over by dogsled every week for eight months, and have come to think of as a solid piece of the earth, you wake one day to find a heaving jumble of ice. The spring silence is broken by pistol reports of cracking on the river, and then the sound of breaking branches and the whining pop of a falling tree as the careening blocks of ice gouge the riverbanks. A related but far eerier phenomenon occurs in the coastal ice. Suddenly in the middle of winter and without warning a huge piece of sea ice surges hundreds of feet inland, like something alive. The Eskimo call it *ivu*.* The silent arrival of caribou in an otherwise empty landscape is another example. The long wait at a seal hole for prey to surface. Waiting for a lead to close. The Eskimo have a word for this kind of long waiting, prepared for a sudden event: *quinuituq*. Deep patience.

As I moved through the Arctic I thought often about a rhythm indigenous to this land, not one imposed on it. The imposed view, however innocent, always obscures. The evidence that there *is* a different rhythm of life here seemed inescapably a part of the expression of the animals I encountered, though I cannot say precisely why. A coherent sense of the pervasiveness of such a rhythm is elusive.

The indigenous rhythm, or rhythms, of arctic life is important to discern for more than merely academic reasons. To understand why a region is different, to show an initial deference toward its mysteries, is to guard against a kind of provincialism that vitiates the imagination, that stifles the capacity to envision what is different.

Another reason to wonder which rhythms are innate, and what they might be, is related as well to the survival of the capacity to imagine beyond the familiar. We have long regarded animals as

---

* Eskimo descriptions of this phenomenon were not taken seriously until 1982, when archaeologists working at Utqiagvik, a prehistoric village site near Barrow, Alaska, discovered a family of five people that had been crushed to death in such an incident.

a kind of machinery, and the landscapes they move through as backdrops, as paintings. In recent years this antiquated view has begun to change. Animals are understood as mysterious, within the context of sophisticated Western learning that takes into account such things as biochemistry and genetics. They are changeable, not fixed, entities, predictable in their behavior only to a certain extent. The world of variables they are alert to is astonishingly complex, and their responses are sometimes highly sophisticated. The closer biologists look, the more the individual animal, like the individual human being, seems a reflection of that organization of energy that quantum mechanics predicts for the particles that compose an atom.

The animal's environment, the background against which we see it, can be rendered as something like the animal itself—partly unchartable. And to try to understand the animal apart from its background, except as an imaginative exercise, is to risk the collapse of both. To be what they are they require each other.

Spatial perception and the nature of movement, the shape and direction something takes in time, are topics that have been cogently addressed by people like Werner Heisenberg, Erwin Schrödinger, Paul Dirac, and David Bohm, all writing about subatomic phenomena. I believe that similar thoughts, potentially as beautiful in their complexity, arise with a consideration of how animals move in their landscapes—the path of a raven directly up a valley, the meander of grazing caribou, the winter movements of a single bear over the sea ice. We hardly know what these movements are in response to; we choose the dimensions of space and the durations of time we think appropriate to describe them, but we have no assurance that these are relevant. To watch a gyrfalcon and a snowy owl pass each other in the same sky is to wonder how the life of the one affects the other. To sit on a hillside and watch the slow intermingling of two herds of muskoxen feeding in a sedge meadow and to try to discern the logic of it is to grapple with uncertainty. To watch a flock of snow geese roll off a headwind together is to wonder where one animal begins and another ends. Animals confound us not because they are deceptively simple but because they are finally inseparable from the complexities of life. It is precisely these subtleties of fact and conception that comprise particle physics, which passes for the natural philosophy of our age. Animals move more slowly than beta particles, and through a space bewildering larger than that encompassed by a cloud of electrons, but they urge us, if we allow them, toward a consideration of the same questions about the fundamental nature of life, about the relationships that bind forms of energy into recognizable patterns.

In trying to discover the route and the time of man's arrival in the New World, science has had little to work with but bits of charcoal and an occasional broken tool or weapon retrieved from ancient fires and hunting sites. There is little disagreement about how man came to North America—people migrated across a broad, dry plain called Beringia from Asia during several different periods in the late Pleistocene. But evidence that would confirm man's arrival at some time earlier than 35,000 years ago, or even 20,000 years ago, is in dispute. The certain evidence is that people have been living in North America for at least 14,000 years.

Assuming that man arrived in North America on foot instead of by boat, and gradually at that, he crossed from Asia either sometime before 35,000 years ago, when the Bering land bridge was open, or not until much later, about 25,000 to 23,000 years ago. (The Bering land bridge was present from about 25,000 years ago until about 11,000 years ago, but it was only during the period from 25,000 to 23,000 years ago that man could have both crossed from Asia and traveled south to the central plains of North America. After that the Wisconsin Ice Age climaxed; the eastern and western North American ice sheets met, closing off the way south and separating the American prairie from the Arctic. Western Alaska remained free of ice during this period, and no doubt people continued to live farther east in Beringia until Bering Sea rose with meltwater from the ice sheets, flooding the land bridge and separating Asia and North America.)

Many archaeologists believe man came to North America in two waves. The first (the one that might have crossed 25,000 to 23,000 years ago, or earlier) brought with it flaked stone and bone tools comparable to Neanderthal man's Mousterian tools.* The second wave came about 13,000 years later and brought with it a more advanced tool tradition, comparable to the Aurignacian tools of Cro-Magnon man.† Both immigrant groups were big-game hunting cultures, subsisting on animals like large-horned bison, ground sloth, and woolly mammoth.

How the Arctic itself, the land east and north of the land bridge, became inhabited is unknown. The early hunting cultures in Alaska were succeeded about 5000 years ago by what some archaeologists regard as a less robust and impressive cultural tradition, one distinguished only by its very finely worked small tools. These microblade cultures were very likely the first human cultures to move into the North American Arctic.

Archaeologists know of two periods in the recent past when the climate warmed enough in the Arctic to allow human beings in skin boats easy summer passage through the islands of the Canadian Archipelago. These two "climatic optimums" occurred between about 3500 and 4500 years ago and again about 1100 to 900 years ago, and people migrated into the high Arctic on both occasions.

Louis Giddings, an archaeologist with a gift for locating important prehistoric sites, discovered cultural sequences at Onion

---

* The Mousterian tradition, named for tools discovered near Le Moustier in the Dordogne in France, marks the high point of Neanderthal culture in the Middle Paleolithic, 40,000 to 100,000 years ago. See chart, Appendix III.

† The Aurignacian was one of several traditions that emerged in the upper Paleolithic in western Europe between ten and forty thousand years ago, when Cro-Magnon people displaced the Neanderthal culture.

Portage on the Kobuk River in Alaska and at Cape Krusenstern, Alaska, that provided basic chronologies for Arctic cultural phases. With Giddings's findings and those of archaeologists working in northern Canada and in Greenland, it has become possible in recent years to organize a relatively coherent picture of early human occupation of the North American Arctic.

Before setting this forth, I should make two points. First, human beings migrating into this region were making a very bold move. Survival here required skills and technologies unknown to these hunters, not the least of which were qualities of a psychological nature. Second, the arctic migrations represent movements of very small numbers of people. It is not out of the question to consider that all the microblade sites archaeologists have discovered so far from western Canada to northern Greenland were created by fewer than 500 people. The Arctic offered man scant resources, which were widely scattered and sometimes difficult to retrieve. Even at the height of their success during the Thule cultural phase, about A.D. 1000, the number of arctic residents from Point Barrow to Peary Land may have been no more than 5000.

The first people to cross into North America were probably paleo-Indians, people who settled in the interior of Alaska and spread south. The geographical point of origin of paleo-Eskimos, people who remained in the Arctic, is unknown, but archaeologists generally favor the Bering Sea region and eastern Siberia. These arctic mongoloids may or may not have been the ancestors of modern Eskimos; in any case, paleo-Eskimos were in arctic Alaska by about 5000 years ago, having perhaps crossed the open water of Bering Strait in skin boats. It was their culture that was typified by minutely flaked chert and obsidian cutting tools about one inch long and one-quarter inch wide. This culture and its variations are referred to as the Arctic Small Tool tradition (ASTt).

ASTt campsites have been found as far east as Peary Land in northern Greenland (where the culture is called Independence I, after a site on Independence Fiord) and more or less continuously across the American and Canadian Arctic. Many of these sites appear to have been inhabited for only a single night or, at most, for a couple of weeks before the people moved on. These people hunted muskoxen, polar bear, arctic fox, arctic hare, and sea ducks, and the tools they left behind suggest theirs was a harsh and meager life. A Canadian archaeologist named Robert McGhee has written that ASTt peoples migrated into "the coldest, darkest and most barren regions ever inhabited by man." He speculates that during the winters when they were hard-pressed for food, these people "may have almost hibernated in their unlit and unheated dwellings." One looks today upon the remains of their dwellings—a fox-bone awl, a quartz arrowhead, the ring of stones that held down their skin tents—with profound respect.

With a gradual cooling, the Arctic Ocean ice front came farther south, and ASTt peoples apparently retreated. The next culture to make its presence known was another ASTt culture called Pre-Dorset, which appeared about 3500 years ago. This was a more communal, more technologically advanced people. They carved soapstone bowls in which they burned oil rendered from marine mammal blubber for heat and light, and they fashioned small wood sleds on which to pull their belongings. (Many Pre-Dorset campsites have been found at caribou river crossings and at fish-trapping locations that have been used by subsequent cultures well into modern times.)

Pre-Dorset peoples seem to have been concentrated in a core area around Foxe Basin, a region of land and sea mammal abundance. During periods when the climate ameliorated, they may have migrated out to other regions as well. The remnants of many different technologies have been uncovered at Pre-Dorset sites. (A technology is an assemblage of tools, utensils, weapons, and other implements designed for a specific task, such as the preparation of skins for clothing or caribou hunting.) The materials for construction and manufacture have included stone, bone, skin, ivory, antler, and, very rarely, wood. Some of the tools are highly specialized, designed, for example, for use in hunting a certain animal only in a specific season or under specific circumstances—to take a seal in open water or, alternately, at its winter aglu. About 2800 years ago, the Pre-Dorset sites gave way to evidence of a new culture called Dorset.

Many archaeologists speculate that the Dorset culture grew out of various elements of Pre-Dorset culture. Perhaps, too, there was an infusion of ideas and technologies from a contemporaneous culture in Greenland called Independence II; or from Alaskan cultures; or from archaic Indian cultures living to the south. However they arose, Dorset people seem to have appeared first in the Foxe Basin region of northern Canada. They had skin boats, small sleds, and better sea-hunting equipment than their forebears, and they built houses of snow.

Dorset carving is by far the most developed art in Eskimo prehistory. (The artwork of Okvik and Ipiutak culture in the Bering Sea area, contemporaneous with Dorset artwork, is comparable.) And most archaeologists agree that there is something unique about it. In contrast to other cultures, Dorset people decorated very few utilitarian objects, and single pieces of artwork, all carvings, are rather rare. The general feeling is that the carvings were connected with shamanistic magic, and many think there is something decidedly dark about them. These caribou antler, bone, and walrus ivory carvings are of single animals, most often polar bears; of human figures and human/animal figures; and of human faces in chaotic tableaux. The representations are both realistic and stylized, and most of the carvings are of inconspicuous size.

The eye for detail is so sharp and the execution so deft that you can readily tell a carving of a common loon from one of a red-throated loon. The style, writes Canadian artist and critic George Swinton, "exudes intensity and power . . . despite its remarkable subtlety and delicacy." The human faces in some of the carvings that seem tortured and psychotic to some viewers, Swinton compares stylistically with German Expressionism, saying that their form "emphasizes content, vigour, and involvement (as opposed to style, elegance, and detachment)." The primitive quality in them, in other words, is more brutal than fetching.

Perhaps too much has been made of this Dorset "darkness"; but the observation that Dorset art is unsettling, while the art that preceded it and followed it is not, is common among archaeologists dealing with this period. Giddings describes the Dorset-like art of the Ipiutak to the west, in Alaska, as "grotesque and bizarre" and the Old Bering Sea culture art that followed as "balanced and pleasing, as though the artists led a secure—even serene— existence." The circumstances under which these carvings are found sometimes augment feelings of apprehension. Froelich Rainey, excavating an Ipiutak burial site at Point Hope, Alaska, found a small carved caribou hoof protruding on a shaft from the pelvic region of a human skeleton. He cleared more dirt away to find that this long ivory shaft penetrated the entire vertebral column and emerged in the skull, where it curved forward into the space where the mouth would have been. It terminated in a miniature human hand, opened in supplication.

In July 1979, a young archaeologist working at a Dorset site in the high Arctic uncovered a caribou scapula that left him shaken. Both surfaces of this flat bone were incised with scores of small human faces with gaping mouths. He remembers sitting with the scapula in his hands on a cool and overcast morning and dumbly contemplating the agonized expressions. "I was frightened out of my wits by it," he told me. Then he handed me his notes for that day and said, "Which is why the entry is so mundane." He got up twice in the night to unpack the piece and look at it, he was so disturbed.

When I have held these objects in my hand, I have marveled most at the skill of the carvers, and found them more provocative than dark.

THE Dorset came into their ascendancy during a period of cooling in the Arctic. During the warming trend that followed, the climatic optimum of A.D. 900–1100, they were displaced by a quite different culture called Thule (pron. too' lē). Archaeologists don't know whether the Dorset were absorbed by the Thule or forcibly driven east and south out of the Foxe Basin area. (Remnant bands of Dorset survived in the fastness of northern Quebec and Labrador until about A.D. 1400.)

The Thule, a vigorous, highly skilled, whale-hunting culture originating in the region of Bering Strait, grew out of Old Bering Sea culture. Robert McGhee has written that Old Bering Sea people had a hunting technology "that gave them an abundant and secure economy [and] they developed a way of life that was probably as rich as any other in the nonagricultural and nonindustrial world."

Old Bering Sea culture was succeeded by a richer culture around Saint Lawrence Island, called Punuk. Punuk people may have moved north about A.D. 900, to hunt whales and other sea mammals along the northwest coast of Alaska during the warming trend. There they either mingled with, or passed right over, a culture called Birnirk. A Punuk or Birnirk-like group then continued east across the Beaufort Sea in large skin boats, or umiaks, and established themselves in northern Canada as the Thule.

The Thule, directly ancestral to modern Eskimos, moved east very quickly. They may have traveled the 2600 miles from Point Barrow to Peary Land, in fact, in only two or three generations. With the climate warming up, bowhead whale populations from the western and eastern Arctic likely met in Parry Channel (M'Clure Strait, Viscount Melville Sound, Barrow Strait, and Lancaster Sound); and herds of narwhals and belukhas and walrus must have penetrated far north into the Canadian Archipelago as well. In the west, spotted and ribbon seals would have wintered and summered farther to the north, the same being true for gray, harp, and hooded seals in the eastern Arctic. The whole ecosystem shifted north. The sea ice and the scarcity of animals in certain seasons that had once discouraged east-west travel were no longer impediments. (The increase in average annual temperature during the climatic optimum was not much more than 3°F, but the effects were dramatic. The tree line in North America, for example, shifted north about 60 miles.)

The Thule were superb hunters. They possessed an elaborate

marine-mammal hunting technology, which they used from the umiak in pursuit of whales and walrus, on the sea ice, and from the kayak.* They developed the dog-drawn sled and made sophisticated refinements in the harpoon technology of the Dorset. Their winter homes were warm, semisubterranean shelters with lower walls and floors of stone and upper walls and roofs of turf over a skin covering, which was supported by whale ribs and jawbones.

The Thule stand out as a highly successful people. They compare well in spirit, though not in fact, with the Magdalenian caribou-hunting culture of Europe during the final phase of the Upper Paleolithic. The Magdalenian period is characterized by an apotheosis in cave painting (at Altamira and Lascaux, for example) and a lavish and skillful decoration of hunting weapons and other, utilitarian objects, including beautifully carved, fine-eyed bone needles. Magdalenian hunters lived almost 10,000 years before the Thule; but they, too, flourished during a climatic optimum. This advantage, together with a knowledge of their own capacity to succeed as a culture, seems to have infused them with vigorous confidence. Their caribou-hunting way of life, with its refined artistic overtones, was perfectly suited to the landscape they found themselves in.

The same sophisticated kind of hunting culture continued to make ecological sense in the Far North long after farming and pastoral cultures supplanted hunting cultures in Europe during the Neolithic. The Paleolithic-Mesolithic-Neolithic sequence of Europe, thought to be a natural and even necessary progression for mankind, is a model that applies poorly in a land of permafrost and

---

* The umiak, a Thule invention, is an open, walrus- or bearded seal-skin boat, about 30 feet long, sometimes fitted with a square sail and a single, stepped mast. On long journeys it was commonly rowed by women, while the men followed in shorter, lower, decked-over, single-seat, and more seaworthy kayaks, free to hunt. For this reason the boat is also called "a women's boat."

long winters. Farmers and herdsmen did not move into the Arctic for good reason. (The Samis, or Lapps, of northern Scandinavia and the Kola Peninsula are the only far northern people to have voluntarily turned to a life of seminomadic herding.)

The climatic optimum that brought the Thule so swiftly to northern Greenland, and which brought the Norse to southern Greenland at the same time, ended about A.D. 1100. The cooling trend that followed drove the Thule out of the high Arctic (and proved disastrous for the Norse, who were dependent in part on agriculture to sustain themselves and could not adapt). The Thule culture fragmented into several distinct traditions. These cultures —Polar Eskimo living around Inglefield Fiord in Greenland, Central Eskimo living on Baffin Island, Caribou Eskimo living on the mainland to the west of Southampton Island—were the tribes that met the second wave of European explorers (after the Norse) in the sixteenth and seventeenth centuries.

The cooling trend that culminated in the Little Ice Age of 1650–1850 changed both the type and the numbers of animals living in the Arctic. As a consequence, the hunting tradition the Eskimos inherited from the Thule, its tools and methods, had to be altered or abandoned in order for the different, isolated groups to survive. They met the first European explorers, therefore, during a transitional period between a Thule phase and a more distinctly Eskimo phase in their culture.

The latter transition—archaeologists regard the Thule as directly ancestral to modern Eskimos—is an important one. The tendency of almost all Europeans was to regard the Eskimos they met as brutish people living unrefined lives. No sense of transition between high and low phases in a culture, no sense of environmental necessity, no sense, even, that the various Eskimo cultures were different, informed these early observations. And these early judgments fixed an image of the Eskimo people as a backward race in the European imagination. Had the second, decisive wave of European culture met Thule people as the Norse had, instead of the historic Eskimo, they might have taken a different view of their culture. (Though, to judge from Cortés's response to the Aztecs, it is unlikely.)

When archaeologists sketch the broad outline of Arctic prehistory, they are inclined to make comparisons among the various cultural phases, based in part on the wealth of the respective material cultures, and to stress that the transitions between them occurred at different times in different places. Thus, it might have been remnants of the earlier Dorset that the first Europeans met on the coast of Labrador, in southern Greenland, and on the Ungava Peninsula, not post-Thule Eskimos. And so, too, the ASTt cultures are called "impoverished" compared with the later Thule, or with the Siberian hunting cultures that preceded them into North America. Western society on its own has long held in low esteem human cultures that matured outside the Temperate Zone, a confusion, in large part, about what the landscapes these people lived in demanded of them.

There is a tendency among archaeologists and many modern arctic observers to look back wistfully to the period of Thule culture, to regard it as not only more highly achieved than that of the smaller groups of more nomadic historic Eskimo but also more coherent. They were the last Arctic culture to close their doors before Western man arrived. Because of this, and the obvious comparison with high cultures of the European Paleolithic, there is a certain allure about them. From their tools and homes comes a substantive feeling of energy, of passion and enthusiasm. A student working at a Thule site on Ellesmere Island told me about a harpoon head she had found. "All they had to do with it was catch walrus. But they made it beautiful," she said.

The admiration one feels kneeling over the pathetic remains of an early ASTt campsite can be very deep. What tenacity. What courage. Another sort of feeling comes over one at a Thule site. One misses any sense of remoteness or separation and feels instead profound respect. A powerful, dignified people, one imagines. The delicate and robust tools, as the student said, are beautiful. Peter Schledermann, who has excavated prehistoric sites across most of

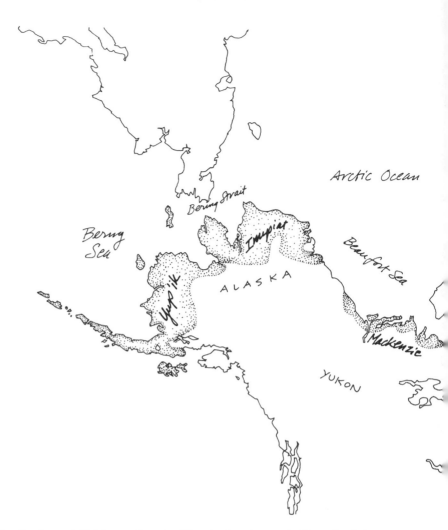

Distribution of Eskimo tribes in North America and Greenland in historic times.

the Canadian Arctic, said to me one evening over dinner in Calgary, "Everything we are is in our spirit. In archaeology, you are examining the long line of what we are."

WE owe much of our understanding of the distinctions among the groups of historic Eskimo to a handful of exceptional ethnographers who lived for various periods of time with them—Knud Rasmussen, Kaj Birket-Smith, Diamond Jenness, Franz Boas, and Hans Steensby. Beginning in the West, these groups include the

North Slope Eskimo, who perhaps retained more of their Thule heritage than the others, and who include an inland-dwelling component called the Nunamiut; the Mackenzie Eskimo, dwelling near the delta of the Mackenzie River; the Copper Eskimo, who inhabited Victoria Island and the Coronation Gulf area and traveled to the *Investigator* cache at Mercy Bay, and were the last of the historic groups to be discovered; the Central Eskimo of Baffin Island and Melville and Boothia peninsulas; the Caribou Eskimo, who dwelled on the tundra northwest of Hudson Bay; and the Polar

Eskimo, the most isolated of the groups, in northwest Greenland. (This last small group served many Arctic expeditions, including those of Robert Peary and Frederick Cook. In 1949 their central settlement, Uummannaq, was moved 60 miles farther north by the Danish government to permit construction of a strategic NATO air base.)

Among the Central Eskimo were other, smaller, distinct traditions, including the Netsilik, known for their soapstone carvings; the Igloolik, the people the British whalers met at Pond's Bay; and the Sadlermiut of Southampton Island, all of whom died in an epidemic in 1900 after a visit by a Scottish whaler, the *Active*. What shreds of information exist suggest that the Sadlermiut retained, perhaps, a significant amount of Dorset culture within their own tradition. Aivilik Eskimo, related to Caribou Eskimo people, now live on Southampton Island.

In modern times, of course, tribes like the Sadlermiut still disappear with regularity in different parts of the world, or they are absorbed into Western culture in a way that obscures or even obliterates their intellectual and material traditions. These losses seem tragic and consequential, and they are frustrating because they sometimes occur for reasons of indifference or greed. They are not like the loss of the Thule. The Thule, one can feel, are extinct on natural grounds, an event arbitrated by the landscape. The eclipse of the Sadlermiut, however, seems to diminish us, because we are their contemporaries, because we claim to be enlightened about the intrinsic worth of life, and because we esteem compassion. The Sadlermiut were a way to understand Southampton Island. A reflection on that harsh landscape and the evidence of their success there leads to the conclusion that we lost some wisdom about life with their passing. We cannot anymore pick up their things and ask, "Why did you make this?" or "What is this for?," and hope to hear the answer that would come in any case only once in a thousand times, the answer that reveals what it *means*. The answer that opens the timeless interior of the human mind, that collapses centuries of distance and transcends the object at hand.

Wherever I went I felt the loss of the Sadlermiut and so a sharper sense of gratitude toward those who once wrote down the observations of arctic peoples, described their skills, and saw to the preservation of the objects of their culture. Even if we cannot say what an object meant, we can still marvel today at what it did and at the people who made it. With a minimum of materials historic Eskimos created a wealth of utilitarian implements, distinguished by ingenuity in design, specificity of purpose, and appropriateness of material to the task.*

I think first of the clothing. Winter clothing was almost always made from caribou skin. The fur of arctic fox and, in the western Arctic, Dall sheep, was warmer, but those skins were too delicate. Caribou hair is not hollow the way polar bear hair is—it consists of large, multichambered cells—but the effect is the same: excellent lightweight insulation. The skins of adult cows, taken early in the fall, before their winter coats got too thick, provided the best combination of warmth and lightness. (Late-fall cow skins, like those of bull caribou or of muskoxen, were too heavy to be comfortable but made excellent bedding.) Caribou calf skins were used for underclothing and boot liners. The skins of the caribou's forelegs were used for boot uppers and in the palms of mittens because they resisted abrasion. The ruff of the parka was of wolverine or wolf, furs that easily shed the ice crystals that form there from breathing. The tightly spaced stitching was overcast or blind, as the situation required, to keep out

---

* The materials they worked with, of course, came almost entirely from the animals they hunted. Eskimos generally regarded these materials as gifts given in accordance with ethical obligations they felt toward the animals. The two parallel cultures, human and animal, were linked in biological ways and, for the Eskimo, in spiritual ways that are all but lost to our understanding today. It was the gift rather than the death that was preeminent in the Eskimo view of hunting.

wind and snow or to forestall the wicking of moisture. Sealskins were more often used in place of caribou in summer clothing because they were waterproof. They were sewn together with sinews that swelled slightly when wet (making the stitching waterproof) and were soled with a hide as tough as walrus but lighter, that of the bearded seal.

Slippers inside the winter boots were sometimes made of whole bird skins turned inside out. Waterproof rain gear was made from seal intestine. For walking quietly on the snow, boots were sometimes soled with polar bear fur.

Eskimo clothing required daily attention—sewing, softening, and drying—because it was somewhat fragile. It was lighter and warmer, however, than any clothing Western explorers brought with them to the Arctic, and after several fatal lessons, expedition leaders began to insist on Eskimo clothing for everyone. In some respects it remains superior for general use to modern Western expeditionary clothing.

Eskimos utilized the caribou completely. They made clothing, bedding, and bags from its skin and tools and weapons from its bones and antlers. Noting that fats in the caribou's leg joints congealed at lower temperatures the farther they were from the body core, they took the fat from the foot to use as a lubricant for bowstrings in freezing temperatures. (Western civilizations made the same discovery with cattle, whence neat's-foot oil.) They used the marrow of its bones for fuel; its blood in glues; its sinews for lashings, bindings, and thread. What they did not eat they cached, against the lean months of spring. (The anthropologist Richard Nelson marveled during his modern fieldwork at the still thorough anatomical knowledge of Eskimo women, at the way they could quickly cut up a large animal "into smaller and smaller pieces without a saw, without breaking a bone.")

What is so consistently striking about the way Eskimos used parts of an animal is the breadth of their understanding about what would work. Knowing that muskox horn is more flexible than caribou antler, they preferred it for making the side prongs of a fish spear. For a waterproof bag in which to carry sinews for clothing repair, they chose salmon skin. They selected the strong, translucent intestine of a bearded seal to make a window for a snow house—it would fold up for easy traveling and it would not frost over in cold weather. To make small snares for sea ducks, they needed a springy material that would not rot in salt water—baleen fibers. The down feather of a common eider, tethered at the end of a stick in the snow at an aglu, would reveal the exhalation of a quietly surfacing seal. Polar bear bone was used anywhere a stout, sharp point was required, because it is the hardest bone.

One notices many subtle, imitative correspondences in their creations: the drag handle at the end of a thong used to pull a seal home over the ice is carved in the shape of a polar bear. The beak of a fish-hunter, the loon, forms the point of a fish spear. Appropriate or fine distinctions: a preference for belukha sinew over caribou sinew to stitch sealskin. Snowy owl or cormorant feathers chosen over others for arrow fletchings. And signs of resourcefulness: tightly wrapping fresh char, lapped head to tail in a wet sealskin, and letting it freeze to form the runner for a sled.

The sled itself was a remarkable piece of equipment. The sled runners were cross-braced with lengths of caribou antler, lashed to the runners with sealskin thongs. The bottoms of the runners were shod with a mixture of pulverized moss and water, built up in layers. On top of the peat shoeing came an ice glaze, carefully smoothed and shaved. The result was a flexible sled that could be sent over the surface of the snow with a flick of the wrist, and that moved over irregularities in the sea ice without tipping unduly.

Otto Geist, excavating a Punuk site on Saint Lawrence Island in the 1920s, made a list of items these people made solely from walrus ivory, each one designed to perform a specific task or serve a specific purpose. A dog-harness buckle. A wound pin to keep a seal from bleeding. Part of a fox trap. A tent-line tensioner. His list ran to more than a hundred items.

In *Eskimo Realities* Edmund Carpenter remarks on a well-known phenomenon, that Eskimos quickly grasp the essence of any mechanical problem and solve it. Even when the object is something they've never seen before, they will select from "scrap" or "waste" material something with the right tensile strength or capacity for torsion or elasticity, something with the necessary resistance to heat, repeated freezing or corrosion, and shape it with simple tools into a serviceable if not permanent solution. Nineteenth-century explorers remarked on this capacity often, as have modern scientists with broken outboard engines and wristwatches.

Very sharp, someone once said, these broadly smiling men with no pockets, no hats, and no wheels.

THERE is a small village in the central Brooks Range today called Anaktuvuk Pass. The Eskimos there are called Nunamiut, a group that until recently subsisted largely on caribou, Dall sheep, and moose. Originally nomadic, they spent winters in the Brooks Range and summers with relatives on the Beaufort Sea coast, trading caribou skins for sealskins and blubber. Their initial experience with modern trade goods was with such things as Russian tobacco in the eighteenth century, which they obtained from Eskimos living around the mouth of the Colville River, who had traded for it with Bering Sea Eskimos. After 1850 American whalers brought in large quantities of flour, tea, coffee, sugar, and tobacco, as well as guns, ammunition, and alcohol to the northwest coast of Alaska. The Nunamiut were less directly involved in this trade than their coastal relations, but they were profoundly affected nevertheless. The caribou herds they depended on were decimated to feed the whaling crews, and the Nunamiut were forced to abandon their life in the mountains. They shifted away from an economy based on hunting toward one based on trade. A few found seasonal employment on the coast, and most began trapping for furs in earnest.

A change came over the Nunamiut in the 1930s when the market for fur collapsed and the trading posts were closed, distant effects of economic depression in the United States. In 1934 a handful of families, knowing the caribou population had recovered and was again migrating through the mountains, sought to return to an earlier, more satisfying way of life. They set up a camp that first year at the junction of the Anaktuvuk and Colville rivers. For a few years they continued to travel regularly to the coast, where they fished and hunted seals, but in 1939, after this short period of readjustment, they returned to their homeland in the Brooks Range.

Ten years later the promise of trade goods to be brought into the mountains by airplane and the services of a temporary teacher in the summer induced several bands of Nunamiut to gather at a place called Tulugak Lake. In 1951 this group of sixty-five people moved a few miles farther south and a United States post office was established at Anaktuvuk Pass at the skin tent of a hunter named Homer Mekiana. A permanent school was built in 1961, by which time many of the Nunamiut were staying in or near the village year-round. Today about 180 people live there. There is a village store; satellites provide both telephone and television service; and there is a new school with sauna baths and a swimming pool, built with royalty money from Alaskan oil discoveries.

This story has been repeated many times in the same sequence across the Arctic in the past fifty years. Nomadic hunters are consolidated in one place for purposes of trade; radical changes are made in the native way of life in order to adapt to a trade-based or cash-based economy; some make strenuous efforts to return to a semblance of the older way of life; and, finally, large segments of the native language are lost, and the deep erosion of social, religious, political, and dietary customs occurs under intense pressure from missionaries, bureaucrats, and outside entrepreneurs. Hunting expertise, the ability of a man and a woman to keep a family going, the kind of knowledge of life that grew from patience and determination—such attributes were not as highly regarded by the interlopers, who sought to instill other virtues: promptness, personal cleanliness, self-improvement, and a high degree of orderliness and scheduling in daily life.*

Among those in the outside culture whom the Nunamiut have counted as friends in modern times are several anthropologists and biologists who recognized a repository of knowledge in the Nunamiut, particularly about the natural history of the local landscape, and who honored them for it. Some of the Nunamiut men and women who have led balanced and dignified lives through all the changes they have had to face have become symbols of unpretentious wisdom to visiting scientists. The situation, of course, is not unique to Anaktuvuk Pass. Many scientists comment in their papers and books and in private conversation about the character of their Eskimo companions. They admire their humble intelligence, their honesty, and their humor. They find it invigorating to be in the presence of people who, when they do speak, make so few generalized or abstract statements, who focus instead on the practical, the specific, the concrete.†

I visited Anaktuvuk Pass in 1978 with a friend, a wolf biologist who had made a temporary home there and who was warmly regarded for his tact, his penchant for listening, and his help during an epidemic of flu in the village. We spent several days watching wolves and caribou in nearby valleys and visiting at several homes.

---

* It is easy to impugn the worth of such nebulous virtues, and to find among the interlopers venal and self-aggrandizing people. But it disparages Eskimos to see them as helpless in this situation. Most Eskimos are not opposed to changing their way of life, but they want the timing and the direction of change to be of their own choosing. "There is no insistence," a man once told me, "on living as hard a life as possible." In passing, it should be noted that many people have offered genuine assistance to Eskimos. One frequently hears praise in the Canadian Arctic, for example, for Catholic missionaries, because of their long-term commitment to a single village, their practice of learning to speak the language and to hunt, and their emphasis on good schooling.

† For a list of publications that grew out of work with the Nunamiut, see note 4.

The men talked a lot about hunting. The evenings were full of stories. There were moments of silence when someone said something very true, peals of laughter when a man told a story expertly at his own expense. One afternoon we left and traveled far to the west to the headwaters of the Utukok River.

The Alaska Department of Fish and Game had a small field camp on the Utukok, at the edge of a gravel-bar landing strip. Among the biologists there were men and women studying caribou, moose, tundra grizzly, wolverine, and, now that my companion had arrived, wolves. The country around the Utukok and the head-waters of the Kokolik River is a wild and serene landscape in summer. Parts of the Western Arctic caribou herd are drifting over the hills, returning from the calving grounds. The sun is always shining, somewhere in the sky. For a week or more we had very fine, clear weather. Golden eagles circled high over the tundra, hunting. Snowy owls regarded us from a distance from their tussock perches. Short-eared owls, a gyrfalcon. Familiar faces.

A few days after we arrived, my companion and I went south six or seven miles and established a camp from which we could watch a distant wolf den. In that open, rolling country without trees, I had the feeling, sometimes, that nothing was hidden. It was during those days that I went for walks along Ilingnorak Ridge and started visiting ground-nesting birds, and developed the habit of bowing to them out of regard for what was wonderful and mysterious in their lives.

The individual animals we watched tested their surroundings, tried things they had not done before, or that possibly no animal like them had ever done before—revealing their capacity for the new. The preservation of this capacity to adapt is one of the central mysteries of evolution.

We watched wolves hunting caribou, and owls hunting lemmings. Arctic ground squirrel eating *irok*, the mountain sorrel. I thought a great deal about hunting. In 1949, Robert Flaherty told an amazing story, which Edmund Carpenter was later successful in getting published. It was about a man named Comock. In 1902, when he and his family were facing starvation, Comock decided to travel over the sea ice to an island he knew about, where he expected they would be able to find food (a small island off Cape Wolstenholme, at the northern tip of Quebec's Ungava Peninsula). On the journey across, they lost nearly all their belongings—all of Comock's knives, spears, and harpoons, all their skins, their stone lamps, and most of their dogs—when the sea ice suddenly opened one night underneath their camp. They were without hunting implements, without a stone lamp to melt water to drink, without food or extra clothing. Comock had left only one sled, several dogs, his snow knife, with which he could cut snow blocks to build a snow house, and stones to make sparks for a fire.

They ate their dogs. The dogs they kept ate the other dogs, which were killed for them. Comock got his family to the island. He fashioned, from inappropriate materials, new hunting weapons. He created shelter and warmth. He hunted successfully. He reconstructed his entire material culture, almost from scratch, by improvising and, where necessary, inventing. He survived. His family survived. His dogs survived and multiplied.

Over the years they carefully collected rare bits of driftwood and bone until Comock had enough to build the frame for an umiak. They saved bearded-seal skins, from which Comock's wife made a waterproof hull. And one summer day they sailed away, back toward Ungava Peninsula. Robert Flaherty, exploring along the coast, spotted Comock and his family and dogs approaching across the water. When they came close, Flaherty, recognizing the form of an umiak and the cut of Eskimo clothing but, seeing that the materials were strange and improvised, asked the Eskimo who he was. He said his name was Comock. "Where in the world have you come from?" asked Flaherty. "From far away, from big island, from far over there," answered Comock, pointing. Then he smiled and made a joke about how poor the umiak must appear, and his family burst into laughter.

I think of this story because at its heart is the industry and competence, the determination and inventiveness of a human family. And because it is about people who lived resolutely in the heart of every moment they found themselves in, disastrous and sublime.

During those days I spent on Ilingnorak Ridge, I did not know what I know now about hunting; but I had begun to sense the outline of what I would learn in the years ahead with Eskimos and from being introduced, by various people, to situations I could not have easily found my way to alone. The insights I felt during those days had to do with the nature of hunting, with the movement of human beings over the land, and with fear. The thoughts grew out of watching the animals.

The evidence is good that among all northern aboriginal hunting peoples, the hunter saw himself bound up in a sacred relationship with the larger animals he hunted. The relationship was full of responsibilities—to the animals, to himself, and to his family. Among the great and, at this point, perhaps tragic lapses in the study of aboriginal hunting peoples is a lack of comprehension about the role women played in hunting. We can presume, I think, that in the same way the hunter felt bound to the animals he hunted, he felt the contract incomplete and somehow even inappropriate if his wife was not part of it. In no hunting society could a man hunt successfully alone. He depended upon his wife for obvious reasons—for the preparation of food and clothing, companionship, humor, subtle encouragement—and for things we can only speculate about, things of a religious nature, bearing on the mutual obligations and courtesies with which he approached the animals he hunted.

Hunting in my experience—and by hunting I simply mean being out on the land—is a state of mind. All of one's faculties are brought to bear in an effort to become fully incorporated into the landscape. It is more than listening for animals or watching for hoofprints or a shift in the weather. It is more than an analysis of what one *senses*. To hunt means to have the land around you like clothing. To engage in a wordless dialogue with it, one so absorbing that you cease to talk with your human companions. It means to release yourself from rational images of what something "means" and to be concerned only that it "is." And then to recognize that things exist only insofar as they can be related to other things. These relationships—fresh drops of moisture on top of rocks at a river crossing and a raven's distant voice—become patterns. The patterns are always in motion. Suddenly the pattern—which includes physical hunger, a memory of your family, and memories of the valley you are walking through, these particular plants and smells—takes in the caribou. There is a caribou standing in front of you. The release of the arrow or bullet is like a word spoken out loud. It occurs at the periphery of your concentration.

The mind we know in dreaming, a nonrational, nonlinear comprehension of events in which slips in time and space are normal, is, I believe, the conscious working mind of an aboriginal hunter. It is a frame of mind that redefines patience, endurance, and expectation.

The focus of a hunter in a hunting society was not killing animals but attending to the myriad relationships he understood bound him into the world he occupied with them. He tended to those duties carefully because he perceived in them everything he understood about survival. This does not mean, certainly, that every man did this, or that good men did not starve. Or that shamans whose duty it was to intercede with the forces that empowered these relationships weren't occasionally thinking of personal gain or subterfuge. It only means that most men understood how to behave.

A fundamental difference between our culture and Eskimo culture, which can be felt even today in certain situations, is that we have irrevocably separated ourselves from the world that animals occupy. We have turned all animals and elements of the natural world into objects. We manipulate them to serve the complicated ends of our destiny. Eskimos do not grasp this separation easily, and have difficulty imagining themselves entirely removed from the world of animals. For many of them, to make this separation is analogous to cutting oneself off from light or water. It is hard to imagine how to do it.

A second difference is that, because we have objectified animals, we are able to treat them impersonally. This means not only the animals that live around us but animals that live in distant lands. For Eskimos, most relationships with animals are local and personal. The animals one encounters are part of one's community, and one has obligations to them. A most confusing aspect of Western culture for Eskimos to grasp is our depersonalization of relationships with the human and animal members of our communities. And it is compounded, rather than simplified, by their attempting to learn how to objectify animals.

Eskimos do not maintain this intimacy with nature without paying a certain price. When I have thought about the ways in which they differ from people in my own culture, I have realized that they are more afraid than we are. On a day-to-day basis, they have more fear. Not of being dumped into cold water from an umiak, not a debilitating fear. They are afraid because they accept fully what is violent and tragic in nature. It is a fear tied to their knowledge that sudden, cataclysmic events are as much a part of life, of really living, as are the moments when one pauses to look at something beautiful. A Central Eskimo shaman named Aua, queried by Knud Rasmussen about Eskimo beliefs, answered, "We do not believe. We fear."

To extend these thoughts, it is wrong to think of hunting cultures like the Eskimo's as living in perfect harmony or balance with nature. Their regard for animals and their attentiveness to nuance in the landscape were not rigorous or complete enough to approach an idealized harmony. No one knew that much. No one would say they knew that much. They faced nature with fear, with *ilira* (nervous awe) and *kappia* (apprehension). And with enthusiasm. They accepted hunting as a way of life—its violence, too, though they did not seek that out. They were unsentimental, so much so that most outsiders thought them cruel, especially in their treatment of dogs. Nor were they innocent. There is murder and warfare and tribal vendetta in their history; and today, in the same villages I walked out of to hunt, are families shattered by alcohol, drugs, and ambition. While one cannot dismiss culpability in these things, any more than one can hold to romantic notions about hunting, it is good to recall what a *struggle* it is to live with dignity and understanding, with perspicacity or grace, in circumstances far better than these. And it is helpful to imagine how the forces of life must be construed by people who live in a world where swift and fatal violence, like *ivu*, the suddenly leaping shore ice, is inherent in the land. The land, in a certain, very real way, compels the minds of the people.

A good reason to travel with Eskimo hunters in modern times is that, beyond nettlesome details—foods that are not to one's liking, a loss of intellectual conversation, a consistent lack of formal planning—in spite of these things, one feels the constant presence of people who know something about surviving. At their best they are resilient, practical, and enthusiastic. They pay close attention in realms where they feel a capacity for understanding. They have a quality of *nuannaarpoq*, of taking extravagant pleasure in being alive; and they delight in finding it in other people. Facing as we do our various Armageddons, they are a good people to know.

In the time I was in the field with Eskimos I wondered at the basis for my admiration. I admired an awareness in the men of providing for others, and the soft tone of voice they used around bloodshed. I never thought I could understand, from their point of view, that moment of preternaturally heightened awareness, and the peril inherent in taking a life; but I accepted it out of respect for their seriousness toward it. In moments when I felt perplexed, that I was dealing with an order outside my own, I discovered and put to use a part of my own culture's wisdom, the formal divisions of Western philosophy—metaphysics, epistemology, ethics, aesthetics, and logic—which pose, in order, the following questions. What is real? What can we understand? How should we behave? What is beautiful? What are the patterns we can rely upon?

As I traveled, I would say to myself, What do my companions see where I see death? Is the sunlight beautiful to them, the way it sparkles on the water? Which for the Eskimo hunter are the patterns to be trusted? The patterns, I know, could be different from ones I imagined were before us. There could be other, remarkably different insights.

THOSE days on Ilingnorak Ridge, when I saw tundra grizzly tearing up the earth looking for ground squirrels, and watched wolves hunting, and horned lark sitting so resolutely on her nest, and caribou crossing the river and shaking off the spray like diamonds before the evening sun, I was satisfied only to watch. This was the great drift and pause of life. These were the arrangements that made the land ring with integrity. Somewhere downriver, I remembered, a scientist named Edward Sable had paused on a trek in 1947 to stare at a Folsom spear point, a perfectly fluted object of black chert resting on a sandstone ledge. People, moving over the land.

Six

ICE AND LIGHT

THE RADIO REPORT the evening before had been terse and ominous: gale warnings for the northern Labrador Sea. Our apprehension was over more than heavy seas, however. There were icebergs ahead—and we would be steaming into those waters in darkness, straight into a picket line of ice the size of cathedrals, borne slowly south on the Canadian Current. Implacable icebergs from the tidewater glaciers of West Greenland, the towering, gray marble walls at Savissivik and Torsukattak and Upernavik. But in those heavy seas, we knew, the ship's radar would not be able to distinguish even those fifty times larger than the ship from the wild crests of windblown waves.

The heavily laden vessel, the MV *Soodoc*,* carrying equipment and a year's supplies to an arctic mine, plowed resolutely into the dark water, taking spray over her bows. The wind vibrated cables until they moaned; it wailed through the ship's deck cranes. Waves began to wash over us amidships. The crew secured portholes and hatches on the ship's upper deck and prepared for the violent pitching and rolling to come.

We passed into Davis Strait in peace. The storm passed us to port and fell away behind, one of those strange reprieves that leave you in momentary disbelief.

In the morning I stood in the bow, watching the ship's prow split smoothly the six-foot swell of green-black water. Looming in the fog, those ice massifs that had left some of us sleepless were moving inexorably south, wreathed in gray silence, inchoate in the cold air. If we had but touched last night, the ship would have been torn by the noise of alarms and Klaxon. We would have bolted up the companionways in our storm gear for the tiny lifeboats, hobbled by half-donned clothing, brought down to the raw edge of life. Lowering away into ice and darkness in 20-foot seas, terror like a wild dog in your chest.

We passed in peace. I stared at the dark swell and thought how gently is the sparrow held that lights on a ship at sea. And then went aft, for the first meal of the day.

Montreal was far behind us. We were on the stretch, bound for the Northwest Passage; cutting the same water, seeing the same colors and animals and clear currents that Frobisher and Davis and Baffin had seen. Which is why I had asked to come. And to see the ice that had silenced them all. If I had a desire simply to be with anything in the North, it was to be with icebergs. I do not know if I had had this wish for years or if it only intensified as the prospect of the voyage loomed. But when I saw them, it was as

---

* For M[otor] V[essel] Sault ("Soo") [Sainte-Marie, Ontario] d[ominion] o[f] c[anada], a 355-foot, 7000 dead-weight-tonnage bulk cargo ship, with a complement of twenty-three.

though I had been waiting quietly for a very long time, as if for an audience with the Dalai Lama.

On the afternoon of the day we knew the storm had passed, I stood on the starboard side of the bridge at a window, with the heavy protective glass lowered. I rested my forearms on the sill, feeling the warmth of the bridge heaters around my legs and a slipstream of cool air past my face. The first icebergs we had seen, just north of the Strait of Belle Isle, listing and guttered by the ocean, seemed immensely sad, exhausted by some unknown calamity. We sailed past them. Farther north they began to seem like stragglers fallen behind an army, drifting, self-absorbed, in the water, bleak and immense. It was as if they had been borne down from a world of myth, some Götterdämmerung of noise and catastrophe. Fallen pieces of the moon.

Farther to the north they stood on their journeys with greater strength. They were monolithic; their walls, towering and abrupt, suggested Potala Palace at Lhasa in Tibet, a mountainous architecture of ascetic contemplation. We would pass between them, separated from them by no more than half a mile. I would walk from one side of the ship to the other, wondering how something so imposing in its suggestion of life could be approached so closely, and yet still seem so remote. It was like standing in a dirigible off Annapurna and Everest in the Himalayas.

The suggestion of life around them was not an illusion. Harp seals and flocks of seabirds were drawn to fish schooling in the nutrient-rich waters at their base—an upwelling driven by fresh-water runoff from the iceberg, pouring into the lighter water of the salty ocean. With my binoculars I could follow the scarves of turquoise meltwater unfurling 400 feet to the sea.

I occasionally drew back from the starboard window to make a sketch, or to bring the binoculars up to my eyes. I marveled as much at the behavior of light around the icebergs as I did at their austere, implacable progress through the water. They took their color from the sun, and from the clouds and the water. But they also took their dimensions from the light: the stronger and more direct it was, the greater the contrast upon the surface of the ice, of the ice itself with the sea. And the more finely etched were the dull surfaces of their walls. The bluer the sky, the brighter their outline against it.

I wrote words down for the tints—the grays of doves and pearls, of smoke. Isolated in my binoculars, the high rampart of a mesa-like berg seemed sheared off like a wall of damp talc. Another rounded off smoothly, like a human forehead against the sky, and was pocked and lined, the pattern of a sperm whale's lacerated tun. Floating, orographic landscapes—sections broken out of a mountain range: snow-covered ridges, cirque valleys, sharp peaks. The steep walls often fell sheer to the sea, like granite pitches, their surfaces faceted like raw jade, or coarser, like abraded obsidian.

Where the walls entered the water, the surf pounded them, creating caverns, grottoes, and ice bridges, strengthening an impression of sea cliffs. At the waterline the ice gleamed aquamarine against its own gray-white walls above. Where meltwater had filled cracks or made ponds, the pools and veins were milk-blue, or shaded to brighter marine blues, depending on the thickness of the ice. If the iceberg had recently fractured, its new face glistened greenish blue—the greens in the older, weathered faces were grayer. In twilight the ice took on the colors of the sun: rose, reddish yellows, watered purples, soft pinks. The ice both reflected the light and trapped it within its crystalline corners and edges, where it intensified.

The burden of rocks, gravel, silt, and sand that icebergs carry within them streaks their sides; as they melt, they rise higher in the water and the debris in their shoal water creates a series of waterline marks. As they fracture and tilt, the patterns of waterline marks cross at odd angles and slant skyward.

It seemed almost superfluous, but the third mate took the measure of one with his sextant: 64.7 meters high by 465.4 meters long (212.27 by 1526.88 feet). Another is 70.4 meters high by 371.0 meters long (230.97 by 1217.19 feet); but the numbers cannot encompass them. The ice reaches far below the surface of the water and stretches away in a third dimension. It is impossible to know how much of it lies beneath the water—four-fifths of its height and seven-eighths of its mass is the mariner's general rule. And the shape of each one changes as our ship passes. New valleys, slopes of wind-packed snow, ramparts and spires, and columnar bluffs come into view. Another set of measurements of the same iceberg turns out differently.

One day, low decks of cumulus clouds bearing off to the southeast open up a horizon to the west and north. In brilliant sunshine the icebergs now gleam as crisp a blinding white in the black water as storm-lit sails. After a while icebergs near the horizon break with the surface of the ocean to float low in the pale blue sky. Four or five of them, distant mirages, not seeming to take the moment seriously at all. I return, smiling, to those immediately before me, and renew my faulty sketching. I remember the church at Ranchos de Taos, New Mexico, Saint Francis of Assisi; photographers have gone there for decades, impassioned with a desire to render it in shades of black and white only. What would an Edward Weston or a Wynn Bullock or a Paul Strand have thought of these? I stare for hours from the starboard window at these creatures I have never seen before. They drift past in the spanking, beautiful weather. How utterly still, unorthodox, and wondrous they seem.

In the interior of Greenland the Wisconsin Ice Age continues, as it were, unabated. The Greenland ice cap, forming continuously from layers of compacted snow and trapped air and expanding at varying rates, is 1500 miles long, 450 miles wide, and up to 11,000 feet thick. It bears down with such force that the center of the island is warped some 1180 feet below sea level. The glacial tongues and margins of the ice cap reach the sea at several prominent points, where enormous sections of ice break off and float away in the currents. One of the most imposing of them is the 400-foot-high palisade of Humboldt Glacier, which stretches north and south for 50 miles at the edge of Kane Basin.

Most of the icebergs of the Northern Hemisphere are calved from the western glaciers of the Greenland ice cap, into Disko and Melville bays. They drift north in the West Greenland Current for a while and then come south that year or the next with the Canadian Current to the Labrador Sea. As imposing as they are, icebergs are dwarfed by ice islands, a kind of ice calved along the north coast of Greenland and the northwest coast of Ellesmere Island from ice shelves that extend offshore into embayments of the ocean. (The structure and behavior of shelf ice have been likened to those of both glacial ice and sea ice, though strictly speaking it is neither.) These ice islands, up to 300 square miles in extent but only 150 to 165 feet thick, become incorporated in the polar ice pack, where they make ideal, long-term drift bases for scientific research. They are structurally sound, and their flat tops, uniformly corrugated like a tin roof, offer a working platform close to the surface of the water. (Fletcher's Ice Island [T-3], a 50-square-mile platform spawned from the Ward Hunt Ice Shelf at Disraeli Fiord, Ellesmere Island, was used by scientific parties for twenty-five years before work there was terminated in the mid-1970s.) Ice islands normally drift for decades in the ice gyre north of Alaska before being caught, finally, in the East Greenland Current, in whose waters they eventually disintegrate and melt.

Almost as extensive as ice islands but much thicker are tabular icebergs, which break off whole from the foot of a tidewater glacier. With a volume of 40 or 50 cubic miles, they are the largest objects afloat in the Northern Hemisphere. Other sorts of freshwater arctic ice include the ice that forms on arctic rivers and on tundra lakes and ponds (which may freeze to the bottom in winter), and the lenses and wedges of ground ice within permafrost. The latter influence the formation of a distinctive geometry of frost cracks in the tundra called "patterned ground," and raise the hemispherical mounds, or frost boils, called pingos. (A well-known cluster of some 150 pingos, from 3000 to 5000 years old, rises near Toker Point, just east of the mouth of the Mackenzie River.)*

The sea ice that forms on the surface of the ocean behaves in less predictable ways than freshwater ice, depending on how it is formed and altered and on how old it is. Its physics—the distribution of forces within it, the range of its elasticity and plasticity, the structural quality of its crystal lattices—is highly complex. "Scarcely a substance on earth," writes one scientist, "is so tractable, so unexpectedly complicated, so deceptively passive."

Freshwater ice usually begins to crystallize at 39.2°F, the temperature at which fresh water is densest. Sea ice does not achieve its maximum density, or start freezing, until it is cooled to 28.6°F. In its initial stages, the crystalline structure of sea ice incorporates brine and is not solid. It will therefore bend under a load before it fractures, while newly formed freshwater ice, brittle and also more transparent, will fracture suddenly, like a window-pane. (Because of its elasticity, even sea ice four inches thick is unsafe to walk on, while freshwater ice only half as thick will support a human being.)

In the absence of any wind or strong current, sea ice first appears on the surface as an oily film of crystals. This frazil ice thickens to a kind of gray slush called grease ice, which then thickens vertically to form an elastic layer of ice crystals an inch or so thick called nilas. Young nilas bends like watered silk over a light ocean swell and is nearly transparent (i.e., dark like the water). When it is about four inches thick, nilas begins to turn gray and is called young ice, or gray ice. When gray ice finally

---

* Permafrost, a unique substance, is frozen soil, not ice. Part of the confusion over how to classify it, however, arises from the fact that it behaves somewhat like ice, extending itself through the soil by a process of crystalline growth. The complex pattern of its development accounts for the facts that it underlies ground in the Arctic that was never covered by glacial ice and that east of the Taimyr Peninsula it reaches a depth of 1900 feet.

becomes opaque it is called first-year ice. And in these later stages it thickens more slowly.

By spring, first-year ice might be four to six feet thick. If it doesn't melt completely during the summer, it becomes second-year ice in the fall, tinted blue and much harder. (Brine in the upper layers has drained out during the summer and fresh ice crystals have filled the interstices.) Second-year ice continues to thicken, until it stabilizes after a few years at about 10 to 12 feet. If it remains unmelted through a second summer, it is simply called multiyear ice, or polar pack ice, to distinguish it from first- and second-year pack ice.* A more formidable version of multiyear ice, paleocrystic ice, forms in the open polar sea and may be 50 feet thick.

Pack ice may be consolidated in great expanses of rubble called field ice, or broken up by lanes of open water (leads) to a lesser or greater degree, creating various types of close and open pack ice —for example "close pack" (seven-tenths to nine-tenths coverage of the sea).†

Winds and currents almost always affect the formation of sea ice. If a swell comes up in a sludge of grease ice, for example, the crystals congeal in large, round plates that develop upturned edges from bumping against each other—a stage called pancake ice. If nilas is broken up by the wind, the separate sheets often ride up over each other in a characteristic interlocking pattern called finger-rafting. Heavier ice may ride up cleanly over itself or create low ridges of rubble or piles of crumbled fragments as it grinds

---

* The term "pack ice" is used in a wide sense to include any accumulation of sea ice other than fast ice (ice attached to the shore), no matter what form it takes or how disposed.

† Because sea ice presents such a grave danger to ships, precisely defined terms are critical for accurate reporting. Terms that refer to the type and extent of ice coverage are standardized in the Scott Polar Institute's *Illustrated Glossary of Snow and Ice* and the Canadian Hydrological Services' *Pilot of Arctic Canada*.

against itself. Weathered by wind-driven snow, this debris forms rounded hills called hummocks. Ice of sufficient thickness, fractured by wind, tide, and currents and then driven in on itself by these same forces, may create a huge riprap of rubble, 20 to 40 feet high and extending as far below the ice, called a pressure ridge.

Wind and current affect sea ice formation to such an extent that very little smooth ice occurs anywhere in the Arctic except in bays and along shallow coastlines. In spring the ice surface develops puddles and melt holes (often at old aglus) and a complex pattern of surface drainage. Second-year ice is likely to produce needle ice at the bottom of these melt pools, sharp spikes diligently avoided by men, dogs, and bears. In the upper layer of first-year ice that has been drained of brine candle ice sometimes forms, which tinkles like a glass chandelier as it collapses before a gust of wind or at the touch of a hand.

Because sea ice responds to wind and current and because winds and currents have predominant patterns, researchers look for the same kind of sea ice to form in the same places every year. In Coronation Gulf, where winds and currents are light, the ice may be unusually smooth for many miles in every direction. In Nares Strait (Kennedy Channel, Hall Basin, and Robeson Channel) between Ellesmere Island and Greenland, multiyear ice driven down from the north piles up in ridges 80 feet high, a violently fractured landscape that extends north and west to the extremely rugged ice of the Lincoln Sea.

The variety of ice types and the many patterns of its fracture and dislocation amaze a first-time visitor. What could become as ordinary underfoot as soil or rock remains as exotic as the surface of another planet. When nilas sags beneath you, your legs have no idea what to do. If you are forced to cross a series of pressure ridges with a heavy sledge, or must fight constantly to keep a small boat from being crushed in moving pack ice, you have difficulty imagining any landscape more exhausting or humbling.

Flying over the ice is an easy way to appreciate its tectonic activity on a larger scale, to better understand it as the never-quite-settled surface of the Arctic Ocean. From above, the finger-rafting of huge, transparent sheets of nilas seems like a delicate and regular joinery of panes of glass. The rafting of sheets of young nilas creates a pattern of scattered, altostratus-like shapes. Dark ice cakes below prove to be ones covered with epontic algae and flipped over by animals, or places where walrus have hauled out, rested, and defecated. Long streaks of gray-white ice cutting across a broad, snow-covered expanse show where leads have recently frozen over. A low pressure ridge may lead to a dark hole and a patch of reddish snow, a polar bear kill. Streamers of grease ice in patches of open water line up with the wind. In winter the leads steam with frost smoke where the (relatively) warm water meets the frigid air.

A geometry of lightning-bolt-shaped leads, of long black ponds, jagged rills, and ridges of debris that meander like eskers stretches as far as light and the atmosphere let you see. In a wide lead, small floes roll slowly off the wind to the right, on a heading of 30° to it. (All windblown ice in the North behaves this way because of the coriolis effect, the tendency of a moving body on the earth's surface to drift sideways because of the earth's rotation.)

Because of the constant, accordian-like adjustment of the ice surface, there is always open water in the Arctic Ocean, even in the coldest weather. Along the coast, where a band of stable, shorefast ice forms, a predictable flaw lead often separates shore-fast ice from the moving pack, particularly when offshore winds are blowing. (This flaw zone is a regular highway for sea mammals and the most heavily hunted area of the sea ice by both bears and men.)

In addition to these flaw leads and the numerous leads that open and close regularly in the pack, there are relatively large areas of persistent open water called polynyas that stay open all winter. They are maintained by unique current and wind patterns and occur in the same places year after year. Depending on their size and location, polynyas can harbor significant concentrations of overwintering seabirds and marine mammals. (The whaler's West Water in Baffin Bay was actually the southern end of the largest polynya in the North American Arctic, the North Water.)

SHOREFAST ice, embayed ice, or sea ice that has formed in regions where there are no appreciable currents can offer a serene and dependable surface over which to travel, even at night. Pack ice, the ice beyond the flaw lead, holds a different sort of attraction because of its constant motion, varied topography, and the access it provides to certain animals. But to venture out there on foot is, to put it simply, to court death. Pack ice moves irregularly before the wind, and the change in orientation of an individual piece of ice is unpredictable. Commonly, especially on larger pieces of ice, there is no sensation at all of movement or change. A person might discover suddenly that he was far from shore, or realize he had no idea of his position. In every coastal village from Inglefield Fiord to Saint Lawrence Island there is a story of someone who got caught out there by mistake, often pursuing a polar bear, and who was never seen again.

The crushing power of moving pack ice is not a great threat to people traveling with dogs or on foot. They can usually move nimbly enough over its surface. To be at its mercy in a boat or small ship, however, is to know an exhausting, nerve-wracking vulnerability. In May 1814, with his whaling ship beset off the east coat of Greenland, William Scoresby set out on foot to reconnoiter the final mile of maneuvering that he hoped would set him free. Like many men caught in such circumstances, Scoresby was terrified. But he was mesmerized as well by the ice, by its sheer power, its daunting scale, the inexorability of its movement. The sound of its constant adjustment before the wind was like "complicated machinery, or distant thunder," he wrote. Even as he sought a way out, he marveled at the way it distracted him. He lost the sense of plight that spurred him, the pleading whining that came from his ship's pinched hull; he became a mere "careless spectator." It was as though he were walking over the back of some enormous and methodical beast.

The sea ice was a more perilous environment in the era of wood ships than it seems today from the bridge of a steel-hulled icebreaker, but no arctic sailor was or is ever at ease in it. The whalers forced their way in with poorly fitted ships and lived for months at the extreme limits of their ability to cope. To get through a stretch of ice and out to open water, or to survive in a stream of ice driven down on them in a storm, nineteenth-century sailors had to employ several operations. With a favorable wind and an ice-strengthened prow, they could "bore" their way through, following the shouted directions of a lookout in the crow's nest. But a sail ship has no reverse, no reliable "dead slow," no instant "hard-to-port" response. More often they had to take the ship in tow behind their whaleboats and row through the ice. Or "warp" it forward, winching from the windlass against anchors set in the ice ahead. Or "mill-doll," by dropping a boat with three or four men from the bowsprit, to fracture ice in advance of the prow.

In the shifting pack, even a 250-ton ship could conceivably be crushed in two or three minutes, forced up in the air with an explosion of its oak ribs and driven under with a grunt, like a grand piano caught in an industrial press. To protect it during a storm in the ice front, or at night when they could not find open water, the crews sawed temporary docks in the floes. As often as not they lost that protection and had to begin all over again the wearying task of cutting and removing blocks of ice. In heavy weather the pack moved like a jigsaw puzzle; loose ice hit them repeatedly, "hard enough to knock the ship's brains out." Officers tried to mete out a crew's strength over the course of a storm, or until they got out of the ice. But any situation could change instantly—ice at rest one minute was moving the next. Officers felt the strain of unceasing responsibility and vigilance. "During that time," wrote one captain of a harrowing seventeen hours he spent running a shore lead, "I did the heaviest smoking of my life. I smoked twenty-two cigars and numerous pipes, and I had coffee brought to me every hour. I don't know whether it was the tobacco or the coffee that brought us through, but we made it with no damage."

Damage was routine, some of it serious. "Relays of men at the pumps and others working with buckets," wrote a captain of his stove ship, "succeeded in raising seven to eight tons of water per minute, [but] the sea came in quicker than it could be thrown out." And the sea was a frigid 30°F. They fothered their broken hulls with wads of sail and filled the cracks as well as they could with cordage and oakum. They sought a desperate protection up-current of icebergs.* But the icebergs sometimes disintegrated and the ships were swamped or crushed. Once a storm passed and the menacing ice was still, they no longer had to lie in their bunks and listen to the "rending, crashing, tearing noise," the screech and detonation of a ship's timbers. But until they were clear of it, its capricious and unappeasable nature preyed on their imaginations.

If it got very cold, as often happened toward the end of the whaling season, ice might congeal around a ship, creating in only a few hours "a crystal pavement by the breath of Heaven cemeted firm." Then a man stood on the deck in such stillness, he could hear his watch ticking in his pocket. Men who had collapsed at the pumps or lost their appetites when ice peeled the copper sheathing off the ship's bottom now went out on the ice for a stroll and flew kites or tossed a ball, as though they were on a commons.

When a ship was seriously beset, the crew packed their belongings, set them on deck, and waited. The slow compression of the ship could go on for weeks before the keel finally broke or the holds flooded. When a ship was lost, however, it rarely sank right away—the men had time to step overboard and walk away, if

---

* Icebergs, because of their deep keels, move with the current, while sea ice moves before the wind. An iceberg can therefore plow a course through oncoming sea ice, providing shelter for a ship in its wake.

they were lucky, to another ship. In the fall of 1777, more than 350 such shipwrecked men, whalers and sealers, were to be found hiking over the ice off the southeast coast of Greenland. About 140, given food and clothing at native settlements, eventually reached Danish villages on the west coast. The others perished. In 1830, so many ships were destroyed in Melville Bay (the place they called "the breaking-up yard") that at one point nearly 1000 men were camped on the ice. Legally under the command of no captain, they set fire to the broken ships and milled about for weeks in drunken celebration. (Not a man was lost in this weird catastrophe.)

Five years later an isolated group of British ships, fishing too late, became for the first time irrevocably beset in Baffin Bay. The men had neither proper clothing nor food enough to see them through the winter. Most died of starvation, exposure, and despair during the four months they were carried passively south in the Canadian Current. The ships' logs are poignant. On November 11, 1835, an officer of the *Viewforth* wrote: "Weather milder. A great many fish have been playing around the ship to-day, amongst which we observed unicorns and white whales. We are now to the southward of Cape Searle, a sublime object. The moon has been in sight all day—it never sets—a thing I never saw before." On November 13 a mate aboard the *Jane* wrote: "Strong breezes with snow; heavy press, ship suffering greatly, how she can bear it God only knows. It's awful work; long dark nights, no hope for us if she goes. May God preserve our shelter."

When they reached the ice front in February, the floes opened and then closed, opened and then closed on them. Each day they built up their hope from scratch. One of the whalers sank. When the others were finally released, too few men were still alive aboard some of the ships to hoist sail. They drifted aimlessly in weather so foul that for days on end they could not take a bearing or fix their position. Some were met by outwardbound whalers; miraculously, every ship eventually reached England. The following year, a dozen vessels froze in again. Half these ships sank, and the loss of life was extensive—forty-four of fifty-eight aboard the *Dee*, forty-two of forty-nine aboard the *Advice*.

Sometimes it was over very quickly. At 3:30 A.M. on the 26th of April 1832, the whaler *Shannon* of Hull, running before a southeast gale, slammed bow first into an iceberg. The captain ran forward in the darkness and laid his hands to the wall of ice even as it continued past them, ripping open the ship's starboard side. They were awash in minutes. Sixteen men and three boys were swept away. The survivors clung to each other beneath a sail, on a part of the ship kept afloat by trapped air. They were without food or fresh water. They survived, with the death of but three more, by bleeding each other and drinking the blood from a shoe. A man who left their deck shelter to commit suicide spotted two Danish brigs on the 2nd of May. The survivors, save the captain, were all frostbitten. "The rescue," writes a historian of the arctic whale fisheries, "was one of those providential affairs of which many instances could be related."

I think of a final image of devastation: the remnant of several whaling crews found in a frozen stupor behind a sea wall of dead bodies, stacked up to protect them from the worst of the heavy seas in which their small floe rolled and pitched.

The horror and loss of life are remote from us now. Our assessment of arctic seas is today more often made from an airplane, amid the crackle of constant radio contact, or from the warm bridge of an icebreaker, guided by the lugubrious movement of a gyrocompass and the deep-space silence of satellite navigation systems. This machinery compresses time and space, and comforts us because of the authority with which it keeps danger at bay. From these quarters, its scale reduced, we appraise the landscape very differently.

Few men in northern ships today, however, are without regard for the human history that preceded their own in those waters. And no arctic ship's master, his Lloyd's of London Ice Class IA Super ship boring through four feet of sea ice at a steady five knots, sleeps free of the stories that have been passed down. They are ignored only by men for whom the recalcitrance of the land is but a distraction, a disturbance to be quelled by machinery.

The frozen ocean itself still turns in its winter sleep like a dragon.

MAX Dunbar, a pioneering arctic oceanographer, has described the Arctic Ocean with some wistfulness. Because of a paucity of seismic and magnetic research, and a lack of core samples from the seabed, the evolution of the Arctic Basin is a puzzle; and because so much of its waters are covered with ice, the Arctic Ocean remains the least understood of the world's seas. Its waters are relatively sterile when compared with those of the highly productive subarctic seas. Their lack of productivity, however, is not due to coldness or to lack of light as much as to the water's vertical stability. Without an upwelling of inorganic salts (phosphates, nitrates, and silicates) from the bottom, a rich life in the sunlit upper layers cannot be sustained. (The lack of any endemic genera, the low number of plankton species, and small plankton populations are all signs of the ocean's youth as well as its sterility, in Dunbar's view.)

Oceanographers divide the Arctic Ocean into five regions, according to the relatively few species of life to be found in each one. Farthest north is the high Arctic abyssal region, perpetually ice-covered and least known. Between there and the coasts lies a high Arctic shallow region of drifting annual ice, which enjoys periods of summer sunshine and some upwelling. Along the North American and Eurasian coasts is a brackish water region, a zone of fluctuating temperatures and salinity due to a tremendous outpouring of freshwater rivers from the northern rims of the two continents. (More meltwater flows in spring from the Lena into the Laptev Sea than from any other river in the Northern Hemisphere.)

Most of the Arctic is without tide pools and that array of life typified by the presence of sea grasses, kelp, and barnacles, because the near-shore bottom is scoured by ice every year. Some areas, however, do harbor small populations of intertidal creatures, and these constitute a fourth zone, the Boreal littoral faunal region. Soviet scientists, far and away the most experienced of arctic oceanographers, also recognize a fifth zone between brackish coastal waters and the high Arctic shallow region, which they call the low Arctic shallow region (essentially a broad shelf sea, the continental shelf north of Russia being the most extensive sea shelf in the world).

The life of the polar seas is structured around a spring bloom of epontic phytoplankton that initiates a period of active feeding by herbivorous zooplankton. Carnivorous zooplankton, various crustaceans, and a small number of fish species, principally polar and arctic cod, extend this food web, as we have seen.* The sea ice prevents 99 percent of the sun's light from reaching these active layers of the water, but it also insulates creatures in the food web from the extreme cold of winter, and it has profoundly shaped their evolution and development. The Arctic Ocean, in fact, cannot be explained ecologically without taking the sea ice into account. Because of this, many oceanographers have come to regard the Arctic Ocean as unique, a landscape that requires a special point of view.

The foundations of Western ecology were laid down by scientists working almost exclusively with temperate-zone eco-systems. The violent fluctuations characteristic of arctic eco-systems played no role in their original conceptions, and certain conditions that typify arctic ecosystems were treated as impediments rather than normal circumstances for the development of life. Snow and ice, for example, were at first regarded as temporary

---

* Arctic fish have adapted to their unusual circumstances in several striking ways. The mouth of the arctic cod opens forward and up, allowing it to feed on the underside of the ice. Because of low light conditions the eyes of arctic species are somewhat larger, and because cold water is denser than warm water, arctic species also tend to be stronger swimmers than their southern counterparts.

and relatively unimportant conditions in the environment, not as integral components of the ecosystem. Snow, however, proved to be as fundamental in shaping an animal's life in the Arctic as rainfall is in the Philippines or sunlight in the Arabian Desert. It creates the stable platform from which certain animals reach browse unreachable in the summer. It forms the barrier that, more than cold temperatures, sends seed-eating birds south in the fall. It provides cover for the ermine and other weasel-like animals that plunge into snow at the approach of a predator and burrow long distances through it without surfacing. It provides insulation for ptarmigan, which dive into it in the evening to sleep. It provides the contours that conceal predators from their prey; at the same time, it founders predators and allows longer-legged and broader-footed prey to escape. It shelters a creature like the lemming, too small to grow hair long enough for insulation and still be able to walk. It creates a greenhouse effect for some plants in the spring and protects them from drying winds in the winter. It is snow that determines that a ground-dwelling squirrel that cannot migrate must hibernate, while an arboreal squirrel, living high above the ground, can remain active all winter.

Winter, not summer, is more the season of record in the Arctic for the evolutionary biologist. A northern ecologist looking at snow sees an element as integral to the landscape as soil. It is snow that cuts some animals off from their food, makes heavy energy demands on others, and insulates a third group.

Ice, to the ecologist, is but an extreme form of snow, and it alters the landscape and affects the lives of animals in ways as profound and subtle. The quality and type of sea ice are as crucial in shaping the lives of arctic marine mammals as topographic relief and the presence of plant food are in directing the movements of land animals. Seals and walrus depend on the ice to carry them passively to new feeding grounds and to function as a platform upon which they can rest, molt their hair, and give birth to their young. Ice floes also serve as temporary islands where these animals are safe from orcas and landbound predators. As a seaward extension of the land, the ice becomes as a winter highway for migrating muskoxen, caribou, polar bears, and arctic foxes. Icebergs and large remnant pieces of pressure ridges that ground in coastal bays and continue to shift in the tides all winter, can keep enough water open to maintain a herd of walrus at a new feeding ground until spring. In November, after a river has frozen over and its channel has drained (no water flows into it after the watershed above freezes), you can sometimes drop through the ice and walk around on the empty riverbed—one of the polar bear's favorite places for a winter bivouac.

The most dramatic association between ice and arctic life, perhaps, and still largely an unexplained mystery, involves events at polynyas in winter and spring. Polynyas occur both along the coast (long, narrow shore polynyas) and at sea (more lakelike, flaw polynyas). The open water, which occurs in the same places every year, offers an overwintering refuge to some animals and a staging ground to other animals migrating north in the spring. (The consistent pattern of open water has no doubt been crucial in shaping the migratory routes of many seabirds and marine mammals.)

Polynyas are kept free of solid ice all winter by a complex interaction of forces—prevailing winds, currents, and tides, and perhaps local upwelling. They seem especially important for walrus and bearded seals as winter refuges, less so for ringed seals, narwhals, and belukhas. Some seabirds, such as the black guillemot, eiders, and oldsquaw, as well as Ross's gulls and ivory gulls, may also benefit by wintering in these places, though scientists are hard-pressed to explain how a food web can function in these dark, bitterly cold places.

Polynyas seem really to come into their own in the spring. The annual phytoplankton bloom may start in them as much as two months before it begins in adjacent, ice-covered areas, offering migrating colonial seabirds (northern fulmars, kittiwakes, dovekies, murres) a significant head start. Polynyas also seem vitally important as feeding areas for early-arriving narwhals and bowhead and belukha whales.

Areas of year-round open water in the Canadian Arctic. Adapted from Ian Stirling and Holly Cleator, Polynyas in the Canadian Arctic.

One cannot consider polynyas, of course, without recalling images of narwhals and belukhas fatally trapped in savssats; and the precipitate oscillations in normal sea-ice formation that can catch tens of thousands of early-arriving or molting seabirds by surprise. (In the spring of 1964, 100,000 king eiders—one-tenth of the regional population—were frozen-in in the Beaufort Sea.) A very real sense of loss in the face of large-scale catastrophe, however, can obscure how integral to the nature of northern ecosystems this edge between life and death is, an edge the annual formation of sea ice sharply accentuates.

One fall afternoon a friend, an ornithologist, was counting migrating birds near Demarcation Bay on the north coast of Alaska, at a place called Pingokralik. On several tundra ponds he was also following the progress of three or four families of red-throated and arctic loons. Loons are unable to walk on land, and they require plenty of open water for taking off. Early in September, when the red-throated loon chicks were barely half their parents' size, the coast was buffeted by snow squalls. Within a few days the tundra ponds were frozen over. My friend emerged from his tent one morning to find a red-throated loon and its chick paddling about energetically in an effort to maintain a small patch of open water. The other parent, which had spent the night at sea, flew by every half hour or so with food in its beak, but it could no more land than the other bird could take off.

The next day it warmed up enough so the pondbound adult could take off and the other bird could land with food for the chick. The loons—there were other families in similar straits nearby—persevered in this manner, even as the human observer was driven off to a more permanent shelter. He did not know the fate of the loon chicks (the adults may well have abandoned them). What he remembers seeing were the adults flying back and forth strongly from the sea, dark spots fading in the snow squalls. Resolute, even in the face of poor timing. Successful animals.

DURING parts of one summer I lived at the Canadian government's Polar Continental Shelf camp at Resolute, Cornwallis Island, a staging area for scientific research in the Arctic. During those weeks I was able to speak with a number of scientists—archaeologists, biologists, geologists, ornithologists; but one of my strongest memories is of an evening I spent with a retired geologist named Maurice Haycock, talking about painting. Haycock was in his eighties when I met him. He had had a long and successful career as a geologist with the Canadian government and had played the

French horn for many years in the Ottawa Symphony Orchestra. He had also traveled occasionally with the Canadian landscape painter A. Y. Jackson, both of them painting in the Northwest Territories on geological field trips.

One afternoon Haycock and I walked down to the edge of Barrow Strait together to look at a hazy apparition of distant Somerset Island, which had been lifted above the horizon in an imposing mirage. (*Puikartuq*, the Eskimo call it, "coming up for air.") We also examined a Thule campsite together. And he told me stories of his experiences in the Arctic in the 1920s, when travel was by dog sledge. He described one time in particular, of sledging across smooth coastal ice in brilliant spring weather, mile after mile. Time fell away. He experienced a detachment so peaceful, he said, that in his scientific mind he solved problem after problem. He spoke to me with the tones of someone remembering once having fallen in love. He was charming, a man nearing the end of a life of rich, authentic moments.

The evening I am thinking of, I was sitting in his room in camp. He lay on his bed with one arm across his forehead. In his other hand he held several brushes, from which he meant shortly to wash the residue of the day's efforts. He was trying to capture in words his admiration for the land. He recalled having painted once at the Grand Canyon and the trouble he had had in painting the air, the space between the south rim where he stood and the far north rim.

He was trying to speak about the difficulty of painting air. And he said he liked to paint here on Cornwallis Island, the fields of glacial till where there was hardly a plant, because he enjoyed the subtleties. "A close-toned land," he said. The brushes clicked in his hand as he rolled them against each other. He thought in silence. "The tones of the land here," he said, "are lighter than the tones of the midday sky."

As I listened, I felt the evening sun pouring through the windowpane onto the side of my head. The room was airy with sunlight, flushed, like an empty summer bedroom in one of Edward

Hopper's paintings. I could see how brightly Haycock's eyes shone as he moved through the forests of his own memory; his large, roughened hands; and the sheen on a painting he'd done that morning on a small piece of birch plywood. I was acutely aware of listening to him, though for long periods neither of us spoke. He reminisced about days painting on the tundra near Great Slave Lake with Jackson, one of Canada's radical Group of Seven, landscape painters who gained prominence for their indigenous Canadian style in the 1910s. He talked about why one went out to paint like that. It was a conversation with the land, he said.

The evening slipped quietly away from both of us. Eventually he went to wash his brushes and I went to my room and lay down to think. If I were a painter, I, too, would be taken with the fullness and subtle quality of the light here. You have the color balances from all twenty-four hours from which to choose, the sweeping lines of crisp desert vistas under huge prairie skies, and the rarefied air with which to work. Ice and water push the light up beneath cliffs and into other places where you would expect to find shadows, and back into the sky where it fills the air. At certain hours the land has the resolution of a polished diamond.

This obvious and disarming beauty, oddly, is absent from nineteenth-century European landscape paintings of the region. But the subject of virtually all of that work was British arctic exploration, and the theme was remarkably consistent—a nation blessed by God, at war with the elements in a treacherous landscape. The Arctic they painted was a place beyond the pale of civilization, a beast that preyed on virtue and enterprise. Among the most famous of these paintings are Caspar David Friedrich's *The Polar Sea* (1824), in which a ship of exploration (the *Hope*, in an early sketch) lies crushed amid huge, rafted floes; William Bradford's *An Arctic Summer, Boring through the Pack Ice in Melville Bay* (1871), in which a distant three-masted ship, although itself bathed in light, is headed for a foreground of ice overshadowed by cloud and upon which rests a cruciform fragment from another vessel's mast; and Edwin Landseer's *Man Proposes, God Disposes*, in which two imposing polar bears are tearing apart the wreckage of yet another ship crushed in the ice.

The luminist tradition in nineteenth-century American landscape painting found itself only on the fringes of the Arctic, but it was a movement far better suited to an evocation of the North than the European tradition. Luminist painters sought out a soothing and restful light, which they found along the New England coast at places like Provincetown, Massachusetts. The art critic John Russell, alluding to the nation's mood after the Civil War, has called it "a healing light." I think of these New England paintings because the light in them, the plein-air essence of it, is a familiar light in the Arctic. As I traveled to and from Resolute, especially in the evening hours around midnight, I beheld scenes that reminded me forcefully of the work of luminists like Fitz Hugh Lane. At Cape Vera, Devon Island, one evening, the water in Jones Sound was so black and matte-finished it looked like scorched earth, and the icebergs floating in it were so brilliant my eye could not rest on their surfaces. Another time, off the west coast of Ellef Ringnes Island, the air, not the sun, seemed to be the source of a flat, breathy light, within which I saw only long, restful lines: a bare strand meeting the dark water, and the water the vacant blue of the sky. And yet again on Banks Island, at two in the morning, I saw a herd of muskoxen moving across a shallow slope of green grass in strong light, through air as bright as if it had just been washed in a summer rain, with brilliant, individual pinpoints of purple lousewort and white avens in the foreground. As in the New England paintings, it was as though "all that one beheld was full of blessing."

The evening I spoke with Haycock, I came across, in my notes about light, the words of a prisoner remembering life in solitary confinement. He wrote that the only light he experienced was "the vivid burst of brilliance" that came when he shut his eyes tight. That light, which came to him in a darkness that "was like being in ink," was "like fireworks." He wrote, "My eyes *hungered* for light, for color. . . ." You cannot look at Western painting, let alone the work of the luminists, without sensing that hunger. Western civilization, I think, longs for light as it longs for blessing, or for peace or God.

The night I spoke with Haycock, in a building on Cornwallis Island in which no one but scientists slept (a scientific background was Haycock's entrée), I felt because of his artistic passion the great range of human inquiry. We desire not merely to know the sorts of things that are revealed in scientific papers but to know what is beautiful and edifying in a faraway place. Considering the tradition of distant travelers, the range of their interests and the range of their countrymen's desire to know, the government camp on Cornwallis Island seemed an impoverished outpost. There were no provisions there for painters, for musicians, for novelists. And there were no historians there. If the quest for knowledge in any remote place is meant in an egalitarian sense to be useful to all, then this is a peculiar situation. Yet it is no different from what one would find in a hundred other such remote places around the world. Whenever we seek to take swift and efficient possession of places completely new to us, places we neither own nor understand, our first and often only assessment is a scientific one. And so our evaluations remain unfinished.

Whatever evaluation we finally make of a stretch of land, however, no matter how profound or accurate, we will find it inadequate. The land retains an identity of its own, still deeper and more subtle than we can know. Our obligation toward it then becomes simple: to approach with an uncalculating mind, with an attitude of regard. To try to sense the range and variety of its expression—its weather and colors and animals. To intend from the beginning to preserve some of the mystery within it as a kind of wisdom to be experienced, not questioned. And to be alert for its openings, for that moment when something sacred reveals itself within the mundane, and you know the land knows you are there.

AT first it seems that, except for a brief few weeks in autumn, the Arctic is without color. Its land colors are the colors of deserts, the ochers and siennas of stratified soils, the gray-greens of sparse plant life on bare soil. On closer inspection, however, the monotonic rock of the polar desert is seen to harbor the myriad greens, reds, yellows, and oranges of lichens. The whites of tundra swans and of sunlit ice in black water are pure and elegant. Occasionally there is brilliant coloring—as with wildflowers in the summer, or a hillside of willow and bearberry in the fall; or a slick of vegetable oils shining with the iridescent colors of petroleum on a tundra puddle; or the bright face of a king eider. But the bright colors are more often only points in a season, not brushstrokes; and they are absorbed in the paler casts of the landscape.

Arresting color in the Arctic is found more often in the sky, with its vivid twilights and the aurora borealis. (The predominant colors of the aurora are a pale green and a soft rose. I turned over a weathered caribou antler once on the tundra and found these same two colors staining its white surface. Such correspondence, like that between a surfacing guillemot and an Eskimo man rolling upright in his kayak, hold a landscape together.)

Arctic skies retain the colors of dawn and dusk for hours in winter. On days when the southern sky is barely lit for a while around noon, layers of deep violet, of bruised purples and dense blues, may stretch across 80° of the horizon, above a familiar lavender and the thinnest line of yellow gold. The first sunrise/sunset of spring may glow "carmine and lake [red], fading off into crimsons, yellows, and saffrons," as a British naval surgeon wrote in his winter journal. In the spring and fall, when sunrises and sunsets are more widely separated, vivid reds, oranges, and yellows shine through washes of rose and salmon, of pale cyan, apricot and indigo, as they do in other latitudes. In summer, the skies have a nacreous quality, like the inside of an abalone shell. The colors of summer skies are pastel; the temperature of the light, however, varies enough so that around midnight yellows in the landscape fade noticeably and blues deepen.

The striking phenomena in the arctic sky for a newcomer are the unsuspected variety of solar and lunar rings, halos, and coronas;

the aurora borealis itself; and the mirages that occur at sea, including fata morganas. These events are especially apparent in the Far North for several reasons. The kinds of ice crystals that cause solar and lunar refraction are often present in the arctic atmosphere. The air itself is clear. Slight inversions in the lower atmosphere and sharp temperature differentials at the surface of the ocean in summer, which cause mirages, are common. And the arctic region lies directly underneath the part of the earth's atmosphere that makes the auroral display, or northern lights, visible.

When he was in winter quarters on the coast of Melville Island in 1819–20, William Parry drew a picture of the sun's halos, arcs, and parahelia, or sun dogs, that is now famous. He captured in that single drawing many of the effects that are regularly seen in the Arctic either alone or in some combination. The sun, at the time, was about 22° above the southeastern horizon. It was surrounded by a halo that measured 44° across the horizon and by a second halo 92° across the horizon, part of which was cut off below by the line of the earth. (These are called, after their degree of radius, the 22° and 46° solar halos.) Both these halos were subtended by other arcs, while yet another arc cut across the sun and swept away east and west, parallel to the horizon (the parahelic arc). Where the parahelic arc crossed the 22° halo, two brilliant sun dogs appeared. And below the sun, just at the horizon, gleamed a third sun dog (actually a subsun).

This picture can be readily explained by physicists in terms of ray mechanics, a precise bending of sunlight through certain types of ice crystals aligned in a specific way. In fact, a physicist named Robert Greenler reproduced the elements of Parry's drawing almost perfectly in a computer illustration generated by the formulae involved—a tribute to the accuracy and completeness of Parry's work.

Francis M'Clintock, another British explorer, was presiding at a burial through the sea ice in Baffin Bay in 1857 when he took

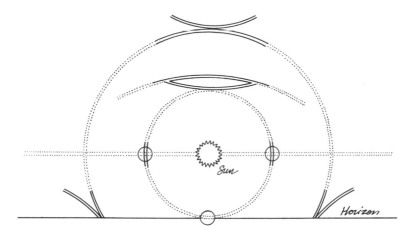

William Parry's drawing of solar arcs and halos.

notice of a stark December moon. A "complete halo encircl[ed] the moon," wrote M'Clintock, "through which passed a horizontal band of pale light that encompassed the heavens; above the moon appeared the segments of two other halos, and there were also mock moons or paraselenae to the number of six. The misty atmosphere lent a very ghastly hue to this singular display, which lasted rather more than an hour."

The physics involved in the refraction and reflection of sunlight by ice crystals and water droplets, and its diffraction by airborne particles, is dauntingly complex. The arcs and halos produced are sometimes very faint; they also occur in unexpected combinations. Seeing them, however, is largely a matter of training yourself to look. On a single spring day over Lancaster Sound I saw a soft, opaque white pillar or feather (the shape was like a passerine bird's tail feather) standing between the sun and the southeastern horizon (a sun pillar); and that evening, a few minutes after midnight, two long, rainbow-hued shields standing on the horizon on opposite sides of the sun, an unusual pair of sun dogs.*

THE aurora borealis, pale gossamer curtains of light that seem to undulate across arctic skies, are transfixing in part because of their diffidence. "It is impossible to witness such a beautiful phenomenon without a sense of awe," wrote Robert Scott, the British Antarctic explorer, "and yet this sentiment is not inspired by its brilliancy but rather by its delicacy in light and colour, its transparency, and above all by its tremulous evanescence of form. There is no glittering splendour to dazzle the eye, as has been too often described; rather the appeal is to the imagination by the suggestion of something wholly spiritual. . . ."

It is unusual in the literature of exploration to find a strictly consistent reaction, but virtually everyone who wrote down his thoughts about the aurora described, first, the inadequacy of his language and, second, a pervasive and stilling spiritual presence. Among Eskimos the descriptions are often of events that precede or follow life on earth, of the play of unborn children, or of torches held by the dead to help the living hunt in winter. In more southerly latitudes of the Northern Hemisphere, where the aurora is occasionally visible, its connotations are much different, largely because its predominant color when it becomes visible that far south is a deep red. The apparition suggested conflagration and holocaust to Europeans in the Middle Ages. Vikings thought it a reflection in the sky of Vulcan's forge. Miners in Alaska at the

---

* Once I developed the habit of looking into the "empty" part of the arctic sky opposite the sun, and at sections of the sky that spanned more than 60°, I began to notice much more in temperate-zone skies—the mother-of-pearl iridescence of the sun's or moon's corona in clouds, for example, or noctilucent clouds in the stratosphere late in the evening. The most complex and spectacular display of solar arcs and halos I ever saw was in the winter sky over Los Angeles. At first, out of the corner of my eye, I thought they were only wind-distorted jet contrails. I almost didn't look up.

turn of the century, of a more scientific and prosaic bent, thought the aurora was a gaseous form of lightning or the glow from radium mines.

The first time I recognized the northern lights was on a flight from Seattle to Anchorage, when I saw them above the Wrangell Mountains. It was a clear night, and at first I thought it was only a long, moonlit orographic cloud, the kind one often sees isolated over a mountain. Then I saw it move. Completely absorbed, I watched the long banner of pale light, unfurling in lateral movements over the snow-white mountains until the plane turned away. The motions were like a t'ai chi exercise: graceful, inward-turning, and protracted.

The bottom of an auroral display rarely comes as close as 100 miles above the earth. To the human eye, however, the thin wall of light sometimes appears actually to touch the earth because of a problem of depth perception with objects of unknown size in space. Accurate descriptions are further complicated by its overwhelming size, and its movement. The light wall is often hundreds of miles long and 150 miles or more high; as the intensity of auroral activity increases, the "curtain" of light begins to undulate in a horizontal direction, folding back on itself in huge S-curves and then unfurling again.

There are additional problems with perspective and scale. To someone underneath the display (the top of the wall is tipped toward the south), the aurora may appear like a convergence of rays toward an apex above. Seen edge-on (from directly beneath the bottom edge), the display may seem like luminous smoke rising from the earth. From a distance it may look like a weightless curtain of silk, hanging straight down and rippling in the night air.

The aurora occurs in a thin corridor called the auroral oval centered on the North Magnetic Pole. The display is created by an electric discharge in the earth's ionosphere and is apparent to us because some of the energy released is visible light. The most common tinting, of pale, whitish green and pinkish rose, is light emitted from oxygen atoms. During intense periods of auroral activity, nitrogen molecules release a crimson light, usually apparent only at the bottom edge of the auroral curtain.

Imagine that your view is from the sun and that you are facing the earth. To your far left on the earth's surface are the penumbral shadows of dawn. Before you is the bright light of noon. To your far right the border between evening and night. Streaming outward from the sun is a gas of ionized, or charged, particles, mostly helium and hydrogen nuclei, called the solar wind. These particles pass around the earth as though it were a rock in a stream of water. In doing so they flatten the planet's magnetic field (the magnetosphere) on the near side (day) and elongate it on the far side (night). As it flows past the earth, the solar wind generates an electric current from left to right. The path of least resistance for the solar particles that carry this current is along force lines in the earth's magnetic field that curve down to the earth's surface in the polar regions (like the embrasure of an apple, where the stem is). Particles pouring into the polar regions from a positive terminal on the left create the aurora. As they flow up and out to a negative terminal on the right, they constitute a separate invisible phenomenon, the polar wind.

As the stream of particles flows earthward down the funnel-shaped surface of the magnetosphere at the Pole, it excites electrons in oxygen atoms and nitrogen molecules which, as they settle back into a stable state, emit energy—X rays, infrared and ultraviolet light, radio waves, and visible light.

The still wall of light we perceive curved along an east-west arc is the calmest sort of auroral display. The more energetic the sun's streaming particles, the deeper they penetrate into the earth's ionosphere and the taller the wall of light becomes. Varying intensities in the electric field produced by the solar wind, and in the solar wind's own magnetic field, cause the wall to develop a series of fine corrugations and folds perpendicular to its east-west extension, to surge in several directions, and to break up into patches. The changes in the electric and magnetic fields that produce, respectively, the changes in color and motion are caused by magnetic storms on the sun. Major magnetic storms occur in an eleven-year cycle, in association with solar flares in the vicinity of sunspots and in solar features called coronal holes. Magnetic sub-storms, far more common, create the sequence of auroral events that arctic viewers think of as "typical" for an arctic winter evening. First, a sudden brightening resolves itself into a transparent auroral curtain. Its fine corruscations (rays) become more prominent. There are surges of movement east and west across the curtain, which starts to develop deep folds. The entire display may then move steadily north. Toward dawn it breaks up into isolated luminous patches, like clouds.

The power produced in this generator is astonishing—1 trillion watts with a current of 1 million amperes. The most violent solar storms affect magnetic compasses, wreak havoc with radio communications and certain navigational systems, and create induced electric currents in long conductors like the trans-Alaska pipeline.

Many people claim the aurora makes a sound, a muffled swish or "a whistling and crackling noise, like the waving of a large flag in a fresh gale of wind," as the explorer Samuel Hearne wrote. And some Eskimos say "the lights" will respond to a gentle whistling and come nearer. They easily evoke feelings of awe and tenderness; the most remarkable effect they seem to have, however, is to draw a viewer emotionally up and out of himself, because they throw the sky into a third dimension, on such a vast scale, in such a beautiful way, that they make the emotion of self-pity impossible.

I remember flying from Prudhoe Bay to Fairbanks one winter night. The sky was clear and the aurora borealis was very strong. With moonlight from the south the snow-covered landscape below was bright, its relief evident in ground shadows. Even the faint line separating the snow-covered tundra from the snow-covered ice was apparent. The auroral curtain stretched out to the west from my view, toward the village of Wainright and the Chukchi Sea. It was in its early, quiescent form of diaphanous rays, a long, pale ghost fire. I could see the edge of the Brooks Range and the plain of the North Slope below. I recalled days of camping in the mountains, of traveling on the tundra, and the times I'd camped on the arctic coast west of Prudhoe. I could see these places clearly, but it was the aurora, towering over the earth, that resolved what could have been only a map into a real landscape, making the memories seem immediate and tangible.

No one knows whether the first Europeans found their way to Iceland, and thence to Greenland and North America, by accident or by design. A reasonable thought is that Iceland occasionally appeared to people in the Faroe Islands as a great looming mirage, like the one of Somerset Island I saw that day. Such mirages often occur whenever a mass of warm air lies over a body of cold water. Light rays that under other conditions might travel straight off into space are bent, or refracted, back earthward in a series of small steps as they pass through layers of air at different temperatures.

Mirages are usually divided into two categories: in superior mirages, like the one of Somerset, the image the eye sees of an object is a false image above the actual object; in an inferior mirage, the false image occurs below the object. Superior mirages are commonly seen at sea in the Arctic in summer, especially late in the afternoon of a clear day. Distant islands, ships, coastlines, and icebergs lying beyond the real horizon all appear to be closer than they are, the sea itself appears slightly concave, and the horizon seems unusually far off.

Superior images are created when light waves pass from denser (or cooler) air in the lower atmosphere into air that is less dense (or warmer). Evenly spaced layers of successively warmer air (i.e., layers of air arranged in a perfect temperature gradient) work like a series of eyeglass lenses, each of which is successively less corrective. A ray of light passing through them all is bent back earthward in a smooth arc. The viewer sees a single clear image of the real object.

If the lenses are arranged, however, so that a more corrective lens comes between two less corrective lenses, the ray of light is turned back on itself. If it is turned back sufficiently (e.g., because of a strong temperature inversion in the lower atmosphere), a viewer will see not only the primary image but a second, inverted image on top of it. Another series of corrective lenses "out of sequence" (i.e., a second temperature inversion in the lower atmosphere) will create a third image, this one right-side-up on top of the second image. With other changes in the order of the lenses, the primary image itself will disappear entirely, leaving an empty space between the horizon and the second, inverted image.

The degree of "stooping" (the vertical compression common with superior mirages), as well as the number of images that appear, and any apparent magnification of the image, depend on the rate of change of air temperature vertically and the presence of reversals in that rate of change. Mirages, of course, are always imprecise. The distortions come about because of shimmering (due to slight turbulence in the air) and because the entire atmospheric lens itself is astigmatic—it curves more strongly in one direction (vertically) than the other (horizontally). All mirages, therefore, are vertically fuzzy. It is this astigmatic quality of the atmosphere, in combination with complex atmospheric inversions above uniformly bright objects like the sea ice, that gives rise to the most impressive of arctic mirages, the fata morgana. These extensive "mountain ranges" or "urban skylines" seem utterly real to the soberest viewer because of the combined effect of several optical phenomena.

Under mirage conditions, sunlight reflecting off the sea ice, through layers of successively warmer air, in which there is a sequence of slight temperature inversions, creates the appearance of a high grayish rampart in the distance. The wall appears in outline and detail exactly like a distant palisade seen through the earth's blue haze because the astigmatic atmospheric lens has broken the white ice up into areas of light and shadow, and vertical blurring has eliminated any recognizable features. If the layers of air are then slightly tipped by a breeze and return to the horizontal in a regular rhythmic pattern (which occurs because of gravity), the alternation will produce permanent peaks and spires on an already steady image and the illusion is complete. The upper edge of the mirage appears serrated, like the arête of a mountain range; the gray walls suggest snow-covered slopes, even down to dark ridge lines where wind has apparently blown the snow away; and the clefts of steep montane valleys are apparent.

Mirages were a source of delight and amusement to many arctic travelers. They brought lighthearted feelings and a sense of mock astonishment to the serious, sometimes tedious business of making coastal surveys and plotting a course. Fata morganas stand somewhat outside this tradition of innocent whimsy. Seasoned explorers, vehemently insisting on what they had seen, set down mountains and islands on their charts where there was nothing but empty sky. So convincing were these apparitions that the skepticism of other explorers (or even a member of the same expedition) was met with contempt. Expeditions sent out later to verify these new lands sometimes saw the same fata morgana, further confusing the issue. Only by prolonging their arduous journeys, thereby observing a constant receding of the image, did they prove that the land was not there at all.

So it was for the Macmillan Expedition (1913), sent to confirm the existence of a "Crocker Land," reported by Robert Peary northwest of Cape Thomas Hubbard, northern Axel Heiberg Island. The "Barnard Mountains," reported by John Ross in 1818 to extend from Devon Island to Ellesmere Island across Jones Sound, were found not to exist by Edward Inglefield in 1852. American explorer Charles Francis Hall's "President's Land" proved an ephemera. The "King Oscar Land" and "Petermann Land" described by an Austrian army officer from Cape Fligeli, Franz Josef Land, in 1884 were never seen again. Vilhjalmur Stefansson set off twice in search of "Keenan Land" in the Beaufort Sea.

Some arctic experts conjecture, especially in Stefansson's case, that these fata morganas were actually tabular bergs or ice islands. It may, indeed, have been a tabular berg hundreds of square miles in extent that a Cossack explorer named Alexei Markoff found far north of the Yana River delta in 1715. The "prodigious mountains" of ice that blocked his path were never reported again.

THE monotonic surfaces of the Arctic create frequent problems with scale and depth perception, especially on overcast days. Arctic hare and willow ptarmigan sometimes disappear against the snow when they are only two or three yards away. Even when a contrasting animal like a caribou or a brown bear is visible on snow or ice, it is sometimes hard to determine whether it is a large animal at a distance or a small animal at close range. In *My Life with the Eskimo* Stefansson recalls spending an hour stalking a tundra grizzly that turned out to be a marmot. A Swedish explorer had all but completed a written description in his notebook of a craggy headland with two unusually symmetrical valley glaciers, the whole of it a part of a large island, when he discovered what he was looking at was a walrus. Johann Miertsching, traveling with M'Clure aboard the *Investigator*, wrote of a polar bear that "rose in the air and flew off" as the hunting party approached. A snowy owl. "These comical deceptions," wrote Miertsching, "are a frequent occurrence."

The white-out is another familiar deceptive phenomenon. It commonly occurs under an overcast sky or in a fog bank, where light traveling in one direction at a certain angle has the same flux, or strength, as light traveling at any angle in any other direction. There are no shadows. Space has no depth. There is no horizon. On foot you stumble about in missed-stair-step fashion. On a fast-moving snow machine your heart nearly stops when the bottom of the world disappears.

William Scoresby, in his *Account of the Arctic Regions* (1820), offered an original explanation for mistakes in depth perception that are frequently made along certain arctic coasts. The coasts he had in mind are characterized by an extreme degree of contrast between their barren rock walls and expanses of snow and ice. With no middle tones to work with, the eye has trouble resolving these two-dimensional vistas into three dimensions. The human eye also commonly uses the relative density of blue light scattered in the air to judge distance (this is the light that softens the edge of a far mountain); but the clear arctic atmosphere scatters very little light. Faced with these high-contrast, black-and-white coasts, having no knowledge of their real height, and staring at them through an exceedingly clear atmosphere, early mariners had no idea whether they were 5 or 25 miles offshore. Mogens Heinson, sent out to search for lost colonies in Greenland by Frederick II of Denmark in the sixteenth century, battled ice and snow squalls across the North Atlantic for weeks before he raised Greenland's southeast coast. With a fresh gale blowing favorably and clear skies, he laid a course for those towering cliffs. After several hours he appeared to be no closer to the coast than when he began. The effect was so convincing that he succumbed to the belief that his ship was being held motionless over an under-sea lodestone. Frightened, he put about until the coast of Greenland was far behind, and then set course for Denmark.

It is my habit when I travel to note resemblances, particularly of form and color. For example, that between the bones of a lemming and a strand of staghorn lichen next to it on the tundra. Or the sound of a native drum made from walrus intestine and its uncanny resemblance to the underwater voice of the walrus. Or between an object I have never seen before and objects I am familiar with—the head of an arctic hare's rib and the rainspout gorgons of cathedrals. Scoresby's observation is memorable; a pure contrast of black and white draws much in the Arctic together. Sunlit icebergs on a matte-dark sea are a very common example. But I also remembered this point when looking up to see arctic hares feeding on a shadowed hillside. Or any of the white summer birds against dark hills or soil—ivory gulls and tundra swans. Or the other way around—black guillemots flying over the white ice. Or any of the arctic birds in which the black-and-white pattern is so apparent—snowy owl, snow bunting, dovekie, common loon, snow goose. The black bowhead with its white chin patches. Walrus on an ice floe. Leads in the spring ice.

The startling contrast in these images became a reminder for me of the tendency to register only half of what is there in a harsh land, to ignore the other part, which is either difficult to reach or unsettling to think about. The dim-lit ocean beneath the ice, so difficult of access, remains unknown, as do the winter lives of many of the animals and plants. The ice life of the ribbon seal is known, but not its pelagic life. The beautiful throat-singing of the Eskimo, *katajak*, is heard by the winter visitor but not the shouts of a shaman bound by his helpers with walrus-hide cord and "traveling" in a trance. Caribou moving through the Ogilvie Mountains like wood smoke in a snowstorm, that image, but not the caribou cow killed by ravens in her birthing.

I would remember a flock of jet-black guillemots, streaking low over the white ice.

In the middle of summer, lying on my back on the warm tundra, I would think about the winter, because the summer by itself was so peaceful and I was trying to understand how the *whole* landscape fit together. Winter, with its iron indifference, its terrible weight, explained the ecstasy of summer. The effects of winter were disquieting to contemplate. Not the cold, though that could make you whimper with pain; it could, they would say, make rocks give up and shatter. Not the cold but the oppression. The darkness that came down. The winter wind that picked up a boat in a village and pitchpoled it across the frozen beach, as if darkly mad. The oral literature of the Eskimo is full of nightmare images from the winter months, images of grotesque death, of savage beasts, of mutilation and pain. In the feeble light between the drawn-in houses of a winter village, you can hear the breathing of something with ice for a heart.

I remember a January in Fairbanks when the temperature

stayed around —45°F for a week. Any bit of moisture in the air turned to crystals, creating an ice fog. It is haunting and beautiful to see the exhalations of a herd of caribou hanging over them like a cloud in that cold, or breath trailing behind a gliding snowy owl. But in Fairbanks, where the fog from furnaces and cars and wood fires was suspended just above the streets, it was oppressive. It blurred the edges of buildings and muffled the sound of the already obscure passing car. Snow as hard as concrete took the curbs away from the streets. In the witless gray light, huge ravens walked the alleys behind stores, tearing at bits of garbage. They hunkered on the tops of telephone poles in the white vapor, staring down, cawing that ear-splitting caw. I never felt anything so prehistoric.

Winter darkness shuts off the far view. The cold drives you deep into your clothing, muscles you back into your home. Even the mind retreats into itself.

In winter I try to remember the spring: light so brilliant the eyelid by itself is no protection. You sleep with a strip of felt tied over your eyes. (I would think of Winifred Petchey Marsh, wearing snow goggles with thin slits while she painted on the tundra at Eskimo Point, because sunglasses distorted the colors.) Of air so clear, a vista so open, you thought you would be able to see Iowa from the banks of the Colville, with just a little elevation. But in winter I would also dwell on darkness. A kind of darkness, for example, that afflicts the Kaminuriak caribou: excess killing at the hands of Eskimos, in modern times. Everyone is afraid to say something about it, for fear of being called a racist. It is easier to let the animals go than to confront that tenebrous region in ourselves. The darkness of politics, in the long hours, runs into the darkness of the land. Into anger.

I would think of the Eskimo. The darker side of the human spirit is not refined away by civilization. It is not something we are done with. Eskimo people, in my experience, have, still, a sober knowledge of their capacity for violence, but are reluctant to speak of it to whites because they have been taught that these are the emotions, the impulses, of primitives. We confuse the primitive with the inability to understand how a light bulb works. We confuse the primitive with being deranged. What is truly primitive in us and them, savage hungers, ethical dereliction, we try to pass over; or we leave them, alone, to be changed. They can humiliate you with a look that says they know better.

In the modern ironies of a remote village—satellite televising of game shows, a small boy wearing a Harvard sweatshirt, pasta for dinner with cloth napkins, after a sermon in the Baptist church about the scourge of Communism—even here, especially here, it is possible to catch a glimpse, usually in the preparation for a hunt, of the former power, the superhuman strength and unflinching intensity, of the *angakoq*. He is an intermediary with darkness. He has *qaumaneq*, the shaman light, the luminous fire, the inexplicable searchlight that enables him to see in the dark, literally and metaphorically. He reaches for the throat of darkness; that is the primitive, as primitive as an explosion of blood. Out hunting, in the welter of gore, of impetuous shooting, that heady mixture of joy and violence, sometimes it is possible for an outsider to feel the edge of the primitive. Unbridled, it is frightening. It also defeats starvation. And in its enthusiasm for the concrete events of life, it can defeat what weighs against the heart and soul.

Winter darkness brings on the extreme winter depression the Polar Eskimo call *perlerorneq*. According to the anthropologist Jean Malaurie, the word means to feel "the weight of life." To look ahead to all that must be accomplished and to retreat to the present feeling defeated, weary before starting, a core of anger, a miserable sadness. It is to be "sick of life" a man named Imina told Malaurie. The victim tears fitfully at his clothing. A woman begins aimlessly slashing at things in the iglu with her knife. A person runs half naked into the bitter freezing night, screaming out at the village, eating the shit of the dogs. Eventually the person is calmed by others in the family, with great compassion, and helped to sleep. *Perlerorneq*. Winter.

I would turn over a tiny Dorset mask, the anguished face, in my mind. I recall a day of errors, hunting seals in the ice of the Beaufort Sea. I felt whatever trouble we had had that day was due to my own failures of attitude, though this was self-indulgent thinking. I was skinning a bearded seal on a small ice cake with another man, in silence. The ocean—still as a pane of glass. One call only, from a loon. I thought how the ice under my feet *could suddenly melt*. I was standing on water over the water. My heart went into my neck. Later we ate. I ate the meat of the seal.

No summer is long enough to take away the winter. The winter always comes. You try to get a feeling for the proportions of a full life, one that confronts everything. An animal dies. You face two central, philosophical questions: What is death, and what is the nature of an animal? You fall asleep on the summer tundra in the streaming light. You awake to the sound of birds—plovers and Lapland longspurs. Inches from your eye, an intense cluster of Parisian blue flowers. A few inches farther a poppy nods under the weight of a bumblebee. Above, cumulus clouds as voluptuous as summer fruits. You roll over and embrace the earth.

A black guillemot flies over the white ice, and then disappears against the dark water.

DURING the sea-lift passage of the *Soodoc* north through Davis Strait, en route to Little Cornwallis Island, I got in the habit of spending afternoons in the cab of a large front-loader that was chained down on the deck alongside other pieces of heavy machinery. I could sit there out of the wind and occasional rain, looking out through its spacious windows at the sea and ice. Sometimes I would read in the *Pilot of Arctic Canada*. Or I would read arctic history with a map spread out in my lap.

The days among the icebergs passed slowly. I sat in my makeshift catbird seat on the deck, or stood watching in the bows, or up on the bridge with my binoculars and sketchbook.

The icebergs were like pieces of Montana floating past. A different geography, I thought, from the one I grew up knowing.

Icebergs create an unfamiliar sense of space because the horizon retreats from them and the sky rises without any lines of compression behind them. It is this perspective that frightened pioneer families on the treeless North American prairies. Too much space, anchored only now and then by a stretch of bur oak savanna. Landscape painting of the T'ang and Sung dynasties (seventh to twelfth centuries) used this arrangement of space to create the sense of a large presence beyond. Indeed, the subject of such paintings was often their apparent emptiness.

American landscape painting in the nineteenth century, to return to an earlier thought, reveals a struggle with light and space that eventually set it apart from a contemporary European tradition of pastoral landscapes framed by trees, the world viewed from a carriage window. American painters meant to locate an actual spiritual presence in the North American landscape. Their paintings, according to art historians of the period, were the inspirations of men and women who "saw the face of God" in the prairies and mountains and along the river bottoms. One of the clearest expressions of this recasting of an understanding of what a landscape is were the almost austere compositions of the luminists. The atmosphere of these paintings is silent and contemplative. They suggest a private rather than a public encounter with the land. Several critics, among them Barbara Novak in her study of this period in American art, *Nature and Culture*, have described as well a peculiar "loss of ego" in the paintings. The artist disappears. The authority of the work lies, instead, with the land. And the light in them is like a creature, a living, integral part of the scene. The landscape is numinous, imposing, real. It ceases to be, as it was in Europe, merely symbolic.

At the height of his critical and popular acclaim in 1859, Frederic Edwin Church, one of the most prominent of the luminists, set sail for waters off the Newfoundland coast. He wanted to sketch the icebergs there. They seemed to him the very embodiment of light in nature. Following a three-week cruise, he returned to his studio in New York to execute a large painting.

The small field sketches he made—some are no larger than the palm of your hand—have a wonderful, working intimacy about them. He captures both the monolithic inscrutability of icebergs and the weathered, beaten look they have by the time they arrive that far south in the Labrador Sea. Looking closely at one drawing, made on July 1, I noticed that Church had penciled underneath it the words "strange supernatural."

The oil painting he produced from these sketches came to be called *The Icebergs*. It is so imposing—6 feet by 10 feet wide— a viewer feels he can almost step into it, which was Church's intent. In the foreground is a shelf of ice, part of an iceberg that fills most of the painting and which rises abruptly in the left foreground. On the right, the flooded ice shelf becomes part of a wave-carved grotto. In the central middle ground is a becalmed embayment, opening onto darker ocean waters to the left, which continue to a stormy horizon and other, distant icebergs. Dominating the background on the far side of the embayment is a high wall of ice and snow that carries all the way to the right of the painting. In the ocean air above is a rolling mist. The shading and forms of the icebergs are expertly limned—Church was an avid naturalist, and conscientious about such accuracy—and the colors, though slightly embellished, are true.

There are two oddities about this now very famous American landscape painting. When it was undraped at Gaupil's Gallery in New York on April 24, 1861, the reaction was more reserved than the lionized Church had anticipated. But *The Icebergs* differed from the rest of Church's work in one, crucial aspect: there was no trace of man in it. Convinced that he had perhaps made a mistake, Church took the work back to his studio and inserted in the foreground a bit of flotsam from a shipwreck, a portion of the main-topmast with the crow's nest. The painting was then exhibited in Boston, where it was no better received than it had been in New York. Only when it arrived in London did critics and audiences marvel. "A most weird and beautiful picture," wrote a reviewer in the *Manchester Guardian*. England, with its longer history of arctic exploration and whaling and but a few years removed from the tragedy of Sir John Franklin, was certainly more appreciative, at least, of its subject matter.

The second oddity is that Church's painting "disappeared" for 116 years. It was purchased in 1863 by a Sir Edward Watkin, after the London showing, to hang at his estate outside Manchester, called Rose Hill. It then passed by inheritance through Watkin's son to a purchaser of the estate; and then, by donation, to Saint Wilfred's Church nearby (which returned it to Rose Hill with regrets about its size). By 1979 Rose Hill had become the Rose Hill Remand Home for Boys, and *The Icebergs*, hanging without a frame in a stairwell, had been signed by one of the boys. Unaware of its value and seeking funds for the reform school's operation, the owners offered it for sale. The painting was brought back to New York and sold at auction on October 25, 1979, for $2.5 million, the highest price paid to that time for a painting in America. It now hangs in the Dallas Museum of Fine Arts, in Texas.

CHURCH's decision to add the broken mast to *The Icebergs* speaks, certainly, to his commercial instincts, but the addition, I think, is more complex than this; and such a judgment is both too cynical and too simple.

Try as we might, we ultimately can make very little sense at all of nature without resorting to such devices. Whether they are such bald assertions of human presence as Church's cruciform mast or the intangible, metaphorical tools of the mind—contrast, remembrance, analogy—we bring our own worlds to bear in foreign landscapes in order to clarify them for ourselves. It is hard to imagine that we could do otherwise. The risk we take is of finding our final authority in the metaphors rather than in the land. To inquire into the intricacies of a distant landscape, then, is to provoke thoughts about one's own interior landscape, and the familiar landscapes of memory. The land urges us to come around to an understanding of ourselves.

A comparison with cathedrals has come to many Western minds in searching for a metaphor for icebergs, and I think the reasons for it are deeper than the obvious appropriateness of line and scale. It has to do with our passion for light.

Cathedral architecture signaled a quantum leap forward in European civilization. The gothic cathedral churches, with their broad bays of sunshine, flying buttresses that let windows rise where once there had been stone in the walls, and harmonious interiors—this "architecture of light" was a monument to a newly created theology. "God is light," writes a French cultural historian of the era, Georges Duby, and "every creature stems from that initial, uncreated, creative light." Robert Grosseteste, the twelfth-century founder of Oxford University, wrote that "physical light is the best, the most delectable, the most beautiful of all the bodies that exist."

Intellectually, the eleventh and twelfth centuries were an age of careful dialectics, a working out of relationships that eventually became so refined they could be expressed in the mathematics of cathedrals. Not only was God light but the *relationship* between God and man was light. The cathedrals, by the very way they snared the sun's energy, were an expression of God and of the human connection with God as well. The aesthetics of this age, writes Duby, was "based on light, logic, lucidity, and yearning for a God in a human form." Both the scholastic monks in their exegetical disquisitions and the illiterate people who built these churches, who sent these structures soaring into the sky—157 feet at Beauvais before it fell over on them—both, writes Duby, were "people trying to rise above their poverty through dreams of light."

It was an age of mystics. When Heinrich Suso, a Dominican monk, prayed at night in church, "it often seemed as if he were floating on air or sailing between time and eternity, on the deep tide of the unsoundable marvels of God." And it was an age of visionaries who spoke of the New Jerusalem of the Apocalypse, where there would be no darkness.

The erection of these monuments to spiritual awareness signaled a rivival of cities, without which these edifices could not have survived. (The money to build them came largely from an emerging class of merchants and tradesmen, not royalty.) In time, however, the cathedrals became more and more esoteric, so heavily intellectualized an enterprise that, today, the raw, spiritual desire that was their original impetus seems lost. To the modern visitor, familiar with an architecture more facile and clever with light, the cathedrals now seem dark. Their stone has been eaten away by the acids and corrosives of industrial air. The age of mystics that bore them gave way rather too quickly to an age of rational intellects, of vast, baroque theological abstraction.

A final, ironic point: the mathematics that made the building of the cathedrals possible was carefully preserved by Arabs and Moors, by so-called infidels.

By the thirteenth century, Europe was starting to feel the vastness of Asia, the authority of other cultures. "The dissemination of knowledge," writes Duby, "and the strides made in the cultural sphere had opened [European] eyes and forced them to face facts: the world was infinitely larger, more various, and less docile than it had seemed to their forefathers; it was full of men who had not received the word of God, who refused to hear it, and who would not be easily conquered by arms. In Europe the days of holy war were over. The days of the explorers, traders, and missionaries had begun. After all, why persist in struggling against all those infidels, those expert warriors, when it was more advantageous to negotiate and attempt to insinuate oneself in those invincible kingdoms by business transactions and peaceful preaching?"

This was the philosophy that carried the Portuguese to India, the Spaniards to Peru, and the French and British into the hinterlands of northern North America. Hundreds of years later, a refinement on this philosophy of acquisition propelled Americans, Canadians, and Russians into the Arctic.

The conventional wisdom of our time is that European man has advanced by enormous strides since the age of cathedrals. He has landed on the moon. He has cured smallpox. He has harnessed the power in the atom. Another argument, however, might be made in the opposite direction, that all European man has accomplished in 900 years is a more complicated manipulation of materials, a more astounding display of his grasp of the physical principles of matter. That we are dazzled by mere styles of expression. That ours is not an age of mystics but of singular adepts, of performers. That the erection of the cathedrals was the last wild stride European man made before falling back into the confines of his intellect.

Of the sciences today, quantum physics alone seems to have found its way back to an equitable relationship with metaphors, those fundamental tools of the imagination. The other sciences are occasionally so bound by rational analysis, or so wary of metaphor, that they recognize and denounce anthropomorphism as a kind of intellectual cancer, instead of employing it as a tool of comparative inquiry, which is perhaps the only way the mind works, that parallelism we finally call narrative.

There is a word from the time of the cathedrals: agape, an expression of intense spiritual affinity with the mystery that is "to be sharing life with other life." Agape is love, and it can mean "the love of another for the sake of God." More broadly and essentially it is a humble, impassioned embrace of something outside the self, in the name of that which we refer to as *God*, but which also includes the self and *is* God. We are clearly indebted as a species to the play of our intelligence; we trust our future to it; but we do not know whether intelligence is reason or whether intelligence is this desire to embrace and be embraced in the pattern that both theologians and physicists call God. Whether intelligence, in other words, is love.

ONE day, sitting in my accustomed spot on the cargo deck of the *Soodoc*, I turned to see the second engineer, who had brought two cups of coffee. He was from Guyana. We talked about Guyana, and about the icebergs, some forty or fifty of which were then around us. He raised his chin to indicate and said, "How would you like to live up there? A fellow could camp up there, sail all the way to Newfoundland. Get off at Saint John's. How about it?" He laughed.

We laughed together. We searched the horizon for mirages with the binoculars, but we were not successful. When his break was over, the engineer went back below decks. I hung over the bow, staring into the bow wave at the extraordinary fluidity of that geometry on the calm waters of Melville Bay. I looked up at the icebergs. They so embodied the land. Austere. Implacable. Harsh but not antagonistic. Creatures of pale light. Once, camped in the Anaktiktoak Valley of the central Brooks Range in Alaska, a friend had said, gazing off across that broad glacial valley of soft greens and straw browns, with sunlight lambent on Tulugak Lake and the Anaktuvuk River in the distance, that it was so beautiful it made you cry.

I looked out at the icebergs. They were so beautiful they also made you afraid.

Seven

THE COUNTRY OF THE MIND

THE DAILY CYCLE of tides rising and falling on the narrow beaches of Pingok Island during the open-water season is hard to read. In this part of the Arctic Ocean, where the Beaufort Sea washes against the north coast of Alaska, the vertical rise of the tide can be measured with a fingertip. On a windless day one can see reflected clouds undisturbed at the rim of the ocean's surface. It is possible to stand toe-to at the water's edge and, if one has the patience, see it gain only the heels of one's boots in six hours. Another peculiarity inherent in the land. In the eastern Arctic, at Ungava Bay and in embayments of the Canadian Archipelago, the tides are more substantial, rising up to 40 feet.

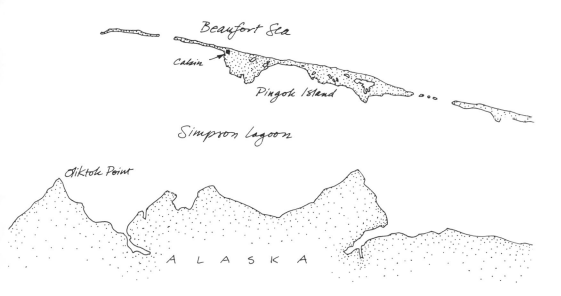

Pingok Island.

Pingok Island lies at 70°35'N and 149°35'W, a few miles off the north Alaska coast, some 30 miles east of the Colville River delta. It is the westernmost of the Jones Islands, a stretch of barrier islands that protects a shallow area along the coast called Simpson Lagoon, favored by migrating ducks.

This particular part of the arctic coast was little visited by Westerners until recently. Prudhoe Bay, where oil was discovered in February 1968, is 40 miles to the east; on clear days black clouds from flare-offs in those oil fields are faintly visible on the horizon. To the southwest a few miles, at Oliktok Point on the mainland, is an operational DEW line station. Pingok Island itself carries traces of modern inquiries into the region: the ubiquitous detritus of industrial reconnoitering and military exercises; and refuse from recent Eskimo and scientific encampments—strands of yellow polyethylene rope, empty wooden boxes and white gas tins, and outboard motor parts.

The most noticeable, man-made features of this island—it is about four and a half miles long and a half-mile wide at several points—are a shed and two pale yellow clapboard buildings that stand at its west end, and a cluster of coastal survey markers erected on the east end. For parts of two summers I lived with several marine biologists in one of the small, one-room buildings at the edge of the western beach. We were at sea most of the time; but on "weather days," when the inevitable August snow squalls or heavy seas prohibited our working efficiently from a small boat, I walked the island's tundra plain.

This is an old business, walking slowly over the land with an appreciation of its immediacy to the senses and in anticipation of what lies hidden in it. The eye alights suddenly on something bright in the grass—the chitinous shell of an insect. The nose tugs at a minute blossom for some trace of arctic perfume. The hands turn over an odd bone, extrapolating, until the animal is discovered in the mind and seen to be moving in the land. One finds anomalous stones to puzzle over, and in footprints and broken spiderwebs the traces of irretrievable events.

During those summers I found, too, the molted feathers of ducks washed up in great wrack lines, in heaps, on the beach. Undisturbed in shallow waters on the lagoon side, I found hoofprints of caribou, as sharp as if the animals had stepped there in fresh clay only a moment before. They must have crossed over in late spring, on the last of the ice. I squatted down wherever the evidence of animals was particularly strong amid the tundra's polygon fractures. Where Canada geese had cropped grass at the edge of a freshwater pond; at the skull of a ringed seal carried hundreds of yards inland by ice, or scavengers; where grass had been flattened by a resting fox.

I saw in the sea face of a low bench of earth along the beach the glistening edge of an ice lens that underlay the tundra. The surface layer of plants and dirt overhung it like a brow-thatch of hair. I tried persistently but without success to sneak up on the flocks of feeding geese. I lost and regained images of ptarmigan against the ground, because of their near-perfect camouflage. I brought back to the cabin to set on a shelf by my bed castings of the landscape, to keep for a while and wonder over. The fractured intervertebral disk of a belukha whale. The prehistoric-looking exoskeleton of a marine isopod. And handfuls of feathers. Tangible things from my gentle interrogations, objects to which some part of a pervasive and original mystery still clung.

In the sometimes disconcerting summary which is a photograph, Pingok Island would seem bleak and forsaken. In winter it disappears beneath whiteness, a flat white plain extending seaward into the Beaufort Sea ice and landward without a border into the tundra of the coastal plain. The island emerges in June, resplendent with flowers and insects and birds, only to disappear again in a few months beneath the first snowstorms. To a Western imagination that finds a stand of full-crowned trees heartening, that finds the flight and voice of larks exhilarating, and the sight of wind rolling over fields of tall grass more agreeable, Pingok seems impoverished. When I arrived on the island, I, too, understood its bleak aspect as a category, the expression of something I had read about or been told. In the weeks during which I made some passing acquaintance with it, its bleakness was altered, however. The prejudice we exercise against such landscapes, imagining them to be primitive, stark, and pagan, became sharply apparent. It is in a place like this that we would unthinkingly store poisons or test weapons, land like the deserts to which we once banished our heretics and where we once loosed scapegoats with the burden of our transgressions.

The differing landscapes of the earth are hard to know individually. They are as difficult to engage in conversation as wild animals. The complex feelings of affinity and self-assurance one feels with one's native place rarely develop again in another landscape.

It is a convention of Western thought to believe all cultures are compelled to explore, that human beings seek new land because their economies drive them onward. Lost in this valid but nevertheless impersonal observation is the notion of a simpler longing, of a human desire for a less complicated life, for fresh intimacy and renewal. These, too, draw us into new landscapes. And desire causes imagination to misconstrue what it finds. The desire for wealth, for revivification, for triumph, as much or more than scientific measurement and description, or the imperatives of economic expansion, resolves the geography of a newfound landscape.

IN 1893, Frederick Jackson Turner read a paper in Chicago before the American Historical Association that changed the course of American historiography—the way historians understand how elements of the past are causally related. Turner's idea, which came to be called the Frontier Hypothesis, has become so much a part of the way we think about the country's past that it now seems self-evident. At the time he presented it, it was unheralded and unique.

Prior to 1893, most historians believed America had been shaped by the desire to separate itself from European influences, or by the economic and social issues that came to a head in the Civil War. Turner offered a third view, that America was shaped by both the fact and the concept of its westering frontier. The national character, so distinguished by enterprise, initiative, and hard work, he said, derived from an understanding of its citizens' experiences on the frontier. Historians generally accepted Turner's hypothesis, and have refined upon and extrapolated from it for nearly a century.

Turner's observation showed at least two things: the narrative direction that a nation's history takes is amenable to revision; and the landscapes in which history unfolds are both real, that is, profound in their physical effects on mankind, and not real, but mere projections, artifacts of human perception. Nowhere in North American history is this more apparent than in the westward movement of the nineteenth century. Politicians and promoters, newspaper editors and businessmen argued hotly over the suitability of the tallgrass and shortgrass prairies for farming. In most of these arguments the political cant of boomers and nay-sayers and the abstractions of agrarian theorists counted for more than the factual testimony of the land in the form of rainfall records or the statements of people who lived there.

Perhaps this is obvious. In the modern age, one of the most irksome, and ironic, of political problems in North America is the promulgation of laws and regulations from Washington and Ottawa that seem grossly ignorant of the landscapes to which they apply. We all, however, apprehend the land imperfectly, even when we go to the trouble to wander in it. Our perceptions are colored by preconception and desire. The physical landscape is an unstructured abode of space and time and is not entirely fathomable; but this does not necessarily put us at a disadvantage in seeking to know it. Believing them to be fundamentally mysterious in their form and color, in the varieties of life inherent in them, in the tactile qualities of their soils, the sound of the violent fall of rain upon them, the smell of their buds—believing landscapes to be mysterious aggregations, it becomes easier to approach them. One simply accords them the standing that one grants the other mysteries, as distinguished from the puzzles, of life.

I recall in this context two thoughts. A man in Anaktuvuk Pass, in response to a question about what he did when he visited a new place, said to me, "I listen." That's all. I listen, he meant, to what the land is saying. I walk around in it and strain my senses in appreciation of it for a long time before I, myself, ever speak a word. Entered in such a respectful manner, he believed, the land would open to him. The other thought draws, again, on the experience of American painters. As they sought an identity apart from their European counterparts in the nineteenth century, they came to conceive of the land as intrinsically powerful: beguiling and frightening, endlessly arresting and incomprehensibly rich, unknowable and wild. "The face of God," they said.

As I step out of our small cabin on Pingok Island, the undistinguished plain of tundra spreads before me to the south and east. A few glaucous gulls rise from the ground and drop back, and I feel the cold, damp air, like air from a refrigerator, against my cheeks. A few yards from the door, stark and alone on the tundra, a female common eider lies dead. A few more yards to the west, a bearded-

seal skin has been expertly stretched between short wooden stakes to
dry. A few yards beyond, a northern phalarope spins wildly on the
surface of a freshwater pond, feeding on zooplankton.

A southwest wind has been blowing for two days; it's the
reason we are ashore today. The sky threatens squalls and snow. I
head south across the tundra toward the lagoon, wondering if I will
find ducks there. In my mind is a vague plan: to go there, then east
along the coast to a place where the tundra is better drained, easier
walking, then back across the island, and to come home along the
seaward coast.

In such flat terrain as this, even with the lowering skies, I brood
on the vastness of the region. The vastness is deceptive, however.
The journals of arctic explorers are full of examples of messages
stashed out there with a high expectation of their discovery, because the prominent places in such a featureless landscape are so
obvious. They are the places a human eye notices right away. And
there is something, too, about the way the landscape funnels human
movement, such that encounters with strangers are half expected, as
is the case in a desert crossing. Human beings are so few here and
their errands such a part of the odd undercurrent of knowledge
that flows in a remote region that you half expect, too, to know of
the stranger. Once, camped on the upper Yukon, I saw a man in a
distant canoe. When he raised his field glasses to look at a cliff
where peregrine falcons were nesting, I surmised who he was (a
biological consultant working on a peregrine census) from a remark
I had overheard a week before in a small restaurant in Fairbanks.
He probably knew of my business there, too. Some of the strangeness went out of the country in that moment.

If the mind releases its fiduciary grip on time, does not dole it
out in a fretful way like a valued commodity but regards it as
undifferentiated, like the flatness of the landscape, it is possible to
transcend distance—to travel very far without anxiety, to not be
defeated by the great reach of the land. If one is dressed well and
carrying a little food, and has the means to secure more food and to
construct shelter, the mind is that much more free to work with the

senses in an appreciation of the country. The unappealing tundra plain, I recall, is to its denizens a storehouse of food and instant tools.

As I thread my way southwest, along the margins of frost polygons, I am aware of the movement of birds. A distant speck moves across the sky with a loon's trajectory. A Savannah sparrow flits away over the ground. The birds come and go—out to sea to feed or to the lagoon to rest—on a seemingly regular schedule. Scientists say the pattern of coming and going, of feeding and resting, repeats itself every twenty-four hours. But a description of it becomes more jagged and complex than the experience, like any parsing of a movement in time.

The sound of my footfall changes as I step from damp ground to wet, from wet to dry. Microhabitats. I turn the pages of a mental index to arctic plants and try to remember which are the ones to distinguish these borders: which plants separate at a glance mesic tundra from hydric, hydric from xeric? I do not remember. Such generalities, in any case, would only founder on the particulars at my feet. One is better off with a precise and local knowledge, and a wariness of borders. These small habitats, like the larger landscapes, merge imperceptibly with each other. Another, remembered landscape makes this one seem familiar; and the habits of an animal in one region provoke speculation about behavior among its relatives in another region. But no country, finally, is just like another. The generalities are abstractions. And the lines on our topographic maps reveal not only the scale at which we are discerning, but our tolerance for discrepancies in nature.

A tundra botanist once described to me her patient disassembly of a cluster of plants on a tussock, a tundra mound about 18 inches high and a foot or so across. She separated live from dead plant tissue and noted the number and kind of the many species of plants. She examined the insects and husks of berries, down to bits of things nearly too slight to see or to hold without crushing. The process took hours, and her concentration and sense of passing time became fixed at that scale. She said she remembered looking up at one point, at the tundra that rolled away in a hundred thousand tussocks toward the horizon, and that she could not return her gaze because of that sight, not for long minutes.

My route across Pingok seems rich, but I am aware that I miss much of what I pass, for lack of acuity in my senses, lack of discrimination, and my general unfamiliarity. If I knew the indigenous human language, it would help greatly. A local language discriminates among the local phenomena, and it serves to pry the landscape loose from its anonymity.

I know how much I miss—I have only to remember the faces of the Eskimos I've traveled with, the constant flicker of their eyes over the countryside. Even inside their houses men prefer to talk while sitting by a window. They are always looking away at the land or looking up to the sky, the coming weather. As I near the lagoon, pondering the identity of something I saw a flock of ptarmigan eating, I smile wryly at a memory: it was once thought that scurvy was induced in the Arctic by the bleakness of its coasts.

There are no ducks nearby in the lagoon. With my field glasses I can just make out the dark line of their rafts on the far side of the water, a lee shore. I settle myself in a crease in the tundra, out of the wind, arrange my clothing so nothing binds, and begin to study the far shore with the binoculars. After ten or fifteen minutes I have found two caribou. Stefansson was once asked by an Eskimo to whom he was showing a pair of binoculars for the first time whether he could "see into tomorrow" with them. Stefansson took the question literally and was amused. What the *inuk* probably meant was, Are those things powerful enough to see something that will not reach you for another day, like migrating caribou? Or a part of the landscape suitable for a campsite, which you yourself will not reach for another day? Some Eskimo hunters have astounding natural vision; they can point out caribou grazing on a slope three or four miles away. But the meticulous inspection of the land that is the mark of a good hunter becomes most evident when he uses a pair of field glasses. Long after the most inquiring nonnative has grown weary of glassing the land for some clue to the movement of animals, a hunter is still scouring its edges and interstices. He may take an hour to glass 360° of the apparently silent tundra, one section at a time.

You can learn to do this; and such scrutiny always turns up a ground squirrel, an itinerant wolverine, a nesting bird—something that tells you where you are and what's going on. And when you fall into the habit, find some way like this to shed your impatience, you feel less conspicuous in the land.

I walk a long ways down the beach before arriving at the place where the tundra dries out, and turn inland. Halfway across I find the skull of a goose, as seemingly random in this landscape as the dead eider in the grass by the cabin. A more thoughtful inquirer, someone dependent upon these bits of information in a way that I am not, would find out why. To the southwest I can see a snow squall—I want to reach the seaward side of the island before it arrives, in case there is something worse behind it. The shoreline is my way home. I put the paper-thin skull back on the ground. Far to the east I see a dilapidated spire of driftwood, a marker erected in 1910 by Ernest Leffingwell when he was mapping these coasts. Leaning slightly askew, it has the aspect of an abandoned building, derelict and wind-punished. It is a monument to the desire to control vastness. It is a referent for the metes and bounds that permit a proper division and registry of the countryside, an assignment of ownership.

THE western history of Pingok Island comprises few events. John Franklin, a young British naval officer, led an overland party almost this far west from the mouth of the Mackenzie in 1826, trying for a rendezvous at Point Barrow, 250 miles farther on. But with bad weather and the physical strain on the men, he "reached the point beyond which perseverance would be rashness," and turned back, in the fall of that year. Robert M'Clure put a party ashore in August 1850, to entreat with a small group of resident Eskimo. The Eskimos regarded *Investigator* as "a swimming island," wrote a thirty-three-year-old Moravian missionary with the shore party.

"At every movement of the ship, though it was half an hour's pull distant, they showed fresh alarm and an electric shock, as it were, went through them all."

Late in the nineteenth century the island was visited by American whalers, who took on fresh water from its ponds. Stefansson abandoned the ill-fated *Karluk* nearby, in September 1913. (Caught in the ice, the ship, a brigantine whaler refitted as a scientific expeditionary vessel, later drifted far to the west, where it was crushed and sank, with the subsequent loss of half the party.) Traders and explorers like Leffingwell were also in the area in these years. In 1952 an archaeologist named William Irving made the first excavations of the island's prehistoric sites. A few years later, the DEW line station was built at Oliktok. In the 1960s the U.S. Navy built two sheds and a 10- by 18-foot cabin for the use of scientific field parties working out of the Naval Arctic Research Laboratory at Barrow, and later for the federal Outer Continental Shelf Environmental Assessment Program and other projects. These buildings also occasionally shelter Eskimos traveling along the coast, whence the bearded-seal skin pegged on the tundra by the door of the cabin we were using.

The aboriginal history of the island is much deeper and also more obscure. It is likely, because of the way it is situated, that the island has been used by hunting peoples for centuries, though probably not continually. Today, a dozen 400-year-old dwellings, outlined on the tundra by protruding driftwood logs and bowhead whale ribs, are the only traces of early occupation left. This stretch of North American coastline was apparently never heavily populated. The Pingok houses, however, constituted the largest prehistoric site on the north Alaska coast in 1981.

An astute archaeologist would have anticipated the remains of such an encampment here. Pingok Island gets its name from an Inupiatun word for "a rising of earth over a dome of ice." The reference is to a long sand dune on the seaward edge of the island which gives protection from storm surges. Such protection is rare along this coast. It would be noticed and taken advantage of.

Hunters camped at Pingok would benefit, too, from early access to bearded and ringed seals around the mouth of the Colville, where freshwater ice begins to disintegrate before the sea ice breaks up. On Simpson Lagoon they would find migrating geese and ducks. Along the beach are great supplies of driftwood (from the Mackenzie River), some of the trees 30 or 40 feet long. There are large freshwater ponds on the island, and from here there is good access to runs of char and to herds of belukha whale, and, in September, to bowhead whales headed west for Bering Strait. On the landward side of the lagoon they could expect to see caribou.

Excavations at the Pingok houses indicate that the people living here between 1550 and 1700 hunted all of these animals, and also walrus and polar bear. Among the more intriguing objects unearthed are a polar-bear-tooth(?) fish lure, a child's miniature hunting bow, and a piece of caribou-antler(?) plate armor.

Standing by the remains of these houses, one is struck by the fact that in the Arctic so much human history lies undisturbed on the surface of the land. And by the contrast with a more easily retrieved past, such as our own. Here is a prong from a bird spear; here is a walrus-tooth pendant; but what were the ideas attached to these objects?

The remains of other, more modern Eskimo dwellings are also found on Pingok—sod and whalebone houses from the 1920s. In recent years ethnohistorians have visited the islands, bringing with them the people who once lived in these houses. The people were interviewed here with these artifacts and the landscape itself close at hand in order to plumb "the memory culture," the culture tied to tools no longer used and still most accurately described in the Inupiatun language, whose vocabulary is rapidly fading.

One Sunday afternoon in the summer of 1981 several Eskimos from the village of Barrow paid us a visit on Pingok. They were conducting a land-use survey, a complex process of land assessment used by native peoples to substantiate their aboriginal claims to certain sections of land. We talked a little about the Eskimo "history" of Pingok Island (as if, without such corroborative details, acceptable to the men who owned the maps, the place would remain vague and unclaimable). Only some sort of acceptable, verifiable history could save it for them now. We all turned, with more ease and enthusiasm, to talk of hunting. Such chance conversations as this, far from the villages, where political and racial tensions can be strong, are often cordial. No one is apt to pursue a point that might lead to disagreement, or to ask a question that might be construed as prying. It is always acceptable, and good, to speak of hunting. A great deal of information about the local landscape passes back and forth in this context. One feels here, sharing the details of animals' lives in the memories of those present, the authority for a claim to the land just as legitimate and important as the things found at a 400-year-old house.

After they left—they were traveling in a small boat toward the east (and to most foreign observers they would have seemed underdressed and poorly provisioned for their journey, a common impression)—we talked among ourselves about the Eskimos' cultural history. The men who left carried with them a borrowed historiography, a matrix they put down like a net in the undifferentiated sphere of time that welled up in their own traditional and unwritten history. It is a system they are becoming familiar, and handy, with. And there was great dignity and authority in the Eskimo women who sat on driftwood logs on Pingok Island, recalling into tape recorders the details of their lives from so many years ago. One could so easily imagine, as memory bloomed before the genuine desire of another to know, filaments appearing in the wind, reattaching them to the land, even as they spoke.

Land-use-and-occupancy projects have been conducted by and with native peoples throughout the Arctic, in furtherance of their land claims and to protect their hunting rights. These studies have revealed a long and remarkably unbroken connection between various groups of indigenous people and the particular regions of the Arctic they inhabit. It is impossible to separate their culture from these landscapes. The land is like a kind of knowledge traveling in time through them. Land does for them what architecture sometimes does for us. It provides a sense of place, of scale, of history; and a conviction that what they most dread—annihilation, eclipse—will not occur.

"We are here [i.e., alive now in this particular place] because our ancestors are real," a man once told an interviewer. The ancestors are real by virtue of their knowledge and use of the land, their affection for it. A native woman, alone and melancholy in a hospital room, told another interviewer she would sometimes raise her hands before her eyes to stare at them: "Right in my hand, I could see the shorelines, beaches, lakes, mountains, and hills I had been to. I could see the seals, birds, and game. . . ." Another Eskimo, sensing the breakup of his culture's relationships with the land, the replacement of his ancient hunting economy by another sort of economy, told an interviewer it would be best all around if the Inuit became "the minds over the land." Their minds, he thought, shaped as they were to the specific contours of the land, could imagine it well enough to know what to do. Like most Eskimos, as the land-use-and-occupancy surveys made clear, he could not grasp the meaning of a life divorced from the landscape—the animals, the weather, the sound of ice, the taste and nourishment that came from "the food that counts."

In a long passage in *The Central Eskimo* (1888), Franz Boas describes the birth of a child and the types of clothing the child wears during the first few days of its life—a cap made of arctic hare fur, underclothes of bird feathers, a hood made of a caribou fawn with the ears attached. One is struck by the great efforts of the mother, especially, to confirm the child immediately in a complex and intricate relationship with "the land," the future source of the child's spiritual, psychological, and physical well-being. Nearly a hundred years later, Richard Nelson, a northern ethnologist, described a similar, modern Koyukon understanding of natural history in *Make Prayers to the Raven* (1983). While many things have changed, the evidence of continued intimacy with a local landscape—a practical knowledge of it, a sensitivity toward it, a supplication of it—is still clear. The incorporation of the land into traditional stories—evidence of close association with the land and the existence of an uncanny and mesmerizing conformity of human behavior in response to subtleties in the landscape—is also still evident. The people, many of them, have not abandoned the land, and the land has not abandoned them. It is difficult, coming from cities far to the south, to perceive let alone fathom the richness of this association, or to assess its worth. But this archaic affinity for the land, I believe, is an antidote to the loneliness that in our own culture we associate with individual estrangement and despair.

I move the glasses off Leffingwell's tower. On the ridge of sand dune along the beach to the north I spot an arctic fox. A great traveler in winter, like the polar bear and the wolf. In summer, when water intervenes in the fox's coastal habitat, he may stay in one place—an island like this, for example. The fox always seems to be hurrying somewhere, then stopping suddenly to sit down and rest. He runs up on slight elevations and taps the air all over with his nose.

The arctic fox's fur runs to shades of brown in summer, which blend with ivory whites on its underparts. (In winter the coat is gleaming white or a grayish blue to pale beige, which is called "blue.") As with any animal, the facets of its life are complexly engaging. The extent and orderliness of its winter caches and its ability to withstand very cold weather are striking. Also its tag-along relationship with the polar bear. It is the friendliest and most trusting of the North American foxes, although it is characterized in many expedition journals as "impudent," derided for its "persistent cheekiness," and disparaged as a "parasite" and a scavenger. Arctic foxes are energetic and persistent in their search for food. They thoroughly scour the coastlines over which they travel and, like polar bears, will gather from miles around at a source of carrion. If it's a cook tent they choose instead, and thirty or forty of them are racing around, tearing furiously into everything, an expedition's initial sense of amusement can easily turn sour or violent. Arctic foxes so pestered Vitus Bering's shipwrecked second

Kamchatka expedition that the men tortured and killed the ones they caught with the unrestrained savagery one would expect of men driven insane by hordes of insects.

In his encounter with modern man in the Arctic, then, the fox's efficient way of life has sometimes gone fatally against him. (His dealings with modern Eskimos have fit more perfectly, though also fatally, with human enterprise. Once largely ignored, he became the most relentlessly pursued fur-bearer in the Arctic with the coming of the fur trade and the advent of the village trading post.)

I watch the fox now, traveling the ridge of the sand dune, the kinetic blur of its short legs. I have seen its (or another's) tracks at several places along the beach. I think of it traveling continuously over the island, catching a lemming here, finding part of a seal there, looking for a bird less formidable than a glaucous gull to challenge for its eggs. I envision the network of its trails as though it were a skein of dark lines over the island, anchored at slight elevations apparent to the eye at a distance because of their dense, rich greens or clusters of wildflowers.

Because the fox is built so much closer to the ground and is overall so much smaller than a human being, the island must be "longer" in its mind than four and a half miles. And traveling as it does, trotting and then resting, trotting and then resting, and "seeing" so much with its black nose—what is Pingok like for it? I wonder how any animal's understanding of the island changes over the year; and the difference in its shape to a gyrfalcon, a wolf spider, or a bowhead echolocating along its seashore. What is the island to the loon, who lives on the water and in the air, stepping awkwardly ashore only at a concealed spot at the edge of a pond, where it nests? What of the bumblebee, which spends its evening deep in the corolla of a summer flower that makes its world 8°F warmer? What is the surface of the land like for a creature as small but as adroit as the short-tailed weasel? And how does the recollection of such space guide great travelers like the caribou and the polar bear on their journeys?

A friend working one summer near Polar Bear Pass on Bathurst

Island once spotted a wolf running off with a duck in its mouth. He saw the wolf bury the duck, and when the wolf left he made for the cache. He couldn't find it. It was open, uncomplicated country. He retraced his steps, again took his bearings, and tried a second time. A third time. He never found it. The wolf, he thought, must have a keener or at least a different way of holding that space in its mind and remembering the approach. The land then appeared to him more complicated.

One day, out on the sea ice, I left the protection of a temporary building and followed a bundle of electric cables out into a blizzard. The winds were gusting to 40 knots; it was −20°F. I stood for a long time with my back to the storm, peering downwind into the weak January light, fearful of being bowled over, of losing touch with the umbilical under which I had hooked a boot. Both its ends faded away in that swirling whiteness. In the 40-foot circle of visibility around me I could see only ice hummocks. I wondered what notions of "direction" a fox would have standing here, how the imperatives for food and shelter would affect us differently.

One can only speculate about how animals organize land into meaningful expanses for themselves. The worlds they perceive, their *Umwelten*, are all different.* The discovery of an animal's *Umwelt* and its elucidation require great patience and experimental ingenuity, a free exchange of information among different observers, hours of direct observation, and a reluctance to summarize the animal. This, in my experience, is the Eskimo hunter's methodology. Under ideal circumstances it can also be the methodology of Western science.†

---

* The world we perceive around an animal is its *environment*; what it sees is its *Umwelt*, or self-world. A specific environment contains many *Umwelten*, no two of which are the same. The concept, developed by Jakob von Uexküll in 1934, assumes that the structure of the organs of perception, the emphasis each receives, the level of their sensitivity, and the ability of each to discriminate, are different in all animals.

† In practice, the two methodologies usually differ. The Eskimo's methods are less formal than those of the scientist, but not necessarily

Many Western biologists appreciate the mystery inherent in the animals they observe. They comprehend that, objectively, what they are watching is deceptively complex and, subjectively, that the animals themselves have nonhuman ways of life. They know that while experiments can be designed to reveal aspects of the animal, the animal itself will always remain larger than the sum of any set of experiments. They know they can be very precise about what they do, but that that does not guarantee they will be accurate. They know the behavior of an individual animal may differ strikingly from the generally recognized behavior of its species; and that the same species may behave quite differently from place to place, from year to year.

It is very hard to achieve a relatively complete and accurate view of an animal's life, especially in the Arctic, where field conditions present so many problems, limiting observation. Many biologists studying caribou, muskoxen, wolves, and polar bear in the North are more distressed by this situation than they otherwise might be. Industry, which pays much of the bill for this arctic research, is less interested in the entire animal than it is in those aspects of its life that might complicate or hinder development—or, to be fair, how in some instances industry might disrupt the animal's way of life. What bothers biologists is the narrowness of the approach, the haste with which the research must be conducted,

---

less rigorous. By comparison, Western scientists often fall far short on hours of observation; and they usually select only a few aspects of an animal's life to study closely. The Eskimo's ecological approach, however, his more broad-based consideration of an animal's interactions with many, some seemingly insignificant, aspects of its environment, is increasingly becoming a Western approach. Western science is better informed about the life history of migratory animals, especially distribution and movement. Eskimos, on the other hand, show a marked reluctance to extrapolate from the individual to include all other animals of that type, as Western scientists do. In recent years some scientists have come to learn more than many Eskimos about specific animals. The last generation of highly informed, broadly experienced native hunters is passing away.

and, increasingly, the turning of an animal's life into numbers. The impersonality of statistics masks both the complexity and the ethics inherent in any wildlife situation. Biologists are anxious about "the tyranny of statistics" and "the ascendency of the [computer] modeler," about industry's desire for a "standardized animal," one that always behaves in predictable ways.

A Canadian scientist told me, "I hate as a biologist having to reduce the behavior of animals to numbers. I hate it. But if we are going to stand our ground against [head-long development] we must produce numbers, because that's all they will listen to. I am spending my whole *life* to answer these questions—they want an answer in two months. And anything a native says about animals, well, that counts for nothing with them. Useless anecdotes."

A belief in the authority of statistics and the dismissal of Eskimo narratives as only "anecdotal" is a dichotomy one encounters frequently in arctic environmental assessment reports. Statistics, of course, can be manipulated—a whale biologist once said to me, "If you punish the data enough, it will tell you anything." And the *Umwelt* of a statistician, certainly, plays a role in developing the "statistical picture" of a landscape. The Eskimos' stories are politely dismissed not because Eskimos are not good observers or because they lie, but because the narratives cannot be reduced to a form that is easy to handle or lends itself to summary. Their words are too hard to turn into numbers.

What the uninitiated scientist in the Arctic lacks is not ideas about how the land works, or a broad theoretical knowledge of how the larger pieces fit together, but time in the field, prolonged contact with the specific sources of an understanding. Several Western scientists, including anthropologist Richard Nelson, marine mammal biologists John Burns, Francis Fay, and Kerry Finley, and terrestrial mammal biologist Robert Stephenson, have sought out Eskimo hunters as field companions in order to get a better understanding of arctic ecology. Nelson, who arrived in Wainwright in the early 1960s quite skeptical about the kinds of animal behavior the hunters had described to him, wrote a line any one of the others might have written after a year of traveling through the country with these people: "[Their] statements which seem utterly incredible at first almost always turn out to be correct."

I walk on toward the dune where the fox has disappeared. The inconspicuous plants beneath my feet, I realize, efficiently harbor minerals and nutrients and water in these acidic, poorly drained soils. They are compact; they distribute the weight of snow, of passing caribou and myself, so it does not crush them. The stems of these willows are shorter than those of their southern counterparts, with many more leaves to take advantage of the light. It may take years for a single plant to produce a seed crop. What do these plants murmur in their dreams, what of warning and desire passes between them?

It is beginning to snow a little, on a slant from the southeast. I walk on, my eye to the ground, out to the horizon, back to the ground. And what did Columbus, sailing for Zaiton, the great port of Cathay, think of the reach of the western Atlantic? How did Coronado assess the Staked Plain of Texas, the rawest space he ever knew, on his way to Quivera? Or Mungo Park the landscape of Africa in search of the Niger? What one thinks of any region, while traveling through, is the result of at least three things: what one knows, what one imagines, and how one is disposed.

What one knows is either gathered firsthand or learned from books or indigenous observers. This information, however, is assembled differently by each individual, according to his cultural predispositions and his personality. A Western traveler in the Arctic, for example, is inclined to look (only) for cause-and-effect relationships, or predator-prey relationships; and to be (especially) alert for plants and animals that might fill "gaps" in Western taxonomies. Human beings, further, are inclined to favor visual information over the testimony of their other senses when learning an area, and to be more drawn to animals that approximate their own scale. Our view is from a certain height above the ground. In any new country we want panoramas.

What one imagines in a new landscape consists of conjecture, for example, about what might lie beyond that near horizon of small hills, or the far line of the horizon. Often it consists of what one "hopes to see" during the trip—perhaps a barren-ground grizzly standing up on the tundra, or the tusk of a mammoth in the alluvial silt of a creek. These expectations are based on a knowledge of what has happened in this land for others. At a deeper level, however, imagination represents the desire to find what is unknown, unique, or farfetched—a snowy owl sitting motionless on the hips of a muskox, a flower of a favorite color never before reported, tundra swans swimming in a winter polynya.

Imagination also poses the questions that give a new land dimension in time. Are these wolverine tracks from *this* summer or the summer before? How old is this orange lichen? Will the caribou feeding placidly in this swale be discovered by those wolves traveling in the distance? Why did the people camped here leave this piece of carved seal bone behind?

The way we are disposed toward the land is more nebulous, harder to define. The reluctant traveler, brooding about events at home, is oblivious to the landscape. And no one is quite as alert as an indigenous hunter who is hungry. If one feels longing or compassion at the sight of something beautiful, or great excitement over some unexpected event, these may effect an optimistic disposition toward the land. If one has lost a friend in the Arctic to exposure after an airplane crash, or gone broke speculating in a northern mine, one might regard the land as antagonistic and be ill-disposed to recognize any value in it.

The individual desire to understand, as much as any difference in acuity of the senses, brings each of us to find something in the land others did not notice.

Over time, small bits of knowledge about a region accumulate among local residents in the form of stories. These are remembered in the community; even what is unusual does not become lost and therefore irrelevant. These narratives comprise for a native an intricate, long-term view of a particular landscape. And the stories are corroborated daily, even as they are being refined upon by members of the community traveling between what is truly known and what is only imagined or unsuspected. Outside the region this complex but easily shared "reality" is hard to get across without reducing it to generalities, to misleading or imprecise abstraction.

The perceptions of any people wash over the land like a flood, leaving ideas hung up in the brush, like pieces of damp paper to be collected and deciphered. No one can tell the whole story.

I must set my face to the wind to head west, back toward the cabin. I drop down to the seaward beach where I will have the protection of the dune. Oldsquaw and eider ducks ride the ocean swell close to shore in the lee of the storm, their beaks into the wind. Between gaps in the dune I catch glimpses of the dark tundra, swept by wind and snow. My thoughts leap ahead to the cabin, to something warm to drink, and then return. I watch the ducks as I walk. Watching animals always slows you down. I think of the months explorers spent locked up in the ice here, some of them trapped in their ships for three or four years. Their prospects for an early departure were never good, but, their journals reveal, they rarely remarked on the animals that came around, beyond their potential as food, as threats or nuisances. These were men far from home, who felt helpless; the landscape hardly registered as they waited, except as an obstacle. Our inattentiveness is of a different order. We insist on living today in much shorter spans of time. We become exasperated when the lives of animals unfold in ways inconvenient to our schedules—when they sit and do "nothing." I search both the featureless tundra to my left and the raft of brown sea ducks to my right for something untoward, something that stands out. Nothing. After hours of walking, the tundra and the ducks recede into the storm, and my mind pulls far back into its own light.

A Lakota woman named Elaine Jahner once wrote that what lies at the heart of the religion of hunting peoples is the notion that a spiritual landscape exists within the physical landscape. To put it another way, occasionally one sees something fleeting in the land, a moment when line, color, and movement intensify and something sacred is revealed, leading one to believe that there is another realm of reality corresponding to the physical one but different.

In the face of a rational, scientific approach to the land, which is more widely sanctioned, esoteric insights and speculations are frequently overshadowed, and what is lost is profound. The land is like poetry: it is inexplicably coherent, it is transcendent in its meaning, and it has the power to elevate a consideration of human life.

The cabin emerges silently up ahead in the flowing snow as the storm closes in. It seems to rest within a white cave or at the far end of a canyon. Sound only comes now from what is immediately around me. The distant voices of birds are gone. I hear the gritty step of my boots in the sand. Splash of wavelets on the beach. Wind rushing over the cones of my ears.

Through a window yellow with light I see a friend at a table, whipping the end of a boat line with waxed thread. I will have hot tea and lie in my bunk, and try to recall what I saw that did not, in those moments, come to mind.

In the 1930s a man named Benjamin Lee Whorf began to clarify an insight he had had into the structure of the Hopi language. Hopi has only limited tenses, noted Whorf, makes no reference to time as an entity distinct from space, and, though relatively poor in nouns, is rich in verbs. It is a language that projects a world of movement and changing relationships, a continuous "fabric" of time and space. It is better suited than the English language to describing quantum mechanics. English divides time into linear segments by making use of many tenses. It is a noun-rich, verb-poor tongue that contrasts fixed space with a flow of time. It is a language of static space, more suited, say, to architectural description. All else being equal, a Hopi child would have little difficulty comprehending the theory of relativity in his own language, while an American child could more easily master history. A Hopi would be confounded by the idea that time flowed from the past into the present.

In 1936 Whorf wrote that many aboriginal languages "abound in finely wrought, beautifully logical discriminations about causation, action, result, dynamic and energetic quality, directness of experience, etc. . . ." He made people see that there were no primitive languages; and that there was no pool of thought from which all cultures drew their metaphysics. "All observers," he cautioned, "are not led by the same physical evidence to the same picture of the universe."

These ideas were anticipated to some extent by the anthropologist Franz Boas, who emphasized the individual integrity of different aboriginal cultures. His was a reaction against the predominant Victorian view that considered all cultures reducible to a set of "true" observations about the world. (Boas's "functionalist" approach has since been replaced by a "structuralist" view, which knowingly imposes abstract and subjective patterns on a culture.)

Whorf, Boas, and others in this tradition urged people after the turn of the century to see human culture as a mechanism for ordering reality. These realities were separate, though they might be simultaneously projected onto the same landscape. And there was no ultimate reality—any culture that would judge the perceptions of another, particularly one outside its own traditions, should proceed cautiously.

In recent years the writing of people like Joseph Campbell and Claude Lévi-Strauss has illuminated the great panorama of human perceptual experience, pointing up not only the different approaches we take to the background that contains us (the landscape) but the similarities we seem to share. For hunting peoples, for example, says Lévi-Strauss, an animal is held in high totemic regard not merely because it is food and therefore good to eat but because it is "good to think." The animal is "good to imagine."

In the Arctic, researchers such as Richard Nelson, Edmund Carpenter, and Hugh Brody, each addressing a different aspect of Eskimo existence, have reiterated these themes in studying the land. Their work has made clear the integrity and coherence of a different vision of the Arctic; misunderstandings that arise when a view of reality similar to our own is assumed to exist; and the ways in which the Eskimo's view of the land presents us with growing ethical, political, and economic problems, because we would prefer that ours was the mind of record in that landscape.

I have already referred to Nelson's work on natural history and hunting. Brody has been influential in the development of land-use-and-occupancy studies. Carpenter has written cogently on Eskimo art and Eskimo perceptions of space. Not surprisingly, each has emphasized that a knowledge of the language, the pertinent regional dialect, is critical to an understanding of what Eskimos are talking about when they talk about the land. Says Nelson, an understanding of the behavior of sea ice off the coast at Wainwright, where the ice is very active, is "difficult to acquire, especially without a full understanding" of Eskimo terminology. Brody, discussing Eskimo concepts of intimacy with the land, says, flatly, "The key terms are not translatable."

Carpenter discerns a correspondence between the Inuktitut language and Eskimo carving: the emphasis in both is on what is dynamic, and on observations made from a variety of viewpoints. In our language, says Carpenter, we lavish attention on concepts of time; Eskimos give their attention to varieties of space. We assume all human beings are oriented similarly in space and therefore regard objects from the same point of view—the top is the top, the bottom the bottom; that direction is north and this south. In describing a distant place, however, says Carpenter, an Eskimo will often make no reference to the mass of the land in between (which would impress us, and which we would describe in terms of distance), but only to geographical points, and not necessarily as seen from the point of one's approach. Thus, to a non-Eskimo observer, the Eskimo might seem to have "no sense of direction." And because he travels somewhat like the arctic fox—turning aside to investigate something unusual, or moving ahead in a series of steps punctuated by short stops for tea, instead of in a straight, relentless dash for a "goal"—the Eskimo might be thought poorly self-disciplined or improvident. But it would only have to do with how the Eskimo saw himself in the fabric of space and time, how he conceived of "proceeding" through the world, where he placed lines or points in the stream of duration.

The Eskimo's different but still sophisticated mind is largely inaccessible without recourse to his language. And, of course, it works the other way around. Each for the other is a kind of primitive.

The Eskimo language reaches its apogee in describing the land and man's activity in it. Young people in modern Eskimo villages, especially in the eastern Arctic, say that when they are out on the land with their parents, they find it much more difficult to speak Inuktitut, though they speak it at home all the time. It is not so much a lack of vocabulary as a difficulty with constructions, with idioms, a lost fluency that confuses them. It is out on the land, in the hunting camps and traveling over the ice, that the language comes alive.* The Eskimo language is seasonal—terms for the many varieties of snow emerge in winter, while those for whaling come into use in the spring. Whole areas of the language are starting to disappear because they refer to activities no longer much practiced, like traveling with dogs; or to the many different parts of an animal like the walrus that are no longer either eaten or used; or to activities that are discouraged, such as the intercession of shamans.

For Whorf, language was something man created in his mind and projected onto reality, something he imposed on the landscape, as though the land were a receptacle for his imagination. I think there are possibly two things wrong with this thought. First, the landscape is not inert; and it is precisely because it is alive that it eventually contradicts the imposition of a reality that does not

---

* So do some people. It is relatively common in the Arctic to meet a person in a village who seems clumsy, irresponsible, lethargic, barely capable of taking care of himself—and then to find the same person in the bush astoundingly skilled, energetic, and perspicacious.

derive from it. Second, language is not something man imposes on the land. It evolves in his conversation with the land—in testing the sea ice with the toe of a *kamik*, in the eating of a wild berry, in repairing a sled by the light of a seal-oil lamp. A long-lived inquiry produces a discriminating language. The very order of the language, the ecology of its sounds and thoughts, derives from the mind's intercourse with the landscape. To learn the indigenous language, then, is to know what the speakers of the language have made of the land.

THE American geographer Yi-Fu Tuan distinguishes in his writing between concepts of space and a sense of place. Human beings, he says, set out from places, where they feel a sense of attachment, of shelter, and comprehension, and journey into amorphous spaces, characterized by a feeling of freedom or adventure, and the unknown. "In open space," writes Tuan, "one can become intensely aware of [a remembered] place; and in the solitude of a sheltered place, the vastness of space acquires a haunting presence." We turn these exhilarating and sometimes terrifying new places into geography by extending the boundaries of our old places in an effort to include them. We pursue a desire for equilibrium and harmony between our familiar places and unknown spaces. We do this to make the foreign comprehensible, or simply more acceptable.

Tuan's thoughts are valid whether one is thinking about entering an unused room in a large house or of a sojourn in the Arctic. What stands out in the latter instance, and seems always part of travel in a wild landscape, is the long struggle of the mind for concordance with that mysterious entity, the earth.

One more thought from Tuan: a culture's most cherished places are not necessarily visible to the eye—spots on the land one can point to. They are made visible in drama—in narrative, song, and performance. It is precisely what is *invisible* in the land, however, that makes what is merely empty space to one person a *place* to another. The feeling that a particular place is suffused with memories, the specific focus of sacred and profane stories, and that the whole landscape is a congeries of such places, is what is meant by a local sense of the land. The observation that it is merely space which requires definition before it has meaning—political demarcation, an assignment of its ownership, or industrial development—betrays a colonial sensibility.

It is easy to underestimate the power of a long-term association with the land, not just with a specific spot but with the span of it in memory and imagination, how it fills, for example, one's dreams. For some people, what they are is not finished at the skin, but continues with the reach of the senses out into the land. If the land is summarily disfigured or reorganized, it causes them psychological pain. Again, such people are attached to the land as if by luminous fibers; and they live in a kind of time that is not of the moment but, in concert with memory, extensive, measured by a lifetime. To cut these fibers causes not only pain but a sense of dislocation.

The expansion of nations into lands beyond their borders, and the rearrangement of these lands, conceptually and in real terms, to serve the expanding nation's ends, are among the most perplexing political problems of our time. A traveler often differs from a nation-state, however, in wishing to disturb nothing in the land beyond his borders, but only to visit and somehow arrive, through the inevitable contrasts, at a renewed sense of the worth of his own place, of the esteem in which he wishes to hold the landscape that originally shaped him.

In setting out, however, the traveler immediately confronts the problem of the map, an organization of the land according to a certain sense of space and an evaluation of what is important. I traveled everywhere with maps, no one of which was ever entirely accurate. They were the projection of a wish that the space could be this well organized. You cannot blame the maps, of course; nor can you travel without them. I was glad to pull them out of a pack or a back pocket and find clarification. I have leaned over the navigator's shoulder in a C-130 to get a better idea of where we were going and where at that moment we were. I have drawn maps in a notebook to explain to someone where I had been, to see if he could corroborate or amplify what I had seen. I knew that mixture of satisfaction and desire—to know exactly how one is situated in the vastness; and that wish to fully comprehend the space a map renders and sets borders to. But I would try to be wary. Even a good map, one with the lines and symbols of a hand-written geography on it, where Tuan's "spaces" have been turned into "places," masquerades as an authority. What we hold in our hands are but approximations of what is out there. Neatly folded simulacra.

The perspective of most maps of the land, to begin with, is an abstraction, because it represents what the moving eye, not the stationary eye, sees in an overview. The map is two-dimensional, while the earth is three-dimensional and curved in two planes; neither the renderings nor the projections are ever quite accurate, and if the scale is large, the distortion can be extreme. (The most familiar sort of world map, the Mercator projection, in which the Arctic looms larger than all the Russias, and Greenland is almost the size of North America, is a distortion that takes a long while and some thought to unlearn.) Maps organize space mathematically. They set down outlines over various kinds of coordinates and use a distribution of names to make an abstraction—sometimes beautiful or astonishing—of what is real. The orderliness, simplicity, and clarity of the presentation, of course, is often seductive.

The variety of Arctic maps is enormous, and the information they provide is astonishing. If you could sit in a room with them undisturbed and digest the information they represent, you would become an Arctic Marco Polo. Beyond the predictable high-resolution, satellite- and U-2-generated, computer-enhanced assembly of physiographic maps, there are ones that show the migration routes of caribou with ten years of acetate overlays; the cobweb of electronic surveillance at sensitive military points such as northern Bering Sea; daily updates of ice coverage in summer shipping lanes, sent electronically and rendered on Thermofax paper; and maps that require much pondering, with isotherms (temperature gradients), isograms (magnetic gradients), and isanthers (time gradients for the blooming of flowers). And maps of archaeological sites, polar bear denning sites, and the distribution of sources of gravel in the Arctic.*

Of them all, the one I carry in my mind most prominently is a polar projection, a physiographic map with the Arctic Ocean centrally located. The northern reaches of Eurasia and North America and the whole of Greenland form a perimeter. The narrow entrance to the ocean between Greenland and Svalbard stands out because the deep waters there are a darker shade of blue than those over the continental shelf. (Here is the only place a deep current can move in and out of the Polar Basin.) And all the obscure places —the New Siberian Islands, the Kara Sea, Franz Josef Land, places banished to regions of distortion in the Mercator projection—are accorded their proper proportions.

When I look at this map on my wall, I am reminded of the geographical continuity of the region, which is unique—no matter how far east or west you go, you are still there. I can see how much shorter the route from Rotterdam to Yokohama is via Bering Strait than through the Panama Canal. And there is a fetching remoteness to northern Greenland when the island is seen in its entirety, not distorted or truncated. And I can put my fingers on wild Ellesmere, with its Agassiz Ice Cap and exotic plateaus, a daydreamed landscape of my youth. The Baffin Island Eskimos call it *ooming-mannuna*, where the muskoxen have their country.

THE earliest maps of the Arctic reflected the skills and conceptions (and misconceptions) of the cultures that produced them. Long before it became a field science, cartography was a contemplative pursuit; cartographers drew fabled landscapes and imaginary lands

---

* Gravel deposits are second only to hydrocarbon (gas and oil) deposits in their importance to arctic villages. Vast quantities of gravel are needed to prepare airstrips and construction pads because of the difficulty of building over permafrost.

of their own divining. The Arctic they depicted was a dark, mountainous, icy region of "brutes with neither language nor reason [who] hiss like geese"; or, alternately, an idyllic place of perpetual sunshine and warm seas. Either Asgard, the Norse citadel of zephyrs, brilliant light, and reigning power; or Niflheim, a cold wasteland of unending darkness hung with the stench of death.

The discovery of Svalbard by Dutch whalers in the sixteenth century and explorations north and west toward Novaya Zemlya by Willoughby and Chancellor (1553), and Barents (1596), and to the west by Frobisher (1576–1578), Davis (1585–1587), Hudson (1607–1610), and Baffin (1616), brought the Arctic to a more empirical definition. In succeeding centuries, it was discovered, piece by piece, beneath the ice and snow. Its lands were mapped and its waters charted. The final break with an Old World image of the Arctic was made when a Norwegian ship called the *Fram* completed a spectacular circumarctic voyage (1893–1896). Robert Peary proclaimed Greenland an island in 1892. In 1915–1917 Stefansson discovered the last, large pieces of land in the Far North. The coastline of the Canadian Archipelago was extensively redrawn during and immediately after World War II, as a result of military reconnaissance, and the last large islands in the south were discovered, in Foxe Basin west of Baffin Island (including Air Force Island, approximately 500 miles square).

Part of the allure of the Arctic has always been the very imprecision of its borders. The flat topography of the land becomes part of the frozen sea in winter. In summer, in some regions, low-lying land extends so far into shallow seas it is hard to tell them apart. It is easy to imagine that small bits of land might still lie hidden—and this indeed recently proved true in a dramatic way. In 1968, geographers finally determined mathematically that a small island called Kaffeklubben, which Peary had discovered in 1900, not Cape Morris Jesup, Greenland, was the northernmost point of land. In 1978, however, a tiny new island was discovered in the ice, 1500 yards north of Kaffeklubben. It was named

Oodaaq for a Polar Eskimo who accompanied Peary on his 1909 trip to the Pole.*

In time, then—and more sophisticated satellite-mapping technology continues to improve the accuracy of arctic maps—the lands that were imagined to exist in the Arctic were slowly replaced on the maps by the outlines of the lands that were actually found to be there. "Frobussher's Straights," which cut across northern Canada from the Atlantic to the Western Ocean in George Best's 1587 map; the Open Polar Sea, which Henry Hudson confidently sailed for in 1607; and the land bridge from Norway to Svalbard—all these misconceptions faded from the maps.

Many of the old maps of the Arctic, with their fabled islands, were only expressions of a wish for something better, for an easing of human travail—to find the Blessed Isles of the West, or a route to the Moluccas, the "Spice Islands," free of Spanish ships or Turkish middlemen. One folds such maps and puts them gently back in the drawer, out of a certain regard for human history, the long reach of human desire, and a search for contentment that goes beyond the borders of one's homeland.

To set these maps aside makes the colonial tragedies they record no less tragic; the admonition against imperious delusions no less sharp; and evidence of the real landscape no less insubstantial. Another age will surely find us as headstrong and avaricious as our exploring ancestors, and our plans as disrespectful and unwise

---

* Oodaaq was born in 1878 or 1879 and lived until the mid-1950s. He assisted a number of explorers and scientists, most of whom introduced different spellings of his name into the historical records—Ootah (Peary), Odârk (Mylius Erichsen), Odaq (Rasmussen), and Ûtâq (Jean Malaurie). Oodaaq Island was discovered on July 26, 1978, by Uffe Petersen during a Danish Geodetic Institute survey of regional topography in northern Greenland. "It is a rather small [patch of gravel]," a colleague of Petersen wrote me, "only 30 m (98.4 feet) in diameter and less than 1 m (3.28 feet) over sea level at its highest point. Its position is 83°40′32.51″N 30°40′10.12″W."

as some of these earlier schemes for prosperity seem to us now. Perhaps they will be forgiving as well.

WE have come to think of the Arctic as vast because in the familiar
Mercator projection it stretches from one side of the world to the
other. The suggestion that the region never comes together, however, that its various sections are "a world apart," is false. The
region turns in on itself like any nation. It is organized like Australia,
around an inland desert sea, with most of its people living on the
coastal periphery. It is not vast like the Pacific. It is vast like the
steppes of Asia. It has the heft, say, of China, but with the population of Seattle.

    The Arctic's geographical unity derives from the sameness of
its climate and seasons of light, and the similarity of its animal
populations east and west—polar bear, bowhead whale, arctic fox,
ringed seal, snowy owl. There are relatively few localized arctic
species, such as the narwhal; and very few circumpolar animals
show any subspecific differences (the walrus is one).*

    To a modern traveler the arctic landscape can seem numbingly
monotonous, but this impression is gained largely, I think, from
staring at empty maps of the region and from traveling around in it
by airplane. The airplane, like the map, creates a false sense of
space; it achieves simplicity and compression, however, not with
an enforced perspective but by altering the relationship between
space and time. The interior of a plane is artificially lit, protected
from weather, full of rarefied air cut with the odor of petroleum

---

* Further enhancing a sense of the region's natural homogeneity is the
fact that the native people of half the Arctic, from Bering Strait to
northern Greenland, speak nearly the same language. A linguistic
continuity like this is not known anywhere else in the world. The
mutual intelligibility of Eskimo dialects has facilitated the formation of
a political body, the Inuit Circumpolar Conference, which now assists
Alaskan, Canadian, and Greenlandic Eskimos in the settlement of land
claims and in their pursuit of self-determination.

distillates and tobacco, and far noisier than the ground below. Many who fly in arctic aircraft, often crowded together with sled dogs and boxes of freight, incur slight headaches, and many experience some sort of spatial or temporal disorientation. Stories of government officials and reporters who arrive in northern villages by jet from somewhere in southern Canada, hear little of what is spoken to them, and insist on departing the very same day, are legion. Their haste, their cool insensitivity and aura of power seem, somehow, a part of the aircraft. The great compression of time and space the plane effects is without parallel in the northern villages. The knowledge of the land that such people carry home, therefore, is often false, and their summaries are bitterly resented.

The plane is a great temptation; but to learn anything of the land, to have any sense of the relevancy of the pertinent maps, you must walk away from the planes. You must get off into the country and sleep on the ground, or take an afternoon to take a tussock apart. Travel on the schedule of muskoxen. Camp on a seaward point and watch migrating sea ducks in their days of passage. You need to stand before the green, serpentine walls of the Jade Mountains north of the Kobuk River, or walk out over the sea ice to the flaw lead in winter to hear the pack ice grinding and scraping, a noise like "the whining of puppies and swarming of bees," in the words of the American explorer Elisha Kent Kane. In the stomach of a walrus butchered on the spring ice you will find the sediment of the ocean floor. Slowly comes the realization that 250,000 walrus in the Bering and Chukchi seas are moving tons of sand and fine gravel around, every day. You will think of lemmings and voles turning over thousands of tons of soil on the tundra. And of the Thule, who carried large stones into their camps and set them up in a pattern for a jumping game, like hopscotch. Of the huge stone polar bear traps the Thule built with their sliding stone doors. Residents, moving stones about.

When you have walked for days under the enormous sky; when you have felt the remoteness of the world from the Thomsen

River country of Banks Island; felt the unquenchable exuberance of sled dogs cracking off the frozen miles down a river valley; or been shown how some very small thing, like a Lapland longspur eating the lemming's bones for calcium, keeps the country alive, you begin to sense the timeless, unsummarized dimensions of a deeper landscape.

But you must insist on time to walk away from the plane, which daily enters and leaves the Arctic like some sort of bullet.

Christian Vibe told me a story. He was in northern Greenland, coming and going by dog sledge from the small village of Uummannaq (Thule) on Hayes Peninsula. In the spring of 1940 he was traveling along the east coast of Ellesmere Island, living on supplies he had cached there months before. An Eskimo friend of his from Uummannaq knew that Vibe was a Dane and that some information that had reached Uummannaq in May would be important to him. The man sledged across Smith Sound and found a cache where he knew Vibe would show up. He scratched this message in Eskimo syllabics on the side of a pemmican can:

> germans taking meat from denmark
> the king is still alive
> no gas left in shop.

The meaning was almost instantly clear to Vibe. Germany had gone to war with Denmark (i.e., "was taking her food"); the government of King Christian had not been deposed; and, because of the war, there would be no supplies coming by ship to Uummannaq in the spring. Vibe said he held the can in his gloved hands and looked around in the bright light, at his dogs and his few supplies, and knew he would not get home for a very long time.

SOME early explorers took Eskimos and their knowledge of the land seriously and asked them to draw maps of the surrounding country.* The Eskimos obliged. These maps were a great boon to arctic travel and exploration; today they offer an insight into the way Eskimos perceived the space around them.

A good knowledge of the local landscape and the ability to draw a detailed map are two very different cognitive skills. Nevertheless, many Eskimos, both men and women, produced highly accurate maps of the coastal and interior regions of their homeland. Robert M'Clure told his biographer in 1856 that the Eskimo of western Victoria Island drew expertly with pencil and paper "as if they were accustomed to hydrography." Another British naval officer marveled at a map created for him on the beach by Eskimos at Cape Prince of Wales in 1826, where stones, sticks, and pebbles were used "in a very ingenious and intelligible manner" to create a scaled replica of the region. Franz Boas reported Eskimos in the eastern Arctic drawing maps so fine he could recognize their every point in comparison with his own charts. "It is remarkable," wrote Boas, "that their ideas of the relative position and direction of coasts far distant from one another are so clear." The linear distances involved were as much as 1000 miles, and the areas represented as large as 150,000 square miles. Eskimos could also read European maps and charts of their home range with ease, in whatever orientation the maps were handed to them—upside down or sideways. And they had no problem switching from one scale to another or in maintaining a consistent scale in a map they drew.

Eskimos were making and using maps long before they met Europeans, both as mnemonic devices for ordering extensive sys-

---

* Mapmaking in the Arctic presented Europeans with several problems. The season for ship travel, to begin with, was very short, and during these summer months much of the coastline was either shrouded in fog or blocked by ice. Alternately, the same conditions that created mirages distorted the coasts and caused inconsistent readings when the ship tried to fix its own position. The sheer length of the coastline, and the barrenness and ruggedness of the land where survey parties had to put ashore, made this formidable task even more daunting.

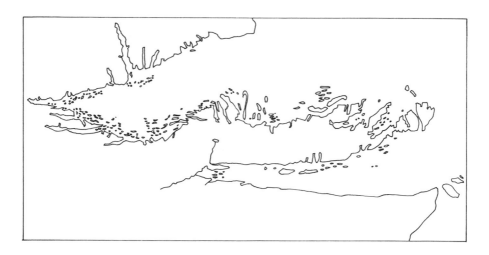

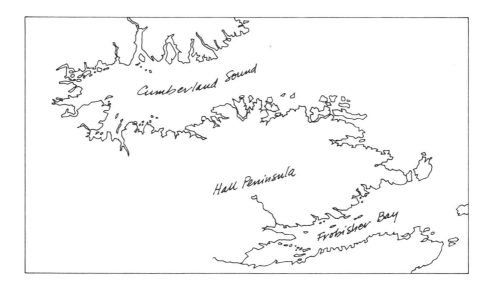

Above, map of the Cumberland Sound–Frobisher Bay region, drawn from memory by an Eskimo named Sunapignanq. Below, map of the same area generated with modern cartographic techniques.

tems of place names and as navigational aids. Some of the latter were
carved of wood—excellent for sea travel because they rendered
coastlines in three dimensions (very useful in the eastern Arctic),
were impervious to weather, and would float if dropped overboard.

Edmund Carpenter, with his particular interest in Eskimos'
differing appreciation of the volume of space and their lack of a
preferred orientation in it, has noticed that in maps of Southampton
Island that the Aivilik prepared for him, the only distortions
appeared in areas that were hunted very intensively. These regions
were drawn larger than those visited less frequently. Contemporary Eskimo maps evince the same accuracy and richness,
testifying to the continued maintenance of local geographic knowledge by those for whom this aspect of the culture is still alive, the
astonishing degree to which the faculty of memory is cultivated
among them, and their enduring penchant for long journeys over
the land and sea ice. All this, despite their having moved into
permanent settlements in most cases.

Traces of human presence in the land, like maps, organize undifferentiated space in certain ways, and the effect, especially in
open country, is soothing. To come upon a series of Dorset campsites adds dimension and direction to the land; and one of course
takes pleasure in the objects seen at these places. The same is true
of a place where caribou for hundreds of years have crossed a
river, or moved between mountains.

Distinctive landmarks that aid the traveler and control the
vastness, as well as prominent marks on the land made inadvertently
in the process of completing other tasks, are very much apparent in
the Arctic. The most evocative are the *inuksuit* (stones piled up
in the shape of human beings) that dot the eastern arctic landscape.
They once funneled herds of caribou into depressions or rock
corrals and marked lake shores at points where the fishing was good.
One also finds stone fish dams and ptarmigan fences that date from
Thule times. Rock cairns raised by early European explorers still
stand out crisply in the landscape, on hills and headlands, and at

turns of the coastline; and they are still utilized by bush pilots and others as navigational aids.

More modern traces of man on the land, infinitely more prevalent, are not as charming. Canada's recently awakened sense of a northern destiny, for example, initiated a contemporary period of fervent cairn-building that proceeds unabated. Geological survey crews, oil-drilling crews, and various bureaucratic officials and dignitaries now routinely erect commemorative cairns. A simple cigar tube placed inside might contain a Polaroid print of mugging pals, or a more substantial metal case might hold a large color print of a government official and his family. (The diminishment of genuine exploration history suggested by these acts infuriates some northerners. They regard such cairn-building as pompous or silly, and dismantle the cairns whenever they come upon them.)

More irritating to the eye than these gratuitous monuments are the tens of thousands of miles of seismic trails generated in a continuing search for oil and gas, and the hundreds of thousands of empty aviation gas barrels scattered across the tundra at thousands of spike camps used by scientists, technicians, and, in recent years, by Eskimo hunters. As the science of seismic surveying improves, the same areas are surveyed all over again, and the system of trails left in the tundra by the cleat-footed tractor trains is extended. Vegetation does not grow back; the compressed soil does not rebound; spring rains do not wash the trails away. If anything, they occasionally grow worse. The exposed soil absorbs more sunlight, permafrost below begins to melt, and the tractorway begins to sink and separate, like a prairie gully in soil held together by no roots.

PULUWATAN natives in the Caroline Islands are famed for the accuracy with which they navigate on the high seas between distant archipelagos of the South Pacific. They align their boats with certain rising and setting stars, and note the presence at sea of particular species of birds, the salinity of the water, the set of currents, and the behavior of swell systems. Likewise, an Eskimo navigating in polar darkness and white-outs and across featureless stretches of ice and snow makes full and efficient use of the few clues available to him. On shorefast ice in summer fog he travels between the voices of seabirds on landward cliffs and the sound of surf on the seaward edge of the ice. When he begins a journey over open terrain he marks the angle of the wind and checks his bearing periodically by glancing at the fur of his parka rim, at its alignment with the breeze. He bends down to feel the trend of sastrugi (ridges of hard snow that form in line with the prevailing wind) when he cannot see them in darkness or blowing snow. He notes the trend of any cracks in the ice as he crosses them. Sea ice cracks can reveal the presence of a cape or headland invisible in the distance, or they may confirm one's arrival at a known area, where the pattern of cracks is the same, year after year. The need to pay attention to the smallest clues is essential—a dark object on the ice could be a stone, revealing a hidden shoreline.

Constant attention to such details, memories of the way the land looks, and stories told by other travelers and hunters about the region are used together with the movements of animals, especially those of birds, and "sky maps" to keep the traveler on course.* Searching for such small but crucial clues, especially in the tremendous glare of light in spring (the traditional season for long journeys, because of the combination of good light and firm ice) or in the low-contrast conditions of winter, can be exhausting for a man who does not know what to ignore.

These navigational skills are still part of village life for some in the Arctic, used just as often today in traveling long distances

---

* A distant body of open water in the sea ice will often cast a dark shadow in the clouds above, producing a "water sky," while ice lying over the horizon often produces a soft white reflection in the air above it called "ice blink." The term "sky map" refers to either phenomena or to the pattern of light and dark they create together in the sky. A very discerning eye can distinguish among several sorts of ice blink. Snow-covered land appears yellowish white in the sky. Field ice is a lucid white, tinged with yellow. Pack ice is a pure white. Sea ice in embayments is a grayer white.

by snow machine as they were once by people traveling by dog sledge or on foot. And such skills still remain more critical for the success of a journey, especially over the sea ice, than even the best maps and navigation aids. Fogs and blizzards obscure the reference points important in navigation by topographic map—even compasses can't be consistently relied on here. The closer one gets to the magnetic pole, the stronger the vertical component and the weaker the horizontal component of this electromagnetic field become, causing the needle to wander listlessly, east and west of magnetic north. Corrections for compass declination at certain longitudes and latitudes are useless. Ionospheric disturbances, including magnetic storms and a phenomenon called "polar cap absorption," adversely affect radio direction-finding equipment. The frequency of temperature inversions in the summer makes it difficult to align a sextant on an undistorted horizon. And satellite-generated maps showing the extent of the sea ice, sent electronically to ships, are dated in twenty-four hours.

In the Arctic the sun does not rise reliably in the east and set in the west, and the farther north one goes, the fewer are the stars that rise and set. The summer moon is so dim that its presence is barely noticed. The most dependable sources of direction for most Eskimos, therefore, are the behavior of the wind and ocean currents, the consistent alignment of a flaw lead, and such things as the direction of flow of a river. You hardly ever hear someone say he is going to head "east" to hunt or visit or look around.

ONE September morning I traveled east (the way I envisioned it) with several friends in a small boat from our scientific base camp at Beaufort Lagoon, near the Canadian border. It was a balmy day, exhilarating weather after a week of cold wind and rain and overcast skies during which we had been working at sea. We were headed for the Yukon border, which had for all of us a romantic allure. We traveled about 25 miles along the coast before we were cut off in the shore lead by ice. Fortuitously, we were within a hundred yards of the border.

We doffed our parkas and wandered about the tundra somewhat aimlessly, in the vicinity of a cluster of weathered driftwood
piles that marked the dividing line between the two countries.
Caribou trails and the sight of migrating ducks and geese, the
absence of immigration officials, and, not least, the sun shining
brightly in a cloudless sky made us all take crossing the border less
seriously. We found tufts of polar bear fur caught in the dry
tundra grasses, and the tracks of a bear in the steep embankment,
where it had descended the coastal bluff to the ice and headed out
to sea.

In such benign circumstances it was hard to imagine the
deadly tension that characterized other national borders on that
same day. We were all of us more affected by an exotic childhood
idea—reaching the Yukon Territory. We took our bearings from a
country in our heads—it was an *idea* that brought us here, to a
spot on the tundra we would be hard pressed to distinguish in
terms of plant life or animal life or topography from the tundra
a mile farther to the east, or back to the west. To come here at all
was an act of carefree innocence. We stood around for nearly an
hour. We took each other's pictures. We were delighted by the
felicitous conjunction of this good weather and our idea of "the
Yukon Territory."

Ideas no less real and far more affecting brought European
explorers into the Arctic hundreds of years ago. They were searching for lands and straits they knew existed but which they had
never seen; and they could not believe they did not exist when they
failed to find them. As there was a Strait of Magellan at Cape Horn,
they thought, so too should there be a northern strait, a Strait of
Anian, just as there were Western and Eastern, Northern and
Southern oceans. Did not the most learned references of the day,
the sea charts, depict such a passage? And did it not make sense
that Frobisher should find gold in the Arctic, just as the Spaniards
had in the tropics?

When the early arctic explorers wrote down in official com-
mentaries what they had seen, they were hesitant to criticize the

wisdom of the day, what the esteemed maps indicated. They were prone, in fact, to embellish, in order to make themselves seem more credible. They even believed on occasion that they *had* sensed something where there was nothing because it seemed ordained that it should happen—did not the eye glimpse faintly a shore before the fog closed in? Had not the ear recorded a distant surf before darkness and a contrary wind conspired against it? The land, they believed, should corroborate, not contradict, what men knew from sources like Ptolemy about the shape of the world. The accounts of such explorers were read and passed on; the entangled desires and observations of the writers, with a liberal interpretation by cartographers with reputations of their own to protect, perpetuated a geography of hoped-for islands and straits to the west of Europe that could not be substantiated, a geography only of the mind.

The influence of these images, of course, was considerable. Such a mental geography becomes the geography to which society adjusts, and it can be more influential than the real geography. The popular image of a previously unknown region, writes J. Wreford Watson, is "compounded of what men hope to find, what they look to find, how they set about finding, how findings are fitted into their existing framework of thought, and how those findings are then expressed." This, says Watson, is what is actually "found" in a new land.

Another geographer, John L. Allen, pondering the way we set off for a fresh landscape, writes, "When exploration is viewed as a process rather than as a series of distinct events, its major components [are seen to be] clearly related to the imagination. No exploratory adventure begins without objectives based on the imagined nature and content of the lands to be explored." The course of discovery is guided, then, by preconceived notions. Field observations, writes Allen, "are distorted by these images. The results of exploration are modified by reports written and interpreted in the light of persistent illusions and by attempts made to fit new information into partly erroneous systems and frameworks of geographical understanding."

Over the past twenty years, some of the focus of academic geography has shifted away from descriptions of the land and focused instead on landscapes that exist in the human mind. The extent and complexity of these geographical images, called mental maps, are wonderful. An urban resident, for example, sees himself situated in urban space with specific reference to certain stores, parking spaces, and public transportation stations. He assigns one street or building more importance than another as a place for chance meetings with friends. He knows which routes between certain points are safest and how to get to a certain restaurant even though he doesn't know the names of any of the streets on the way. The mental map of an Eskimo might be an overview of the region where he customarily hunts—where caribou are likely to turn up in the spring, where berries are to be found, where consistent runs of char are located, where the ground is too swampy to walk over in June, where good soapstone is to be had, or a regular supply of driftwood.

The mental maps of both urban dweller and Eskimo may correspond poorly in spatial terms with maps of the same areas prepared with survey tools and cartographic instruments. But they are proven, accurate guides of the landscape. They are living conceptions, idiosyncratically created, stripped of the superfluous, instantly adaptable. Their validity is not susceptible of contradiction.

Our overall cultural perception of a region requires another term. Mental maps are too personal; and the term does not convey sufficiently the richness of the invisible landscape, that component of a regional image that aboriginal groups dwell on at least as much as they consider a region's physiographic components. Jahner's term, the spiritual landscape, refers more specifically to relationships inherent in the physical landscape which make us aware of the presence of the forces and relationships that infuse our religious thought. If one can take the phrase "a country of the mind" to mean the landscape evident to the senses, as it is retained in human memory and arises in the oral tradition of a people, as a repository of both mythological and "real-time" history, then perhaps this phrase will suffice.

Amos Rapoport, an Australian architect, and like Tuan and Carpenter curious about the meaning of "place," made a landmark study among Kurna, Arunda, Walbiri, and other Australian aborigines. He mapped their mythological landscapes. He understood that the stories that compose a tribe's mythological background, their origin and their meaning and purpose in the universe, are "unobservable realities" that find their expression in "observable phenomena." The land, in other words, makes the myth real. And it makes the people real.

The stories that unfold against the local landscape, and that give expression to the enduring relationships of life, said Rapoport, are as critical for people as food or water. The mythic landscape is not the natural landscape, Rapoport concluded, but the mythic and natural landscapes overlap at certain visible points in the land. And the limits of the local landscape, he emphasized, are not something that can be politically negotiated; they are fixed in mythology. They are not susceptible of adjustment. Rapoport's study made it eminently clear, as he put it, that Europeans may "completely misunderstand the nature of the landscape because of their point of view."

It is always somewhat risky to extrapolate from one aboriginal culture to another. I know of no work comparable to Rapoport's in the Arctic, however, and his observations come as close to being generically sound as any anthropologist's I know. The journals of the most attentive arctic explorers, those with both a flair for listening and a capacity to record metaphorical impressions without judgment, are filled with references to mythological events that occurred at particular places. Eskimos are not as land-conscious as aborigines; they are more sea-conscious, and the surface of the sea is impermanent, new every year. Still, the evidence for a landscape in the Arctic larger than the one science reports, more extensive than that recorded on the United States Coast and Geodetic Survey quadrangle maps, is undeniable. It is the country the shamans shined their *qaumaneq*, their shaman light, into.

The aspiration of aboriginal people throughout the world has been to achieve a congruent relationship with the land, to fit well in it. To achieve occasionally a state of high harmony or reverberation. The dream of this transcendent congruency included the evolution of a hunting and gathering relationship with the earth, in which a mutual regard was understood to prevail; but it also meant a conservation of the stories that bind the people into the land.

I recall a scene in one of the British discovery expeditions to the Arctic of a group of ship's officers standing about somewhat idly on a beach while three or four Eskimo men drew a map for them in the sand. The young officers found the drawing exotic and engaging, but almost too developed, too theatrical. I can imagine the Eskimos drawing a map they meant not to be taken strictly as a navigational aid, but as a recapitulation of their place in the known universe. Therefore, as they placed a line of stones to represent a mountain range and drew in the trend of the coast, they included also small, seemingly insignificant bays where it was especially good to hunt geese, or tapped a section of a river where the special requirements for sheefish spawning were present. This was the map as mnemonic device, organizing the names of the places and the stories attached to them, three or four men unfolding their meaning and purpose as people before the young officers. They did not know what to leave out for these impatient men. There was no way for them to separate the stories, the indigenous philosophy, from the land. The young officers later remembered only that the maps were fascinating. Had the Eskimos told them that the Pentateuch was merely fascinating, they would have thought them daft.

The place-fixing stories that grew out of the land were of two kinds. The first kind, which was from the myth time and which occurred against the backdrop of a mythological landscape, was usually meticulously conserved. (It was always possible that the storyteller would not himself or herself grasp completely the wisdom inherent in a story that had endured, which had proved its value repeatedly.)

The second kind of story included stories about traveling and what had happened to everyone in the years that could be recalled. It was at this place that my daughter was born; or this is where my brother-in-law killed two caribou the winter a bear killed all my dogs; or this, Titiralik, is the place my snow machine broke down and I had to walk; Seenasaluq, this is a place my family has camped since before I was born.

The undisturbed landscape verifies both sorts of story, and it is the constant recapitulation in sacred and profane contexts of all of these stories that keeps the people alive and the land alive in the people. Language, the stories, holds the vision together.

To those of us who are not hunters, who live in cities with no sharp regret and enjoy ideas few Eskimos would wish to discuss, such sensibilities may seem almost arcane. And we may put no value to them. But we cut ourselves off, I think, from a source of wisdom. We sometimes mistake a rude life for a rude mind; raw meat for barbarism; lack of conversation for lack of imagination. The overriding impression, I think, for the visitor in the Arctic who walks away from the plane, and waits out the bouts of binge drinking, the defensive surliness and self-conscious acting in the village, is that a wisdom is to be found in the people. And once in a great while an *isumataq* becomes apparent, a person who can create the atmosphere in which wisdom shows itself.

This is a timeless wisdom that survives failed human economies. It survives wars. It survives definition. It is a nameless wisdom esteemed by all people. It is understanding how to live a decent life, how to behave properly toward other people and toward the land.

It is, further, a wisdom not owned by anyone, nor about which one culture is more insightful or articulate. I could easily imagine some Thomas Merton–like person, the estimable rather than the famous people of our age, sitting with one or two Eskimo men and women in a coastal village, corroborating the existence of this human wisdom in yet another region of the world, and looking around to the mountains, the ice, the birds to see what makes it possible to put it into words.

ONE July evening I flew with two paleontologists from Ellef Ringnes Island some 400 miles southwest to their new camp near Castel Bay on Banks Island. In the years before, these two people had elucidated a wonderful bit of arctic history. A collection of fossils they assembled from a thick layer of interbedded coal and friable rock called the Eureka Formation on Ellesmere Island indicated that 40 to 50 million years ago, during the Eocene, the Arctic was a region forested with sequoias and ginkgo trees. It enjoyed a moist and temperate, almost warm climate and a collection of animals that showed a resemblance to the kinds of animals that have been discovered in Eocene deposits in Europe. At the time, the Eurasian and North American crustal plates were just beginning to separate at the northern end of the Atlantic Ocean, and animals had only recently ceased moving back and forth.

Robert West and Mary Dawson and I sat in the jump seats of an aircraft called a Twin Otter, amid their camp gear and fossil collections, for several hours. I listened to them explain their work, and took pleasure in it, in the fulfilled hopes and dashed dreams of a field season, and in some of the scenes they envisioned in the land below us during the Eocene, when three-toed horses, ancestral flying lemurs, and prehistoric crocodiles lived. It was not something they could see clearly, only imagine. They recounted their patient search through frost-riven rubble in the Arctic, looking for bits of mineralized bone, teeth, and shells, for pieces of petrified wood and casts of fallen leaves, the shreds of evidence that suggested a landscape.

It was a long flight. To be heard we had to shout a little over the sound of the engines or draw things on pieces of paper. Somewhere over Melville Island the pilot, Duncan Grant, turned around in his seat to listen. The copilot flew on. Grant began to tell us about the history of arctic exploration, a subject upon which he was keen and knowledgeable. We were approaching Dealy Island on the south coast, where Kellett and his crew wintered in 1852 aboard HMS *Resolute*. He wanted us to see that, and, farther on, the winter quarters of Parry at the bay now called Winter Harbor.

As we crossed from Melville Island to Banks Island we looked down on massive pressure ridges, the jumbled, very heavy ice of M'Clure Strait. As we neared the coast, Grant, shouting, tried to get us to see what Pim had seen as he approached Banks Island, when he made a dash from Dealy Island in the spring of 1853 to rescue M'Clure and the men aboard the *Investigator*. Even though it was July, a different cast of light entirely, you could see what Grant meant and how the event loomed for him as we approached. We all stopped talking. For the last half hour we just looked out the windows.

We flew over herds of muskoxen. The slanting light was so bucolic in its effect on the hillsides that they looked like herds of black angus grazing in English pastures. We crossed the mouth of the Thomsen River and then circled while West and Dawson surveyed the terrain and decided where to camp. Grant landed on a gravel ridge, where only a few plants were growing—a good exposure of the Eureka Formation. We unloaded their gear and then stood there, just looking around. It was a beautiful evening. We were all smiling with an unspoken hope that their work would be successful.

Dawson handed me a packet of letters they had written to their families and asked me to mail them when we got back to Resolute. We waved, a mixture of regret and good wishes at parting. I rode for hours with the letters on the seat beside me. I thought about the great desire among friends and colleagues and travelers who meet on the road, to share what they know, what they have seen and imagined. Not to have a shared understanding, but to share what one has come to understand. In such an atmosphere of mutual regard, in which each can roll out his or her maps with no fear of contradiction, of suspicion, or theft, it is possible to imagine the long, graceful strides of human history.

I thought about it all the way back to Resolute, watching Melville Island and then Bathurst disappear beneath the clouds, as weather moved in from the west.

Eight

THE INTENT OF MONKS

W E LEFT OUR CAMP on Pingok Island one morning knowing a storm was moving in from the southwest, but we were not worried. We were planning to work in open water between the beach and the edge of the pack ice, only a few miles out, making bottom trawls from an open 20-foot boat. The four of us were dressed, as usual, in heavy clothes and foul-weather gear.

You accept the possibility of death in such situations, prepare for it, and then forget about it. We carried emergency and survival equipment in addition to all our scientific gear—signal flares, survival suits, a tent, and each of us had a pack with extra clothing, a sleeping bag, and a week's worth of food. Each morning we completed a checklist of the boat and radioed a distant base camp with our day plan. When we departed, we left a handwritten note on the table in our cabin, saying what time we left, the compass bearing we were taking, and when we expected to return.

My companions, all scientists, were serious about this, but not solemn or tedious. They forestalled trouble by preparing for it, and were guided, not deterred, by the danger inherent in their work. It is a pleasure to travel with such people. As in other walks of life, the person who feels compelled to dramatize the risks or is either smugly complacent or eager to demonstrate his survival skills is someone you hope not to meet.

Our camaraderie came from our enthusiasm for the work and from exhilaration with the landscape, the daily contact with seabirds, seals, and fish. We rarely voiced these things to each other; they surfaced in a word of encouragement or understanding around rough work done in unending dampness and cold. Our mutual regard was founded in the accomplishment of our tasks and was as important to our survival as the emergency gear stowed in a blue box forward of the steering console.

We worked through the morning, sorting the contents of bottom trawls and vertical plankton tows. Around noon we shut the engines off and drifted under overcast skies, eating our lunch. The seas were beginning to slap at the hull, but we had another couple of hours before they built up to three or four feet—our match, comfortably. We decided, then, to search for seals in the ice front before heading in. An hour later, by a movement of the ice so imperceptible it was finished before we realized it, we were cut off from the sea. The wind, compacting the ice, was closing off the channels of calm water where we had been cruising. We were suddenly 200 yards from open water, and a large floe, turning off the wind and folding in from the west, threatened to close us off even deeper in the pack. Already we had lost steerageway—the boat was pinned at that moment on all four sides.

In those first hours we worked wordlessly and diligently. We all knew what we faced. Even if someone heard our distress call over the radio, we could not tell him precisely where we were, and we were in pack ice moving east. A three-day storm was coming on. The floes might crush the boat and drive it under, or they could force it out of the water where we would have it for shelter.

We took advantage of any momentary opening in the ice to move toward open water, widening the channels with ice chisels, pushing with the twin 90-horsepower engines, the four of us heaving at the stern and gunnels. We were angling for a small patch of water within the pack. From there, it seemed, after a quick reconnoiter ahead on foot, we might be able to get out to the open sea. Thirty feet shy of our patch of water, we doubted the wisdom of taking ice chisels to one particular chunk of weathered pressure ice that blocked our path. Fractured the wrong way, its center of gravity would shift and the roll could take the boat under. The only way around it was to pull the boat, which weighed 3000 pounds, completely out of the water. With an improvised system of ice anchors, lines, and block and tackle, and out of the terrific desire to get free, we set to. We got the boat up on the floe, across it, and back into the water.

Had that been open water, we would have cheered. As it was, we exchanged quick glances of justifiable but not foolish hope. While we had been winching the boat over the ice toward it, this patch of water had been closing up. And another large floe still separated us from the ocean. Where the surf broke against it, it fell a sheer four feet to the sea. Even if we got the boat over that ice, we could never launch it from such a precipice.

Two stayed in the boat. I and one other went in opposite directions along the floe. Several hundred yards to the east I found a channel. I looked it over quickly and then signaled with the up-raised shaft of my ice chisel for the others. It was barely negotiable to begin with, and in the few minutes it took to get the boat there, the channel closed. We put the prow of the boat against the seaward floe and brought both engines up to full power, trying to hold it against the wind. The ice beside it continued to move east. The channel started to open. With the engines roaring, the gap opened to six feet. With a silent, implicit understanding each of us acted decisively. The man at the helm reversed the engines, heeled the boat around, and burst up the channel. We made 20 quick feet, careened the boat over on its port gunnel, and pivoted through a 120° turn. One ran ahead, chopping swift and hard at the closing ice with a chisel. Two of us heaved, jumping in and out of the boat, stabbing at chunks of ice closing on the props. One man remained at the throttles. Suddenly he lunged away, yanking the starboard engine clear of fouling ice. The man ahead threw his ice chisel into the boat and jumped across to help lift at the port gunnel. We could *feel* how close. The starboard side of the boat slid off the ice, into the water. The bow lifted on the open sea. There was nothing more for our legs to strain against. We pulled ourselves over the gunnel and fell into the boat, limp as feed sacks. Exhausted. We were out.

We were out, and the seas were running six feet. And we were miles now from a shore that we could not see. In the hours we had been in the ice, the storm had built considerably, and we had been carried we did not know how far east. The seas were as much as the boat could handle, and too big to quarter—we had to take them nearly bow-on. The brief views from wave crests showed us nothing. We could not see far enough through the driving sleet and spray, and the arctic coast here lies too low, anyway. We could only hope we were east of Pingok, the westernmost of the barrier islands, and not to the west, headed down into Harrison Bay, where the wind has a greater fetch and the shore is much farther on.

We took water over the bow and shouted strategy to each other over the wind and the sound of engines screaming as the props came out of the water. We erected a canvas shelter forward to break the force of the sea and shed water. We got all the weight we could out of the bow. A resolute steadiness came over us. We were making headway. We were secure. If we did not broach and if we were far enough to the east, we would be able to run up on a leeward shore somewhere and wait out the storm.

We plowed ahead. Three of us stood hunched backward to the weather.

I began to recognize in the enduring steadiness another kind of calmness, or relief. The distance between my body and my thoughts slowly became elongated, and muffled like a dark, carpeted corridor. I realized I was cold, that I was shivering. I sensed the dry pits of warmth under my clothes and, against this, an opening and closing over my chest, like cold breath. I realized with dreamlike stillness that the whole upper right side of my body was soaked. The shoulder seams of my foul-weather gear were torn open.

I knew I had to get to dry clothes, to get them on. But desire could not move my legs or arms. They were too far away. I was staring at someone, then moving; the soaked clothes were coming off. I could not make a word in my mouth. I felt suspended in a shaft in the earth, and then imagined I was sitting on a bare earthen floor somewhere within myself. The knowledge that I was being slammed around like a wooden box in the bottom of the boat was like something I had walked away from.

In dry wool and protected by a tarp from the seas, I understood that I was safe; but I could not understand the duration of time. I could not locate any visual image outside myself. I concentrated on trying to gain a sense of the boat; and then on a rhythmic tensing and loosening of my muscles. I kept at it and at it; then I knew time was passing. There was a flow of time again. I heard a shout. I tried to shout myself, and when I heard an answer I knew that I was at the edge of time again, and could just step into it. I realized I was sitting up, that I was bracing myself against heavy seas.

The shouts were for the coast. We had found Pingok.

We anchored the boat under the lee shore and went into the cabin and changed clothes and fixed dinner. Our sense of relief came out in a patter of jokes at each other's expense. We ate quietly and went to bed and slept like bears in winter.

*　*　*

THE storm blew for two days. We nearly lost the boat when an anchor line parted, and got wet and cold again trying to secure it; but that seemed no more than what we had chosen by coming here. I went for a long walk on the afternoon of the second day, after the storm had become only fretful gusts and sunlight threatened to break through the low clouds.

I still felt a twinge of embarrassment at having been reduced from a state of strength to such an impassive weight, to a state of disassociation, so quickly. But I did not dwell on it long. And we would go out again, when the seas dropped. We would go into the ice again. We would watch more closely; but nothing, really, had changed.

With the experience so fresh in my mind, I began thinking of frail and exposed craft as I walked down the beach, of the Irish carraughs and Norse knarrs that brought people across the Atlantic, bucking pack ice streaming southward on the East Greenland Current. My God, what had driven them? All we know is what we have deduced from the records of early historians. And the deference those men showed to their classical predecessors, to Ptolemy, Solinus, and Isidore, their own nationalism and religious convictions, their vanity, and the shape of the ideas of their age— all this affected what they expressed. And when it was translated, or when they themselves translated from others, interpolations, adaptation, and plain error colored the historical record further. So the early record of arctic exploration is open to interpretation. And this refined history is less real, less harrowing than what had happened to us in the boat. It is events mulled and adjudicated.

I wanted to walk the length of the seaside beach on Pingok, knowing the storm was dying away. I brooded over the fates of those early immigrants, people whose names no one knows, who sailed in ships of which there are neither descriptions nor drawings, through ice and storms like this one—but so much farther from a shore, with intentions and dreams I could only imagine.

The earliest arctic voyages are recorded in the Icelandic sagas and Irish imramha. But they were written down hundreds of years after the fact by people who did not make the journeys, who only heard about them. The Norse Eddas and Icelandic sagas, wrote the arctic explorer and historian Fridtjof Nansen, are "narratives somewhat in the light of historical romances, founded upon legend and more or less uncertain traditions." The same can be said of the imramha and the records of Saint Brendan's voyage, though in tone and incident these latter are different from the sagas.

In the following pages, beginning in a time before the sagas, the notion of a road to Cathay, a Northwest Passage, emerges. The quest for such a corridor, a path to wealth that had to be followed through a perilous landscape, gathers the dreams of several ages. Rooted in this search is one of the oldest of all human yearnings— finding the material fortune that lies beyond human struggle, and the peace that lies on the other side of hope.

I should emphasize two points. Few original documents point up the unadorned character, the undisguised sensibilities, of the participants in these dramas. And the most common simile of comparison for these journeys—the exploits of astronauts—falls short. The astronaut is suitably dressed for his work, professionally trained, assiduously looked after en route, and nationally regarded. He possesses superb tools of navigation and observation. The people who first came into the Arctic had no photograph of the far shore before they left. They sailed in crude ships with cruder tools of navigation, and with maps that had no foundation or geographic authority. They shipwrecked so often that it is difficult to find records of their deaths, because shipwreck and death were unremarkable at the time. They received, for the most part, no support—popular or financial. They suffered brutally and fatally from the weather and from scurvy, starvation, Eskimo hostility, and thirst. Their courage and determination in some instances were so extreme as to seem eerie and peculiar rather than heroic. Visions of achievement drove them on. In the worst moments they were held together by regard for each other, by invincible bearing, or by stern naval discipline. Whether one finds such resourceful courage among a group of young monks on a spiritual voyage in a carraugh, or among worldly sailors with John Davis in the sixteenth century, or in William Parry's snug winter quarters on Melville Island in 1819–20, it is a sterling human quality.

In the journals and histories I read of these journeys I was drawn on by a sharp leaning in the human spirit: pure desire—the complexities of human passion and cupidity. Someone, for example, had to pay for these trips; and whoever paid was looking for a way to be paid back. Rarely was the goal anything as selfless as an increase in mankind's geographical knowledge. An arctic voyage in quest of unknown riches, or of a new passage to known riches, could mean tangible wealth for investors, and it could mean fame and social position for a captain or pilot. For a common seaman the reward might only mean some slip of the exotic, or a chance at the riches himself—at the very least a good story, probably something astounding. Enough, certainly, to sign on.

As I read, I tried to imagine the singular hunger for such things, how desire alone might convey a group of people into those fearsome seas. The achievement of one's desires may reveal what one considers moral; but it also reveals the aspiration and tack of an individual life, and the tenor of an age. In this light, one can better understand failures of nerve in the Arctic, such as Bering's in the Chukchi Sea in 1728—he simply did not have Peter the Great's burning desire to define eastern Russia. And one can better understand figures in arctic exploration so obsessed with their own achievement that they found it irksome to acknowledge the Eskimos, unnamed companions, and indefatigable dogs who helped them.

Arctic history became for me, then, a legacy of desire—the desire of individual men to achieve their goals. But it was also the legacy of a kind of desire that transcends heroics and which was privately known to many—the desire for a safe and honorable passage through the world.

As I walked the beach I stopped now and then to pick over

something on the storm-hardened shore—bits of whale vertebrae, waterlogged feathers, the odd but ubiquitous piece of plastic, a strict reminder against romance.

The narratives I carried in my head that afternoon fascinated me, but not for what they recorded of geographic accomplishment or for how they might be used in support of one side or another of a controversy, such as whether Frederick Cook or Robert Peary got to the Pole first. They held the mind because of what they said about human endeavor. Behind the polite and abstemious journal entries of British naval officers, behind the self-conscious prose of dashing explorers, were the lives of courageous, bewildered, and dreaming people. Some reports suggest that heroic passage took place for many just offstage. They make clear that others struggled mightily to find some meaning in what they were doing in those regions, for the very act of exploration seemed to them at times completely mad. They wanted to feel that what they were doing was necessary, if not for themselves then for the nation, for mankind.

The literature of arctic exploration is frequently offered as a record of resolute will before the menacing fortifications of the landscape. It is more profitable I think to disregard this notion— that the land is an adversary bent on human defeat, that the people who came and went were heroes or failures in this. It is better to contemplate the record of human longing to achieve something significant, to be free of some of the grim weight of life. That weight was ignorance, poverty of spirit, indolence, and the threat of anonymity and destitution. This harsh landscape became the focus of a desire to separate oneself from those things and to overcome them. In these arctic narratives, then, are the threads of dreams that serve us all.

APSLEY Cherry-Garrard, a companion of Robert Scott, said that exploration was the physical expression of an intellectual passion. His remark was made in an age when royal societies and governments underwrote most expeditions, out of a Victorian sense of duty, curiosity, and orthodoxy. More exploration, by far, was instigated, and more geographical knowledge gained, with the underwriting of men of commerce, war, and religion, who went out for commercial gain or for national or religious conquest. Still, Cherry-Garrard's observation, concise and idealistic, is worth remembering. It points up the relationship between toil and belief, and alludes to the hope of reward that is so much a part of a decision to enter the unknown. It might at first seem to be no visionary Elizabethan merchant's slogan; nor serve to explain the voyages of Irish monks in search of *Terra Repromissionis Sanctorum*, the blessed landscape where one stepped over that dark abyss that separated what was profane from what was holy. But, in a sense, Cherry-Garrard's summation describes all arctic travel—the intellectual passion is whatever anyone imagined would be there for him.

Desire for material wealth, for spiritual or emotional ecstasy, for recognition—strains of all three are found in nearly every arctic expedition. From the beginning, however, the promise of financial reward proved the most enduring. Nansen, writing in 1911, regarded all arctic exploration as simply evidence of the power of the unknown over the human mind. "Nowhere else," he wrote, "have we won our way more slowly, nowhere else has every new step caused so much trouble, so many privations and sufferings, and certainly nowhere have the resulting discoveries promised fewer material advantages."

Leaving aside the Irish *peregrinatores* and the Norse for the moment, it became clear fairly quickly to early European explorers that beyond furs in the subarctic and fisheries at the arctic periphery, the land held no tangible wealth. Cartier's famous remark about southern Labrador came to stand for a general condemnation of the whole region: it looked like "the land God gave to Cain." "*Praeter solitudinem nihil video*," wrote one early explorer—"I saw nothing but solitude." And yet, fatal shipwreck after shipwreck, bankruptcy after bankruptcy, the expeditions continued, strung out on the thinnest hopes, with the most sanguine expectations. Men of character continued to sail to their death for men of greed. And unscrupulous promoters and aggrandizing individuals of every stripe continued to manipulate and take advantage of whatever new was learned.

One looks in vain for a rational explanation for this dedication —the exploration of the Arctic made as little sense as Pizarro's march in search of El Dorado, or Coronado's surreal wandering over the trackless llanos of the Southwest. There was at least gold and silver to be had in the Spanish conquest, high-grade ore in record time. Hiking down the empty beach at Pingok, my head full of the volumes of Hakluyt, the scholarly deliberations of Samuel Eliot Morison, the personal narratives of John Davis, of William Parry, I arrived always at the same, disquieting place: the history of Western exploration in the New World in every quarter is a confrontation with an image of distant wealth. Gold, furs, timber, whales, the Elysian Fields, the control of trade routes to the Orient—it all had to be verified, acquired, processed, allocated, and defended. And these far-flung enterprises had to be profitable, or be made to seem profitable, or be financed until they were. The task was wild, extraordinary. And it was complicated by the fact that people were living in North America when we arrived. Their title to the wealth had to be extinguished.

The most philosophically troubling issue of our incursion in the New World, I think, grows out of our definition of wealth— the methods for its acquisition and our perception of what sorts of riches can actually be owned and transferred. A fresh landscape brings out awe, desire, and apprehension in us. But one like North America, undeveloped, also encourages a vague feeling that we can either augment or waste our lives in such places, depending on what we do. Our colloquy with the original inhabitants, of course, is unfinished. And we are still asking ourselves: What is worth acquiring here?

In the following narratives, it is not solely the desire of some men for different sorts of wealth that becomes clear but the suspicion that North America offered more than material wealth. It offered wealth that could not be owned, like the clarity of the air and the sight of 300,000 snow geese feeding undisturbed on the Great Plain of the Koukdjuak. One cannot change the historical fact that the air is no longer clear in some places and that geese no longer feed in such numbers along the Koukdjuak, while the silver mines in the great mountain of Potosí are entering their fifth century of production in an atmosphere of urban despair and destitution. And that the native people have been abused.

Our anxieties about these things are honest and deeply perplexing. Our difficulty lies in part, I think, with our insistence on defining completely the terms of our encounter with new-found wealth. We do not like to be countermanded in our categories by having something define itself. We seem vaguely uneasy, too, with the notion that a flock of snow geese rising like a snowstorm over Baffin Island is as valuable or more to mankind than the silver, tin, and copper being dug out of the Bolivian Andes at Potosí. These are not modern misgivings; they date in North America from the time of Columbus and John Cabot.

What every culture must eventually decide, actively debate and decide, is what of all that surrounds it, tangible and intangible, it will dismantle and turn into material wealth. And what of its cultural wealth, from the tradition of finding peace in the vision of an undisturbed hillside to a knowledge of how to finance a corporate merger, it will fight to preserve.

Walking down the long beach at Pingok that day I understood something else about our encounter with North America, which I did not at first have words for. It had to do with tolerance. It seemed clear to me that we need tolerance in our lives for the worth of different sorts of perception, of which the contrasting *Umwelten* of the animals on the island are a reminder. And we need a tolerance for the unmanipulated and unpossessed landscape. But what I came to see, too, was that we need to understand the relationship between tolerance and different sorts of wealth, how a tolerance for the unconverted things of the earth is intertwined with the substance of a truly rich life.

WHEN Pytheas sailed from Marseilles through the Gates of Hercules (the Strait of Gibraltar) and turned north in search of tin and amber, he was likely not the first. Carthaginians probably preceded him. His journals and maps are lost. Roman historians, jealous of his success, later disparaged his accomplishment, which was probably the circumnavigation of Britain and the discovery of the Orkneys. He sailed as far as the north coast of Norway or perhaps as far as Iceland—both have been suggested as his *Thule*.* Pytheas' journey (330–325 B.C.) commonly serves as a starting point for a history of arctic exploration, but this is history from a Mediterranean point of view. People ancestral to the Celts of northern Europe and to the Norse no doubt plied the same waters Pytheas sailed, at the same time.

The Mediterranean view of the Arctic, down to the time of the Elizabethan mariners, was shaped by two somewhat contradictory thoughts. The Arctic represented both threat and salvation. In the classical mind—which means in most learned European minds in the Middle Ages—invasion and destruction came from the North, at the hands of roving warrior peoples, from vaguely known Cimmerians about 800 B.C., to the Teutonic tribes that fought the Romans, to the Norse and Saxons of later centuries. The North was a region of fierce, fabulous people like the Amazons and the Cynocephali, or dog-headed people. Of barbaric Sythians whose lands bordered the bleak prospect of the Northern Ocean. One might go there for tin or amber, or for horses and furs, but these lands "under the pivot of the stars" were held by "hasty and evil-tempered folk" who had "the nature of bears." They ate raw meat and fat, and the eggs of "fen fowl" (plovers, gulls, and geese), and were as curious and dangerous as nightmares.

---

* In the writings of Pytheas the term "Thule" refers to a place six days' sail north of Britain.

The Northern Ocean itself was a place of whirlpools (*Chaos* and *Maelstrom*) and rip tides. (Mediterranean sailors did not discover tides until they left that inland sea.) The Hyperborean Sea, wrote a sixth-century monk, "was one known only to Him who created it." *Oceanus innavigabilis* and *Oceanus caligans vel rigens*, it said on the maps. Unnavigable. A hardened ocean shrouded in darkness. Beyond this, however, beyond Boreas, Caecias, Argestes, Thrascis, and the other northern winds, on the other side of the Rhipaean Mountains, "terrible with snow," was a land more graceful and sweet, less troubled and more fecund than any anyone had ever known. The pastures were so excellent that "if the cattle were allowed to graze more than a small part of the day, they burst in pieces." The sound of moving water was as the music of a string quartet. Vines bore fruit twelve times a year. Wheat headed not in grains but in loaves. People lived in perfect peace, "far from the evils of tyranny and war." Their place of worship was within clouds of wheeling swans.

The Land of the Hyperboreans, which lay beyond all the malevolence symbolized by the barbarians, was in its different guises, including the various Isles of the Blessed in the Western Ocean and the "Wineland" of the Norse, one of the most powerful projections of the Western imagination. These same ideas of a land where "no enemy pursues" (the Elysian Fields, the Hesperides, Avalon, El Dorado, and Irish Brasil) were inseparably a part of early arctic exploration.*

The Irish imramha, or sea sagas, recount the voyages of monks searching for the Isles of the Blessed and, as it happened, for bleak outposts in the "desert of the Ocean" suitable for contemplation. The most widely known of these was written down sometime in

---

* Most maps located these fabulous islands to the west of Europe, but their association was with visions of the North as well. The discovery of the Azores and Madeira by the Portuguese in the fifteenth century (they may have been known earlier to Phoenician traders) lent support to the notion that there were other isles farther to the west.

the ninth or tenth century, the *Navigatio Sancti Brendani Abbatis*, the story of the seven-year voyage of the abbot Saint Brendan, in a carraugh with seventeen monks. Brendan was born about A.D. 489 in County Kerry and was abbot at Clonfert in East Galway when he left on his journey (or a series of journeys).

Their craft, the carraugh, was a long, narrow, open but seaworthy boat consisting of a wickerlike basket frame covered with oak-tanned oxhide caulked with tallow. Brendan and his monks sailed with wine and cold food, used oars and a single stepped mast to convey themselves, slept on a mattress of heather, and dropped a stone anchor in bays where they explored. Their journey is a wondrous epic, filled with ecstatic visions and astounding events. They met strangers with gestures of courtesy and used their healing arts among them. They took little note of the hazards they faced. The themes are of compassion, wonder, and respect (as distinct from the themes of property, lineage, bloodshed, and banishment that distinguish the later, Icelandic sagas).

Reading loosely, it is possible to imagine that Brendan reached the Faroes and Iceland, and perhaps saw the towering volcanic peak of Beerenberg on the eastern end of Jan Mayen Island. At one point the monks saw an iceberg that took three days of hard rowing to reach. Transfixed by its beauty, Brendan suggested they row through a hole in it, which in the evening light seemed "like the eye of God."

These impeccable, generous, innocent, attentive men were, one must think, the perfect travelers.

In the fifth and sixth centuries Ireland was the center of high culture in Europe. Its tribal monasteries were refugia for intellectual thought and spiritual practice. Under pressure from Rome to bring their tradition into line with Christian orthodoxy and pressed as well by barbaric Vikings, these monks, like fierce Essenes, moved north and west to the Faroes and to Iceland, where they built their cells and monasteries on promontories and plains facing the Western Ocean. Tradition, but scant reliable record, holds that they moved on to Greenland ahead of the Norse, and thence to Labrador, Newfoundland, and the Saint Lawrence River Valley.

The Norse who came in their tracks, the second European culture after the Celts to enter the Arctic, are often cast as plunderers and wastrels, but the characterization is inaccurate. Many of the Norse who came to Iceland—the country was discovered in 860, according to the sagas, by Gardar Svavarsson, a Swedish-born Dane—were fleeing the tyrannic reign of Harald Haarfager or the rebellion of local inhabitants in Norse-occupied Ireland, Scotland, and Normandy. They were farmers and fishermen, not sea raiders. They began arriving in Iceland sometime after 870. Greenland, which may have been discovered by a Norwegian named Gunnbjörn Ulfsson, was made famous by Eirik Raude, made an outcast in Iceland in 982 for twice taking human life without reason. His banishment lasted three years, during which time "Eric the Red" stayed in present-day Julianehåb District in Greenland, on Eriks Fiord.*

In 986 Eric again sailed for Greenland from Iceland with twenty-five ships, of which fourteen, with about 500 people, arrived at Eriks Fiord. The settlers built houses of stone and turf, with turf roofs over driftwood frames. They raised a small breed of cattle, sheep, and goats, hunted seals and walrus, and caught fish. The community at Eriks Fiord, called the Eastern Settlement, and another 175 miles farther up the coast called the Western Settlement, came near to thriving during periods in the eleventh and twelfth centuries when there was some regular trade with northern Europe—walrus ivory, gyrfalcons, polar bear hides, and sealskins for iron, grain, manufactured implements, and simple machinery. It was a self-governing free state but, because of its tenuous economy, never politically stable. In 1261 it came under

---

* Most Norse and Danish place names in Greenland are being changed to Greenlandic Eskimo names. To avoid confusion I have used the older, more familiar names. The modern terms appear in the gazetteer.

Norwegian rule. The trade on which it depended, strictly regulated by a Norwegian charter, withered for a variety of reasons—the rise of the Hanseatic League, the shift of the Norwegian capital to Copenhagen in 1397, and financial collapse in Bergen, the Norwegian city from which ships for the Greenland trade sailed. The two colonies in Greenland were soon forgotten. Without trade to sustain them, a subsistence economy never being their forte, the remnant Norse population died out or intermarried with their Eskimo neighbors. Some last few may have been abducted by English slave traders in the sixteenth century.*

According to a widely accepted interpretation of the two pertinent sagas, that of Eric the Red (also called the Saga of Thorfinn Karlsevni) and the Tale of the Greenlanders, one Bjarni Herjulfsson, en route to Greenland in 986 and blown far to the west in a storm, stood off the coast of Labrador and then Baffin Island before arriving in Eriks Fiord. Eric's son Leif sailed in 1001 for the lands Bjarni had seen, in search of a precious commodity—timber. He landed first at Baffin Island (Helluland, "the country of flat stones"); then on the Labrador coast, perhaps at about 54°N, where there is a dense strip of coastal timber (Markland, "the forest land"); then, finally, on the northeast coast of Newfoundland, near the Strait of Belle Isle (Vinland).†

The Norse settlement at L'Anse aux Meadows, Newfoundland, excavated in the 1960s by Helge Ingstad, may have been used continuously by Leif and his brothers and Thorfinn Karlsevni before being abandoned in 1014. Apparently Norse skirmishes with

---

* There is a poignant line in the seventeenth-century *Annals* of the Icelandic Bishop Gisli Oddsson. He writes that the Norse, who had adopted Christianity about A.D. 1000, finally abandoned their morals, their faith, and their superior culture "*et ad Americae populos se converterunt*"—"and converted to the way of the American people."

† The sagas were not written down for another 200 years. The authors of the sagas, with a penchant for making what they heard fit what they believed (i.e., had read), may have invented this last name to signify a land of self-sown wheat and wild grapes suitable for winemaking.

the Indians and Eskimos proved too troublesome and costly. A child, Snorri, was born to Gudrid, the widow of Leif's brother Thorstein, and to Karlsevni at L'Anse aux Meadows in the autumn of 1009.

When the Greenland colonies faded away, Europe's sense of the Arctic receded to include only Iceland, with which she maintained a regular trade. Well into the sixteenth century, in fact, western Europe remained more aware of the voyage of Saint Brendan than of the existence of the Greenland colonies and Leif Ericsson.

A European understanding of world geography in the thirteenth, fourteenth, and fifteenth centuries was derived from wheel maps and older T-maps. The former presented the world arranged as a disk, with the Mediterranean at the center of a large continent and with a watery border beyond. The continent's outer shore was indented with the three embayments of the Outer Ocean—the Red Sea, the Persian Gulf, and the Caspian Sea. The T of the latter map was formed with the Mediterranean as a vertical line and with the Nile and Don rivers connecting horizontally through the Black Sea. Islands on the wheel maps were "distributed more or less according to taste, and as there happened to be room." At the utmost edge of the world, the realms of the sky, the sea, and the underworld met—but this was a cartographic abstraction. The idea that the world was a sphere was widely held. (It was the absence of spherical projections—the modern globe was not introduced in Europe until about 1492—that led people to talk about the earth as though it were flat.)

Beginning in the fourteenth century, cartographic representation of the world from Ptolemy's point of view slowly changed. With the development of compass, or portolano, charts, the coasts became better defined. The fanciful *Insulae Fortunatae*, variously titled, were moved farther north and west, into lesser-known waters. (Brasil, moved hither and yon, could still be found on British Admiralty charts in 1873.) Greenland, the quintessential remote Arctic for Europeans in the fifteenth century, was drawn in on maps and the first globes as a peninsula stretching north and west from Scandinavia (as on the Fra Mauro map of 1459); or as land extending north from central Asia (Clavus' Nancy map of 1472); or as the farthest-east extension of Asia (Contarini map, 1506). The region of the North Pole was depicted as open water; as a separate continental mass (*Terra Septemtrionalis* [Land of the North] or *Terrae Polaris Pars* [Part of the Polar Land]); and later in the fifteenth century, after the magnetic compass had come into use in Europe, as a dark, magnetic mountain.

Fifteenth-century Europe was neither empirical nor discriminating in its geography. The spurious geographical entertainments of Sir John Mandeville's *Travels* (1356) were read as avidly as the eyewitness accounts of Marco Polo (1298), and both were held in the same regard. As was the case with the mariner's compass and the portolano chart, the introduction in Europe of authentic new geographic knowledge was no guarantee it would be welcomed and acted upon. When John Cabot sailed from Bristol to find Newfoundland, he held a letter patent from Henry VII; but what he found was of little interest to Englishmen and was soon all but forgotten. His vision, wrote Samuel Eliot Morison, was "like an exotic flower springing up in untilled soil" in England.

Bristol fishermen, in the view of American geographer Carl Sauer, had been fishing on the Newfoundland banks for several years before Cabot arrived, with no great concern for who owned the land or what sovereign might claim it. Their business was cod. Cabot's arrival, however, began the modern period of an Arctic more rigorously defined in the European mind. His voyage (1497) stirred the first serious European interest in the possibility of a Northwest Passage—through a strait separating North America from Polo's Chinese province of Ania, down which ships could sail unimpeded to the harbors of Cathay, the Moluccas, and the ports of India.

Before such a passage was sought to the north of Cabot's Newfoundland landfall by the English, the region to the south was explored for the French by Verrazano and Cartier. Verrazano was Italian, from Tuscany. Like Columbus, a Genoese sailing for the Spanish, and like Cabot, a Genoese sailing for the English, Verrazano was a freelance explorer in an age when monarchs and merchants were not as enthusiastic about New World as Old World prospects. Their overriding interest was in finding a protected, unencumbered trade route to China. The Caribbean was a Spanish ocean, and the route around Africa was Portuguese. The overland route through the Middle East entailed payments to Turkish middlemen. (As far as England was concerned Spain also posed a threat to her export trade with continental Europe.)

The possible routes for the French and the English, then, were to be found, it was thought, either southward along Cabot's new coast (if his New Founded Isle was the hoped-for Asian promontory); to the north of his landfall if North America was a continent; or somewhere to the west, Newfoundland being just one more of the many islands thought to comprise "the western lands." The English also knew of the possibility of a Northeast Passage, around Norway's North Cape; Alfred the Great had transcribed the sober and accurate report of Ottar about his and his Norse companions' voyage into the White Sea about 880. Since England was looking for markets for its West Country woolens, the northeastern route was especially appealing. But it was not tried until 1553.

Verrazano was sent west in 1524 by the French, who were constrained as much as the English by Spanish and Portuguese control of the Southern Ocean and by middlemen in the Levant; and as much in need of "spices" from the Orient—not only condiments to preserve food (or enhance the taste of spoiling food) but drugs, dyes, oils, cosmetics, and perfumes. He coasted the eastern shore of North America, eliminating the possibility of any passage between Florida and Nova Scotia (except at North Carolina's Outer Banks, where Pamlico Sound looked like the Pacific to him). Ten years later Cartier sailed into the Gulf of Saint Lawrence for the first time. Again, there were Spanish, French, Portuguese, and

English cod fishermen there ahead of him—not to mention Estevão Gomes (a Portuguese sailing for Spain) and João Alvares Fagundes, a Portuguese shipowner with colonial ideas.

On his second voyage (1535), Cartier pursued a search for "Saguenay" (a land invented by a Huron named Donnaconna to flabbergast the French), and an exploration of the Saint Lawrence River. The rapids at this farthest-west point he named, sardonically, "La Chine" (China) Rapids. (The French interest in a western passage would continue to be a middle-latitude search for a river route, a guiding vision in North American exploration, for another 300 years.)

Because they thought Cabot's Newfoundland might lie to the east of the meridional line of demarcation established in the Treaty of Tordesillas (at roughly 45°W), and therefore belong to them, the Portuguese sailed from both Lisbon and the Azores to explore. João Fernandes, a *lavrador*, or small landed proprietor like a Spanish hidalgo, sailed as far as Cape Farewell, Greenland, in 1500. (The landfall was initially named for him, an Anglicized version, Labrador, later being shifted to the west by mapmakers.) Also in that year, Gaspar Corte Real landed on Newfoundland, found relics of Cabot's (lost) second expedition, and kidnapped fifty-seven Beothuk Indians, whom he took back to Lisbon. He returned to the region in 1501, and he too disappeared. He was followed by a brother, Miguel, on a similar voyage in 1502; his caravel vanished as well.

An English merchant, Robert Thorne, was of the opinion that Cathay could be reached on two tacks—straight over the Pole, or west through a strait somewhere north of Newfoundland, which was coming to be called *Fretum Trium Fratrum*, the Strait of the Three Brothers (whether for the three Corte Real brothers or John Cabot's three sons is not known). Henry VIII obliged Thorne and sent out two ships in 1527—the *Dominus Vobiscum*, which was lost, and the *Mary of Guilford*, John Rut, master. Rut went a third of the way up the Labrador coast and then lost his nerve. He reversed course and sailed for the West Indies.

Henry VIII was notably uninterested in finding a Northwest Passage; but the idea was fertile in the minds of northern European entrepreneurs, who, if not sanguine, were at least hopeful. America, before and after Verrazano's and Cartier's voyages, was viewed by the English as a land discovered by accident and around or through which it was desirable to sail. The northern route was not encouraging because of the ice. Those who still subscribed to Parmenides' theory of geographical zones believed the frigid zone was impenetrable or represented too dangerous a passage to be feasible as a trade route. Others, like Robert Thorne, thought that the worst ice lay on the Arctic Circle—beyond that was an open ocean, good weather, and clear sailing all the way to the Strait of Anian, the western counterpart to the Strait of the Three Brothers.

The attitude among investors in England and the Netherlands, the two nations in most pressing need of a reliable, tariff-free route to the East, was cautious. Sebastian Cabot, a charming and forceful man trading on his father's reputation, and a fabricator of northern voyages in which he claimed to have participated, was as persuasive in arguing for venture capital for a northern voyage as geographers, who sensed North America taking shape out there on the horizon, were eloquent. In 1553, as governor of what came to be called the Muscovy Company, he sent three ships to the Northeast under the command of Sir Hugh Willoughby. (The ships were hopefully sheathed with lead to protect them against shipworms when they reached the warm Southern Ocean.) Willoughby and the officers and men of two ships froze to death on the north coast of the Kola Peninsula. The third ship, under the command of Richard Chancellor, reached the White Sea. During the winter, Chancellor made a 600-mile journey to Moscow and established what would become an overland trade route for Russian furs.

In 1556, a Muscovy ship passed through Karskiye Vorota Strait, and its master, Stephen Borough, became the first European to see the Kara Sea, the vast and intimidating icescape that lay beyond Novaya Zemlya. Daunted, Borough returned to England. Cathay seemed suddenly closer by way of Moscow.

The Dutch also tried in this direction. In 1596 Willem Barents, pilot for Jacob van Heemskerke, accompanied by a second ship under the command of Jan Cornelis Ryp, discovered the archipelago they called Spitsbergen (probably known 500 years earlier to Norse sailors, who named a land in this region Svalbard, "the cold coast"). The two ships later parted, Ryp returning to Amsterdam and Barents sailing west for Novaya Zemlya, thinking a way across the Kara Sea might be found to the north of the island. He rounded the island's northern cape before he was forced into winter quarters by heavy ice. At Ice Haven the men built a hut of driftwood, burned polar bear fat for light, and skirmished with curious foxes. They felt terrorized by polar bears; they were weakened by scurvy; and they endured relentless, crushing cold. Heat from a fire kept blazing in the hut did not melt ice on the floor only a few feet away. In the spring they refitted one of the ship's boats (the ship itself having been crushed during the winter, a sight that "made all the hairs of our heads rise upright with fear") and made a spectacular 1600-mile journey across ice and open water to the Kola Peninsula. Barents died on the way, of scurvy. Gerrit de Veer's narrative of this adventure, *The True and Perfect Description of Three Voyages, so strange and woonderfull, that the like has never been heard of before* . . . , chronicles the awful conditions they endured and conveys a certain nightmarish aspect, particularly because of their fear of the animals.

Finding a Northeast Passage was of no further interest to the Dutch or anyone else, until the opening of Russia's far eastern frontier by Cossacks, expanding the Stroganov fur empire, and the expeditions of Peter the Great.*

---

* Some of the impetus to open a Northeast Passage, across Asia and south through a "Strait of Jezzo," was a restriction imposed by the emperor of Japan against trade in the Kamchatka region for vessels coming up from the south. Japan took a significant tribute from Kamchatka, from silver mines it was thought. The Dutch were certain such a northern passage existed because Dutch traders wrecked on the

Under Elizabeth I, daughter of Anne Boleyn and Henry VIII, England became a formidable maritime power and achieved, as well, a national sense of identity and purpose, of which Elizabeth was the embodiment. These were the years (1558–1603) when Shakespeare wrote, when Francis Bacon established the scientific method, when Richard Hakluyt wrote *The Principal Navigations*, and when the queen's "West Country sailors" greatly expanded England's sphere of political influence. Francis Drake sailed around the world. Walter Raleigh organized the English colonization in Virginia. John Hawkins, a freebooter like both Drake and the circumnavigator Thomas Cavendish, made numerous improvements in ship design and distinguished himself with some of the others, including Martin Frobisher, at the defeat of the Spanish Armada (1588). In 1587 John Davis, the least warlike and piratical of them all, would sail up the west coast of Greenland and quietly into Baffin Bay.

Belief in a navigable Northwest Passage flourished under Elizabeth. It was energetically promoted by a highly visible merchant, Michael Lok, and it had the support of well-regarded minds, like Hakluyt's and the philosopher John Dee's. It was hotly argued for by Sir Humphrey Gilbert, a favorite of the queen (and yet another Devon neighbor of Drake, Raleigh, and Davis, though not their match at sea), in *A Discourse of a Discoverie for a New Passage to Cathaia*. Finally, at least two well-touted stories in support of a Strait of Anian were circulating in England at the time. A monk, one Antonio Urdaneta, claimed to have sailed through it in the 1550s; and a Portuguese mariner, Martin Chacque, claimed to have come through in 1556, west to east like Urdaneta. (Both tales were unfounded.)

In the thrall of this enthusiasm, Michael Lok founded the

Korean coast in those years found a stranded whale with a harpoon in it from the Spitsbergen fishery. The whale could only have gotten there through a strait between Asia and North America.

Cathay Company and outfitted Martin Frobisher for a voyage of discovery in 1585. Frobisher sailed from London in a small bark, the *Gabriel*, with a crew of eighteen, accompanied by another small bark, the *Michael*, and an even smaller, unnamed pinnace with a crew of four. The pinnace went down in a gale that sprung the *Gabriel*'s mainmast and tore away her fore-topmast. The captain and crew of the *Michael*, "mistrusting the matter" as they neared Greenland, "conveyed themselves privilie away" from Frobisher and returned home, reporting the *Gabriel* lost in a storm.

Frobisher entered what he thought was a strait (actually Frobisher Bay, Baffin Island) on August 11. He spent fifteen days exploring both coasts, thinking the west one North America, the east one Asia, before he sailed for home, convinced this was the eastern opening of the Passage. A stone picked up by a sailor on the east shore, "merely for the sake of the place from whence they came," fell into the hands of Michael Lok, who had it declared gold-bearing ore, drummed up financial support, and dispatched a second expedition in 1577. Frobisher, with a belief in the Passage and a master mariner's keen desire to find it, probably cared very little for these plans, but went mining as directed and limited his explorations to Frobisher Bay.

The three ships, *Gabriel*, *Michael*, and the *Aid*, a flagship ten times the size of the two former ships, returned to England on September 23 with 200 tons of worthless bronze-lustered mica (amphibolite and pyroxenite). In hopes of gaining new investors, Lok arranged for the rock to be assayed at a high value. He was partly successful in attracting investors, though the canny stayed away. The third voyage ended in tragedy. Fifteen ships sailed in May 1578. The *Denys* was lost in a storm when they arrived, and on the return voyage, with 1350 tons of the spurious ore, they encountered more storms and forty men drowned, many of them Cornish miners.

Queen Elizabeth did not lose faith in Lok's enterprise until the very end. On their first voyage she waved to the ships from the palace window at Greenwich, as they passed by on the Thames.

On the eve of the second voyage she let Frobisher kiss her hand. Before the third, she placed a gold chain around his neck and extended her hand for each of the captains to kiss. Frobisher's men, during the second voyage, and on the peninsula Elizabeth herself had named Meta Incognita, found a badly decomposed narwhal, from which they took the tusk. In his account of the voyage, Dyonyse Settle writes that the men placed spiders in the hollow base of the tooth and that the spiders died. "I saw not the triall hereof," he writes. "But it was reported unto me of a trueth: by the vertue whereof we supposed it to be the sea Unicorne." Frobisher made a present of the tusk to Elizabeth.

This enterprise left Lok in debt and the Cathay Company bankrupt. The transparent greed of some of the investors, chicanery to keep the scheme alive, and the loss of workingmen's lives left a foul taste in many mouths. Frobisher cleared his own name in battle, was knighted, and died in 1594 fighting the Spanish.

Voyages of a very different sort were undertaken eight years later by John Davis, perhaps the most highly skilled of all the Elizabethan navigators, a man of a more serene disposition than the volatile Frobisher, much less the disciplinarian among his men, less acquisitive and less self-promoting of his achievements—part of the reason that he, of all the West Country mariners, was the one never knighted.

With the backing of Adrian Gilbert, a prominent Devonshire physician, and William Sanderson, a London merchant-adventurer, and under the patronage of the Duke of Walsingham, Davis outfitted two small ships, the *Sunneshine* and the *Mooneshine*, the former with a four-piece orchestra, and sailed from Dartmouth on the Devon coast on June 7, 1585.

Their first landfall was near present-day Cape Walløe on the southeast coast of Greenland, but fog and the ice stream in the East Greenland Current held them off. "[T]he irksome noyse of the yse was such, that it bred strange conceites among us, so that we supposed the place to be vast and voyd of any sensible or vegitable creatures, whereupon I called the same Desolation." The

two ships stood out from Cape Farewell (Davis would so name
it on his second voyage) and came to shore, finally, near the old
Norse settlement at Godthåb on July 29. And here took place
one of the most memorable of meetings between cultures in all of
arctic literature.

Davis and several others were reconnoitering from the top
of an island in what Davis had named Gilbert Sound when they
were spotted by a group of Eskimos on the shore, some of whom
launched kayaks. They made "a lamentable noyse," wrote John
Jane, ". . . with great outcryes and skreechings: wee hearing them,
thought it had bene the howling of wolves." Davis called on the
orchestra to play and directed his officers and men to dance. The
Eskimos cautiously approached in kayaks, two of them pulling
very close to the beach. "Their pronunciation," wrote Jane, "was
very hollow through the throate, and their speach such as we
could not understand: onely we allured them by friendly imbrac-
ings and signes of curtesie. At length one of them poynting up to
the sunne with his hande, would presently strike his brest so hard,
that we might hear the blowe." John Ellis, master of the *Mooneshine*, began to imitate, pointing to the sun and striking his breast.
One of the Eskimos came ashore. They handed him pieces of their
clothing, having nothing else to offer, and kept up their dancing,
the orchestra playing all the while.

The following morning the ships' companies were awakened
by the very same people, standing on the same hill the officers had
stood on the day before. The Eskimos were playing on a drum,
dancing and beckoning to them.

(Davis's courteous regard for the Eskimos is unique in early
arctic narratives. He found them "a very tractable people, voyde
of craft or double dealing. . . ." He returned to the same spot on
his second voyage; the moment of mutual recognition, and his
reception, were tumultuous.)

Two days after meeting the Eskimos, Davis crossed the strait
later named for him and sailed far up Cumberland Sound, which
he judged, from the lack of ice, the breadth of the channel, the

set of the tides, the sight of whales passing to the east, and the "colour, nature, and qualities" of the water, to be the entrance to the Northwest Passage. Satisfied, he sailed for home. (There was no thought of overwintering on these early voyages. The ships were too small to carry a year's provisions.) On October 3 he wrote Walsingham that the passage was "nothing doubtfull, but at any tyme [of year] almost to be passed, the sea navigable, voyd of yse, the ayre tollerable, and the waters very depe."

Gilbert, Sanderson, and Walsingham were pleased with Davis's progress, and, with additional backing from merchants in the city of Exeter, he sailed again on May 7, 1586, with a fleet of four ships—the large ship *Mermayde*, the barks *Sunneshine* and *Mooneshine*, and a small pinnace, the *North Starre*. Davis sent the *Sunneshine* and the *North Starre* up the east coast of Greenland with instructions to explore as far as they could in search of a route over the Pole. With the other two ships he sailed for Godthåb, where he assembled a second, prefabricated pinnace on the beach, launched with the help of forty Eskimos.

The meeting with the people at Godthåb was marked initially by a spirit of fellowship, but the mood began to deteriorate once the Eskimos became "marvellous theevish, especially for iron." Davis tried to ameliorate the situation. He continued to trade generously with the Eskimos, and he cajoled his men to forbear. One afternoon a rock-throwing incident escalated into a fight and one of his men was wounded. That was enough for Davis. With a fair wind he sailed north.

On the 17th of July the two ships and the pinnace fell in with an enormous tabular iceberg "which bred great admiration to us all," a sight so incredible to them that Davis declines to write about it, saying only, "I thinke that the like before was never seene." They coasted its perimeter for thirteen days. Davis Strait, as it was later named, was full of ice where they had seen none the year before; the sight so worked on the minds of the men that they begged Davis to turn for home. He landed on the Greenland coast, disassembled the pinnace, transferred stores, and sent those who wished to go home on the *Mermayde*. With the rest he sailed in the *Mooneshine* for Baffin Island. He passed the entrance to Cumberland Sound without recognizing it, crossed Hudson Strait in a snowstorm, and then sailed south along the Labrador coast, where they made several prodigious hauls of codfish on improvised hooks.

At Trunmore Bay (perhaps), where they anchored to dry fish, they were attacked by "the brutish people of this countrey." Two of Davis's men were killed and three wounded. Immediately afterward the ships were all but driven onshore by a storm when an anchor cable parted. On September 11 Davis turned for home, arriving to find that the *Sunneshine* and *North Starre* had been turned back by the ice before advancing very far, and that the *North Starre* had gone down with her crew in a storm.

Though not as enthusiastic as they had been, Davis's supporters underwrote a third voyage in 1587, with the understanding that while Davis himself sailed into the places he now thought might offer passage (Davis Strait, Cumberland Sound, Hudson Strait, and Hamilton Inlet on the Labrador coast), the accompanying ships would fish for cod to defray the expense of the expedition. Davis's own ship, a small, clincher-built pinnace, the *Ellen*, broke her tiller the first day out and, overall, sailed "like to a cart drawn with oxen."

At Godthåb, Davis explored the interior of the fiord while the crew of one of the other ships assembled a fourth craft, another pinnace on the beach. (Davis intended to explore in this pinnace while the other three ships went south to fish for cod.) Again hostilities broke out, with the Eskimos stealing nails from the shipwrights. Davis could not settle the issue. After a gunner fired a blank shot from a cannon, Davis ordered the half-assembled pinnace knocked down and stowed aboard the *Elizabeth*. With the *Sunneshine* leaking badly and that crew and the *Elizabeth*'s nearly mutinous with a desire to be off, Davis bade them adieu. He set a course north in the *Ellen* along the Greenland coast, sailing as far as 72°46′N, which he named Sanderson's Hope for

Greenland

Sanderson's Hope

Baffin Bay

Baffin Island

Mercy Cape

Cumberland Sound

Godthåb

Hudson Strait

Frobisher Bay

Cape Chidley

Hudson Bay

Cape Farewell

Labrador Sea

the Passage. The ocean was open far to the north and west, and of "an unsearcheable depth." But there was no wind to take him in either direction. He made southwest. After being beset for two days when he tried to penetrate the pack ice, he doubled the Cape of God's Mercy (named on the first voyage for the cape that pointed him into what he thought was the Passage), and headed up Cumberland Sound. When the wind fell off, he sailed back to the entrance and south past Frobisher Bay, which he named Lumley's Inlet. (With no reliable method to determine longitude, and under the pervasive influence of the problematical Zeno map, which showed Frobisher Strait at the southern tip of Greenland, Davis thought he was the first to visit here.)

He noted again, as he had the year before, the "furious overfall" of tides in Hudson Strait, "lothsomly crying like the rage of the waters under London Bridge." They cruised along the Labrador coast looking for the *Sunneshine* and *Elizabeth*, which, owing to the poor sailing characteristics of the *Ellen*, were to escort him home. They had not waited. On August 15, Davis set sail for Dartmouth. It took him a month to make the crossing.

Davis's accomplishments on these trips are stunning. He laid down most of the Labrador coast on sailing charts, some 700 miles of the west coast of Greenland, and most of southwest Baffin Island. His notes on ice conditions, plants, animals, currents, and the interior of Greenland, as well as his ethnographic descriptions of the Eskimos, were the first of their kind. He brought these lands not only onto the maps but into the realms of science. The "Traverse-Booke" he developed on the voyages became the model for a standard ship's log. The backstaff he developed anticipated the reflecting quadrant and the modern sextant. And *The Seaman's Secrets* (1594), much of it based on these three voyages, became a seventeenth-century bible for English mariners.

In subsequent years Davis discovered the Falkland Islands and sailed into the Pacific, hopeful of finding a western entrance to the Passage. He was killed by Japanese pirates in the Strait of Malacca, off Singapore, in 1605, at the age of fifty-five. He was a loyal and courageous man, tolerant of other people's differences. His knowledge of navigation was a fine blend of scientific acumen and practical experience. In *The Worlde's Hydrographical Description* (1595), reflecting on the light that fell on the northern regions in the summer, he wrote that because of this suffusion of light the land beneath the Pole Star is "the place of greatest dignitie" on earth.

DAVIS's expeditions went out uninsured, like all others at the time —the risk of shipwreck due to crude instruments, errors in the charts, or inexperienced command was simply too high. A master mariner like Davis could determine his latitude with a quadrant, astrolabe, or backstaff. He had declination tables to compensate for compass errors. And he might be fortunate enough to have the journal or rutter of another pilot who had been to the area he was sailing, to warn him about reefs or give helpful advice about tides. But not until John Harrison built his first chronometer in 1735 would there be a reliable way to determine longitude.

The charts and maps available to expeditions, especially for westering mariners, were of little help. Too much of the information was whimsical or groundless, and updating maps often meant contending with theoretical concepts of geography with which practical mariners had little patience. Furthermore, with no way to determine longitude and scant information on compass variation in different parts of the hemisphere, they found it hard to place new lands accurately and so improve old maps. The Zeno map (1558), a fictitious compilation showing many large islands in the western North Atlantic, was of such intimidating authority, on the other hand, that even John Davis believed he had to "harmonize his work with universally received errors."

A competent mariner, observing of the weather and attentive to the subtle behavior of the sea and the movement of his ship, especially a known ship, frequently had an intuitive feeling for what he was doing, even along an unknown coast. If he was sailing "by ghesse and by God," he was mostly guessing right. He preferred a small, maneuverable vessel to a large cargo ship—a frequent point of disagreement with an expedition's backers—and tried, if possible, to sail in company with another ship. (It was not until 1821, when Parry set off on his second trip to the Arctic with *Hecla* and *Fury*, that anyone saw the wisdom of embarking in duplicate ships with interchangeable parts.)

Sailors, the best of them, had an astounding ability to keep their ships running, and were as resourceful as Eskimos with a handful of scraps in improvising a repair. They often pulled a small ship completely out of the water on a foreign beach and heaved it over to patch its hull. Their lot in arctic waters, where they ran the constant risk of being stove by ice, was dreadful. Their fare was utterly simple: salt beef and codfish, bread and dried peas, cheese and butter, and beer. All eaten cold. There were no hot liquids like coffee or tea. Sailors slept wherever there was room among the stores and provisions, and felt fortunate to have a change or two of clothing if they got wet or cold. The possibility of scurvy and shipwreck were always "hard by."*

Shipboard conditions slowly improved, the maps became more accurate, and better navigational instruments were developed. Books such as Davis's *The Seaman's Secrets* spread a technical knowledge of navigation. By the seventeenth century, cartographers were not so disposed to conjecture by filling in with an island or two. They left large areas like the Arctic blank now, something that would have astounded their predecessors. The maze of portolano lines on coastal charts became, in time, a circular arrangement of thirty-two winds, drawn like the petals of

---

* The cause of scurvy, a vitamin-C deficiency disorder that induces capillary hemorrhaging, loosening of the teeth, anemia, and general debilitation, was unknown. Victims showed "a tottering gait, attenuated form, and care-wore expression of countenance." James Lind, a Scottish naval surgeon, successfully treated scurvy-ridden sailors with oranges and lemons in 1747. A ration of lemon juice became the standard preventative in the British navy by 1795, though it was sometimes inadequate to stave off symptoms on a long cruise.

a flower—the wind, or compass, rose. Exploration, however, continued to be an arrangement between bankers and dreamers, carried out by tough, sagacious pilots and resourceful crews. And because the bills had to be paid, remuneration in trade from the newly discovered lands was never far from the minds of those who wished to pursue these journeys.

SEVERAL important voyages followed soon after Davis's last. Henry Hudson sailed for the Pole in 1607 with ten men and a boy in a small pinnace. They got as far as 73 °N on the east coast of Greenland, where Hudson named a promontory Hold with Hope. On the return voyage he discovered Jan Mayen Island and the whale fishery at Spitsbergen. After a voyage to Novaya Zemlya, and a second voyage that started in that direction but turned for the east coast of North America and became an exploration of the Hudson River, he sailed in 1610 for arctic waters. That year he overwintered in James Bay, south of the strait and bay which today bear his name. In the spring some of the crew, fearing starvation, mutinied. They put Hudson and his son, three loyal men, and four of the sick in a boat and set them adrift, never to be seen again. The alleged ringleaders of the mutiny were later killed by Eskimos; those left alive sailed the *Discovery* home in a pitiful condition, reduced to eating candles, grass, and shreds of bird skin.

The entrepreneurs who employed Hudson, more interested in refitting for another voyage than in any trial for mutiny, sent the same ship back out under Thomas Button in 1612. He reached the far shore of Hudson Bay, realized Hudson's Sea was an embayment, and named a point there Hopes Checked. (Hudson, who thought he was sailing into the Pacific, named the southern cape at the entrance to Hudson Strait Hopes Advance.) Button, who overwintered at the mouth of the Nelson River, where he lost many men, discovered Coats, Southampton, and Mansel islands, and in the spring sailed to 65 °N in Roes Welcome Sound.

In 1615 William Baffin, pilot, and Robert Bylot, captain, made the first of two important journeys together, this one into Foxe

Channel and Frozen Strait, north of Hudson Bay, where they determined that there was no Northwest Passage to be found via Hudson Strait. Baffin, a gifted navigator and an astute and accurate observer, saw the tide flooded from the southeast and ebbed from the northwest. He guessed, correctly, that the Passage lay through Davis Strait, and in 1616 he and Bylot went there. (Hudson's voyage, Button's voyage, and both of Baffin's were made in the *Discovery*, a bark the size of Davis's *Sunneshine*.)

The second voyage took Bylot and Baffin to 78°N, above Davis Strait and farther north than anyone else would sail for 200 years.* They named many of the sounds, bays, and capes for their investors, the same men who had sent Hudson and Button out before them—Smith, Jones, Lancaster, Digges, and Wolstenholme. Returning to the south, Baffin surveyed the east coast of the island that would be named for him, laying down charts until his work intersected that of John Davis.

When Baffin's journal and charts were prepared for publication, they were heavily censored; in time, his discoveries came to be disbelieved and were removed from contemporary maps. (It was not until 1818 that Sir John Ross would confirm everything Baffin had set down.) Baffin's work, and Button's journals and maps, were suppressed, probably, by investors who didn't want rivals nosing about for a passage in Baffin Bay. The early history of Hudson Bay after Button's voyage there in 1612 is a woeful chronicle of fatal disasters and bravado in search of a Northwest Passage and a fortune in furs and gold. When Charles II granted a permanent charter to Prince Rupert and other "Gentlemen Adventurers trading into Hudson's Bay" in 1670, he offered that company, in effect, a sovereign right to all lands drained by the

---

* Norse seamen went as far as "Norðrsetur," which may have been in the vicinity of Sullorsuaq Strait (70°12′N), and they likely sailed farther. Norse artifacts have been found in a Thule village on Bache Peninsula on Ellesmere Island (79°N), but it is uncertain how they got there.

rivers emptying into Hudson Bay. This sweeping privilege was made contingent, however, upon the Bay's efforts to find a Northwest Passage. Once the Gentlemen Adventurers saw the bales of lustrous furs brought out of the subarctic hinterlands by Pierre Radisson and Médard Chouart des Groseillers, they were disinclined to pursue any such geography. They were staring at a fortune. In order to protect it and create a trade monopoly, the Bay deliberately obstructed (initially) the search for a Passage in the region, since any business along such a route would bypass them on the way to China. The size of the bribe they reportedly paid to one Christopher Middleton to falsify his records of exploration induced the British Admiralty to set aside in 1734 a huge sum as a reward for the discovery of a Northwest Passage— £20,000.

The story of the Hudson's Bay Company is the story of an enormously powerful, nearly autonomous special-interest group that for hundreds of years strongly influenced the political, social, economic, and environmental fate of a country larger than most sovereign nations. Its stable base of remuneration in the New World—fur trapping—changed the whole focus of arctic exploration. Given the desolate aspects of the land, no one had suspected what a staggering number of high-quality furs would be brought out year after year, and for how many years this would go on.*

The other, earlier foundation of wealth found by merchant-adventurers in the Arctic was the whale fishery, first in the vicinity of Spitsbergen where it was shore-based and extremely competitive, especially between the Dutch and the British, and then in the open waters of the "whale-fisher's bight," a tongue of water that extends

---

* Between 1769 and 1868, the Hudson's Bay Company sold at auction in London, among other furs and skins, the following: 891,091 fox, 1,052,051 lynx, 68,694 wolverine, 288,016 bear, 467,549 wolf, 1,507,240 mink, 94,326 swan, 275,032 badger, 4,708,702 beaver, and 1,240,511 marten. During parts of this same period two other companies, the North West Company and the Canada Company, were trading furs in numbers as large.

unfrozen in winter into the northern Greenland Sea west of
Spitsbergen, the last trace of the Gulf Stream.* Sealing took place
here, too, in the spring on the "west ice," to the west of the whale–
fisher's bight. (The whale and seal fisheries would thrive in the
Greenland and Norwegian seas for more than a hundred years
before whalers shifted to Davis Strait and North American sealers
began to exploit a sealing ground just as large on the sea ice north
and east of Newfoundland.)

When Henry Hudson returned to England in 1607 with
stories of whales in the waters west of Spitsbergen, the Arctic was
perceived for the first time as something of innate value, not solely
the region of a problematical route to the Pacific. And its potential
could not have been more emphatically set forth than by Radisson
and Groseilliers, when they walked into the court of Charles II
beneath armloads of marten, beaver, lynx, and wolverine furs from
subarctic Canada. The Arctic would yield little else in the next
300 years except coal from places like Spitsbergen, but the furs
and expanding seal, whale, and cod fisheries seemed adequate rec-
ompense from so bleak an area for investors who felt, in some
instances, that they had been bullied into geographic exploration
when all they wanted was a return on their (considerable) invest-
ments. With the growth of the Hudson's Bay Company's fur
empire and the development of the fisheries, the staggering wealth
of North America being shipped to Europe, and an opening of
the southern Atlantic to less restricted trade, the idea of a Northwest Passage ceased to be commercially attractive. It became,
instead, the solution to a geographic puzzle.

---

* The current, properly speaking, is the West Spitsbergen Current. It is
a continuation of the warm Norwegian Current, which is a continua-
ton of the North Atlantic Current, where the Gulf Stream terminates
semantically for oceanographers. The warm West Spitsbergen Current
rounds the northwest cape of Spitsbergen, where some of it flows
beneath the polar ice for another 1500 miles, emerging in the vicinity
of the New Siberian Islands—an indication of the enormous volume of
Caribbean water involved.

DURING the time of the first European voyages into the Arctic, the northern rims of Asia and North America remained unknown. In 1725 Peter the Great sent Vitus Bering, a Dutchman, to reconnoiter the eastern margins of Siberia and to see if Siberia and North America were connected. In 1728 Bering sailed through the strait that now carries his name and then bore northwest to 67°N.* Though the way was clear to round the Chukchi Peninsula and to sail west to the mouth of the Kolyma River, Bering turned back. In the fog in the strait he also missed the coast of North America. A geodesist named Gvozdev reached it in 1732 in the ship Bering left behind, landing in the vicinity of present-day Point Hope. In 1741 Bering tried a second time to determine the lay of the North American coast, this time with the naturalist Georg Wilhelm Steller along.† Bering shipwrecked on the return voyage in the Commander Islands, where he died, bringing to thirty the number of men who perished on the voyage.

Between 1733 and 1742 Russian explorers made a prodigious and nearly successful attempt to explore and map the whole of the north coast of Asia from the mouth of the Ob River to Bering's East Cape. The last section, from Bear Cape to East Cape, was not completed until 1824, by Ferdinand von Wrangel. (In 1867 an American whaling captain, Thomas Long, named Wrangel Island for him.)

The strait that separates the two continents (the western

---

* The Yearbooks of the Sung dynasty record a much earlier voyage in these waters. In A.D. 458 a Buddhist monk, Hwui Shan, together with four other monks, sailed north past the Kuril Islands and up the coast of the Kamchatka Peninsula, then east through the Aleutian Islands to mainland Alaska.

† Steller discovered and named many new animals on this trip, including Steller's jay (a verification of their North American landing) and Steller's sea cow, which was never seen again by scientists. The sea otter furs brought back by the expedition's survivors drew Russian free trappers into the region, who subsequently embarked on a bloody suppression of native coastal peoples.

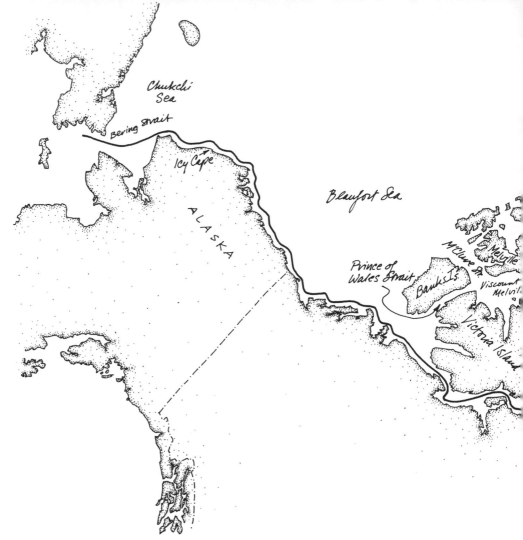

The Northwest Passage. To clear the middle Baffin Bay pack ice, ships must approach Lancaster Sound from the northwest. An alternate route passes west through Barrow Strait and Viscount Melville Sound,

entrance to the Northwest Passage) was, according to some historians, first discovered by a Cossack named Simon Dezhnev in 1648. The Spaniards also sent explorers in this direction, but they never came this far north. A Greek pilot, Apostolos Valerianos (Juan de Fuca) told Michael Lok in Venice in 1595 that he had sailed into the Strait of Anian at 47°N three years before. Many suspect he didn't get even that far north, but there is a strait at that latitude, and it was named after him in 1788. Other, clearly un-

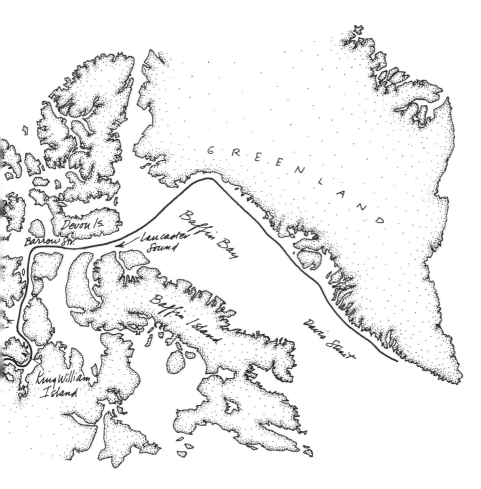

then south through Prince of Wales Strait. The exit through M'Clure Strait is almost always blocked by heavy ice as is the exit through M'Clintock Channel.

founded claims for entering the Strait of Anian were made for Maldonado (1588) and de Fonte (1640). The first ship from Europe to reach Bering Strait was under the command of James Cook, who arrived in 1778 and sailed north and west until he was within sight of Icy Cape (70°20′N). (In expectation of this development, the British Admiralty had altered the provisions of its £20,000 Northwest Passage prize to include royal as well as private ships, and success by any route, not necessarily one via

Hudson Bay—a clear indication that the search for the Passage was now a matter of state, not commerce, and that Baffin's observation, that there was no route through Hudson Bay, had finally been heeded.)*

At the time Cook sailed into the Chukchi Sea the northern reaches of North America and most of the Canadian Archipelago were unknown. On July 14, 1771, an indefatigable and persistent overland traveler named Samuel Hearne reached a spot near the mouth of the Coppermine River on Coronation Gulf with a group of Slavey Indians and a Chipewyan guide, Matonabbee. On this, his third attempt to reach the area, he fixed the first point of geographical reference on the American shore of the Northern Ocean. In 1778, Alexander Mackenzie reached an island in the delta of the river that now bears his name, and a second point was fixed. Between 1819–1822 and 1825–1827 British overland naval parties under the command of John Franklin mapped the North American coast from the Return Islands (149°W) to Turnagain Point on Kent Peninsula (107°W). Hearne's and Mackenzie's overland routes, together with exploration of the southern British Columbian coast by George Vancouver (1792), and of the North American coast from south of the Columbia River to Icy Cape by Cook, eliminated the possibility of a Northwest Passage south of approximately 68°N. If there was a passage, it lay north of the explored North American coast, in an unknown region.

*   *   *

---

* A second award of £5000 was also established at this time for the first ship to sail within 1° of the Pole. And a third prize of £5000 was authorized for the first ship to sail past 110°W, since longitude could now be accurately determined. Cook had on board one of John Harrison's clocks, for precisely fixing longitude west of the Greenwich meridian. He called it "our never-failing guide." An imperious Admiralty Board gave the chronometer its stamp of approval but made Harrison, a cabinetmaker, wait thirty-seven years for his reward (another £20,000). They couldn't believe a commoner had actually solved the problem.

THE reasons for pursuing the search for a passage in the west—the ice in the east, north of Russia, was thought simply too formidable, too extensive—changed over the years. By 1820 no one was advocating the commercial feasibility of such a route. William Scoresby put the case succinctly in his *Account of the Arctic Regions*: annual ice conditions are too variable, the latitude is too high, the season is too short. But the possibility of obtaining new geographical knowledge, the opportunity for scientific investigation in the Arctic, and a broadening awareness of natural history, together with simple curiosity and the slim possibility of locating an arctic mine, were sufficient to keep an interest in the Passage alive.

In 1815, the war with France finally over, Sir John Barrow, Second Secretary of the Admiralty and founder of the Royal Geographic Society, could turn his full attention to his passion, geography, in particular the question of the Passage. Empowered to send British ships and naval officers on the expeditions he devised, he infused the endeavor with a lofty sense of purpose. Barrow had a disdain for crass motives of any sort—he deplored the Hudson's Bay Company's arctic hegemony as "a preposterous state of affairs"; he also trusted naively in the superior worth of rank and social position over practical experience, a trait, of course, that distinguished many Englishmen of his and later generations.

Scoresby, the experienced whaler, may have had Barrow's arrogance in mind, in fact, when he politely raised an objection in 1820 to "the want of experience in the navigation of icy seas" among the officers of the Royal Navy who figured in Barrow's plans. "No judgement, however profound, no talent, however acute," wrote Scoresby, "can supersede the necessity of practice." Certainly Barrow read these words, but he did not entirely heed them. No great disasters, save one, ensued during the twenty-seven years he directed his arctic enterprises, but it is worth noting Scoresby's general observation on those seeking "imperishable renown" in the Arctic.

Working fishermen were no doubt off the coast of New-foundland before Cabot got there, in Frobisher Bay before Frobisher got there, in Hudson Strait before Hudson, and in Lancaster Sound before Ross arrived. These men, as it were, stepped aside long enough to let the gentlemen discover the land, and then went back to fishing. Fishermen and whalers were disposed to keep "new knowledge" to themselves; and they had few dealings with the social and intellectual strata of men to whom such knowledge might mean political leverage or social rewards.

Since normally there was no intercourse between, say, cartographers and common seamen, the two had different ideas about the state of arctic exploration. Joseph Moxon, an English cartographer living in Amsterdam, met a Dutch sailor in a tavern in 1652. He couldn't help overhearing his conversation with another fellow. The sailor said he worked aboard a shuttle ship, bringing whale blubber south from Spitsbergen during the season. Because they had arrived too early to gain a full load, his captain had taken advantage of open water to sail north. The Spitsbergen whalers kept a tally of such forays beyond 80°N, and this sailor believed they had sailed 2° beyond the Pole. No doubt he was confused, but it was possible in a good ice year for a whaler to get to perhaps 83°N. Moxon was astounded that this information did not circulate, and the sailor was apparently nonplussed by Moxon's interest in the matter.

Not only did men of such different background and pursuits rarely converse, but the field observations of fishermen and whalers, or of common seamen, were thought by the upper classes not quite appropriate to the developing purposes of science, nor useful for the general education of politically or commercially sophisticated men. This singular discourtesy stifled a broad-based understanding of the Arctic early on and contributed to a second problem—the perpetuation of prejudiced, unempirically founded knowledge by special-interest groups. The spheres of separate knowledge of the mapmaker, the able-bodied seaman, the whaling captain, the Eskimo, and the British naval officer were kept segregated through contempt and condescension, and by social policies that divided people on the basis of education, race, social class, and nationality. Although this pattern of intolerance has long been a pattern of human life, it is especially in the area of geographic knowledge that these rifts are lamentable. No one class or culture can pretend to entirely grasp a stretch of land.

The distance that separates most arctic residents on a day-to-day basis from the aspirations and ideas of industrialists and social architects is prefigured in these early divisions. The Bristol fishermen thought Cabot's first voyage an extension of the royal amusement. British officers thought the common seaman too much of a scatterbrain and an adolescent to have anything pertinent to say about navigating through ice. Seasoned HBC factors twitted earnest neophytes newly arrived in the Arctic because they mistook their awkwardness and ineptitude for incompetence and stupidity. And no one took the Eskimo seriously.

Men like Scoresby stand out in arctic history, amid the contentious hegemonies of opinion that characterize especially its economic history, for several reasons: the breadth of his practical experience as an arctic whaling captain, his disinterested scientific observations, his education at Cambridge, and his sense of regard for the ideas of other people. The rarity of such individuals in arctic science, commerce, and public affairs today is as evident as it was in Scoresby's day. In a country in which the future of an entire landscape is at stake, the racial, social, and intellectual barriers remain. The good minds still do not find each other often enough.

JOHN Barrow was adamant and single-minded about what he wanted in the Arctic: a careful accumulation of scientific knowledge. He fervently hoped that his enterprise would bring distinction to all involved, and, not the least of his concerns, enhance English prestige in the world. In 1818, he sent four ships north, all of them several light-years advanced in equipment, provisions, and seaworthiness over the tiny ships Davis and Baffin sailed in. The ships' officers included surgeons, draftsmen, and navigators as well as men able to operate and record from the array of scientific instruments placed on board—barometers, chronometers, artificial horizons, theodolites, pendulums, water-sampling bottles, and several types of thermometer. (Also put aboard, with a deferential nod to Scoresby, were a master and a mate from the Spitsbergen fishery, the former sometimes called the ice pilot or ice master.)

The ships sailed in April, parted company in the North Atlantic, expecting, with bright-eyed optimism, to meet in the Pacific. HMS *Dorthea* and *Trent* shaped their courses north for Svalbard; HMS *Isabella* and *Alexander* for Baffin Bay. The former two, hammered mercilessly by gales and pack ice, took refuge in Magdalena Bay and Fair Haven in Spitsbergen to make repairs before sailing home. The other two ships, under Sir John Ross and Lieutenant William Parry, sailed up Davis Strait in the company of about forty whale ships, entered Melville Bay, which they named, and reached their "farthest north" at the southern entrance to Smith Sound. On the Greenland coast they met a group of Polar Eskimos. Through an interpreter who had come aboard in southern Greenland, a startling and memorable conversation took place. At one point, one of the Eskimos turned to the *Isabella* itself and inquired: "Who are you? What are you? Where do you come from? Is it from the sun or the moon?"

Ross decided Smith Sound offered no good prospect, and so sailed west and south, exploring the entrances to Jones and Lancaster sounds. Lancaster Sound, he reported, was but a bay, closed off by a range of mountains. (No other officer would confirm this observation, and it is impossible to know why he insisted on it. It all but ruined his career.) Coasting south along the east shore of Baffin Island, the officers confirmed the accuracy and completeness of Baffin's disputed report and suppressed charts, and discovered and named Pond's Bay. (Their reports of whales abounding in the new "West Water" brought the first large-scale influx of whalers into that part of Baffin Bay the following year.) Once home, Parry, adamant but discreet, let it be known that no mountain range closed off Lancaster Sound, and that that was the way for the Admiralty to pursue its search.

Parry's excursion into Lancaster Sound the following year is one of the most admirable and engaging, not to mention successful, of all arctic voyages. HMS *Hecla* and *Griper*, provisioned for two years, departed England late in the spring and made for Cape Farewell. The *Griper*, a gun brig, was so "crank" except before the wind that she had to be towed much of the way if the expedition was not to lose time. Parry threw overboard daily a sealed bottle flagged with white cotton cloth which contained a note giving their location and certain scientific particulars, and directing the finder (in six different languages) to return the notice to the Admiralty with an indication of where and when it was found. They sounded at 57°N 30°W for the fabulous Land of Buss, reported by the *Emmanuel* of Bridgewater, homeward bound with Frobisher in 1578, but without success. Entering the East Greenland Current, they passed from the clear blue of the North Atlantic to the earth-stained water of the ice stream. Doubling Cape Farewell, they found the familiar fleets of seabirds: looms (thick-billed murres), Greenland parrots (Atlantic puffins), Mother Carey's chickens (Leach's storm-petrels), sea pigeons (black guillemots), and Greenland swallows (arctic terns). In Davis Strait they killed a horse whale (walrus), which the *Hecla*'s assistant surgeon, Alexander Fisher, carefully necropsied. The men marveled at the walrus's strength: it had broken off the tip of a harpoon driven through two auricles of its heart and fought the boats unceasingly for ten minutes. They also sought out and killed several polar bears, which Fisher thoroughly examined and described.

They were caught in the ice only briefly, as Parry forged his way through the middle Baffin pack and entered Lancaster Sound, more than a month earlier than they had been there in 1818. There was no ice in sight, and no bottom to the bay was visible to the west. One officer indicated in his journal that, though everyone was properly deferential toward Ross's observation of mountains here, they could not "stifle [their] inward pleasures" at the prospect of open waters.

Ice again halted their progress in western Lancaster Sound. Parry made use of the time to explore to the south, in Prince Regent Inlet, before continuing west. On August 21 they were startled to find the broken end of a boat's sail yard floating in the water. Had someone been here before them? No—a seaman remembered its having fallen overboard when they had turned south for the inlet. Parry's progress west was spectacular. Like Verrazano 300 years before, or Cook in Bering Strait, he enjoyed excellent weather and good sailing. Near Fellfoot Point, Devon Island, one of the officers, with a mirthful shrug, figured the bearing and distance for Icy Cape. They came on large pods of belukha, which Parry speculated had come from the mouth of the Mackenzie River, an indication of open water ahead. The crews approached in the boats and "repeatedly urged one another to pull smartly" in order to get closer to the belukhas and hear the "whale-song"— a sound like that made by "passing a wet finger around the edge, or rim, of a glass tumbler."

At 9:15 P.M. on September 4, the ships crossed the meridian at 110°W and claimed the Admiralty prize. Parry was giving names to islands and headlands almost hourly. He paused long enough to land at several places where the men discovered primitive (Dorset?) ruins and brought on board the skulls of musk-oxen. They also found a narwhal tusk inland on Byam Martin Island.

Parry watched the needle in the binnacle compass wander about sluggishly and aimlessly and surmised, correctly, that he had sailed north of the Magnetic Pole. He ordered the binnacle taken below and began to steer by celestial navigation—no mean trick in an arctic summer. Early in September, along Dundas Peninsula, Melville Island, with the weather deteriorating and the ice closing in on them, Parry sensed the end for that year. They reached their farthest west at noon on September 17 at 112°51'W and returned

50 miles up the coast to a place they named Winter Harbor, where they went into winter quarters.

Winter closed quickly—the men had to cut a canal 4082 yards long and 35 feet wide through 7 inches of new ice to get the two ships into the protection of the harbor. The ships were anchored in five fathoms of water, 120 yards apart and 500 feet off the beach. A hut was erected on shore, where the expedition's scientific officer, Edward Sabine, set up his instruments. The ships and the hut were linked with lines, and after two nearly disastrous episodes (which required the amputation of frostbitten fingers and toes), Parry gave orders that no one was to wander out of sight of the ships.

The singular Parry, who turned twenty-nine on the voyage, had made thoughtful preparations for overwintering. Wagoncloth was brought out and run over the spars to create a completely sheltered deck for exercise. On November 5, *Miss in Her Teens, or The Medley of Lovers* was performed on the quarterdeck, and similar farces were produced throughout the winter—with *Miss in Her Teens* getting an encore at the end of the season. Sabine, at Parry's appointment, began to edit and publish *The North Georgia Gazette and Winter Chronicle*, which appeared on November 1 and regularly every Monday thereafter for twenty-two weeks.* It contained strictly anonymous essays, poems, and articles by Peter Pry About, John Slender Brain, and others, and featured adjudication of various issues in the Court of Common Sense. A close reading indicates that several of the officers didn't care for the production and that practical jokes were played on those who wouldn't join in this bit of officers' public-school amusement.

After the first few weeks they saw very few animals, and

---

* Parry had named the first tier of islands north of the Parry Channel the North Georgia Islands for King George III, distinguishing them from South Georgia in the Antarctic. They are now called the Parry Islands.

Parry suggested that the caribou and ptarmigan and other creatures must walk south across the ice to North America for the winter. Only wolves and arctic foxes remained behind. They caught a fox and kept him as a pet, and "Jack" became tame enough to eat from everyone's hand. The dogs on board made a tentative liaison with the wolves that came around. One, a white setter named Carlo, went off and never returned. Parry's black Newfoundland, Boatswain, got in a fight with a wolf in which the wolf, as well, came off poorly.

The officers and men lived in reasonable comfort, with bread baked fresh daily and beer freshly brewed (except when it wouldn't ferment because of the cold). Condensation from cooking and breathing froze to the walls and bulkheads and had to be chipped away regularly. Clothing never seemed to dry; bedding —fumigated weekly with gunpowder and vinegar—was always damp; light, from the single six-inch candle issued each man every six days, became precious. Parry and his officers worried about three things: scurvy, that perennial arctic menace; idleness, which they believed abetted the onset of scurvy and discontent; and their fate. They also expressed concern in their journals about their families, that they might worry too much about them.

The men were regularly inspected for signs of scurvy, and antiscorbutics—three-quarters of an ounce of lemon juice with sugar every morning—were part of every man's ration. (For the worst cases, the enterprising Parry grew mustard and cress near the stovepipe in this room. Daily exercise on deck or ashore if the weather was good was required, and each man had daily tasks to perform—so many that by midwinter the crew was complaining they had too much to do, which pleased Parry.)

In the evenings the officers gathered to read and listen to music, Parry playing his violin and one of the other officers a flute. Religious services were held on Sundays. In spite of the regularity of their lives and "the public obligation to be cheerful," they sensed their vulnerability, a "gloomy prospect which would sometimes obtrude itself on the stoutest heart."

The men amused themselves outside by making mortar barrels out of sea ice and by rendering the blubber of the sea mammals they had killed during the summer for oil, for their winter light. Many of them took long walks, "in a silence far different from that peaceable composure which characterizes the landscape of a cultivated country: it was the death-like stillness of the most dreary isolation, and the total absence of animated existence." Parry wrote of the pleasure of staring at a stone in the snow, for the relief it gave the eye. And of being able to hear a man singing to himself more than a mile away. And the explosive cracking of timbers as cold took the ships.

The return of the sun was so eagerly anticipated that during the time of day when it might be expected to loom early because of refraction, a continuous watch was kept from the top of the *Hecla*'s mainmast. On the fated day, February 3, a relay of men watched—ten minutes each—from the crow's nest. It appeared at 11:40 A.M., Winter Harbor time.

On February 13 two sailors received thirty-six lashes for drunkenness. On the 14th it was $-55°$F and Mr. Fisher poured water through a colander 40 feet up in the *Hecla*'s mast to see if it would freeze before it hit the deck. On February 24 at 10:15 A.M., clothing hung too near the stove in Mr. Sabine's observation hut caught fire and set fire to the building. The blaze was quickly put out, but a man who tried to save the instruments subsequently lost fingers on both hands to frostbite. A young pet glaucous gull died in the fire and was remembered in a dignified eulogy in the next issue of the paper.

March and April came on, but the cold weather did not break; the men suffered the consternation they would have felt had they been in northern England, expecting the return of warmth with the return of the sun, and some signs of spring. On April 9 Parry made his celebrated drawing of the sun's halos and arcs. On April 16 a brilliant solar corona became visible when a layer of light, fleecy clouds passed under the sun, revealing "the most soft and exquisite tints of lake, bluish green, and yellow about their edges, that can possibly be imagined." On June 16 a triple rainbow appeared.*

Parry had not planned for such a long stay as this, and he became anxious about the time of their departure, and their chances of reaching Icy Cape before fall. He decided if he was away before the end of June, he would be fine. In May the men started wearing black crepe veils to prevent snowblindness, and they cheered the sight of the first unfrozen water, on the ship's black paint. On May 24 it rained, but the ice showed no signs of weakening.

On June 1 Parry departed with eleven officers and men to explore to the north and west. The men pulled a cart with 800 pounds of provisions and equipment, on which they rigged a sail to help them over the wet and snowy terrain. Parry named many geographical features for his officers and midshipmen, collected geological samples, examined the remnants of a paleo-Eskimo camp, and constructed several cairns, as was their wont almost everywhere they put ashore. The cairns were roughly 12 feet high and 12 feet across at the base. A tin or copper cylinder, or sometimes one of Messrs. Dankin and Hall's preserved soup tins from the ship, containing the names of the shore party, the date, a short account of the voyage, and perhaps a penny from an officer's pocket, or a uniform button, was buried at the base.

The men returned to the ships on June 15. With no sign of breakup, Parry sent hunting parties out for ten days at a time to secure meat (brant, caribou, muskoxen, ptarmigan), and daily sent members of the crew out to collect sorrel.

Finally, on August 1, the two ships sailed out of Winter Harbor and set out again for Icy Cape. They got no farther west than they had the year before. The pack ice in M'Clure Strait

---

* While the first and second rainbows occur at an angle of 180° from the sun, the third and fourth occur around the sun and are almost never seen. What Parry took for the third rainbow was in fact the fifth level of refraction.

was impenetrable, and the floes humbling—one that had ridden up on another was 42 feet thick. On August 7, far to the southwest, they saw a shore, which they named Banks' Land in honor of Sir Joseph Banks, the proponent of a Northwest Passage whose mantle Barrow had assumed in 1815.

Parry already had his crews on two-thirds rations, in case they were forced to spend a second winter. He tried to get farther south by going back east first. It took him until August 30 to decide that it was hopeless for that year, and he shaped his course for home. On the way out of Lancaster Sound he gave the present Somerset Island the name North Somerset after the homeland of Lieutenant Liddon, the *Griper*'s captain, and the present Devon Island the name North Devon after his own native country. On the 4th and 5th of September they met whalers from Hull. The following day they met four Eskimo men near Clyde Inlet and spent several days with them before sailing for England.

Parry wrote that he had not reckoned with either the severity of the climate or the shortness of the sailing season. But his success was spectacular. It would be eighty years before anyone discovered so much new land in the Arctic in a single voyage—and no one before him had ever seen so much.

A storm the *Hecla* ran into on September 14 tore away the ship's stern boat, broke the foremast off two feet above the forecastle deck, snapped off the main-topmast, and broke away the bowsprit. To get clear of the wreckage they had to cut away their starboard anchor. On the 27th they sighted Foula Island in the Shetlands. On the 29th Parry disembarked at Peterhead and took a coach for London. With him, sealed, were all the journals, drawings, sketches, and notations produced by crew and officers on the expedition, "to be thereafter dispensed of as [the Admiralty] may think proper to determine."

The following spring Parry sailed again, to search for a southern entrance to Prince Regent Inlet, which he would find—Fury and Hecla Strait.

* * *

I thought across the range of these things, walking along the beach at Pingok. The day after a little trouble in the ice it is possible to imagine, if but imperfectly, the sort of reach some of these men made into the unknown, day after day. I think of Brendan asleep on a bed of heather in the bottom of his carraugh, and of the forlorn colonists at Eriks Fiord in the thirteenth century. The exemplary John Davis in his tiny pinnace, the *Ellen*. I think we can hardly reconstruct the terror of it, the single-minded belief in something beyond the self. Davis wrote of the wild coasts he surveyed that he believed God had made no land that was not amenable, that there were no wastelands.

Walking along the beach, remembering Brendan's deference and Parry's and Davis's voyages, I could only think what exquisite moments these must have been. Inescapable hardship transcended by a desire for spiritual elevation, or the desire to understand, to comprehend what lay in darkness. I thought of some of the men at Winter Harbor with Parry. What dreams there must have been that were never written down, that did not make that journey south with Parry in the coach, but remained in the heart. The kind of dreams that give a whole life its bearing, what a person intends it should be, having seen those coasts.

Nine

A NORTHERN PASSAGE

ALL DID NOT GO as smoothly on Parry's first expedition as his *Journal of a Voyage for the Discovery of a North-West Passage from the Atlantic to the Pacific* implies. In the pages of *The North Georgia Gazette* are hints that the officers of the *Griper* were ostracized. The coarser lot of the sailors is made clear in an expedition surgeon's report on the death of one William Scott, from alcoholism and acute psychosis. And the *Hecla*'s assistant surgeon, Alexander Fisher, notes in his journal on February 28, "We had a portion of the Second, Nineteenth, and Twenty-second articles of War read on the quarter-deck

today, and after that a long order relating chiefly to some difference between two officers some days ago."

Such small variation with the pristine image history usually
presents of Parry's voyage might count for nothing but quibbling
if the gentle suppression of these images did not foreshadow a
pattern. Increasingly, afterward, records of arctic exploration presented to the public were arranged to serve a purpose, to bolster a
preconceived vision of the impersonal hostility of the region and
mankind's role in it. The Arctic became an appropriate setting for
a life of national service, and nations touted the success of their
expeditions. Later, the Arctic became a dramatic setting for the
personal quests and heroism of individuals like Robert Peary,
Fridtjof Nansen, and Vilhjalmur Stefansson. Competition for geographic accomplishment in the late nineteenth century became as
keen as the competition had once been for commercial advantage,
and the use of the press to promote these expeditions became increasingly sophisticated.

The Admiralty's demand to control all the records from
Parry's expedition stemmed from the desire—largely Sir John
Barrow's, one suspects—to preserve a successful, coherent, tidy,
and inspiring image of the enterprise. Barrow stressed that these
voyages were for disinterested scientific and geographic discovery;
any mere commercial advantage that might accrue was far less
important. "[W]hatever new discoveries might be made," he
wrote in 1818, with an air of noblesse oblige, were to benefit all
other nations, "without [their] having incurred either the expense
or the risk" of exploration.

Pressed to defend these lofty ideals, which Parry's expedition
so admirably reflected, he remarked summarily, "Knowledge is
power." An enhancement of her international prestige and the
suggestion of an economic hegemony looming in the distance, too,
played a role in an England fresh from the Napoleonic Wars.
When Russia seemed poised to finish what England had begun in
the Arctic, Barrow argued, successfully, to prevent it. He wrote
that to have left the Northwest Passage "to be completed by a

foreign navy, after the doors of the two extremities of the passage had been thrown open by ships of our own [by James Cook (1778) and William Baffin (1616)] would have been little short of an act of national suicide."

The efforts of men such as Barrow to influence public emotions in this arena played a strong role, of course, in determining a public conception of the geography of the region. It is imprecise, however, to call this scheming—even when it involves, as it eventually did, individual men in acts of deception for personal gain; or when, today, it involves a discreet request by industry that scientific consultants structure environmental data in a helpful way. What is involved here, geographers such as John L. Allen have suggested, is a yearning to locate precisely what one has set out to find—and to shape what one finds to suit one's own ends, even if that meets with contradiction.

It is important, I think, not to lose sight of ingenuousness in these episodes. The desire to understand what is unknown is great. And the wish to create some human benefit out of new knowledge, however misconstrued, is one of the graces of Western civilization. Few historians can say precisely where the special interest of a Barrow or a Robert Peary ceased to serve society and served only the man; or where plans for industrialization cross a line and become of greater service to a nation's economy than the well-being of its people.

To travel in the Arctic is to wait. Systems of local transportation, especially in winter and along the fogbound coasts in summer, are tenuous. A traveler may be stranded for days in the vicinity of a small airport, tethered there by the promise of a plane's momentary arrival or by the simple tyranny of plans. In these circumstances I frequently read journals of exploration, especially those dealing with the regions I was in. I read in part to understand human presence in a landscape so emphatically devoid of human life. Slowly in this process a cairn I saw on a headland on Cornwallis Island, or the scattered remnants of a ship's cache at Fury Beach, or the desolate shoreline of King William Island where so many died—all seen from planes—became infused for me with deeper meaning. On seeing them I felt exhilaration, empathy, and compassion—and wistful speculation, that historical sensibility we use, as much as the elements of natural history, to make sense of the regions we inhabit.

In all these journals, in biographies of the explorers, and in modern narrative histories, common themes of quest and defeat, of aspiration and accomplishment emerge. Seen from a certain distance, however, they nearly all share a disassociation with the actual landscape. The land, whatever its attributes, is made to fill a certain role, often that of an adversary, the bête noire of one's dreams. The land's very indifference to human life, ironically, becomes a point in its favor. In the most extreme forms of disassociation, the landscape functions as little more than a stage for the exposition of a personality or for scientific or economic theories, or for national or personal competitions. One rarely finds the lack of overbearing design on the land that distinguished John Davis's voyages, his mature wonder. Encounters with the land in the nineteenth century are more brutal than tender. And are shaped by Victorian sentiment: a desire to exert oneself against formidable odds; to cast one's character in the light of ennobling ideals; to sojourn among exotic things; to make collections and erect monuments. There are no monks intent on cordial visits, moving back and forth between insight and awe, travels without a thought of ownership or utility. And few travelers were not constrained by timetables of accomplishment.

With every expedition into that landscape, however, there went that hope born of a fresh start, that the land would reveal itself; that the maps would turn out splendidly in accuracy and detail; or that feelings of beauty or loneliness would penetrate deeply. For the rare few to whom the land was an unimpeachable source of wisdom, there was also a desire to perceive both its light and its dark sides.

So I read the histories that had been shaped by a sense of

mission or purpose, or that were arranged to fit the times in which they were written, and hoped for a stray remark that would reveal an edge of the land previously undivulged, or an unguarded human feeling that would show the land as something alive.

The expeditions that followed Parry's into the North American Arctic were virtually all British, until the middle of the century when disaster befell Sir John Franklin. Each of these overwintering expeditions disappeared behind a wall of fog—nothing but silence until they emerged somewhere a year later, or three or four years later. Or never. The shorelines and waterways were systematically mapped, but the journals make clear that this reconnaissance called upon a terrible strength in the men who pursued it. Many, boldly led, could not imagine the reason for such hardship; and officers grew weary of trying to impart their visions to reluctant and sullen men.

The cold brought frostbite and amputation, numbing headaches, and stupor to overwintering ships' crews. No kind of clothing or shelter could keep it entirely at bay. The cold made the touch of metal burn and all tasks more difficult, more complicated. Even to make water to drink was a struggle. And the stifling boredom of winter quarters in a dank, freezing ship only compounded apprehension about scurvy and starvation. Men could plan against debilitation, as Parry had; but common seamen still drank themselves into demoralizing unconsciousness with contraband whiskey, and some officers went clinically insane.

The capacity of the frozen sea suddenly to destroy a ship like a nut between two stones was knowledge that pursued people to a state of exhaustion, of abject capitulation. For days the ice seemed only to toy with a ship, to lift it slowly a few feet out of the water, or roll it over 15° to port and hold it. Men slept in their clothes for weeks on end, ready to abandon ship, knowing the bow stem could part suddenly with an explosion and green water pour over them through the fissure. Or any night might be only another when the ice barely murmured against the hull, or screamed like a banshee and hove up shattered in the darkness, but in the distance.

In the spring the light came. It gave men "an extravagant sense of undefined relief," and in their innocence and abandon they became snowblind. Their eyes felt as if they rested on needles in sockets filled with sand. In harness they dragged sledges across the trench and rubble of sea ice and through vast sumps of soft snow. Consumed by the immenseness of the land, men tramped on mindlessly and fell over dead—of exhaustion, of fatal despair, of miscalculation. Died in a tidal crack that suddenly opened, or from a ridiculously simple accident. Starving men ate their dogs, and then their clothing, and then they turned to each other.

Some of this was unnecessary. The strength of British naval exploration was its regimented discipline, exerted by officers who believed completely and indefatigably in what they were doing. Its failure was its ethnocentrism, its attitude of moral and technical superiority to the Eskimo, its perception of the land as deserted and unamenable. The few technical advances the British brought to arctic exploration in the nineteenth century—India-rubber ground cloths, folding canvas boats, portable, alcohol-burning stoves— were all but inconsequential when compared with their failure to understand the advantages of fur clothing, snow houses, and fresh meat over naval uniforms, fabric tents, and tinned food. British ships, it is true, often carried more men than the lands they were exploring could supply with clothing and fresh meat; but, too, they thought in terms of unnecessarily large contingents of men instead of smaller groups better adapted to the land.*

---

* During the years of the Franklin search the British persisted in trusting to the superiority of their terrible winter clothing. They refused to use dog sledges because they felt it demeaned human enterprise to have dogs doing work men could do. Other explorers, particularly Hudson's Bay men like John Rae, and Samuel Hearne earlier, adopted the more serviceable clothing, more nutritious food, and more efficient travel methods of the Eskimos. Both Peary and Stefansson championed various aspects of the local intelligence as indispensable to their successes.

It is worth pointing up the failures of British exploration. The constitutions and desires of all the men involved in this experience were not the same; the complexities of economics and military duty, and the vision of men like John Barrow, placed other men in positions where they struggled for comprehension and meaning in a landscape that contradicted what they did. The geographical knowledge we enjoy now cost some men dearly. It is presumptuous to think they all died believing they'd given their lives for something greater.

IN September 1837, George Back beached a badly leaking HMS *Terror* on the west coast of Ireland. He had spent a monumentally nerve-wracking winter, beset in the ice in Foxe Channel and raked by gales. *Terror*'s bulkheads had started, her deck had been sprung, her eyebolts shot, her bow stoved—she had been squeezed so tight that turpentine had dripped from her timbers. Any other vessel, said the shipwrights who repaired her at Chatham, would have broken apart under the pressure and sunk.

This foray—Back had been sent to map the north coast of America from Fury and Hecla Strait to Kent Peninsula—did not sit well at all in England. A stout ship and an affable, relaxed captain were all that saved crew and officers from near-certain death. The Northwest Passage held no real allure now—Parry had lit the way for whalers from Peterhead and Dundee into the North Water, but that was all the benefit (pure and applied science and a country's honor aside) most could see in these voyages. Besides, public benefactors like Felix Booth, a distiller, were now financing expeditions; and the Hudson's Bay Company was sending out explorers—let them foot the bill, thought Parliament, for whatever gain might be left in it.

Barrow argued, artfully and successfully, however, for yet another voyage, one so completely well outfitted and with objectives so clear it seemed impossible of failure. Thus, HMS *Terror* and *Erebus* sailed from London on May 19, 1845, with 134 men under the command of Sir John Franklin. Their goal was to connect Parry's route through Lancaster Sound and Barrow Strait with the coast of North America, and then to sail west for Bering Strait. The whole of that coast from Icy Cape (Cook's farthest, 1778) to Boothia Peninsula was now known. The endeavor seemed, to most, perfunctory.

Franklin's party, less five men who transferred off before *Terror* and *Erebus* entered the ice, wintered in 1845–46 at Beechey Island, where three men died of unknown causes and were buried. In 1846 Franklin sailed up Wellington Channel to 77°N, then south down the west coast of Cornwallis Island, across Barrow Strait and into Peel Sound. He spent the winter of 1846–47 wedged in heavy multiyear floes in Victoria Strait. What Franklin did not know, and could not have known, was that he had chosen the wrong route. On a route plotted down the *east* side of King William Island and into Queen Maud Gulf via James Ross, Rae, and Simpson straits, he would have encountered only annual ice. Moreover, it was the only practicable route.*

Franklin's tragic error—*Erebus* and *Terror* never got out of the ice, and twenty-one men including Franklin died during a second winter in Victoria Strait—grew out of an incorrect observation by James Ross, exploring the west coast of Boothia Peninsula in 1831. Ross thought King William Island and Boothia Peninsula were connected—he sketched in what would later be named Rae Strait as an isthmus.

By 1848 concern for the missing party had mounted sufficiently for rescue ships to be dispatched. The Admiralty continued the search for Franklin—some forty expeditions, governmental, private, and international, went out over a ten-year period—until March 1854, when Franklin and his men were officially declared

---

* Heavy pack ice enters Victoria Strait annually from the Arctic Ocean via M'Clure Strait, Viscount Melville Sound, and M'Clintock Channel, a pattern of drift unknown in Franklin's time. The alternate route suggested above was the one followed by Amundsen in 1903–1906, on the first successful navigation of the Passage.

dead. Save for evidence of the winter encampment at Beechey Island, not a trace of the expedition had been found. In the spring of 1854, Dr. John Rae, a Hudson's Bay employee, met a group of Eskimos near Pelly Bay who told him they had seen men who had abandoned the ships walking on King William Island and later found their bodies. Rae purchased several relics from them, including a small silver plate with Franklin's name engraved on it. The British government awarded Rae £10,000 for determining the fate of the expedition, but Lady Franklin, Sir John's wife, was not satisfied with this conclusion. She wanted to know how and why such a sterling group (in her estimation) had failed. She continued to spend a large part of her own fortune and to raise public funds as well to outfit private expeditions and pursue the search for her husband's ships. The last of these expeditions, in a small, refitted yacht sent out under the command of Francis M'Clintock, located the only records from the disaster ever found, in the spring of 1859: two notes in separate cairns on the west coast of King William Island and a frozen packet of unreadable letters.

The search for Franklin caught England's imagination as Barrow's quest for a Northwest Passage never had. Scores of expeditions set out from England and America to search the entire unexplored Canadian Archipelago if necessary, especially its coastlines. This approach marked a fundamental change in arctic exploration. Where once the goal had only been to get *through* en route to somewhere else, now expeditions were prepared to overwinter and to make the region itself the focus of their attention. Small detachments of men spread out in the spring in every direction to cover hundreds of miles with man-drawn sledges, discovering new islands, channels, and bays almost everywhere they went. From this enterprise came, ironically, the first extensive and accurate maps of the high Arctic. After six years, however, the British were disenchanted. An oaf of an officer, Sir Edward Belcher, intuiting the Admiralty's growing impatience with an expensive and fruitless endeavor, summarily abandoned the search ships HMS *Resolute*, *Intrepid*, *Assistance*, and *Pioneer* in the ice and departed the Arctic in September 1854.* England's eyes were now on the western Crimea, and her heart with Englishmen dying there.†

The Franklin disaster ended British—indeed, virtually all—interest in finding a Northwest Passage. Franklin's men, said Sir John Richardson, had forged "the last link of the North-west Passage with their lives." They "perished in the path of duty," wrote M'Clintock, and the search for them had been a "glorious mission." These observations were widely endorsed. The Admiralty prize for the first successful navigation of the Passage went, with some grumbling, to Robert M'Clure and the officers and men of *Investigator*, who sailed through Bering Strait in 1850, spent the winters of 1851–52 and 1852–53 beset at Banks Island, and then walked over the ice to *Resolute* at Dealy Island, just west of Parry's old Winter Harbor. They spent the following winter beset off Bathurst Island and sailed home with Belcher in September 1854. (The sledge from *Resolute* that reached *Investigator* at Mercy Bay and escorted the men back in the spring of 1853 was, ironically, called the *John Barrow*.)

In order not to disparage Franklin's efforts, the Admiralty set the prize to M'Clure at £10,000, one-half the £20,000 originally set aside, for having discovered *a* Northwest Passage.

The Franklin search expeditions succeeded in mapping virtu-

---

* The timely arrival of HMS *Phoenix* and *Talbot* at Beechey Island was all that saved the crews of these four ships and the men from HMS *Investigator* from all having to sail home in a single vessel, Belcher's *North Star*.

† The search for Franklin was a many-faceted affair, run on hunch and invention and conducted by people with a variety of motives. Some officers were looking for a quick route to promotion, others were enthralled with delineating a new land. Franklin's fate was, at some points, rather far from many people's minds. One of the oddest plans put into motion was Captain Horatio Austin's to live-trap arctic fox and fix them with metal information tags directing the Franklin party to the search ships and to caches that had been set out for them. Some of the foxes were quietly dispatched by sailors, who valued the fur and thought the plan cockeyed.

ally all the coastline of the arctic islands south and west of the Parry Islands. (Amundsen and Stefansson would complete the survey of the northeast coast of Victoria Island, the most difficult to reach, in 1905 and 1916, respectively.) Prince Patrick, the westernmost of these, was named for the Irishmen who participated in the search.* Several islands were named for groups that donated funds for the search, including the Tasmania Islands at the foot of Franklin Strait, honoring moneys pledged to Lady Franklin's expeditions from that corner of the world (where her husband had been governor-general). Banks Land and King William Land were found to be islands. Bellot Strait was discovered. Virtually all this survey work was done by small sledging parties, a technique brought to perfection by M'Clintock, who set a record in 1853 by traveling over 1328 miles in 105 days.

As interest in Franklin's fate began to wane, attention slowly shifted to two other goals: discovering the waters of a reportedly ice-free polar sea and attaining the Geographic North Pole. These were to be largely American endeavors; indeed, the principal avenue of approach, the channel between Greenland and Ellesmere Island, came to be called the American Route, and the region itself came to be regarded by some, quite erroneously, as part of the United States, especially during the years when Peary was basing his expeditions there.

BY 1850, then, the North had become a region important in its own right. The Hudson's Bay Company was continuing to export a fortune in furs from the Canadian subarctic; some arctic expeditions had reported deposits of coal; American whalers with their "go-aheadism" had met with new success in the Chukchi Sea—perhaps, thought investors, the region had enough potential to warrant

---

* In a most roundabout way. The island was named for Arthur William Patrick Albert, Victoria and Albert's seventh child, born in 1850. The name Patrick was given him in remembrance of his mother's visit to Ireland in 1849.

further exploration. Too, it held out promise of renown and prestige to anyone who could help "extend the charts," who could map what lay north of the Parry Islands or reach the Pole. In 1853, with these sentiments in the wind, American shipping magnate Henry Grinnell, philanthropist George Peabody, and several scientific societies decided to sponsor a single-minded and popular American explorer named Elisha Kent Kane.

Officially, Kane was to become part of the Franklin search when he sailed north. But as nothing had been found to that date but the camp at Beechey Island, Kane felt justified in pursuing the search in an unlikely direction—up Smith Sound and into Kane Basin. He wintered at Rensselaer Harbor in northwest Greenland in 1853–54 and again in 1854–55 when his ship remained beset. His sledge parties pushed up the Greenland coast as far north as 80°N.* In the spring of 1855 Kane and his men packed their journals and maps and rowed and walked out of the Arctic, all the way to Godhavn, where they met a relief expedition.

Arctic exploration had had a military and scientific cast under Barrow's orchestration. It was selflessly performed for God and country. The Americans entered the Arctic with no such illusions. From Kane to Peary, American expeditions were to be characterized by the individuals who led them as much as by the goals their benefactors and sponsors had in mind.

Kane was a diminutive, sickly man, obsessed with arctic exploration, "one of the last of the race of brilliant and versatile amateurs," says Canadian arctic historian L. H. Neatby. His dramatic presence, his brave and sentimental bearing, his romantic vision and virtue captured America's sense of itself. When he died at the age of thirty-seven, he enjoyed a funeral that, at the time, could only be compared with Lincoln's. His very frailty accented the qualities Americans so admired—drive, backbone, and grit.

---

* At the time, William Parry held the record for a farthest north— 82°45′N, a point north of Svalbard reached on a sledge journey in 1827.

With his ship locked up for a second year in the ice, Kane made soup from the ship's rats, burned parts of the ship itself for heat, and rigged mirrors to throw sunlight into the holds where his men lay bedridden with scurvy. In his encounters with the local hunters (characteristically intent on testing newly met people for any weakness, the Eskimos stole from him) he was stern, then vengeful, and finally tactful. He successfully negotiated a treaty with them which required that they provide his party with food.

Kane followed Edward Inglefield, an English explorer, into Smith Sound and generated considerable excitement in the outside world when he reiterated Inglefield's earlier report (1852) that there was open water north of the ice in Kane Basin. The theory of an open polar sea had been advanced numerous times in the previous 300 years, though nineteenth-century arguments for it were "sired by wishful commercial thinking and born to national ambition" in the view of geographer John Kirtland Wright. There was some legitimate reason to speculate about a vast stretch of open water in the Far North. As early as 1810 the Russian explorer Hedenström had described polynyas. The whale–fisher's bight west of Svalbard was known to reach as far north as 82°N in some years. And the extent of annual sea ice, especially in the Greenland Sea, did vary greatly from year to year. But the existence of such a sea was posited largely on scraps of information—about the set of currents, the presence of driftwood from distant coasts showing up in certain areas, a haphazard assortment of sea and land temperatures, and marine-mammal migration patterns. It was poor scientific reasoning, even by the standards of the day.

With the rise of a more rigorous science at the close of the nineteenth century, attempts to find an open polar sea were not taken seriously. They were not, however, loudly disparaged, for the public would not accept such criticism. Between the Civil War and the beginning of the First World War, American audiences were most eager to know and read about polar adventure. Men like Kane and Charles Francis Hall, and later Stefansson and Peary, who journeyed through exotic regions far removed from the factories of industrial America, were fetchingly heroic figures.* Peary especially, the very embodiment of determination, was revered, until his grasping and arrogant nature became too much and public sentiment turned against him.

In September 1875, Karl Weyprecht, an Austrian army officer who discovered Franz Josef Land with Julius von Payer in 1873, urged a group of scientists meeting in Graz, Austria, to make a synchronous and, consequently, more useful examination of the Arctic. Weyprecht regarded recent attempts to reach the North Pole as nothing but stunts; and he criticized the zealous international competition to discover new arctic islands. What was the nature of the arctic climate, he wanted to know, and how did it affect Europe's weather? Could chauvinism be set aside for international cooperation to answer this and other scientific questions in the North? It could, his colleagues believed. Weyprecht's proposals were refined and became the plan for the first International Polar Year. In 1882, eleven countries set up twelve arctic stations for a year of observations.

The station farthest to the north was to be an American one at Fort Conger, Ellesmere Island, commanded by army lieutenant Adolphus Greely. Greely was a humorless, mediocre commander, "an insecure . . . irritable martinet," according to one historian, without arctic experience. He opted, in the American tradition, for spectacular adventure rather than tedious scientific observation, sending a Lieutenant James Lockwood up the coast of Greenland to best, if possible, the current British farthest north of 83°20'N. Lockwood reached 83°24'N with Sergeant David Brainard and an Eskimo companion on May 15, 1883, four nautical miles farther

---

* Hall, a small businessman and obsessed visionary, endured hardship in the Arctic with almost neurotic indifference. In 1862 he took down the story of Frobisher's visits to Baffin Island from resident Eskimos who had kept the details perfectly in order in oral tradition for 275 years. He died in 1871 in his winter quarters at Thank God Harbor, northern Greenland, a victim, apparently, of murder by arsenic poisoning.

north than the Nares Expedition had got on that same shore. "We shook each other's hands from very joy," wrote Brainard later, "and even hugged the astonished Eskimo who wondered what it was all about." Sergeant Brainard, one is chagrined to note, also carved an advertisement for a well-known ale into the rock before turning back.

Greely had been put on Ellesmere Island to build Fort Conger, to make meteorological and magnetic observations, and to explore both Ellesmere and northern Greenland. The party was to be picked up in the summer of 1883. The relief ship did not show up that year, nor did it appear in the summer of 1884. Desperate, Greely led his men south along the coast to Cape Sabine in hopes of finding a cache, either one left by his would-be rescuers or one from the 1875–1876 Nares Expedition. (They found both. The former was pitifully inadequate and retrieving the latter proved too arduous.) Sixteen of the twenty-five men on Pim Island at Cape Sabine died of starvation that winter, including the young and very likable Edward Israel.

The failure to rescue all the men in the party—Greely, himself, survived—is one of the most shameful episodes in American history. The rescue efforts of both 1883 and 1884 were inept, half-hearted affairs. The saddest part, perhaps, was the disparagement heaped on Greely by the very politicians who would not underwrite a serious effort to rescue him. Heroic attempts apparently did not count for much against unqualified success in America. Not to have rounded the tip of Greenland or discovered new land, to have bested the British by only four miles—it wasn't enough. Greely was written off, a cruel and inhumane treatment of a man who did the best he could to keep his men alive. One of the loudest voices of condemnation was that of Robert Peary, who lived to greatly regret his self-indulgence.

By this time, 1900, arctic exploration had largely become the story of two men, Fridtjof Nansen and Peary. Robert Peary, the older of the two, was a shrewd salesman, desperate for acclaim. His accomplishments were genuine—explorations of northern Greenland and his arrival at the North Pole in 1909, arduous journeys requiring a determination that staggers the imagination. His bluster and his ability to command, however, concealed loneliness and insecurity, which he sought to assuage by his accomplishments and by maneuvering to gain the favor and companionship of powerful people. He embodied the bearing and to some extent the ideals of Theodore Roosevelt, one of his staunchest supporters.

Nansen, a Norwegian scientist and humanitarian, was a different sort of man—nearly as driven as Peary, but not a showman, not an imposing presence. He had a larger view of the world than Peary did, a better understanding of the scale of human events, and he made lasting contributions in several fields. He was the first explorer to cross the Greenland ice cap; he derived and then proved a theory of polar drift; and he wrote a scholarly two-volume work on early arctic exploration, *In Northern Mists*. In 1923 he was awarded the Nobel Peace Prize for his efforts on behalf of refugees after World War I.

While there is an aura of the unrequited lover about Peary, the proportions of Nansen's life seem ideal. Nansen, however, was not harried the way Peary was, dogged by a bewildering series of misfortunes that culminated in a self-destructive dispute with Dr. Frederick Cook over who had gotten to the North Pole first.

WHEN he read in 1884 that part of the wreckage of a ship called the *Jeannette* had turned up on the southwest coast of Greenland, Nansen began to speculate about polar drift in the Arctic Ocean.*

With Scottish ship architect Colin Archer, Nansen built the *Fram*, a 128-foot, broad-beamed, three-masted schooner designed

---

* The *Jeannette*, an American vessel, was crushed in the ice in the Laptev Sea in 1881. Most of the members of the expedition, including its commander, naval lieutenant George De Long, perished. They proved Wrangel Island was an island, however, and discovered the De Long and New Siberian islands, indicating the great seaward extent of the Siberian continental shelf. At about the same time, July 20, 1879, a Swedish geologist and explorer, Adolf Erik Nordenskjöld, rounded Cape Dezhnev in a steam sail ship, completing the Northeast Passage. (In 1913 Severnaya Zemlya, the last arctic archipelago, was discovered by a Russian officer, to complete a picture of the Siberian high Arctic.) Nordenskjöld's voyage opened a trade route for Siberian furs, lumber, and ore, which became the impetus for the development of the modern Soviet fleet of cargo ships and nuclear-powered icebreakers. The completion of the Northwest Passage by Amundsen in 1906, by comparison, aroused very little interest in Canada or the United States until the discovery of oil in the Arctic in 1968.

to survive in the polar pack.* The *Fram* was outfitted for five years, and on June 24, 1893, with eleven companions, Nansen set his course from Norway to intersect the *Jeannette*'s. By the end of September the *Fram* was beset as intended, north of the De Long Islands. For two years Nansen drifted in safety, making numerous observations. The ship rode beautifully in the ice; the drift, though slow, went as Nansen had expected, a clockwise movement westward from the De Long Islands. Bored and eager for a struggle, Nansen left the ship on March 14, 1895, with Frederik Johansen and twenty-six dogs in an effort to reach the North Pole. They passed beyond 86°N, but spring was upon them and they dared go no farther. As it was, they barely reached Franz Josef Land with two of the dogs. They overwintered there and sailed for Norway in August, with the English explorer Frederick Jackson, whom they were fortunate enough to meet there, quite by accident.

The *Fram*'s captain, Otto Sverdrup, brought the ship safely out of the ice and into the Greenland Sea in August 1896. Two years later, on another expedition, Sverdrup was forced into winter quarters with the *Fram* by heavy ice on the eastern coast of Ellesmere Island. A suspicious Peary suddenly showed up in Sverdrup's camp—he wanted to know what Sverdrup's intentions were. To explore to the west and not try for the Pole, said the Norwegian. Peary, snubbing a courteous offer of coffee, bade the Norwegians an abrupt adieu. Another slight Peary would regret.

Between 1898 and 1902 Sverdrup and his companions explored southern and western Ellesmere and discovered Axel Heiberg

---

* The *Fram*'s smooth, round-bottomed shape offered no projections for sea ice to grip. Its rudder and the cast-iron propeller of its auxiliary engine were housed in protective wells and could be hoisted on deck quickly in an emergency. The oak hull itself, with an aggregate thickness of four feet, was reenforced with extra frames and an internal bracing of wood and iron. Layers of heavy felt, cork, and reindeer-hair insulation made the cramped quarters more comfortable. A windmill on board provided power for a system of electric lights.

Island and Amund and Ellef Ringnes islands to the west.* Not since Parry's first expedition had so much new land been discovered and mapped. It was thorough, competent exploration, which went largely unheralded in America, like the Danish exploration of east Greenland.

ONE winter in Yellowknife, in the Northwest Territories, when the temperature did not get above −40°F for seven weeks, I found plenty of time to read. Ringing in my mind was a conversation about the perception of landscape that I had had with a man named Richard Davis, at his office at the Arctic Institute of North America in Calgary. I had explained my fascination with a set of journals, written about travels over the tundra north and east of Yellowknife, those of Samuel Hearne, John Franklin, Warburton Pike, and Ernest Thompson Seton.† Hearne had lived off the land like his Slavey and Chipewyan companions on a journey to the Northern Ocean (1770–1772). The land does not take on the proportions of an enemy in his journal, nor does it seem bereft of life. A different understanding emerges from Franklin's journal, in which the land reflects the name it was to bear ever after—the Barrens. (Franklin's 1819–1822 expedition was troubled by execution, starvation, murder, and cannibalism.) In Pike's journal (1890) the tundra is construed as a wild place that sagacious and incessantly tough men are meant to subdue, to survive in. For Seton (1907) the same tundra is so benign, its economic promise so bright, he even attempts to change its name from the Barrens to the Arctic Prairies.

The same land—plants, animals, small trees, weather, the low hills, rivers, and lakes—is, as one might easily guess, seen differently in different eras by men of dissimilar background. I speculated about

---

* Count Axel Heiberg and two wealthy brewers, Amund and Ellef Ringnes, contributed heavily to Nansen's and Sverdrup's expeditions.
† See note 5 for titles and dates of publication.

the overlap and contrast in the journals with Davis, who had himself written a paper comparing the journals of twentieth–century travelers in the subarctic. Something that comes up in a comparison of such journals, he said, is how much a description of the land in an early report affects the description of the same landscape in a later report. Confirming the existence, in other words, of a landscape like Pike's in the North—"the most complete desolation that exists on the face of the earth"—is partly the result of choosing that writer over another to read before departing.

As I sat reading in Yellowknife I was mindful of this, of the caution with which one should approach any journal, of the tendency to make a single appealing narrative stand for the entire experience or, worse, to stand in place of the experience. I also felt a sense of privilege, having been able to walk over some of the same country these explorers traversed. Even if I did not always care for the shape of the mind, I could see they had been there. Hearne's journal rings with authentic detail, some of it quite subtle. I reflected that week in Yellowknife how infrequently any of us is able to do this, to verify what is given to us to read about a far place. And how in reading three or four journals about the same region one sees even better the gaps, the strange lacunae that emerge in our understanding of anything. And something else: one wants to get a sense of the land itself, to know what it is; but one is also drawn irresistibly to the people who walk around on it, figuring out both the landscape and themselves.

The literature of nineteenth-century arctic exploration is full of coincidence and drama—last-minute rescues, a desperate rifle shot to secure food for starving men, secret letters written to painfully missed loved ones. There are moments of surreal stillness, as in Parry's journal when he writes of the sound of the human voice in the land. And of tender ministration and quiet forbearance in the face of inevitable death. As if caught up in the plot of a great Victorian novel, ships and people often turn up again in ironic circumstances—Sir John Ross was rescued in 1831, after being trapped in the ice of Prince Regent Inlet for four years, by the

Isabella, the ship he had sailed into Smith Sound in 1818, since converted to a whaler. The *Terror*, which George Back barely got clear of Foxe Channel in 1837, the near-disaster that almost ended British arctic exploration, was Franklin's flagship in 1845.

Francis M'Clintock, who would be the first to find records from the Franklin Expedition, on King William Island in 1859, also had a hand in M'Clure's completion of the Northwest Passage. In the spring of 1851 he left a message under a rock at Winter Harbor, Melville Island, giving the location of his ship's winter quarters. It was found the following spring by M'Clure, who, realizing the note was now dated, added information to it about the location of *Investigator* at Mercy Bay and the dire circumstances there. M'Clintock's note was checked by a colleague in the fall of 1852 and, the ship's fate then known for the first time, preparations were made for a rescue expedition in the spring of 1853. (A single member of *Investigator*'s crew, Samuel Cresswell, was fortuitously present when a supply ship, HMS *Phoenix*, departed Beechey Island for London on August 24, 1853. He thus became the first person to travel through the Northwest Passage—the rest of the crew spent another winter in the Arctic.) Another note left by M'Clintock, on the north shore of Prince Patrick Island, was discovered in 1915 by Stefansson and delivered, still legible, to his widow in 1921.

Of the many dramatic events, several became fixed in my mind.

In 1900, Peary placed a cairn on the northeast shore of Greenland at 82°37′N. In the previous twenty-five years the Danes had been making a systematic reconnaissance of Greenland's remote east coast. The only hole in their map was that between Peary's cairn and Cape Bismarck (76°45′N), a distance of about 400 miles. In August 1906, the Danmark Expedition arrived at Cape Bismarck to complete the coastal survey. On May 1, 1907, having spent the previous autumn laying down caches, Mylius Erichsen, Höeg Hagen, and an Eskimo companion named Jörgen Brönlund parted company with J. P. Koch and his party, after traveling north from Cape Bismarck with them. Koch headed for Peary's cairn. Erichsen turned west into Independence Fiord, the east entrance to a channel that Peary had reported led to the west coast of Greenland. On May 27, by accident, the parties met again. Koch had found Peary's cairn while Erichsen had traveled 125 miles into Danmark Fiord and found his way blocked. He told Koch he was going to run up Independence Fiord to the vicinity of Academy Glacier, from where he thought he might be able to look westward into Peary Channel. He thought it would take only a few days.

Erichsen's party never returned. Koch and the others searched unsuccessfully for them in the fall, laying down emergency supplies along the coast as they went. The following spring they began a careful check of the depots. In a small cave, which served as a cache on the coast of Lambert Land, they found Brönlund's body. At his feet were a bottle containing all of Hagen's maps and his diary, all but the last page written in Eskimo syllabics. On the final page, in Danish, Brönlund had written:

> Perished 79 Fiord after attempt to return over inland ice in November. I arrive here in waning moonlight, and could not go farther for frozen feet and darkness. Bodies of the others are in middle of Fiord off glacier (about 2½ leagues). Hagen died 15th of November, Mylius about ten days later.

The three of them, it turned out, had run into warm weather on the way back, which made travel over the sea ice impossible. They ran out of food and their dogs perished. They had found a geography Peary's descriptions did not prepare them for. Hagen's maps, which the Eskimo had carried with him to the end, corrected the errors.

There was no Peary Channel. Where Peary had reported the frozen northern reaches of the Greenland Sea, they had found two enormous peninsulas, Crown Prince Christian Land and land now named for Erichsen. (In fairness to Peary, other explorers made such errors, though few were ever pointed up in such a regrettable way.)

Peary's own journeys were full of desperate moments, including one of the most harrowing in arctic literature. In 1906, retreating south across the ice after an unsuccessful attempt to reach the Pole, Peary found his way blocked by a lead a half-mile wide. The party, camped on the north side, sent men to reconnoiter east and west, and waited, day after day, for the lead either to close or to freeze over. Peary's provisions ran perilously low. The men finally killed their dogs for food and broke up their sleds for fuel. The lead was by then two miles wide, but some distance from camp a thin film of ice had formed over it. The ice would not support a man without snowshoes—to stumble, even to pause, would mean breaking through. They tied on their snowshoes with great care, spread out in a wide line abreast, and set out in silence. Each man moved with a rhythmic shuffle. The young ice rose in bow waves like water at the tips of their snowshoes. When the toe of his rear shoe broke through the ice on two successive steps, Peary thought his life was finished. He heard someone cry out behind him but did not dare stop or turn around. "God help him," he thought. When they reached solid ice on the other side no one spoke. Peary heard the quivering sighs of the two men nearest to him. The shout had been from a man whose snowshoes, like Peary's, had broken through. But everyone had made it.

That moment, indeed the intensity with which Peary lived, contrasts sharply with the highly accomplished but unsung arctic voyage of one Richard Collinson. Collinson left England in January 1850 in HMS *Enterprise*, with his consort M'Clure in *Investigator*. Somewhere en route to the Bering Sea, around Cape Horn and via Hawaii, M'Clure decided he would just as soon be the first ship through the Northwest Passage as to find Sir John Franklin. M'Clure was already forty-three, and his chances for promotion were not good. Accordingly, he slipped ahead of his commanding officer.

Collinson, a few weeks behind M'Clure (who had made a bold charge through an uncharted part of the Aleutian chain), arrived

too late to get past the ice at Point Barrow. He turned south and
spent the winter in Hong Kong. In the summer of 1851 he rounded
Point Barrow and, unknowingly, followed M'Clure's 1850 route
up Prince of Wales Strait. On one of the Princess Royal Islands,
Collinson found a note indicating M'Clure had tried to cross Viscount Melville Sound to reach Parry's Winter Harbor but was
prevented by heavy ice. Collinson also tried and was repulsed. He
returned south, doubled Nelson Head, and sailed up the west coast
of Banks Island (unaware, again, that he was just two weeks behind
M'Clure). The ice proved too great an obstacle, however, and he
turned south again. He headed for the southwest shore of Victoria
Island, where he set up winter quarters.

In 1852 Collinson deftly navigated the 300-ton *Enterprise*
through Dolphin and Union Strait, a stunning bit of seamanship, to
winter at Cambridge Bay on the southeast coast of Victoria Island.
Had he had an interpreter along (the interpreter was with
M'Clure), he very likely would have learned the location of
Franklin's tragedy. As it was, he only collected some relics of the
expedition from local Eskimos. In the spring of 1853 he explored
the east coast of Victoria Island as far as Gateshead Island, finding
that he had been anticipated there by Rae in 1851. (The relics Rae
collected among the Pelly Bay Eskimos in 1854 would also arrive
in England a year before Collinson was able to get back with his.)
Collinson set sail for England in the summer of 1853. After again
navigating unscathed through the treacherous shoal water south of
Victoria Island, he was forced into winter quarters at Camden Bay,
Alaska. He finally reached England via the Cape of Good Hope in
May 1855.

In those five years only three of the sixty-four men with
Collinson died. According to one historian, Collinson exceeded all
his contemporaries in looking after the health and morale of his
men. One of his innovations was a billiard table made of snow
blocks, erected on the sea ice at Cambridge Bay to dispel winter
ennui. The bumpers were made of walrus skin, packed with oakum;

the table surface was a sheet of freshwater ice, finely shaved; and the balls were hand-carved of lignum vitae. "I do not suppose that any of the men had played at billiards before," wrote Collinson, "so they could not complain of the table; but the thing took admirably."

Collinson's journey, for distance traveled, length of voyage, difficulty of navigation, adherence to orders, and overall health of officers and crew upon their return, was singular. His very lack of difficulty, however, obscured his unparalleled achievement and helped to promote M'Clure's somewhat contrived claim. Belcher, it might be noted, knowing full well what had happened to the *Investigator*, abandoned Collinson to the same fate in 1854.

WHEN Collinson headed up the east coast of Victoria Island in 1853, he had two sledges with him. He intended to send one of them across Victoria Strait to King William Island, where he would have found the evidence M'Clintock found six years later—the skeletons, cairns, and abandoned stores that revealed the fate of Franklin's men. As it was, the 55 miles of sea ice looked too formidable, and he decided against it.

On April 25, 1848, Franklin's second-in-command, Captain Crozier of HMS *Erebus*, put a message in a cairn on the northwest coast of King William Island. It stated that he had arrived at this point with 104 men after a journey of some 30 miles across treacherous sea ice. *Erebus* and *Terror* had been frozen in in Victoria Strait for two years. Franklin was dead, as were twenty-three others. He intended to lead these survivors 250 miles south and east to the mouth of Back's Fish River. From there, apparently, he hoped to reach a settlement.

In the vicinity of Cape John Herschel on the south coast of King William Island, Crozier and some forty starving and debilitated men encountered four Eskimo families. Crozier approached them, beseeching them with gestures to open their packs. They held seal meat out to him. He took the meat and began eating and indicated the Eskimos should give meat to the other men, which they did. They spent the night with Crozier's party. In the morning Crozier pleaded with them to stay, saying over and over the word he thought meant "seal." But the families walked away. The thin resources of that part of the Arctic would not support the four families and a party of forty men, and the Eskimos knew it.

Crozier's entreaty—the details were learned from the Eskimos years later—is one of the most riveting moments in arctic history. Crozier had left England in 1845 with every expectation of success. An officer's plum. When technology and British naval tradition proved inadequate to the task, his complacency was shattered. He was reduced to begging from people he regarded as socially and morally inferior, people who counted for nothing against what he felt his own people stood for, by any comparison of accomplishment.

After the encounter on the beach, Crozier and his men became more destitute in every way. The men, for the most part tragically ignorant of where they were, of what they faced, continued to fall in their tracks. A boat abandoned on the beach and later found by M'Clintock contained a kid glove, with measures of powder tied off in each finger; a copy of *The Vicar of Wakefield*; a grass-weave cigar case; a pair of blue sunglasses, folded in a tin case; a pair of calf-lined bedroom slippers, bound with red ribbon; blue and white delftware teacups; and a sixpence, dated 1831.

There is some indication at the place where the last thirty of them died together that they were trying to kill and eat the first snow geese arriving from the south.

In 1923 Knud Rasmussen paused at this place, Starvation Cove near Barrow Inlet on Adelaide Peninsula, to perform a graveside service. It was here, too, that the expedition's journals were found, a waterlogged, wind-scattered, indecipherable mess.

After Rasmussen (and before), others searched for clues to explain this monumental failure. On the basis of Eskimo testimony it is conjectured that one of the ships sank in Victoria Strait and the other went down off Grant Point, Adelaide Peninsula. In 1967 the Canadian military searched the area thoroughly for records,

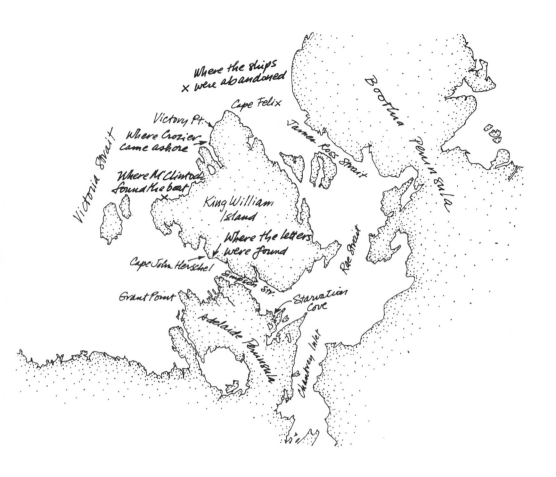

Where the ships
x were abandoned
Cape Felix
Victory Pt.
Where Crozier
came ashore
Where McClintock
found the boat
x
King William
Island
Where the letters
were found
Cape John Herschel
Grant Point
Simpson Str.
Starvation
Cove
Adelaide Peninsula
Chantrey Inlet
Victoria Strait
James Ross Strait
Boothia Peninsula
Rae Strait

relics, and undiscovered grave sites. They found nothing. The desire to write a final epitaph to this story, however, is still very much alive in the North.

ABOUT 1856, two years after the Franklin search officially ended, a shaman named Qillarsuaq, convinced that there were unknown Eskimos living somewhere far to the north, left Baffin Island with a group of about forty people. They traveled to Somerset Island, across to Cornwallis Island, then east along the coast of Devon Island. More than half of the people turned back along the way. Hunting was hard, and they did not entirely share Qillarsuaq's vision. Finally, in 1863, after traveling for several years with none but the map in Qillarsuaq's head, they crossed the sea ice from Cape Sabine, Ellesmere Island, to the coast of Greenland, where they indeed found people. They met two men near Etah. One of them, Aqattaq, had a wooden leg, a gift to him from British whalers. The Baffin Island people had never seen anything like it and marveled.

For the next five or six years the Baffin Islanders lived among the Polar Eskimo, mostly around Siorapaluk. The two groups had been separated during a climatic episode called the Neo-Boreal, or Little Ice Age (1450–1850). With the return of warm weather, the kinds and numbers of animals changed and the Polar Eskimo did not have great success hunting them—in the intervening years they had lost the necessary skills. The Baffin Islanders taught them again: the construction and handling of the kayak, a craft a man could carry with just a forearm thrust in the cockpit, light as a basket; the use of the bow and arrow, to reach out for caribou; and the way to fish for migrating char.

The notion of Eskimos exploring their own lands and adapting anew at the same time Europeans were exploring the Arctic was something the Europeans were never aware of. They thought of the Arctic as fixed in time—a primitive landscape, a painting, inhabited by an attenuated people. They mistook the stillness and the cold for biological stasis. They thought nothing at all changed here. They thought it was a desert, a wasteland.

Stefansson, and others, condescended to Crozier for his inability to survive in a region "teeming with game animals," basing their arguments on the subsequent success of an American cavalry lieutenant in the area.* The criticism is unfair, and revealing. Crozier, if he knew anything about hunting at all, knew it only for a "sport," not as a serious endeavor. It is unlikely that he or any of his men could have survived except in a place that actually did

---

* In 1879 Frederick Schwatka and two companions made a fifty-week, 3200-mile sledge journey from Hudson Bay to King William Island and back, during which time they lived almost entirely off the land.

teem with caribou or muskoxen, apparently never the case in the King William Island–Adelaide Peninsula region. The only food animals that might have sustained them would have been seals, but they did not have the skill to hunt seals—and it is extremely unlikely that there were seals enough to keep so many men alive. That is the reason there were so few Eskimos in the region to begin with. Stefansson's promotion of the Arctic as a land overrun in every sector with animals—he also publicly criticized Greely for failing to feed his men with local animals—showed as poor an understanding of the land as the British misperception of it as a biological desert.

The itineraries of arctic animals are not obvious. Archaeological research has found, however, that the core areas of cultural development in the Arctic, such as Bering Sea and Foxe Basin, have a long history of stable animal populations. Even here, however, their presence is seasonal. Caribou have their ancestral calving areas, the birds their ancestral rookeries. And the narwhal comes predictably to Admiralty Inlet. But if you pick the wrong time to look, it would appear that nothing ever happened at these spots.

The land in some places is truly empty; in other places it is only apparently empty. To those who had no interest in the movement of animals, the entire region seemed empty. They could not grasp a crucial fact—seminomadic people living here in such small numbers were an indication that the animals themselves moved around. Either the animals did not stay long in one place, or there were not very many of them to begin with, or they were very hard to kill. Or there would be more people, living in more permanent dwellings. The land was not empty, but it teemed with animals that would sustain men only in a certain, very limited way. To know this you either had to live there or depend on the advice of the people who did.

Crozier and his men died because they had, truly, no idea of where they were. The cocoon they traveled in split open, exposing them to the elements. Their authority was useless to them. There were too many of them, and they had no idea what to do.

Eskimos willingly escorted a different sort of people in the Arctic, men like Peary and Rasmussen, whose inspirational leadership and skill with dogs they admired. They liked to travel with men who hunted, who became involved in the land. The only strange time that came for them on these journeys was when they had to eat the food that came packed in tin boxes while they were out on that part of the land that was emptiest, on journeys to the Pole and across the Greenland ice cap. They had no great interest in these places; they were, in fact, fearful of them. They went only because they admired the men they were with.

The relief these Eskimos experienced in returning to the coasts, to that living edge of their environment, was extreme. Many of these scenes are touched with a moving and wonderful sentiment. When the Second Thule Expedition arrived back at Uummannaq, Ajako, one of Rasmussen's companions on this starvation journey, went first to the water. "Ajako bends down," writes Rasmussen, "filling his hollow hands with fiord water, which he raises to his face to feel and inhale its salt freshness. In these drops he smells the meat of the walrus, narwhals and seals—flesh of all the blubbery animals which shall now make our days good. Beautiful ocean! I recognize you, now I am home!"

ON the 7th of April 1909, Robert Peary departed the vicinity of the Geographic North Pole, bound for Cape Columbia, Ellesmere Island, and his ship, the *Roosevelt*, which lay beyond at Cape Sheridan. He had arrived the day before, with five men, five sledges, and thirty-eight dogs. In the cross-examination he was subjected to later, Peary was criticized for having no man with him who could vouch for his solar observations, confirming the latitude. Peary's answer was that he wasn't about to share the glory with someone who had not earned the right to be there as he had—and there was no one, in his view.

The men who were with him on that day he regarded as no threat to his prestige. In a photograph, five of them stand on a hummock before a piece of sea ice, on which Peary has planted the

American flag. Ooqueah holds the flag of the Navy League. Ootah has the colors of Peary's college fraternity in his hands. Egingwah holds a flag of the Daughters of the American Revolution, and Seegloo a Red Cross flag. Matthew Henson, Peary's black man-servant, holds the flag that probably meant the most to Peary—a homemade polar flag, pieces of which he had left at four other of his "farthest norths" in the previous nine years.

The blue-eyed, auburn-haired man with the walrus mustache was fifty-three and in robust health at the Pole. Close up, the squinting eyes and weather-polished face showed the wear of twenty-three years in the North. He had wished all of his life to secure some accomplishment that would make him stand out from other men, one awesome, untoppable deed. Now he had it. But this man who so enjoyed the trappings of importance, who wished to be envied, also wished to be liked. He wrote to a woman he loved, after he graduated from Bowdoin, "I should like to gain that attractive personality that when I was with a person, they would always have to like me, whether they wanted to or not." But this was not to be.

As Peary grew older, as the misfortune with bad weather that always seemed to befall his journeys continued, he grew more rigid and less congenial. He exhibited that edge of irritation that emanates from self-important people who think, privately, they may have failed. Toward the end of his life, wounded no one will ever know how deeply by Frederick Cook's claim to have been at the Pole twelve months before him, Peary became recklessly arrogant and despotic.

The few excerpts from Peary's private journals that have been published reveal a man beyond the one who grasped for fame, someone beyond the hauteur, a man with tender regard for his wife and, early on, a certain sensitivity and compassion. He knew that by constantly abandoning his family and pursuing his quest for the Pole, in abandoning certain human duties and obligations, he might be thought "criminally foolish," as he put it. He was troubled by self-doubt and on at least one occasion seems to have toyed with suicide, so bleak did his prospects of making a name for himself seem.

Like all great men, Peary was importuned by oddballs and hounded by dissatisfied people. He grew to hate the parody of himself that grew out of endless public speeches and interviews. For all his disregard and unapproachability, his conniving and maneuvering, a pervading loneliness clung to him. And one is moved to see his life in a less critical way. Something went on inside him that no one else but perhaps his wife understood. After 1902, missing joints from each of his ten toes from frostbite, he walked down Senate corridors and across the streets of Washington, D.C., with a peculiar gliding shuffle. His determination to succeed, the depth and power of this man's obsession, absolutely stills the imagination of anyone who has looked upon the landscape he traversed.

In some ways Peary and Vilhjalmur Stefansson, the most visible twentieth-century arctic explorer, were alike. Both were individualists who built life-long reputations around their arctic exploits. Both were avid, sometimes unscrupulous promoters of their own enterprises and accomplishments. Both were heedless of the slaughter of animals it took to maintain their arctic endeavors. Both were dogged by petty detractors. As they settled into their reputations, they became men who preferred talking to listening, who forgot or denied the others whose lives and toil made their reputations. And, like many explorers, what was in fact nothing more than good luck they came to promote as the result of their own sagacity and careful planning.

Stefansson had a flawed understanding of arctic biology and climate, but he was insistent and dogmatic in his misconceptions. They are most clearly set forth in his book *The Friendly Arctic*, in which he maintains that men, particularly white men, can travel anywhere in the Arctic and the land will provide. Stefansson became so infatuated with this idea, after the book vaulted him to popular acclaim, that he could never see the land as a refutation of it. To prove to people who doubted him that he was right, he killed animals everywhere he went, and left behind what was inconvenient to transport.

Stefansson was also a social Darwinist; he believed in racial superiority and economic destiny. En route to the Arctic in 1908, he was captivated by the sight of natural gas flare-offs burning along the Athabasca River. "It is the torch of Science," wrote Stefansson, "lighting the way of civilization and economic development to the realm of the unknown North." The tundra was for him an extension of the American prairies, and he lamented the fact that "billions of tons of edible vegetation" that could be feeding cattle were going to waste yearly on the northern prairies. He felt that certain wild animals, like the caribou, "cumbered the land" and had to go, because they forestalled the development of ranching and agriculture. Like Theodore Roosevelt, who fought only to save prey species and who reviled predators, Stefansson wanted to make nature over to suit his beliefs about human destiny. His knowledge of the land, despite his great popularity, was selective and self-serving.

Stefansson was an explorer of prodigious determination but not an inspiring leader. He was a poor judge of character, he freely admitted; he could not get some of the people he employed to believe in his work; and he ignored important details in his plans. He was, however, a true visionary. He succeeded between 1913 and 1918 in accomplishing the expeditionary tasks he set for himself despite serious illness, appalling loneliness (he received but a single personal letter in the mailbag one year) and physical hardship, and the rudeness and contempt of some of his companions. (In those years he discovered Brock and Borden islands in the western high Arctic, Meighen Island in the north, defined the previously confused geography of King Christian Island and the Findlay Group, and made extensive pioneering soundings in the Beaufort Sea.)

Stefansson returned from the Arctic in 1919 more convinced than ever that Canada's economic future lay in the North and that the Arctic Ocean was destined to become a "Polar Mediterranean," with large coastal ports, submarine traffic beneath the ice, and a network of transpolar air routes. To convince skeptics, he embarked upon a scheme to raise reindeer on southern Baffin Island, a poorly thought-out project that ended disastrously and showed more than anything how illusionary Stefansson's understanding of the Arctic was.

He nearly wore himself out during this period of his life with lecture tours and commitments to write books and articles, and he made a serious miscalculation in insisting that Canada claim Wrangel Island, a Russian possession, for a future base of operations for arctic transport. Canada's handling of the affair eventually held it up to international embarrassment, and the debacle ended in a tragedy that reminded too many people of the *Karluk:* Stefansson sent his own expedition to Wrangel Island to establish occupation— four young college men and an Eskimo woman (to prepare and mend their skin clothing). The four men, following Stefansson's directions for living off the land, died. The woman survived.

In Ottawa, before he found himself no longer welcome in Canada, Stefansson was called "Windjammer" behind his back, for the loquacious and headlong way in which he promoted his ideas. Stefansson's impetuous insistence on arctic development was based on a distorted view of the land, ironic in the light of his extensive travels. He became an anachronism and then, finally, something of a hero to men promoting oil development, mineral extraction, muskox ranching, and other projects for northern economic development.

Despite his overbearing nature, Stefansson was an approachable and thoughtful man. He willingly shared his moments of geographic discovery. He praised others' skills. And he readily acknowledged his own failures of tact and planning. His compassion toward sled dogs is singular among arctic explorers. (He despised Nansen's and Peary's habit of feeding sled dogs to each other to save weight on long journeys. And in a moving and poignant passage in *The Friendly Arctic*, so revealing of his loneliness, Stefansson assesses the character of a dog named Lindy with great generosity and empathy, concluding, "When he came to die I lost my best friend in the world, whom I shall never forget.")

In his later years, Stefansson became an idol to young men because he irritated self-important and pompous people and because he stood resolutely by his theories. He was pleased to share what he knew and to recommend books from his enormous library; as a friend put it, he had "an unabashed philosophy of eternal youth, complete with revolt and optimism." Stefansson liked young men for the same reason Peary did—they believed in his goals and they threw themselves unquestioningly and energetically into the work at hand. And they were loyal.

Stefansson lived a long life. His energy and independence were an inspiration to many. Peary's life ended in bitterness in 1920. His claim to the Pole was disputed by powerful enemies whom he had publicly ridiculed—Greely in the United States and the Norwegians Sverdrup and Nansen. The confused public image of him is due, in part, to his dedication to achieving a goal that many could not quite catch the importance of. In a speech on the floor of the House of Representatives in 1910, the Honorable J. Hampton Moore of Pennsylvania spoke in support of Peary's claim to have been first at the Pole, and caused to be introduced into the record a number of congratulatory telegrams sent to Peary. They range from President Taft's somewhat quizzical pat on the back to Theodore Roosevelt's cable, sent from his safari camp in Africa and bursting with American pride and hyperbole.

Peary and Stefansson both wrung fame from the Arctic. The distance between the real land and Stefansson's notions about it, or between the unpossessable land and Peary's appropriation of it (both gaps effectively bridged by astute public relations campaigns), is a generic source of trouble in our own time. The landscape can be labeled and then manipulated. It is possible, with insistent and impersonal technology, to deny any innate order or dignity in it.

Peary and Stefansson, too, were public figures, admired for

their energy and vision. The personal insecurity and loneliness that besieged them, and that they sought a way around in the Arctic, however, provokes consideration of several dilemmas. What is the point at which the "tragic" loneliness of an individual, which drives him toward accomplishment, no longer effectively leads but confounds the well-being of the larger society? And what will be the disposition of the landscape? Will it be used, always, in whatever way we will, or will it one day be accorded some dignity of its own? And, finally, what does the nature of the heroic become, once the landscape is threatened?

IN 1918 the American artist and illustrator Rockwell Kent arrived at Fox Island off Alaska's Kenai Peninsula with his nine-year-old son, young Rockwell. "We came to this new land, a man and a boy, entirely on a dreamer's search," he wrote. "Having had a vision of Northern Paradise, we came to find it." He meant to heal himself somehow and to get to know his son. He believed the land would help him to do that, and that it would care for them both.

Kent was a remarkable twentieth-century American. A socialist, he professed himself to the Strenuous Life of Theodore Roosevelt. He delighted in thumbing his nose at social conventions. He identified himself with the drama and characters of the Icelandic sagas, and was fascinated by cold, harsh, testing environments. He was abrasive, self-righteous, and occasionally cruel to people he felt superior to, but he was also a romantic and a man of idealistic visions. And, in spite of the apparent contradiction between his socialist beliefs and his success as an artist and businessman, he was a person of integrity. He argued in his art and in heroic prose for the essential dignity of human beings and for the existence of man's Godlike qualities. His enthusiasm for life was genuine and unbounded, and he was completely dedicated to the work that reflected his beliefs.

On Fox Island, Kent exulted in clearing the land and creating a parklike setting. He was glad to be away from the "confusing intricacy of modern society." His illusions about wilderness were always somewhat at odds with the requirements of daily life on the island, which caused him to reflect that "the romance of [this] adventure hangs on slender threads." Kent realized that what invigorated him in this northern landscape was not so much the land but what he made of the land—what his imagination made of the color, the contours, the shading. His attachment to the landscape was passionate; he responded ecstatically to beauty in the land, in Alaska and on trips to Greenland as well. But his attachment was almost entirely metaphorical; and it was sustained by all the attachments to civilization Kent would not forgo—his mail, trips into the village of Seward for the staples of his vegetarian diet, the neighborly assistance of the island's owner, who lived in a house a few yards from Kent's cabin.

When he and his son left after six months, his neighbor said, "You might as well have spent a couple of months back in the mountains of New York for all you've seen of Alaska." But Kent felt no need to travel further. The invigoration he felt, the renewed sense of wilderness that now compelled his art, made it possible to return to the marital and professional difficulties that he faced in New York.

Kent's metaphorical experience with the land, the way his imagination worked against it, differs markedly from Stefansson's and Peary's manifestly arduous encounters. But it was no less real. And the experience that Kent had—to find oneself in the land, to feel some intrinsic, overwhelmingly sane order in it, to participate in that order—is the aim of many twentieth-century people who travel to such remote regions. Relationships with the land that are intensely metaphorical, like Kent's, are a lofty achievement of the human mind. They are a sophisticated response, like the creation of maps, or the development of a language that grows out of a certain landscape. The mind can imagine beauty and conjure intimacy. It can find solace where literal analysis finds only trees and rocks and grass.

In July 1929, eleven years after the sojourn on Fox Island,

Kent and two companions shipwrecked at Karajak Fiord on the mountainous west coast of Greenland. Walking inland, they came to a lake "round as the moon." The gale that had wrecked them was still blowing. Kent wrote that the lake's

> pebbly shore shows smooth and clean and bright against the deep green water. [We] descend to it and, standing there, look over at the mountain wall that bounds it. The dark cliffs rise sheer from lake to sky. From its high edge pours a torrent. And the gale, lifting that torrent in mid-air, disperses it in smoke.
>
> [We] stand there looking at it all: at the mountains, at the smoking waterfall, at the dark green lake with wind puffs silvering its plain, at the flowers that fringe the pebbly shore and star the banks.

One of them says, "Maybe we have lived only to be here now."

A salient element emerges in Peary's recounting of his arctic journeys, which reminds me of this scene of tranquil beauty after a violent shipwreck. As far as I know, it is consistent with the experience and feelings of most other arctic explorers. The initial trip into that far northern landscape is perceived by the explorer as something from which one might derive prestige, money, social advantage, or notable awards and adulation. Although these intentions are not lost sight of on subsequent trips, they are never so purely held or so highly regarded as they are before the first journey begins. They are tempered by a mounting sense of consternation and awe. It is as though the land slowly works its way into the man and by virute of its character eclipses these motives. The land becomes large, alive like an animal; it humbles him in a way he cannot pronounce. It is not that the land is simply beautiful but that it is powerful. Its power derives from the tension between its obvious beauty and its capacity to take life. Its power flows into the mind from a realization of how darkness and light are bound together within it, and the feeling that this is the floor of creation.

THREE of us were driving north on the trans-Alaska pipeline haul road, pulling a boat behind a pickup. For miles at a time we were the only vehicle, then a tractor-trailer truck—pugnacious and hell-bent—would shoulder past, flailing us with gravel. From Fairbanks to Prudhoe Bay the road parallels the elevated, gleaming pipeline. Both pathways in the corridor have a manicured, unnatural stillness about them, like white-board fences running over the hills of a summer pasture. One evening we passed a lone seed-and-fertilizing operation, spraying grass seed and nutrients on the slopes and berms of the road, to prevent erosion. There would be no unruly tundra here. These were the seeds of neat Kentucky grasses.

One day we had a flat tire. Two of us changed it while the third stood by with a loaded .308 and a close eye on a female grizzly and her yearling cub, rooting in a willow swale 30 yards away. We saw a single wolf—a few biologists in Fairbanks had asked us to watch for them. The truckers, they said, had shot most of the wolves along the road; perhaps a few were drifting back in, with the traffic so light now. Short-eared owls flew up as we drove along. Single caribou bulls trotted off in their light-footed way, like shy waterfowl. Moose standing along the Saga-vanirktok River were nodding in the willow browse. And red foxes, with their long black legs, pranced down the road ahead of us, heads thrown back over their shoulders. That night I thought about the animals, and how the road had come up amidst them.

We arrived at the oil fields at Prudhoe Bay on an afternoon when light blazed on the tundra and swans were gliding serenely in rectangles of water between the road dikes. But this landscape was more austere than any I had ever seen in the Arctic. Small buildings, one or two together at a time, stood on the horizon. It reminded me of West Texas, land throttled for water and oil.

Muscular equipment sitting idle like slouched fists in oil-stained yards. It was no business of mine. I was only here to stay overnight. In the morning we would put the boat in the water and head west to the Jones Islands.

The bungalow camp we stayed in was wretched with the hopes of cheap wealth, with the pallid, worn-out flesh and swollen bellies of supervisors in ball caps, and full of the desire of young men for women with impossible shapes; for a winning poker hand; a night with a bottle gone undetected. The older men, mumbling of their debts, picking through the sweepings of their despair alone in the cafeteria, might well not have lived through the misery, to hear the young men talk of wealth only a fool would miss out on.

We left in the morning, bound for another world entirely, the world of science, a gathering of data for calculations and consultations that would send these men to yet some other site, the deceit intact.

Months later, on a cold March morning, I came to Prudhoe Bay for an official visit. I was met at the airport by a young and courteous public relations officer, who shook hands earnestly and gave me the first of several badges to wear as we drove around the complex. The police at road checkpoints and at building entrances examined these credentials and then smiled without meaning to be cordial. Here was the familiar chill of one's dignity resting for a moment in the hand of an authority of artificial size, knowing it might be set aside like a small stone for further scrutiny if you revealed impatience or bemusement. Industrial spying, it was apologetically explained—disgruntled former employees; the possibility of drug traffic; or environmental saboteurs.

We drove out along the edge of the sea ice and examined a near-shore drill rig from a distance—too chilly to walk over, said my host, as though our distant view met the letter of his and my responsibilities.

We ate lunch in the cafeteria of the oil company's headquarters building, a sky-lit atrium of patrician silences, of slacks and perfume and well-mannered people, of plants in deferential attendance. The food was perfectly prepared. (I recalled the low-ceilinged cafeterias with their thread-bare, food-stained carpets, the cigarette-burned tables, the sluggish food and clatter of Melmac where the others ate.)

On the way to Gathering Station #1 we pull over, to be passed by the largest truckload of anything I have ever seen: a building on a trailer headed for the Kuparuk River. In the ditch by the road lies a freshly fallen crane, the wheels of the cab still turning in the sunshine. The man with me smiles. It is −28°F.

At Gathering Station #1 the oil from four well areas is cooled. Water is removed. Gas is separated off. Above ground for the first time, the primal fluid moves quickly through pipes at military angles and sits under pressure in tanks with gleaming, spartan dials. The painted concrete floors are spotless. There is no stray tool or wipe rag. Anything that threatens harm or only to fray clothing is padded, covered. The brightly lit pastel rooms carry heat from deep in the earth and lead to each other like a series of airlocks, or boiler rooms in the bowels of an enormous ship. I see no one. The human presence is in the logic of the machinery, the control of the unrefined oil, the wild liquid in the grid of pipes. There is nothing here for the oil but to follow instructions.

Tempered, it flows to Pump Station #1.

The pavilion outside the fence at the pump station is drifted in with snow. No one comes here, not in this season. I climb over the drifts and wipe wind-crusted snow from Plexiglas-covered panels that enumerate the local plants and animals. The sentences are pleasant, meant to offend no one. Everything—animals, oil, destiny—is made to seem to fit somewhat naturally together. People are not mentioned. I look up at Pump Station #1, past the cyclone fencing and barbed wire. The slogging pumps sequestered within insulated buildings on the tundra, the fields of pipe, the roughshod trucks, all the muscular engineering, the Viking bellows that draws and gathers and directs—that it all runs to the head of this seemingly innocent pipe, lined out like a stainless-steel thread toward the indifferent Brooks Range, that it is all reduced to the southward journey of this 48-inch pipe, seems impossible.

No toil, no wildness shows. It could not seem to the chaperoned visitor more composed, inoffensive, or civilized.

None of the proportions are familiar. I stand in the wind-blown pavilion looking at the near and distant buildings. I remember a similiar view of the launch complexes at Cape Canaveral. It is not just the outsize equipment lumbering down the roads here but the exaggerated presence of threat, hidden enemies. My face is beginning to freeze. The man in the blue Chevrolet van with the heaters blasting is smiling. No guide could be more pleasant. It is time to eat again—I think that is what he is saying. I look back at the pipeline, this final polished extrusion of all the engineering. There are so few people here, I keep thinking. Deep in the holds of those impersonal buildings, the only biology is the dark Devonian fluid in the pipes.

On the way back to the cafeteria the man asks me what I think of the oil industry. He has tried not to seem prying, but this is the third time he has asked. I speak slowly. "I do not know anything about the oil industry. I am interested mostly in the landscape, why we come here and what we see. I am not a business analyst, an economist, a social planner. The engineering is astounding. The true cost, I think, must be unknown."

During dinner he tells me a story. A few years ago there were three birch trees in an atrium in the building's lobby. In September their leaves turned yellow and curled over. Then they just hung there, because the air in the enclosure was too still. No wind. Fall came when a man from building maintenance went in and shook the trees.

Before we drove the few miles over to Deadhorse, the Prudhoe Bay airport, my host said he wanted me to see the rest of the Base Operations Building. A movie theater with tiered rows of plush red velour seats. Electronic game rooms. Wide-screen television alcoves. Pool tables. Weight-lifting room. Swimming pool.

Squash courts. Running track. More television alcoves. Whirlpool treatment and massage. The temperatures in the different rooms are different perfectly. Everything is cushioned, carpeted, padded. There are no unpleasant sounds. No blemishes. You do not have to pay for anything. He shows me his rooms.

Later we are standing at a railing, looking out through insulated glass at the blue evening on the tundra. I thank him for the tour. We have enjoyed each other. I marvel at the expense, at all the amenities that are offered. He is looking at the snow. "Golden handcuffs." That is all he says with his wry smile.

It is hard to travel in the Arctic and not encounter industrial development. Too many lines of logistic support, transportation, and communication pass through these sites. I passed through Prudhoe Bay four or five times in the course of several years, and visited both lead-zinc mines in the Canadian Archipelago, the Nanisivik Mine on Strathcona Sound on Baffin Island, and the Polaris Mine on Little Cornwallis Island. And one winter I toured Panarctic's facilities at Rae Point on Melville Island, and their drill rigs on the sea ice off Mackenzie King and Lougheed islands.

I was drawn to all these places for reasons I cannot fully articulate. For the most part, my feelings were what they had been at Prudhoe Bay—a mixture of fascination at the sophistication of the technology; sadness born out of the dismalness of life for many of the men employed here, which no amount of red velour, free arcade games, and open snack bars can erase; and misgiving at the sullen, dismissive attitude taken toward the land, the violent way in which it is addressed. At pretensions to a knowledge of the Arctic, drawn from the perusal of a public relations pamphlet and from the pages of pulp novels. A supervisor at an isolated drill rig smiled sardonically when I asked him if men ever walked away from the buildings on their off-hours. "You can count the people who care about what's out there on the fingers of one hand." The remark represents fairly the situation at most military and industrial sites in the Arctic.

Away from the carefully tended environment of a corporate showcase base of operations, the industrial scene is much bleaker. In the most distant camps, to my sensibilities at least, were some of the saddest human lives I have ever known. The society is all male. The tedium of schedules is unrelieved. Drugs and alcohol are smuggled in. Pornographic magazines abound, which seems neither here nor there until one realizes that they are nearly inescapable, and that they are part of a resentful attitude toward the responsibilities of family life. There is a distrust, a cursing of women, that is unsettling. Woman and machinery and the land are all spoken of in the same way—seduction, domestication, domination, control. This observation represents no new insight, of course, into the psychology of development in Western culture; but it is not academic. It is as real as the scars on the faces of flight attendants I interviewed in Alaska who were physically and sexually abused by frustrated workmen flying to and from Prudhoe Bay.

The atmosphere in some of the camps is little different from the environment of a small state prison, down to the existence of racial cliques. This is part of factory life in America, an ugly way the country has arranged itself, a predicament from which economic and political visionaries would extricate us. There is a lurking suspicion among the workers I spoke to that in spite of their good wages they were somehow being cheated, that any chance for advancement from their menial situation was, for most of them, an illusion. And they were convinced that someone, somewhere, was to blame. Their frustration was predictably directed at their employers, at overeducated engineers or petroleum geologists, and at vague political and ethnic groups whom they saw as confused and impractical critics of growth, of progress. Some of these men felt that the Arctic was really a great wasteland "with a few stupid birds," too vast to be hurt. Whatever strong men could accomplish against the elements in such a place, they insisted, was inherently right. The last words of many of these discussions, whether they were delivered quizzically or cynically or in disbelief, were summary—what else is it good for?

Many arctic oil and mine workers are hard-pressed to explain —and mostly not interested in—what it is good for, beyond what is in the ground; or in what its future will be; or in the fate of its people and animals. "Technology is inevitable," a drilling supervisor told me with finality one day. "People just got to get that through their heads." The sensibility of many of the foremen and crew chiefs, to characterize the extreme, is colonial. The tone of voice is impatient and the vocabulary is economic. The mentality is largely innocent of history and arctic ecology, cavalier about human psychological requirements, and manipulative. And the attitude of the extremist, at least in this regard, filters down. These thoughts are parroted by other workers who feel defensive, or embattled by critics. Men who make such extreme statements often give the impression of not having thought through what they are saying. They only mean to keep their jobs, or talk themselves out of doubt.

In the mines and oil fields, of course, were other, different men, who criticized in private conversation what was being done "for the money." As a group, they felt a responsibility for what they were doing. They did not see their jobs solely as a source of income. Many told me they wanted to return to the Arctic after making enough money to go back to school. They wanted to travel in the Arctic and read more about it. They meant no harm, and were uneasy themselves about the damage they were capable of doing. In Canada they feared the collusive force that government and industry were capable of bringing to bear—that the restraints against it were too weak. These were mostly younger men; and the sentiments were not rare among them.

More memorable somehow, and ultimately more gratifying, were the thoughts of several older men who spoke to me on different occasions about the conditions under which they worked. (It was one of them who had suggested the parallel with prison life.) These were seasoned men of dignified bearing in their forties and fifties, the sort of people you have regard for instantly, regardless of the circumstances. They were neither insistent nor opinionated in offering their observations, which made it easier to speculate in their presence; and they gave an impression of deliberation and self-knowledge.

They shook their heads over industrial mismanagement, that humorless, deskbound ignorance that brings people and land together in such a way that both the land and the people suffer. They said, without any condescension, that the companies that employed them sometimes clearly erred, and that they acted in high-handed and sometimes illegal ways. But these were more acknowledgments of a state of affairs than criticism. They spoke as much of their families, of their wives and children. They spoke of them with indulgence and unconscious admiration. You could build anything on the decency of such men.

In the wake of these latter conversations the world seemed on balance to me, or at least well intentioned. Part of what was attractive about these men was that their concern for the health of the land and their concern for the fate of people were not separate issues. They were not for me, either. And one evening, lying in my bunk, it became clear that the fate of each was hinged on the same thing, on the source of their dignity, on whether it was innate or not.

The source of their dignity—not among themselves, but in a larger social context—was the approval of their superiors, an assessment made by people who were not their peers. (Largely unfamiliar with modern Eskimo life, these men nevertheless had an intuitive and sympathetic response to the predicament of Eskimos constantly being scrutinized and judged by outsiders.) Their dignity as workmen, and therefore their self-respect, was not whole. To an outside viewer they, like the land, were subject to manipulation. Their dignity was received. It grew out of how well they responded to directions.

In my experience, most people in the Arctic who direct the activities of employees or who seek to streamline the process of resource extraction without regard to what harm might be done to the land, do so with the idea that their goals are desirable and admirable, and that they are shared by everyone. Their own source of dignity, in fact, derives from a belief that they are working in this way "for the common good." In their view the working man must provide cheerful labor, be punctual, and demonstrate allegiance to a concept of a greater good orchestrated from above. The Eskimo, for his part, must conduct himself either as a sober and aspiring middle-class wage earner or, alternately, as an "authentic, traditional Eskimo," that is, according to an idealized and unrealistic caricature created by the outsider. The land, the very ground itself, the plants and the animals, must also produce something—petroleum, medicines, food, the setting for a movie—if it is to achieve any measure of dignity. If it does not, it is waste. Tundra wasteland. A waste of time.

Without dignity, of course, people are powerless. Strip a person or the land of dignity and you can direct any scheme you wish against them or it, with impunity and with the best of motives. To some this kind of efficiency is a modern technique, lamentable but not evil. For others it is a debilitating degradation, a loss of integrity and spirit that no kind of economic well-being can ever justify.

The solution to this very old and disconcerting situation among the men I spoke to, when I asked, was utopian. They believed in the will of good people. They thought some way could be found to take life–affecting decisions away from ignorant, venal, and unimaginative persons. Yes, they said, an innate not a tendered dignity put individuals in the best position to act, to think through the difficult problems of what to do about technologies that mangled people and mangled the land. But they did not know where you started, where the first, hard changes had to be made.

I was traveling with a friend once, in northern Baffin Island. We were in a hunting camp at the edge of the sea ice with about thirty Eskimos. It was damp and windy—raw weather. Out of the sky one morning—we had been in this atmosphere long enough to make the event seem slightly confusing at first—came a helicopter, which landed at the camp. A man got out and walked over to the tent where we were staying. He was the president of a shipping company. He was concerned that an icebreaking ore ship that had recently been in Admiralty Inlet might have adversely affected hunting for the Eskimos or made travel over the sea ice more difficult for them. (The ship's track had relieved pressure in the ice, which would cause it to break up in an unusual pattern as spring progressed. The track might possibly lure narwhals into a fatal savssat. Or the noise of the ship's engines might frighten narwhals away from the floe edge, where the Eskimos were hunting.)

There were several unusual aspects to this man's visit. First, Eskimos virtually never get to talk directly with "the head man," the person whose decisions vitally affect the direction of their lives. They are usually held at bay by dozens of intermediaries. Second, important men more often have pressing schedules and retinues with them, which preclude protracted or serious conversation. Third, it is unusual for anyone at all to show a concern this pointed, this knowledgeable. The man offered to fly several hunters out along the 40 miles of ship track in the helicopter so they could inspect it. He would land wherever they wanted. The hunters went with him, and were glad for the opportunity to see the situation from the air.

That accomplished, the man could have left, feeling a wave of genuine gratitude from the Eskimos for his thoughtfulness. But he stayed. He sat in a tent in the hunting camp and ate the "country food" that was offered, along with bannock and tea. He did not try to summarize or explain anything. He did not ask a lot of questions to demonstrate his interest. He just sat quietly and ate. He handed a gawking child a piece of bannock and said a few things about the weather. By his simple appreciation of the company, by his acceptance of these unfamiliar circumstances, he made everyone in the tent feel comfortable. The dignity of the occasion arose from an atmosphere of courtesy that he alone could have established.

He sat for more than an hour. And then he said good-bye and left. One incident in the vastness. But it was a fine moment, a gesture you could carry away with you.

ONE brilliant July morning I flew out of Resolute on Cornwallis Island for the Canadian weather station at Eureka, on northern Ellesmere Island. I traveled with a flight map in my lap. From this height, and with the map, I found a corroboration of what I knew of the land—from history books, from walking around in it, from talking to people long resident here, from eating food the land produced, from traveling over it with people who felt defined by it. There were walrus in the upper part of Wellington Channel. We passed over Grinnell Peninsula, long thought an island, named for the generous Henry Grinnell. Far to the west I could see the dark waters of a perennial polynya in the ice in Penny Strait, and to the east country I wanted one day, if ever there was a chance, to see from the ground, at the head of Jones Sound and the southern end of Simmons Peninsula. In winter.

We drew up on the southeast corner of Axel Heiberg Island, which Otto Sverdrup had explored. Good Friday Bay. Surprise Fiord. Wolf Fiord. At the head of these fiords were glaciers that did not reach tidewater—huge hesitations on the brown earth of the valleys. In the east light I was reminded of the mountain ranges of Arizona, of the colors of canyons on the Colorado Plateau—ocherous browns, washed tans, flat yellows. I was mesmerized by the view of Axel Heiberg: distant mountains in a sky of clear air; steep slopes of gray scree tumbled out onto the backs of white glaciers, the lime-green tongues of vegetation etched so sharply against the darker mountains it seemed in the morning light that the scene occurred behind polished glass. I realized this island was as remote as anything I could imagine, and for the first time in all the months I had spent North, I felt myself crossing a line into the Far North. It was as though I had passed through one of those walls of pressure one feels descending from mountains.

I had a clarity of mind that made the map in my lap seem both wondrous and strange in its approximations. I looked west into Mokka Fiord, to a chain of lakes between two whitish gypsum domes. Beyond was the patterned ground of the mesic tundra. The browns and blacks and whites were so rich I could feel them. The beauty here is a beauty you feel in your flesh. You feel it physically, and that is why it is sometimes terrifying to approach. Other beauty takes only the heart, or the mind.

I lost for long moments my sense of time and purpose as a human being. In the walls of Axel Heiberg I found what I had known of mountains as a child; that from them came a knowledge that was received, for which there were no words, only, vaguely, prayers. What I loved as a man, the love for parents and wife and children and friends, I felt suffused with in that moment, flushed in the face. The fierce testament of life in abeyance on the winter tundra, the sharp taste of *irok* on evening walks on Baffin Island, the haunting sound of oldsquaw in the ice, *ahaalik, ahaalik*. At the sudden whiteness of a snowbank on the brown earth at Mokka Fiord, I remembered vividly arctic hares, three feet tall and running on their hind legs, hundreds of them, across Seward Peninsula. In the stillness of Axel Heiberg I felt for the first time the edges of an unentered landscape.

That intense reverie came because of the light, the clearness of the air, and certainly the desire to comprehend, which, however I might try to suspend it, was always there. I found in adumbrations of the land, in suggestions of the landscape and all that it contained, the ways human life sorts through itself and survives. To look at the land was never to forget the people it contained.

For a relationship with landscape to be lasting, it must be reciprocal. At the level at which the land supplies our food, this is not difficult to comprehend, and the mutuality is often recalled in a grace at meals. At the level at which landscape seems beautiful or frightening to us and leaves us affected, or at the level at which it furnishes us with the metaphors and symbols with which we pry into mystery, the nature of reciprocity is harder to define. In approaching the land with an attitude of obligation, willing to observe courtesies difficult to articulate—perhaps only a gesture of the hands—one establishes a regard from which dignity can emerge. From that dignified relationship with the land, it is possible to imagine an extension of dignified relationships throughout one's life. Each relationship is formed of the same integrity, which initially makes the mind say: the things in the land fit together perfectly, even though they are always changing. I wish the order of my life to be arranged in the same way I find the light, the slight movement of the wind, the voice of a bird, the heading of a seed pod I see before me. This impeccable and indisputable integrity I want in myself.

One of the oldest dreams of mankind is to find a dignity that might include all living things. And one of the greatest of human longings must be to bring such dignity to one's own dreams, for each to find his or her own life exemplary in some way. The struggle to do this is a struggle because an adult sensibility must find some way to include all the dark threads of life. A way to do this is to pay attention to what occurs in a land not touched by human schemes, where an original order prevails.

The dignity we seek is one beyond that articulated by Enlightenment philosophers. A more radical Enlightenment is necessary, in which dignity is understood as an innate quality, not as something tendered by someone outside. And that common dignity must include the land and its plants and creatures. Otherwise it is only an invention, and not, as it should be, a perception about the nature of living matter.

The plane, that so well designed, dependable, and ubiquitous workhorse of the Canadian Arctic, the Twin Otter, swung out over Fosheim Peninsula, a rolling upland, far northern oasis, on its approach to the Eureka airstrip. I could see muskoxen feeding to the north.

There is a peninsula at the southern end of Baffin Island called Meta Incognita, named by Queen Elizabeth. The words are often translated as the "Unknown Edge" or the "Mysterious Land."

(Frobisher thought this the shore of North America.) It is possible, however, that Elizabeth had another meaning in mind. The word *meta*, strictly speaking, means "cone." In classical Rome the towers at either end of the race course in the Colosseum, around which the chariots turned, were called *metae*. It may have been that Elizabeth meant to suggest a similar course, with London the *meta cognita*, the known entity, and the land Frobisher found the unknown entity, the *meta incognita*. North America, then, was the turn at the far end of the course, something England felt herself reaching toward, and around which she would eventually make a turn of unknown meaning before coming home.

The European culture from which the ancestors of many of us came has yet to make this turn, I think. It has yet to understand the wisdom, preserved in North America, that lies in the richness and sanctity of a wild landscape, what it can mean in the unfolding of human life, the staying of a troubled human spirit.

The other phrase that comes to mind is more obscure. It is the Latin motto from the title banner of *The North Georgia Gazette: per freta hactenus negata*, meaning to have negotiated a strait the very existence of which has been denied. But it also suggests a continuing movement through unknown waters. It is, simultaneously, an expression of fear and of accomplishment, the cusp on which human life finds its richest expression.

The plane landed. Light was lambent on the waters of Slidre Fiord. From the weather station six dogs came toward us, lumbering like wolves, a movement that suggested they could drop buffalo. I reached out and patted one of them tentatively on the head.

EPILOGUE:
Saint Lawrence Island,
Bering Sea

THE MOUNTAIN in the distance is called Sevuokuk. It marks the northwest cape of Saint Lawrence Island in the Bering Sea. From where we are on the ice, this eminence defines the water and the sky to the east as far as we can look. Its western face, a steep wall of snow-streaked basalt, rises above a beach of dark cobbles, riven, ice-polished, ocean-rolled chips of Sevuokuk itself. The village of Gambell is there, the place I have come from with the Yup'ik men, to hunt walrus in the spring ice.

We are, I believe, in Russian waters; and also, by a definition to them even more arbitrary, in "tomorrow," on the other side of the international date line. Whatever political impropriety might be

407

involved is of little importance to the Yup'ik, especially while they are hunting. From where blood soaks the snow, then, and piles of meat and slabs of fat and walrus skin are accumulating, from where ivory tusks have been collected together like exotic kindling, I stare toward the high Russian coast. The mental categories, specific desires, and understanding of history among the people living there are, I reflect, nearly as different from my own as mine are from my Yup'ik companions'.

I am not entirely comfortable on the sea ice butchering walrus like this. The harshness of the landscape, the vulnerability of the boat, and the great size and power of the hunted animal combine to increase my sense of danger. The killing jars me, in spite of my regard for the simple elements of human survival here.

We finish loading the boats. One of the crews has rescued two dogs that have either run off from one of the Russian villages or been abandoned out here on the ice. Several boats gather gunnel to gunnel to look over the dogs. They have surprisingly short hair and seem undersize to draw a sled, smaller than Siberian huskies. But the men assure me these are typical Russian sled dogs.

We take our bearing from the far prominence of Sevuokuk and turn home, laden with walrus meat, with walrus hides and a few seals, with crested auklets and thick-billed murres, with ivory and Russian dogs. When we reach shore, the four of us put our shoulders to the boat to bring it high up on the beach. A young man in the family I am staying with packs a sled with what we have brought back. He pulls it away across the snow behind his Honda three-wheeler, toward the house. Our meals. The guns and gear, the harpoons and floats and lines, the extra clothing and portable radios are all secured and taken away. I am one of the last to leave the beach, still turning over images of the hunt.

No matter what sophistication of mind you bring to such events, no matter what breadth of anthropological understanding, no matter your fondness for the food, your desire to participate, you have still seen an animal killed. You have met the intertwined issues—What is an animal? What is death?—in those large moments of blood, violent exhalation, and thrashing water, with the acrid odor of burned powder in the fetid corral smells of a walrus haul-out. The moments are astounding, cacophonous, also serene. The sight of men letting bits of meat slip away into the dark green water with mumbled benedictions is as stark in my memory as the suddenly widening eyes of the huge, startled animals.

I walk up over the crest of the beach and toward the village, following a set of sled tracks. There is a narrow trail of fresh blood in the snow between the runners. The trail runs out at a latticework of drying racks for meat and skins. The blood in the snow is a sign of life going on, of other life going on. Its presence is too often confused with cruelty.

I rest my gloved fingers on the driftwood meat rack. It is easy to develop an affection for the Yup'ik people, especially when you are invited to participate in events still defined largely by their own traditions. The entire event—leaving to hunt, hunting, coming home, the food shared in a family setting—creates a sense of well-being easy to share. Viewed in this way, the people seem fully capable beings, correct in what they do. When you travel with them, their voluminous and accurate knowledge, their spiritual and technical confidence, expose what is insipid and groundless in your own culture.

I brood often about hunting. It is the most spectacular and succinct expression of the Eskimo's relationship with the land, yet one of the most perplexing and disturbing for the outsider to consider. With the compelling pressures of a cash-based economy to contend with, and the ready availability of modern weapons, hunting practices have changed. Many families still take much of their food from the land, but they do it differently now. "Inauthentic" is the criticism most often made of their methods, as though years ago time had stopped for the Yup'ik.

But I worry over hunting for another reason—the endless reconciliation that must be made of Jacob with his brother Esau. The anguish of Gilgamesh at the death of his companion Enkidu. We do not know how exactly to bridge this gap between civilized man and the society of the hunter. The Afrikaner writer Laurens van der Post, long familiar with Kalahari hunting peoples as archetypal victims of our prejudice, calls the gap between us "an abyss of deceit and murder" we have created. The existence of such a society alarms us. In part this is a trouble we have with writing out our history. We adjust our histories in order to elevate ourselves in the creation that surrounds us; we cut ourselves off from our hunting ancestors, who make us uncomfortable. They seem too closely aligned with insolent, violent predatory animals. The hunting cultures are too barbaric for us. In condemning them, we see it as "inevitable" that their ways are being eclipsed. Yet, from the testimony of sensitive visitors among them, such as van der Post and others I have mentioned in the Arctic, we know that something of value resides with these people.

I think of the Eskimos compassionately as *hibakusha*—the Japanese word for "explosion-affected people," those who continue to suffer the effects of Hiroshima and Nagasaki. Eskimos are trapped in a long, slow detonation. What they know about a good way to live is disintegrating. The sophisticated, ironic voice of civilization insists that their insights are only trivial, but they are not.

I remember looking into a herd of walrus that day and thinking: do human beings make the walrus more human to make it comprehensible or to assuage loneliness? What is it to be estranged in this land?

It is in the land, I once thought, that one searches out and eventually finds what is beautiful. And an edge of this deep and rarefied beauty is the acceptance of complex paradox and the forgiveness of others. It means you will not die alone.

I looked at the blood in the snow for a long time, and then turned away from the village. I walked north, toward the spot where the gravel spit on which the houses stand slips under the sea ice. It is possible to travel in the Arctic and concentrate only on the physical landscape—on the animals, on the realms of light and dark, on movements that excite some consideration of the ways we conceive of time and space, history, maps, and art. One can become completely isolated, for example, in the intricate life of the polar bear. But the ethereal and timeless power of the land, that union of what is beautiful with what is terrifying, is insistent. It penetrates all cultures, archaic and modern. The land gets inside us; and we must decide one way or another what this means, what we will do about it.

One of our long-lived cultural differences with the Eskimo has been over whether to accept the land as it is or to exert the will to change it into something else. The great task of life for the traditional Eskimo is still to achieve congruence with a reality that is already given. The given reality, the real landscape, is "horror within magnificence, absurdity within intelligibility, suffering within joy," in the words of Albert Schweitzer. We do not esteem as highly these lessons in paradox. We hold in higher regard the land's tractability, its alterability. We believe the conditions of the earth can be changed to ensure human happiness, to provide jobs and to create material wealth and ease. Each culture, then, finds a different sort of apotheosis, of epiphany, and comfort in the land.

Any latent wisdom there might be in the Eskimo position is overwhelmed for us by our ability to alter the land. The long pattern of purely biological evolution, however, strongly suggests that a profound collision of human will with immutable aspects of the natural order is inevitable. This, by itself, seems reason enough to inquire among aboriginal cultures concerning the nature of time and space and other (invented) dichotomies; the relationship between hope and the exercise of will; the role of dreams and myths in human life; and the therapeutic aspects of long-term intimacy with a landscape.

We tend to think of places like the Arctic, the Antarctic, the Gobi, the Sahara, the Mojave, as primitive, but there are in fact no primitive or even primeval landscapes. Neither are there permanent landscapes. And nowhere is the land empty or underdeveloped. It cannot be improved upon with technological assistance. The land, an animal that contains all other animals, is vigorous and alive. The challenge to us, when we address the land, is to join with cosmologists in their ideas of continuous creation, and with physicists with their ideas of spatial and temporal paradox, to see the subtle grace and mutability of the different landscapes. They are crucibles of mystery, precisely like the smaller ones that they contain—the arctic fox, the dwarf birch, the pi-meson; and the larger ones that contain them, side by side with such seemingly immutable objects as the Horsehead Nebula in Orion. These are not solely arenas for human invention. To have no elevated conversation with the land, no sense of reciprocity with it, to rein it in or to disparage conditions not to our liking, shows a certain lack of courage, too strong a preference for human devising.

THE farther I got from the village below Sevuokuk, the more exposed I was to the wind. I pulled my face farther into my parka. Snow squeaked beneath my boots. As I crossed from patches of wind-slabbed snow to dark cobbles, I wobbled over my footing. The beach stones clattered in the wet cold. The violet and saffron streaks of the sunset had long been on the wane. They had gone to pastels, muted, like slow water or interstellar currents, rolling over. They had become the colors of sunrise. The celestial light on an arctic cusp.

I stood with my feet squared on the stones at the edge of the ice and looked north into Bering Strait, the real Estrecho de Anian. To the east was America, the Seward Peninsula; to the west the Magadan Region of Siberia, the Chukchi Peninsula. On each were the burial grounds of archaic Bering Sea–culture people, the richest of all the prehistoric arctic cultures. In the summer of 1976, a Russian group led by M. A. Chlenov discovered a 500-year-old monument on the north shore of Yttygran Island, on Seniavin Strait, off the southeast Chukchi coast. The complex consists of a series of bowhead whale skulls and jawbones set up in a line on the beach that is about 2500 feet long. The monument is associated with several stone and earth structures and also with meat pits. Many of the skulls are still standing up vertically in the ground, in a strict geometric pattern. Chlenov and his colleagues regard the area as a "sacred precinct" and link it to the ceremonial lives of a select group of highly skilled whale hunters, whose culture was continuous from Cape Dezhnev in the north to Providence Bay and included Saint Lawrence Island, where the cultural phase has been named Punuk.

Perhaps the Punuk hunters at Whalebone Alley, as it is known, lived, some of them, exemplary lives. Perhaps they knew exactly what words to say to the whale so they would not go off in dismay or feel the weight of its death. I remember the faces of the walrus we killed, and do not know what words to say to them.

No culture has yet solved the dilemma each has faced with the growth of a conscious mind: how to live a moral and compassionate existence when one is fully aware of the blood, the horror inherent in all life, when one finds darkness not only in one's own culture but within oneself. If there is a stage at which an individual life becomes truly adult, it must be when one grasps the irony in its unfolding and accepts responsibility for a life lived in the midst of such paradox. One must live in the middle of contradiction because if all contradiction were eliminated at once life would collapse. There are simply no answers to some of the great pressing questions. You continue to live them out, making your life a worthy expression of a leaning into the light.

I stood for a long time at the tip of Saint Lawrence Island, regarding the ice, the distant dark leads of water. In the twilight and wind and the damp cold, memories of the day were like an aura around me, unresolved, a continuous perplexity pierced here and there by sharp rays of light—other memories, coherence. I thought of the layers of it—the dying walrus moving through the chill green water, through the individual minds of the hunters, the mind of an observer. Of the very idea of the walrus living on, even as I ate its flesh. Lines in books about the walrus; walrus-hide lines tied to harpoons, dragging walrus-skin boats over the sea. The curve and weight of a tusk in my mind, from a head as dense with bone as a boulder. Walrus-meat stew is waiting back at the house, hot now, while I stand in this cold, thickening wind. At the foot of Sevuokuk, Lapland longspurs build their nests in the walrus's abandoned crania.

Glaucous gulls fly over. In the shore lead are phalaropes, with their twiglike legs. In the distance I can see flocks of oldsquaw against the sky, and a few cormorants. A patch of shadow that could be several thousand crested auklets—too far away to know. Out there are whales—I have seen six or eight gray whales as I walked this evening. And the ice, pale as the dove-colored sky. The wind raises the surface of the water. Wake of a seal in the shore lead, gone now. I bowed. I bowed to what knows no deliberating legislature or parliament, no religion, no competing theories of economics, an expression of allegiance with the mystery of life.

I looked out over the Bering Sea and brought my hands folded to the breast of my parka and bowed from the waist deeply toward the north, that great strait filled with life, the ice and the water. I held the bow to the pale sulphur sky at the northern rim of the earth. I held the bow until my back ached, and my mind was emptied of its categories and designs, its plans and speculations. I bowed before the simple evidence of the moment in my life in a tangible place on the earth that was beautiful.

When I stood I thought I glimpsed my own desire. The landscape and the animals were like something found at the end of a dream. The edges of the real landscape became one with the edges of something I had dreamed. But what I had dreamed was only a pattern, some beautiful pattern of light. The continuous work of the imagination, I thought, to bring what is actual together with what is dreamed is an expression of human evolution. The conscious desire is to achieve a state, even momentarily, that like light is unbounded, nurturing, suffused with wisdom and creation, a state in which one has absorbed that very darkness which before was the perpetual sign of defeat.

Whatever world that is, it lies far ahead. But its outline, its adumbration, is clear in the landscape, and upon this one can actually hope we will find our way.

I bowed again, deeply, toward the north, and turned south to retrace my steps over the dark cobbles to the home where I was staying. I was full of appreciation for all that I had seen.

NOTES

1. Among the more alarming problems and trends in the Arctic are the following. The conviction of Panarctic Oils of Canada, a government-supported consortium, on charges of dumping industrial waste in the Arctic Ocean. A summary declaration by the Quebec government that three Eskimo villages that refused to cede their lands to the province for energy development would thenceforth be political non-entities. The promotion of ill-conceived mega-engineering projects, such as damming Bering Strait to ameliorate harsh weather in the United States or using a nuclear device to create a deep-water harbor at Cape Thompson, Alaska. Poorly planned wildlife research projects, designed in haste to meet pressing deadlines for environmental data, which have resulted in death or injury to the animals involved. A pattern of "destruction by insignificant increments," for example of the migration corridor of the bowhead whale in the West. The extensive vandalization of arctic archaeological sites by oil and mineral exploration crews, government officials, scientists, and wealthy private citizens. A hazy legal understanding of responsibility for the control of arctic pollution in international waters. The reluctance of the Canadian government to protect critical wildlife habitat in the high Arctic from

natural resource exploitation. And, finally, a shift from pure scientific research projects in the Arctic to those associated with industrial expansion. There is also concern over a pall of air pollution emanating from north-central Russia. For an elaboration of these problems, see John Livingston, *Arctic Oil* (1981); Boyce Richardson, *Strangers Devour the Land* (1976); Thomas Berger, *Northern Frontier, Northern Homeland* (1977); Gurston Dacks, *A Choice of Futures* (1981); Milton Freeman, *Proceedings: First International Symposium on Renewable Resources and the Economy of the North* (1981); and David N. Nettleship and Pauline Smith, eds., *Ecological Sites in Northern Canada* (1975).

2. The word "Eskimo" is from the French *Esquimaux*, possibly from *eskipot*, an Algonquian word meaning "an eater of raw flesh." Some Eskimos feel this attribution puts them in a poor light with modern audiences and so use other terms for themselves. "Inuit," the most widely used of these terms, refers specifically to Eskimos of the eastern Canadian Arctic. The Eskimos of the Bering Sea region prefer, instead, to be called "Yup'ik," while North Slope Alaska Eskimos prefer "Inupiat," and Mackenzie Delta Eskimos prefer "Inuvialuit." I have chosen to use the word "Eskimo" throughout in referring to the native arctic people European explorers have met since the sixteenth century. (A fuller explanation of the origin of the word "Eskimo" and of the use of current terms is set forth in David Damas's Introduction to *Arctic* [1984], volume 5 in the *Handbook of North American Indians*, pp. 5–7.)

These Eskimos of the historic period were a short, stocky people, with small feet and hands and relatively short limbs. Their faces were fleshy, often showing the epicanthic eye fold that signaled their comparatively recent Asian origin (more recent than that of the American Indian). Their facial characteristics and their bodily proportions evince some degree of physiological adaptation to the cold, as does their slightly elevated (compared with a Caucasian's) basal metabolism. Their traditional diet, however, which is high in saturated fats, and the exceptional insulation value of their clothing contributed more to their success in the Arctic. Other distinguishing characteristics of the historical Eskimo were a more massive lower jaw and a low-bridged nose. For reflections on Eskimo psychology and thought, see Knud Rasmussen, *Intellectual Culture of the Iglulik Eskimos. Report of the 5th Thule Expedition, 1921–1924*, vol. 7, no. 1 (1929); Jean Briggs, *Never in Anger* (1970); Edmund Carpenter, *Eskimo Realities*

(1973); Richard Nelson, *Hunters of the Northern Ice* (1969); Hugh Brody, *The People's Land* (1975); Franz Boas, *The Central Eskimo* (1888); *Inuit Land Use and Occupancy Project*, vol. 1, edited by Milton Freeman (1976); Jean Blodgett/The Winnipeg Art Gallery, *The Coming and Going of the Shaman: Eskimo Shamanism and Art* (1978); and Edwin S. Hall, *The Eskimo Storyteller: Folktales from Noatak, Alaska* (1975).

3. The uneven pattern of illumination is caused by the tilt of the earth's axis, and by two sorts of movement: the earth's twenty-four-hour rotation (which creates a day), and its annual circuit around the sun (which creates seasons).

Imagine holding a ball in the palm of your left hand at arm's length. At arm's length in your right hand you hold a ruler upright. Incline the ruler toward the ball. Now reverse these positions by crossing your arms. If the ruler is the earth's axis and the ball is the sun, you have just passed from summer solstice to winter solstice in the Northern Hemisphere. At summer solstice the earth's northern polar region is tilted toward the sun. Six months later at winter solstice it is tilted away from the sun, at the same 23½° angle. (On the equinoxes both polar regions—indeed, all places on earth—have a day and night of equal length.)

The varying ratio of daylight to darkness on any given day in the Far North—it remains the same in the tropics and alternates seasonally in the Temperate Zone—is the result of both the earth's inclination on its axis and its daily revolution. The balance of light and dark in any twenty-four-hour period will always be uneven in northern latitudes (except at the equinoxes) because of the earth's inclination. During the seasonal extremes of winter and summer in the North, the effect of the earth's daily rotation may go unnoticed. In the Temperate Zone the effects of both daily rotation and annual revolution on the balance of light are experienced on a regular basis throughout the year.

4. Representative scientific work that grew out of an association with the Nunamiut includes Nicholas Gubser, *The Nunamiut Eskimos: Hunters of Caribou* (1965); Lewis Binford, *Nunamiut Ethnoarcheology* (1978); Helge Ingstad, *Nunamiut: Among Alaska's Inland Eskimos* (1954); Robert Rausch, "Notes on the Nunamiut Eskimos and Mammals of the Anaktuvuk Pass Region, Brooks Range, Alaska," *Arctic* (vol. 4, no. 3 [1951]: 146–195); Laurence Irving, *Birds of Anaktuvuk Pass, Kobuk, and Old Crow*, United States National Mu-

seum, Bulletin 217 (1960); and *Anaktuvuk Pass: Land Use Values through Time*, Grant Spearman, Occasional Paper no. 22, Cooperative Park Studies Unit, Anthropology and Historic Preservation, University of Alaska (1979).

5. The journals are Samuel Hearne's *A Journey from Prince of Wale's Fort in Hudson's Bay to the Northern Ocean* (London: A. Strahan and T. Cadell, 1795); John Franklin's *Narrative of a Journey to the Shores of the Polar Sea* (London: John Murray, 1823); Warburton Pike's *The Barren Ground of Northern Canada* (London and New York: Macmillan and Co., 1892); and Ernest Thompson Seton's *The Arctic Prairies* (New York: Charles Scribner's Sons, 1911).

MAPS

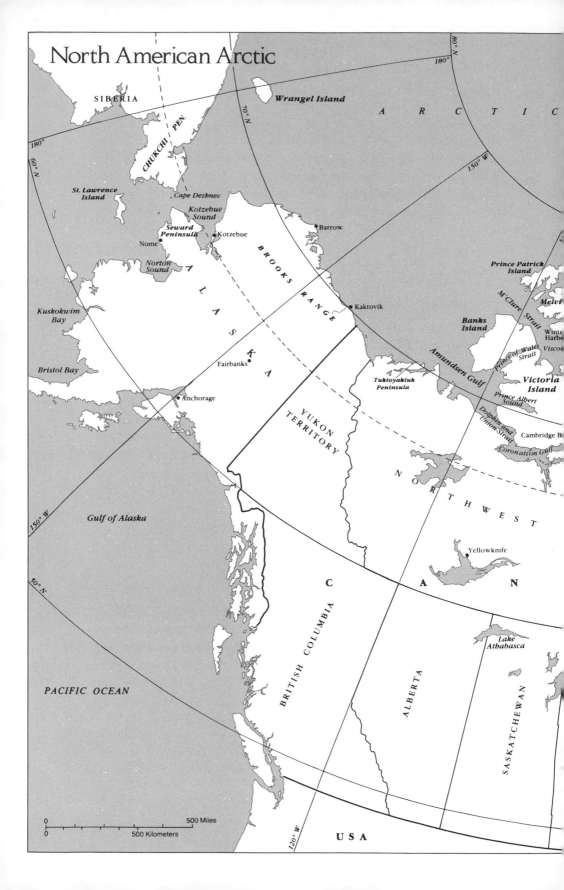

North American Arctic

SIBERIA

Wrangel Island

A R C T I C

CHUKCHI PEN.

St. Lawrence Island

Cape Dezbnev

Kotzebue Sound

Seward Peninsula

Nome

Kotzebue

Barrow

Prince Patrick Island

M'Clure Strait

Melvi

Norton Sound

BROOKS RANGE

A L A S K A

Kaktovik

Banks Island

Winte Harbo

Prince of Wales Strait

Viscou

Kuskokwim Bay

Fairbanks

Amundsen Gulf

Victoria Island

Prince Albert Sound

Bristol Bay

Anchorage

Tuktoyaktuk Peninsula

Dolphin and Union Strait

Cambridge B

Coronation Gulf

YUKON TERRITORY

N O R T H W E S T

Gulf of Alaska

Yellowknife

C A N

PACIFIC OCEAN

C

BRITISH COLUMBIA

Lake Athabasca

ALBERTA

SASKATCHEWAN

0   500 Miles

0   500 Kilometers

USA

NORTH POLE

OCEAN

Wandel Sea

Oodaaq Island

PEARY LAND

Greenland Sea

Cape Bismarck

KNUD RASMUSSEN LAND

30° W

Alert

Fort Conger

Kennedy Channel

Robeson Channel

Axel Heiberg Island

Kane Basin

60° W

G

R

E

E

N

L

A

N

D

Eureka

Ellesmere Island

90° W

Denmark Strait

orden land

Amund Ringnes Island

Thule

30° W

Ellef Ringnes Island

Batburst Island

Melville Bay

land

Jones Sound

Baffin Bay

Cornwallis Island

Devon Island

Resolute

ville Sound

Barrow Str.

Lancaster Sound

Bylot Island

Pond Inlet

Godhavn

Davis Strait

Somerset Island

Brodeur Peninsula

Borden Peninsula

Prince of Wales Island

M'Clintock Channel

Godthåb

Boothia Peninsula

Victoria Strait

Gulf of Boothia

Baffin Island

Cumberland Peninsula

Julianehab

60° N

een Maud Gulf

Melville Peninsula

Air Force Island

Foxe Basin

Hall Peninsula

T   E   R   R   I   T   O   R   I   E   S

Foxe Channel

Foxe Peninsula

Meta Incognita Peninsula

Southampton Island

Hudson Strait

A

D

A

Cape Wolstenholme

Cape Hopes Advanced

Ungava Bay

LABRADOR

Hopes Checked

Hudson Bay

QUEBEC

Churchill

MANITOBA

50° N

Akimiski Island

ONTARIO

Lake Winnipeg

90° W

St. Lawrence River

60° W

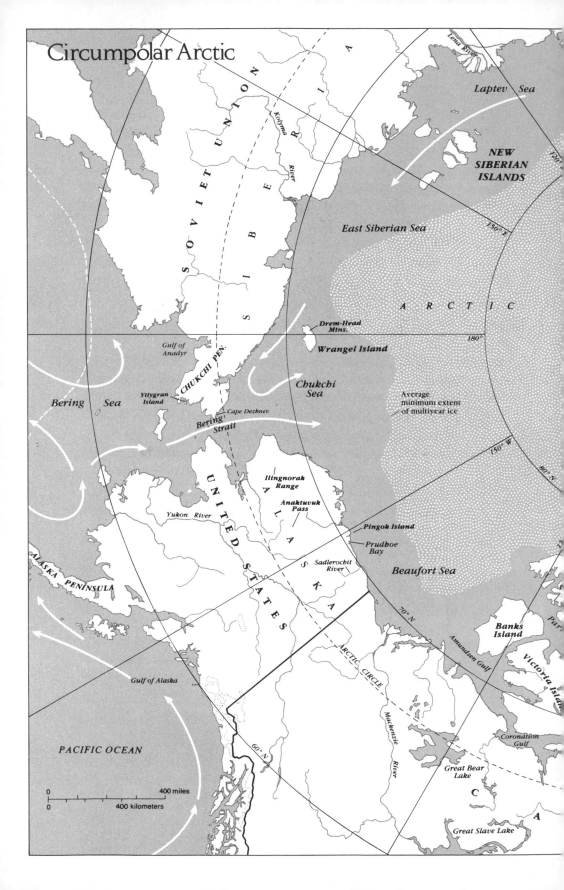

Circumpolar Arctic

SOVIET UNION

S I B E R I A

Lena River

Kolyma River

Laptev Sea

NEW SIBERIAN ISLANDS

East Siberian Sea

120°

150° E

A R C T I C

180°

Drem-Head Mtns.

Wrangel Island

Gulf of Anadyr

CHUKCHI PEN.

Chukchi Sea

Average minimum extent of multiyear ice

Yttygran Island

Cape Dezhnev

Bering Strait

Bering Sea

150° W

80° N

Ilingnorak Range

Anaktuvuk Pass

A L A S K A

Yukon River

UNITED STATES

Pingok Island

Prudhoe Bay

Sadlerochit River

Beaufort Sea

Banks Island

ALASKA PENINSULA

70° N

Victoria Island

Amundsen Gulf

Gulf of Alaska

ARCTIC CIRCLE

Mackenzie River

Coronation Gulf

PACIFIC OCEAN

60° N

Great Bear Lake

C

A

Great Slave Lake

0		400 miles
0		400 kilometers

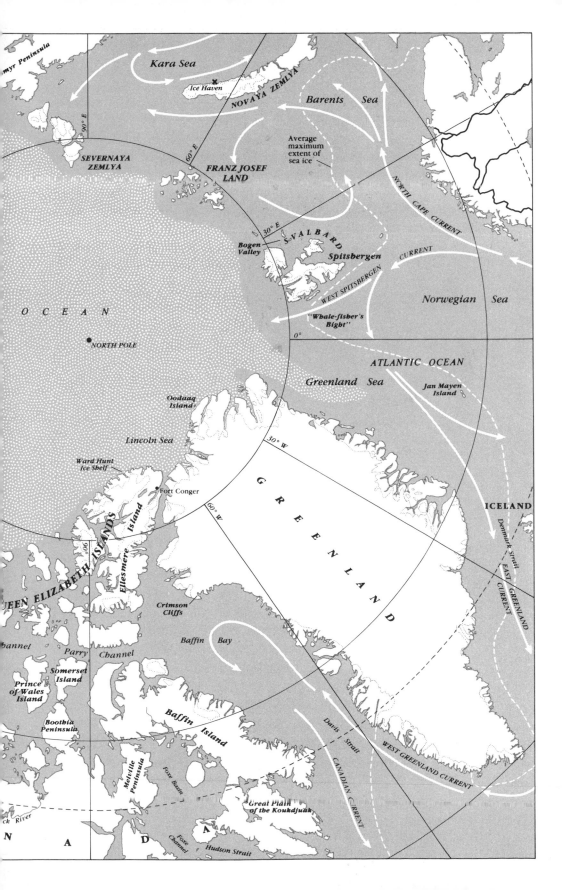

Thaimyr Peninsula

Kara Sea

× Ice Haven

NOVAYA ZEMLYA

Barents Sea

Average
maximum
extent of
sea ice

SEVERNAYA
ZEMLYA

FRANZ JOSEF
LAND

30° E

60° E

90° E

NORTH CAPE CURRENT

Bogen
Valley

SVALBARD

Spitsbergen

WEST SPITSBERGEN

CURRENT

Norwegian Sea

O C E A N

• NORTH POLE

"Whale-fisher's
Bight"

0°

ATLANTIC OCEAN

Greenland Sea

Jan Mayen
Island

Oodaaq
Island

Lincoln Sea

30° W

Ward Hunt
Ice Shelf

• Fort Conger

ICELAND

G
R
E
E
N
L
A
N
D

60° W

Denmark Strait

EAST GREENLAND

CURRENT

QUEEN ELIZABETH ISLANDS

90° W

Ellesmere Island

Crimson
Cliffs

Baffin Bay

Channel

Parry Channel

Somerset
Island

Prince
of Wales
Island

Bootbia
Peninsula

Baffin Island

Melville
Peninsula

Foxe Basin

Davis Strait

WEST GREENLAND CURRENT

CANADIAN CURRENT

ck River

N

A

D

A

Great Plain
of the Koukdjuak

Foxe
Channel

Hudson Strait

Appendix I

Geographic Place Names

	Latitude N.	Longitude W.		Latitude N.	Longitude W.
Able Creek	73 42	120 02	Amundsen Gulf	70 30	123 00
Academy			Anadyr, Gulf of	64 00	178 00
Glacier	81 30	33 30	Anaktiktoak		
Adelaide			Valley	68 09	151 15
Peninsula	68 08	97 30	Anaktuvuk Pass	68 08	151 45
Admiralty Inlet	72 45	86 10	Anaktuvuk		
Agassiz Ice Cap	80 30	76 20	River	69 34	151 28
Air Force Island	68 00	74 30	Anchorage	61 13	149 53
Akimiski Island	53 00	81 20	Anderson River	69 41	128 57
Alaska	65 00	152 00	Anian, Strait of		
Alernerk	69 24	81 48	(*see* Bering		
Aleutian Islands	52 00	174 00	Strait)		
Amchitka Island	51 32	179 00 *E.*	Arctic Bay	73 01	85 08
Ammassalik			Arctic Ocean	85 00	180 00
(now Tasiilaq)	65 36	37 38	Athabasca River	58 27	111 04
Amund Ringnes			Axel Heiberg		
Island	78 15	96 50	Island	79 30	90 00

	Latitude N.	Longitude W.		Latitude N.	Longitude W.
Bache Peninsula	79 08	75 25	Byam Martin		
Back's Fish River			Island	75 13	104 12
(now Back			Bylot Island	73 15	79 00
River)	67 10	95 20			
Baffin Bay	74 00	67 00	Cambridge Bay	69 07	105 02
Baffin Island	68 00	72 00	Camden Bay	70 09	144 45
Bailey Point	74 59	115 00	Canadian		
Baillarge Bay	73 19	84 37	Archipelago	76 00	100 00
Baker Creek	73 38	120 04	Canning River	70 04	145 30
Banks Island	73 00	121 00	Castel Bay	74 11	119 36
Barrow	71 17	156 45	Chukchi		
Barrow, Point	71 23	156 28	Peninsula	66 00	174 00
Barrow Inlet	68 05	96 45	Chukchi Sea	69 00	173 00
Barrow Strait	74 25	95 00	Churchill	58 46	94 10
Barter Island	70 07	143 40	Churchill, Cape	58 46	93 12
Bathurst, Cape	70 35	128 01	Churchill, Fort	58 45	94 00
Bathurst Island	75 40	100 00	Churchill River	58 47	94 11
Bear Cape	55 11	162 00	Clavering Island	74 16	21 00
Beaufort Lagoon	69 52	142 12	Clyde Inlet	70 15	68 50
Beaufort Sea	73 00	140 00	Coats Island	62 35	82 55
Beechey Island	74 44	91 55	Columbia, Cape	83 09	71 11
Beerenberg	71 00	8 20	Colville River	70 27	150 07
Belle Isle,			Commander		
Strait of	51 30	56 30	Islands	55 00	167 00 *E.*
Bellot Strait	72 00	94 45	Conger, Fort	81 45	64 54
Bergen	60 23	5 20 *E.*	Coppermine		
Bering Sea	55 00	175 00	River	67 49	115 05
Bering Strait	66 00	169 00	Cornwallis Island	75 10	95 00
Bismarck, Cape	76 45	18 30	Coronation Gulf	68 00	112 00
Bogen Valley	78 54	28 05 *E.*	Crimson Cliffs	76 08	67 45
Boothia			Crown Prince		
Peninsula	70 30	94 30	Christian Land	80 30	22 00
Borden Island	78 29	111 00	Cumberland		
Borden			Sound	65 20	66 00
Peninsula	72 45	83 00			
Brock Island	77 50	114 15	Dall Point	61 35	166 00
Brodeur			Danmark Fiord	81 00	23 07
Peninsula	72 30	88 00	Davis Strait	65 00	57 30
Brooks Range	68 00	152 00	Deadhorse		
Brother John			Airport	70 18	148 19
Glacier	78 17	72 17	Dealy Island	74 58	108 45

	Latitude N.	Longitude W.		Latitude N.	Longitude W.
De Long Islands	76 30	153 00 *E.*	Faroe Islands	62 00	7 00
Demarcation Bay	69 41	141 20	Fellfoot Point	74 30	88 41
Devon Island	75 00	86 00	Findlay Group	77 20	104 50
Dexterity Fiord	71 15	73 00	Fligeli, Cape		
Dezhnev, Cape			(Cape Fligely)	81 45	59 15 *E.*
(East Cape)	66 05	169 40	Fosheim		
Digges Island	62 35	77 50	Peninsula	79 45	84 00
Disko Bay (now			Foula Island	60 10	2 05
Qeqertarsuup			Foxe Basin	67 00	77 00
Tunua)	69 00	52 00	Foxe Channel	65 00	81 00
Disraeli Fiord	83 00	74 30	Fox Island (now		
Dolphin and			Renard Island)	59 55	149 20
Union Strait	69 00	114 30	Franklin Strait	71 30	96 30
Drem-Head			Franz Josef Land	81 00	55 00 *E.*
Mountains	71 23	179 39 *E.*	Frobisher Bay	62 40	66 20
Dundas			Frozen Strait	65 50	84 25
Peninsula	74 45	112 00	Fury and Hecla		
			Strait	69 56	84 00
East Cape (*see*			Fury Beach	72 49	91 54
Cape Dezhnev)					
Eastern			Gambell	63 47	171 45
Settlement (*see*			Garry Lake	66 00	100 20
Julianehåb)			Gateshead Island	70 30	100 23
Edmund Walker			Gilbert Sound		
Island	77 08	104 05	(now Qussuk)	64 30	51 23
Egg River	72 28	124 05	Godhavn (now		
Ellef Ringnes			Qeqertarsuaq)	69 15	53 33
Island	78 35	102 00	Godthåb		
Ellesmere Island	79 30	81 00	(now Nuuk)	64 11	51 45
Elwin Inlet	73 27	83 45	Good Friday Bay	78 32	92 30
Eriks Fiord (now			Grant Point	68 22	98 42
Tunulliarfik)	60 55	46 04	Great Bear Lake	66 00	120 00
Eskimo Point	61 10	94 15	Great Plain of the		
Etah	78 19	72 38	Koukdjuak	66 25	72 50
Eureka	80 00	85 55	Great Slave Lake	61 30	114 00
			Greenland		
Fairbanks	64 50	147 43	(now Kalaallit		
Fair Haven	77 34	14 40 *E.*	Nunaat)	72 00	40 00
Farewell, Cape			Greenland Sea	75 00	10 00
(now Uum-			Grinnell		
mannarsuaq)	59 46	43 55	Peninsula	76 45	95 00

	Latitude N.	Longitude W.		Latitude N.	Longitude W.
Hall Basin	81 30	63 30	James Ross Strait	69 45	96 20
Hamilton Inlet	54 18	57 42	Jan Mayen Island	71 00	8 20
Harrison Bay	70 40	151 30	John Herschel,		
Hay, Cape	73 42	79 58	Cape	68 39	98 02
Hayes Peninsula	77 00	65 00	Jones Islands	70 32	149 36
Hayes River	67 20	95 02	Jones Sound	76 05	85 00
Hazen, Lake	81 48	71 15	Julianehåb (now		
Hazen Strait	77 10	110 00	Qaqortoq)	60 43	46 02
Hochstetter			Julianehåb		
Peninsula	75 37	20 30	District	60 40	46 10
Hold-with-Hope					
Cape (now			Kaffeklubben		
Cape Broer			Island	83 36	29 48
Ruys)	73 32	20 18	Kaktovik	70 08	143 38
Hold with Hope			Kamchatka		
Peninsula	73 45	21 05	Peninsula	56 00	159 00 E.
Hood River	67 24	108 53	Kane Basin	79 30	69 30
Hope, Point	68 20	166 50	Kara Sea	76 00	80 00 E.
Hopes Advance,			Karajak Fiord		
Cape	61 05	69 33	(now Qarajaq		
Hopes Checked	60 30	94 30	Fiord)	70 25	51 10
Horton River	69 57	126 53	Karskiye Vorota		
Hudson Bay	60 00	85 00	Strait	70 30	58 00 E.
Hudson Strait	62 30	72 00	Kenai Peninsula	60 10	150 00
Humboldt			Kendall Island	69 29	135 15
Glacier (now			Kennedy		
Sermersuaq)	79 30	63 00	Channel	80 45	66 30
			Kent Peninsula	68 35	107 00
Ice Haven	75 40	63 30 E.	King Christian		
Iceland	65 00	18 00	Island	77 52	101 40
Icy Cape	70 20	161 52	King Island	64 58	168 05
Igloolik	69 24	81 48	King William		
Ilingnorak Ridge	68 45	162 00	Island	69 00	97 30
Independence			Kobuk River	66 54	160 38
Fiord	82 08	28 00	Kokolik River	69 45	163 00
Inglefield Fiord	77 27	67 45	Kola Peninsula	67 20	37 00 E.
Inglefield Land	78 40	70 00	Kolyma River	62 20	154 50 E.
			Kongsøya Island	78 55	29 00 E.
ade Mountains	67 14	158 03	Koukdjuak River	66 44	73 02
go River	70 07	143 16	Krusenstern,		
nes Bay	53 30	80 30	Cape	67 08	163 44
Jameson Land	71 10	23 30	Kuparuk River	70 25	148 52

	Latitude N.	Longitude W.
Kuptana Site		
(PjRa-18)	73 39	120 03
Kuril Islands	46 00	150 00 *E.*
Kuskokwim		
River	60 05	162 25
Labrador	54 00	62 00
Labrador Sea	55 00	57 00
Lac St.-Jean	48 30	72 00
Lambert Land	79 15	20 30
Lancaster Sound	74 10	85 00
L'Anse		
aux Meadows	51 36	55 30
Laptev Sea	76 00	126 00 *E.*
Lena River	72 25	126 40 *E.*
Lincoln Sea	83 00	58 00
Little Cornwallis		
Island	75 35	96 30
Lougheed Island	77 30	105 00
Lumley's Inlet		
(*see* Cumber-		
land Sound)		
Mackenzie King		
Island	77 45	111 00
Mackenzie River	69 20	134 00
Magadan Region	65 00	160 00 *E.*
Magdalena Bay	79 35	10 58 *E.*
Mamen, Cape	77 36	110 02
Mansel Island	62 00	80 00
M'Clintock		
Channel	72 00	103 00
M'Clure Strait	74 45	118 00
Meighen Island	79 55	99 00
Melville Bay		
(now Qimus-		
seriarsuaq)	75 45	61 00
Melville Island	75 15	110 30
Melville		
Peninsula	68 00	84 15

	Latitude N.	Longitude W.
Mercy, Bay of		
God's (now		
Mercy Bay)	74 15	118 10
Mercy, Cape of		
God's (now		
Cape Mercy)	64 56	63 40
Meta Incognita		
Peninsula	62 55	68 40
Minto Inlet	71 20	117 00
Mokka Fiord	79 41	87 17
Morris Jesup,		
Cape	83 38	32 31
Mylius Erichsen		
Land	81 10	26 30
Nanasivik Mine	73 02	84 33
Nanortalik	60 07	45 13
Nares Strait	80 10	68 30
Navarin Basin	63 00	174 00
Navy Board		
Inlet	73 13	80 52
Nelson Head	71 02	122 40
Nelson River	57 04	92 30
Newfoundland	52 00	56 00
New Siberian		
Islands	75 00	142 00 *E.*
Newton, Mount	79 02	17 30 *E.*
Nome	64 30	165 25
Nome, Cape	64 26	165 00
Nome River	64 29	165 18
North Cape	71 11	25 48 *E.*
Northern Ocean		
(*see* Arctic		
Ocean)		
North Slope	68 30	152 00
North Water	75 30	75 00
Northwest		
Territories	65 00	105 00
Norton Basin	63 30	164 30
Norton Sound	64 00	164 00
Novaya Zemlya	74 00	57 00 *E.*

	Latitude N.	Longitude W.		Latitude N.	Longitude W.
Nunivak Island	60 10	166 30	Prince Regent		
Nuvua	73 08	85 25	Inlet	73 00	90 30
			Princess Royal		
Ob River	66 45	69 30 *E.*	Islands	72 46	118 03
Ogilvie			Providence Bay	64 23	173 18
Mountains	64 25	133 30	Prudhoe Bay	70 22	148 22
Oliktok Point	70 30	149 51			
Onion Portage	67 07	158 18	Queen Elizabeth		
Oodaaq Island	83 41	30 40	Islands	77 30	95 00
Orkney Islands	59 00	3 00	Queen Louisa		
Owl River	57 50	92 45	Land (now		
			Dronning		
Parry Channel	74 30	105 00	Louise Land)	76 30	24 15
Parry Islands	76 00	100 00	Queen Maud		
Peary Land	82 38	32 30	Gulf	68 25	101 30
Peel Sound	73 00	96 10			
Pelly Bay	68 50	90 10			
Penny Strait	76 37	97 15	Rae Point	75 22	105 35
Peribonka	48 46	72 03	Rae Strait	68 50	94 55
Pim Island	78 44	74 25	Rensselaer		
Pingok Island	70 35	149 35	Harbor	78 51	71 06
Pingokralik	69 42	141 28	Resolute	74 41	94 54
PjRa-18 (*see*			Return Islands	70 27	148 47
Kuptana Site)			Retzius		
Polar Bear Pass	75 45	98 30	Mountain	78 54	28 20 *E.*
Polaris Mine	75 30	96 40	Robeson Channel	82 00	62 00
Pond Inlet	72 47	77 00	Roes Welcome		
Pond Inlet			Sound	64 50	86 40
Settlement	72 42	78 00	[Royal]		
Pond's Bay (*see*			Astronomical		
Pond Inlet)			Society		
Prince Albert			Islands	69 48	91 37
Sound	70 25	115 00	Ruggles River	81 42	68 13
Prince of Wales,					
Cape	65 36	168 05	Sabine, Cape	78 44	74 20
Prince of Wales			Sadlerochit		
Island	72 45	99 00	River	70 03	144 26
Prince of Wales			Safety Sound	64 29	164 45
Strait	72 45	118 00	Sagavanirktok		
Prince Patrick			River	70 18	147 52
Island	76 40	119 30	Saguenay River	48 08	69 43

	Latitude N.	Longitude W.
Saint John's	47 34	56 11
Saint Lawrence, Gulf of	47 00	62 00
Saint Lawrence Island	63 30	170 30
Saint Matthew Island	60 24	172 42
Saint Patrick Canyon	72 51	86 41
Sandersons Hope	72 43	56 11
Sarichef, Cape	54 35	164 55
Savissivik	76 01	65 05
Scoresby Sound	70 30	21 58
Searle, Cape	67 14	62 28
Seenasaluq	72 45	77 27
Seniavin Strait	64 45	172 40
Severnaya Zemlya	79 30	98 00 E.
Sevuokuk Mountain	63 46	171 42
Seward	60 06	149 26
Seward Peninsula	65 00	164 00
Sheridan, Cape	82 29	61 26
Siberia	60 00	100 00 E.
Simmons Peninsula	76 42	89 05
Simpson Lagoon	70 30	149 12
Simpson Strait	68 33	97 30
Siorapaluk	77 47	70 43
Skruis Point	75 09	88 50
Slidre Fiord	79 58	85 50
Smith Sound	78 25	73 50
Smyth, Cape	74 58	115 32
Somerset Island	73 30	93 00
Sons of the Clergy Islands	69 34	91 50

	Latitude N.	Longitude W.
Southampton Island	64 30	84 00
Spitsbergen Archipelago (*see* Svalbard)		
Spitsbergen Island	78 45	16 00 E.
Starvation Cove	68 14	96 35
Strathcona Sound	73 05	84 30
Sullorsuaq	70 12	53 00
Surprise Fiord	78 14	90 00
Svalbard	78 00	19 00 E.
Sverdrup Basin	77 37	94 40
Taimyr Peninsula	76 00	104 00 E.
Tasmania Islands	71 13	96 30
Teddy Bear Island	68 47	114 45
Thank God Harbor	81 36	61 10
Thelon River	64 16	96 05
Thomas Hubbard, Cape	81 21	94 07
Thompson, Cape	68 08	165 58
Thomsen River	74 05	119 49
Three Brothers, Strait of (*see* Hudson Strait)		
Thule (Uummannaq) (before 1949)	76 30	69 00
Thule (now Qaanaaq)*	77 29	69 21

---

* Thule village (Uummannaq) was moved to 77°29′N by 69°21′W in 1949 and is now called Qaanaaq.

	Latitude N.	Longitude W.		Latitude N.	Longitude W.
Titiralik	73 15	80 48	Ward Hunt Ice		
Toker Point	69 39	132 50	Shelf	83 10	76 00
Torsukattak			Wellington		
Fiord	69 58	51 05	Channel	75 15	93 00
Truelove			Western		
Lowland	75 33	84 40	Settlement (*see*		
Trunmore Bay	53 53	57 10	Godthåb)		
Tuktoyaktuk	69 27	133 01	West Water	74 00	76 00
Tuktoyaktuk			Whalebone		
Peninsula	69 30	132 30	Alley	64 37	172 36
Tule Lake	41 54	121 31	Whale-fisher's		
Tulugak Lake	68 17	151 28	Bight	76 00	5 00 *E.*
Tundovaya			White Handker-		
River Valley	71 30	180 00	chief, Cape	59 16	63 23
Turnagain Point	68 38	108 15	White Sea	68 00	38 00 *E.*
			Wilberforce		
Uluksan			Falls	67 07	108 45
Peninsula	73 05	85 25	Winter Harbor	74 47	110 39
Ungava Bay	59 30	67 30	Wolf Fiord	78 30	88 40
Ungava			Wolstenholme,		
Peninsula	60 00	74 00	Cape	62 34	77 30
Unimak Island	54 45	164 00	Wrangel Island	71 00	179 30
Unimak Pass	54 20	164 50	Wrangell		
Upernavik	72 47	56 10	Mountains	62 00	143 00
Utqiagvik	71 17	156 47			
Utukok River	70 03	162 21	Yana River	71 31	136 32 *E.*
Uummannaq	76 30	69 00	Yellowknife	62 27	114 21
			York, Cape	73 48	86 58
Vera, Cape	76 13	89 14	Yttygran Island	64 37	172 36
Victoria Island	70 30	110 00	Yukon-		
Victoria Strait	69 30	100 00	Kuskokwim		
Viscount Melville			(Y-K) Delta	61 30	163 00
Sound	74 15	105 30	Yukon River	62 32	163 54
			Yukon Territory	63 00	137 00
Wainright	70 38	160 01			
Walløe, Cape	60 35	42 50	Zebra Cliffs	82 45	77 26

Scientific Names for Animals and Plants

MAMMALS

Bear
  black   *Ursus americanus*
  brown   *Ursus arctos*
  grizzly* (*see* brown bear)
  polar   *Ursus maritimus*
Beaver   *Castor canadensis*
Caribou
  Alaskan barren-ground   *Rangifer tarandus granti*
  Canadian barren-ground *Rangifer tarandus groenlandicus*
  Peary   *Rangifer tarandus pearyi*
  woodland   *Rangifer tarandus caribou*
Coyote   *Canis latrans*
Ermine (*see* weasel, short-tailed)
Fox
  arctic   *Alopex lagopus*
  red   *Vulpes vulpes*

---

* The terms "tundra grizzly" and "barren-ground grizzly" are used interchangeably to refer to a grizzly bear (*Ursus arctos*) living in such habitat.

Hare
  arctic   *Lepus arcticus*
  snowshoe   *Lepus americanus*
  tundra   *Lepus othus*
Killer whale
  (*see* orca)
Lemming
  brown   *Lemmus sibiricus*
  collared   *Dicrostonyx torquatus*
Lynx   *Lynx canadensis*
Marmot, hoary   *Marmota caligata*
Marten   *Martes americana*
Mink   *Mustela vison*
Moose   *Alces alces*
Muskox
  barren ground or mainland
    Canadian   *Ovibos moschatus moschatus*
  high arctic or Greenland   *Ovibos moschatus wardi*
Narwhal   *Monodon monoceros*
Orca   *Orcinus orca*
Porcupine   *Erethizon dorsatum*
Reindeer   *Rangifer tarandus tarandus*
Sea cow, Steller's   *Hydrodamalis gigas* (extinct)
Sea mink   *Mustela macrodon* (extinct)
Sea otter   *Enhydra lutris*
Seal
  bearded   *Erignathus barbatus*
  gray   *Halichoerus grypus*
  harp   *Phoca groenlandica*
  hooded   *Cystophora cristata*
  ribbon   *Histriophoca fasciata*
  ringed   *Phoca hispida*
  spotted   *Phoca larga*
Sheep, Dall   *Ovis dalli*
Squirrel
  arboreal flying   *Glaucomys sabrinus*
  arctic ground   *Spermophilus undulatus*
Vole
  Alaska   *Microtus miurus*
  tundra   *Microtus oeconomus*
  tundra redback   *Clethrionomys rutilus*

Walrus	
Pacific	*Odobenus rosmarus divergens*
Atlantic	*Odobenus rosmarus rosmarus*
Weasel	
least	*Mustela nivalis*
short-tailed	*Mustela erminea*
Whale	
belukha*	*Delphinapterus leucas*
bowhead	*Balaena mysticetus*
gray	*Eschrichtius robustus*
Greenland right	
(*see* bowhead)	
humpback	*Megaptera novaeangliae*
minke	*Balaenoptera acutorostrata*
Pacific right	*Balaena glacialis*
Polar (*see* bowhead)	
sei	*Balaenoptera borealis*
sperm	*Physeter catodon*
See Narwhal *and* Orca	
Wolf	*Canis lupus*
Wolverine	*Gulo gulo*

BIRDS

Auklet, crested	*Aethia cristatella*
Bluethroat	*Luscinia svecica*
Brant, black	*Branta bernicla*
Bunting, snow	*Plectrophenax nivalis*
Canvasback	*Aythya valisineria*
Cormorant	
Pallas'	*Phalacrocorax perspicillatus*
	(extinct)
pelagic	*Phalacrocorax pelagicus*
Crane, sandhill	*Grus canadensis*

---

* American marine biologists have recently begun to use "belukha" to distinguish the white whale (*Delphinapterus leucas*). In Russian "beluga" refers to the white sturgeon (*Acipenser huso*).

Curlew, Eskimo	*Numenius borealis* (nearly extinct)
Dovekie	*Alle alle*
Dowitcher, long-billed	*Limnodromus scolopaceus*
Duck	
Labrador	*Camptorhynchus labradorius* (extinct)
ruddy	*Oxyura jamaicensis*
Dunlin	*Calidris alpina*
Eagle	
bald	*Haliaeëtus leucocephalus*
golden	*Aquila chrysaëtos*
Eider	
common	*Somateria mollissima*
king	*Somateria spectabilis*
spectacled	*Somateria fischeri*
Steller's	*Polysticta stelleri*
Falcon, peregrine	*Falco peregrinus*
Fulmar, northern	*Fulmarus glacialis*
Gadwall	*Anas strepera*
Goldeneye, Barrow's	*Bucephala islandica*
Goose	
Canada	*Branta canadensis*
emperor	*Chen canagica*
lesser snow	*Chen caerulescens caerulescens*
Ross's	*Chen rossii*
white-fronted	*Anser albifrons*
Guillemot	
black	*Cepphus grylle*
pigeon	*Cepphus columba*
Gull	
glaucous	*Larus hyperboreus*
ivory	*Pagophila eburnea*
Ross's	*Rhodostethia rosea*
Thayer's	*Larus thayeri*
Gyrfalcon	*Falco rusticolus*
Hawk	
marsh	*Circus cyaneus*
red-tailed	*Buteo jamaicensis*
rough-legged	*Buteo lagopus*

Jaeger
 long-tailed   *Stercorarius longicaudus*
 parasitic   *Stercorarius parasiticus*
Jay, Steller's   *Cyanocitta stelleri*
Kittiwake
 black-legged   *Rissa tridactyla*
 red-legged   *Rissa brevirostris*
Lark, horned   *Eremophila alpestris*
Longspur, Lapland   *Calcarius lapponicus*
Loon
 arctic   *Gavia arctica*
 common   *Gavia immer*
 red-throated   *Gavia stellata*
Mallard   *Anas platyrhynchos*
Merganser
 common   *Mergus merganser*
 red-breasted   *Mergus serrator*
Murre, thick-billed   *Uria lomvia*
Oldsquaw   *Clangula hyemalis*
Owl
 boreal   *Aegolius funereus*
 short-eared   *Asio flammeus*
 snowy   *Nyctea scandiaca*
Phalarope
 northern   *Phalaropus lobatus*
 red   *Phalaropus fulicarius*
Pintail, northern   *Anas acuta*
Plover, golden   *Pluvialis dominica*
Ptarmigan
 rock   *Lagopus mutus*
 willow   *Lagopus lagopus*
Puffin
 Atlantic   *Fratercula arctica*
 horned   *Fratercula corniculata*
 tufted   *Fratercula cirrhata*
Raven, common   *Corvus corax*
Redhead   *Aythya americana*
Redpoll
 common   *Carduelis flammea*
 hoary   *Carduelis hornemanni*

Robin	*Turdus migratorius*
Scaup	
greater	*Aythya marila*
lesser	*Aythya affinis*
Shoveler, northern	*Anas clypeata*
Sparrow, Savannah	*Passerculus sandwichensis*
Storm-petrel, Leach's	*Oceanodroma leucorhoa*
Swan, tundra	*Cygnus columbianus*
Teal, green-winged	*Anas crecca*
Tern, arctic	*Sterna paradisaea*
Turnstone, ruddy	*Arenaria interpres*
Wagtail, yellow	*Motacilla flava*
Warbler, arctic	*Phylloscopus borealis*
Wheatear, northern	*Oenanthe oenanthe*
Whimbrel	*Numenius phaeopus*

FISH

Char, arctic	*Salvelinus alpinus*
Cod	
arctic	*Boreogadus saida*
Atlantic	*Gadus morhua*
polar	*Arctogadus glacialis*
Halibut	
Greenland	*Reinhardtius hippoglossoides*
Pacific	*Hippoglossus stenolepis*
Herring	
Atlantic	*Clupea harengus harengus*
Pacific	*Clupea harengus pallasi*
Pollock	*Pollachius virens*
Redfish	*Sebastes marinus*
Salmon	
chinook (king)	*Oncorhynchus tshawytscha*
chum (dog)	*Oncorhynchus keta*
coho (silver)	*Oncorhynchus kisutch*
pink (humpback)	*Oncorhynchus gorbuscha*
sockeye (red)	*Oncorhynchus nerka*
Shark, Greenland	*Somniosus microcephalus*
Sheefish	*Stenodus leucichthys*
Sole, yellowfin	*Limanda aspera*
Trout, lake	*Salvelinus namaycush*

PLANTS

Avens, mountain	*Geum rossii*
Bearberry	*Arctostaphylos rubra*
Birch, dwarf arctic	*Betula nana*
Blueberry	*Vaccinium uliginosum*
Bluegrass	*Poa* sp.
Campion	
bladder	*Lychnis* sp.
moss	*Silene acaulis*
Cinquefoil	*Potentilla uniflora*
Coltsfoot, sweet	*Petasites* sp.
Cottongrass	*Trichacne* sp.
Cowberry (*see* mountain	
cranberry)	
Cranberry, mountain	
(cowberry)	*Vaccinium vitis-idaea*
Crowberry	*Empetrum nigrum*
Fireweed, dwarf	*Epilobium latifolia*
Foxtail	*Alepocurus* sp.
Heather, arctic white	*Cassiope tetragona*
Grass, pendant	*Arctophila fulva*
Lousewort	*Pedicularis sudetica*
Lupine, blue-spike	*Lupinus arctica*
Milkvetch, alpine	*Astragalus alpinus*
Oxytrope	*Oxytropis* sp.
Poppy, arctic	*Papaver* sp.
Saxifrage	*Saxifraga* sp.
Sedge, water	*Carex aquatilis*
Sorrel, mountain	*Rumex paucifolius*
Sweetbroom, northern	*Hedysarum mackenzii*
Tamarack	*Larix laricina*
Tea, Labrador	*Ledum groenlandicum*
Willow	
arctic	*Salix arctica*
barren-ground	*Salix brachycarpa*
blue	*Salix subcoerulea*
diamondleaf	*Salix planifolia pulchra*
feltleaf	*Salix alaxensis*
Richardson	*Salix richardsonii*

tea-leaf	*Salix phylicifolia*
veiny-leafed	*Salix phlebophylla*
Willow herb	*Epilobeum* sp.
Woodrush	*Luzula* sp.

Appendix III

Human Culture and Civilization

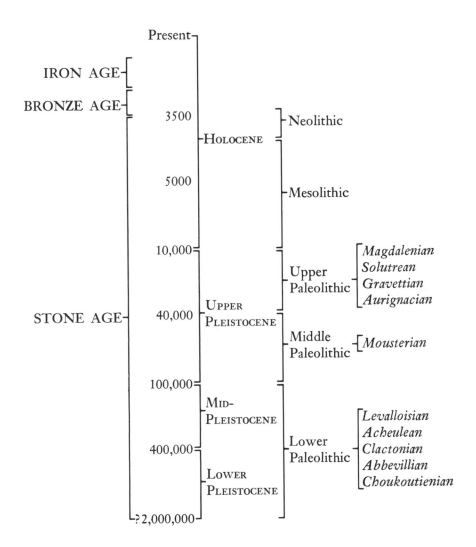

NB Dates refer to Years Before Present and are approximate. Cultural sequences are from Europe and Asia only.

BIBLIOGRAPHY

I HAVE TRIED to indicate in the text and in notes throughout, the titles of various books, articles, and reports I found useful. The literature on the Arctic, of course, is vast and diverse. As political and industrial pressures to organize and allocate portions of the land have increased, the number of publications, especially of technical papers, has grown even larger.

The following bibliography is intended to provide the general reader with a broad understanding of the biology, ecology, archaeology, ethnography, and history of the Arctic. These books, I trust, will lead an interested reader to more specific works.

For readers with specific questions about sources for material in the text, I would be glad to answer queries directed through the publisher.

ANDRASKO, KENNETH. *Alaska Crude: Visions of the Last Frontier.* Photographs by Marcus Halevi. Boston: Little, Brown and Company, 1977.

ARMSTRONG, TERENCE, et al., editors. *The Circumpolar North: A Political and Economic Geography of the Arctic and Sub-Arctic.* London: Methuen and Company Ltd., 1978.

445

BERGER, THOMAS R. *Northern Frontier, Northern Homeland.* Report of the Mackenzie Valley Pipeline Inquiry. Ottawa: Department of Indian Affairs and Northern Development, 1977.

BLISS, L. C., editor. *Truelove Lowland, Devon Island, Canada: A High Arctic Ecosystem.* Edmonton, Alberta: University of Alberta Press, 1977.

BOAS, FRANZ. *The Central Eskimo.* United States Bureau of American Ethnology, Sixth Annual Report, 1884–1885. Washington, D.C.: Government Printing Office, 1888.

BODFISH, HARTSON. *Chasing the Bowhead.* Cambridge: Harvard University Press, 1936.

BRODY, HUGH. *The People's Land: Eskimos and Whites in the Eastern Arctic.* Middlesex, England: Penguin Books, 1975.

BRIGGS, JEAN. *Never in Anger: Portrait of an Eskimo Family.* Cambridge: Harvard University Press, 1970.

CARPENTER, EDMUND. *Eskimo Realities.* New York: Holt, Rinehart and Winston, 1973.

DACKS, GURSTON. *A Choice of Futures: Politics in the Canadian North.* Toronto: Methuen, 1981.

DAMAS, DAVID. *Arctic.* Handbook of North American Indians, Vol. V. Washington: Smithsonian Institution, 1984.

DUNBAR, MAX. *Ecological Development in Polar Regions: A Study in Evolution.* Englewood Cliffs, N.J.: Prentice-Hall, 1968.

FREEMAN, MILTON. *Inuit Land Use and Occupancy Project.* Vol. I. Ottawa: Department of Indian and Northern Affairs, 1976.

———, editor. *Proceedings: First International Symposium on Renewable Resources and the Economy of the North.* Ottawa: Association of Canadian Universities for Northern Studies, 1981.

GIDDINGS, LOUIS. *Ancient Men of the Arctic.* New York: Alfred A. Knopf, 1967.

HALL, EDWIN S., JR. *The Eskimo Storyteller: Folktales from Noatak, Alaska.* Knoxville, Tenn.: University of Tennessee Press, 1975.

HOPKINS, DAVID M., JOHN V. MATHEWS, JR., CHARLES E. SCHWEGER, and STEVEN B. YOUNG. *Paleoecology of Beringia.* New York: Academic Press, 1982.

IRVING, LAURENCE. *Arctic Life of Birds and Mammals.* New York: Springer-Verlag, 1972.

KENT, ROCKWELL. *Salamina.* New York: Harcourt, Brace and Company, 1935.

KERSTING, RUDOLF, editor. *The White World.* New York: Lewis, Scribner, 1902.

KIMBLE, GEORGE, and DOROTHY GOOD. *Geography of the Northlands.* Special Publication Number 32. New York: American Geographical Society, 1955.

LIVINGSTON, JOHN. *Arctic Oil: The Destruction of the North?* Toronto: Canadian Broadcasting Corporation, 1981.

LUBBOCK, BASIL. *The Arctic Whalers.* Glasgow: Brown, Son and Ferguson, Ltd., 1937.

MALAURIE, JEAN. *The Last Kings of Thule.* New York: E. P. Dutton, 1982.

MCCLINTOCK, FRANCIS. *The Voyage of the "Fox" in the Arctic Seas: A Narrative of the Discovery of the Fate of Sir John Franklin and His Companions.* London: John Murray, 1859.

MCGHEE, ROBERT. *Canadian Arctic Prehistory.* Toronto: Van Nostrand Reinhold Ltd., 1978.

MIRSKY, JEANNETTE. *To the Arctic!: The Story of Northern Exploration from Earliest Times to the Present.* Chicago: University of Chicago Press, 1970.

MORISON, SAMUEL ELIOT. *The European Discovery of America: The Northern Voyages, A.D. 500–1600.* New York: Oxford University Press, 1971.

MULLER, FRITZ. *The Living Arctic.* Toronto: Methuen, 1981.

NANSEN, FRIDTJOF. *In Northern Mists: Arctic Exploration in Early Times.* London: W. Heinemann, 1911.

NEATBY, L. H. *In Quest of the Northwest Passage.* New York: Thomas Y. Crowell, 1958.

NELSON, RICHARD. *Hunters of the Northern Ice.* Chicago: University of Chicago Press, 1969.

PARRY, WILLIAM EDWARD. *Journal of a Voyage for the Discovery of the North-West Passage from the Atlantic to the Pacific.* London: John Murray, 1821.

RASMUSSEN, KNUD. *The Intellectual Culture of the Iglulik Eskimo. Report of the Fifth Thule Expedition.* Vol. VII. Copenhagen: Gyldendalske Boghandel, 1929.

REMMERT, HERMANN. *Arctic Animal Ecology.* New York: Springer-Verlag, 1980.

SCORESBY, WILLIAM. *An Account of the Arctic Regions, with a History and Description of the Northern Whale-Fishery.* Vol. I. London: Archibald Constable, 1820.

STEFANSSON, VILJHALMUR. *The Friendly Arctic.* New York: Macmillan, 1921.

———. *My Life with the Eskimo.* New York: Macmillan, 1923.

VIBE, CHRISTIAN. *Arctic Animals in Relation to Climatic Fluctuation.* Copenhagen: C. A. Reitzels Forlag, 1967.

WEEMS, JOHN EDWARD. *Peary: The Explorer and the Man.* Boston: Houghton Mifflin Company, 1967.

ZASLOW, MORRIS, editor. *A Century of Canada's Arctic Islands: 1880–1980.* Ottawa: Royal Society of Canada, 1981.

REFERENCE

Ecological Sites in Northern Canada. David N. Nettleship and Pauline A. Smith, editors. Ottawa: Canadian Committee for the International Biological Programme, 1975.

The Exploration of Northern Canada. Alan Cooke and Clive Holland, editors. Toronto: The Arctic History Press, 1978.

Illustrated Glossary of Snow and Ice. Terence Armstrong et al., editors. Cambridge, England: Scott Polar Research Institute, 1973.

Pilot of Arctic Canada. Ottawa: Department of Energy, Mines and Resources, 1970.

INDEX

Able Creek, 43
Account of the Arctic Regions
    (Scoresby), 10, 239–40, 343
Adaptations to the land, failure of
    explorers', 360
Admiralty Inlet, 119, 123
Agape, 250
Akimiski Island, 93
Alaska, xix, 252
    polar bears in, 78–80
    seal hunting in, 76–78
    See also individual place names
Alernerk, 107
Algae, 8n, 123–24
Allen, John L., 294, 357
Anadyr, Gulf of, 155
Anaktuvuk Pass, 194–96
Anian, Strait of, 323, 325, 340, 412
Animals of Arctic, 30–31, 34–38
    adaptations of, 30, 67, 75

encounters with, 4, 13, 36–37, 72,
    78–79, 111–12, 118, 126–27
extinction of, 49–52
migrations of, 152–78
muskox, 42–75
narwhals, 119–51
pagophylic, 124
polar bears, 76–118
prehistoric, 51
route-finding by, 66, 98, 100, 268
sacred relationships with, 199–203
Umwelt (German) self-world,
    268–69, 313
unknowability of, 177, 269
See also individual animal names;
    Capture of animals
Archeology, arctic pre-history,
    50–52, 176n, 180–82, 187,
    412–13
Arctic Circle, 18n, 21

Arctic region
  boundaries, 18–19, 282
  changes in, xxvi, 290
  compasses in, 292
  cf. desert, xxiii, 30, 43, 96, 255, 258
  discoveries in, 282
    See also Explorers in Arctic
  historical ideas of, 16–17, 314–16
  perceptions of, 295
    See also Land; Landscape
  problems in, 417–18
Arctic Ocean
  fish adaptations to, 220n
  life in, 220
  map, description of, 281
  regions of, 219–20
  silence of, 138
Arctic Small Tool tradition
    (ASTt), 180–81
  campsites, 180, 187
Arktikós, 16
Aurora borealis, *See* Northern lights
Axel Heiberg Island, 403–4

Back, George, 361
Baffin, William, 335–37
Baffin Bay, 2, 217
Baffin Island, 119, 149, 156, 318, 330,
    401
Bailey Point, 69
Baker Creek, 43–44, 74–75
Banks Island, 42–75, 152, 299
Barents, Willem, 23–24, 110, 324
Barrow, Sir John, 343, 345
  version of Parry expedition, 356
Barrow, Point, 77
Barrow Strait, 96
Bear, grizzly (brown), xix, 85–86
Bear, polar, *see* Polar bear
Beaufort Sea, 252, 255, 387
Beechey Island, 362, 364n, 375
Belukha whales, 133
  See also Whales; Whaling

Bering, Vitus, 339
Bering Sea and Strait, 125–26,
    162–63, 165, 285, 339
Biological diversity in Arctic,
    xxiv–xxv, 24–25
Birds of Arctic, 120–21
  breeding colonies, 157
  migration routes of, 155, *156*
  migrations of, 151–78
  and muskox, 72
  pagophylic, 124
    See also individual bird names
Blessed Isles, *See Insulae Fortunatae*
Blubber
  of narwhals, 133
  of polar bears, 84, 87–88
  of whales, 3
Boas, Franz, 275, 287
  The Central Eskimo, 265
Bogen Valley, 81, 91–92
Bowhead whales, 2–4, 10, 166–67,
    184
  named Greenland right, 4
    See also Whaling
Brendan, Saint, 316
  arctic voyage, 316
Brody, Hugh, 275–76
Brönlund, Jörgen, 375–76
Brooks Range, xix, 28, 194
Brown, Robert, 82
Bureau of Land Management/Outer
    Continental Shelf study, 77n
Bylot, Robert, 335–37
  journals and charts, 336

Cabot, John, 320–21
Cabot, Sebastian, 323
Cairns, 290, 352, 375, 379
California
  Tule Lake migrations, 152–58, *156*
Campbell, Joseph, 275
Canada, *See* individual place names

Capture of arctic animals
  muskox, 74
  narwhal, 143
  polar bear, 112
Caribou, *170–71*, 254, 260
  Eskimo use of, 192–93
  mating and reproduction of, 169
  migration of, 168–71
Carpenter, Edmund, 197, 275–77,
  289
  Eskimo Realities, 194
Cartier, Jacques, 321–22
Cathay Company, 325–27
Cathedrals, 248–49
The Central Eskimo (Boas), 265
Change in Arctic, xxv–xxvii, 290,
  417–18
Cherry-Garrard, Apsley, 310–11
Chukchi Sea, 76–78, 85, 126, 285, 365
Church, Frederic Edwin, 245–47
  Icebergs, The (painting), 246
Churchill, 114–16
Churchill, Cape, 104, 115
Climate changes in Arctic, 173–75
Clothing of Eskimos, 190–93
Collinson, Richard, 377–79
Comock, 197–98
Concentrations of life in Arctic, 34,
  157
Conceptions of Arctic
  historical, 16–17, 314–16
  modern, 11–12
  See also Explorers in Arctic;
    Landscape
Conger, Fort, 368–70
Cook, Frederick, 310
Cook, James, 341
Copper Eskimos, 46–48
Copper Eskimo site (Kuptana,
  PjRa-18), 45, 52, 74–75
"Country of the mind," 295
Crane, sandhill, 44–45, 164
Crimson cliffs, 7–8

Crozier, Captain Francis, 379–380
Cumbrian (whaling ship), 1–10

Darkness, 183, 241–44
Davis, John, 327–33, 358
  accomplishments, 332–33
  meeting with Eskimos, 328
  The Seaman's Secrets, 332, 334
Davis Strait, 4, 205, 346
De Long, George, 171, 371n
Desire, xxi, xxvii, xxviii, 13, 255,
  257, 309, 311
de Veer, Gerrit, 324
DEW Line station, xxvii, 253, 262
Dezhnev, Cape (East Cape), 99, 339,
  371n, 413
Dignity, 151, 400, 402, 405–6
Discovery (ship), 335–36
Disassociation state in storm, 306–7
Discoveries of arctic lands, 282
  See also Explorers in Arctic
Diseases of Eskimos from Europeans,
  7, 10
Dogs, xxvii, 48, 198, 286, 309, 377,
  384, 406
Dorset culture, xxv, 182–83
  art and culture, 107, 244
  carvings, 182–83
  "flying" bear, 107
  See also Pre-Dorset culture
Dovekie, 121, 133n
Dreams, xxi, xxviii, 14, 405, 414
Duby, Georges, 248–49
Dunbar, Max, 219

East Cape. *See* Dezhnev, Cape
Ecosystems of Arctic, 25–26, 31, 33
  "stressed" and "accident prone,"
    32–33
Edmund Walker Island, 18
Electronic tracking of bears, 87
Elizabeth I, 325, 405–6
Ellen (ship), 330, 332

Ellesmere Island, xxi, xxii, 209, 281, 299, 368–70

Enterprise, HMS, 378

Erebus, HMS, 361–63, 379

Erichsen, Mylius, 375–76

Eric the Red, 317–18

Eriks Fiord, 317–18

Eskimo Realities (Carpenter), 194

Eskimos

    arrival in North America, 178–203

      See also Arctic Small Tool tradition; Pre-Dorset; Dorset; Thule

    Baffin Island contacts, 382

    caribou, use of, 192–93

    carvings, 107, 181, 182–83

    clothing, 190–93, 265

    Comock, 197–98

    contemporary change among, xxvi–xxvii, 195, 402

    Copper Eskimos, 46–48

    Davis meeting with, 328–29

    derivation of word, 418

    dietary changes of, xxvi

    diseases from Europeans, 7, 10

    and dogs, xvii, 48, 198

    and Europeans, 6–7

      diseases from, 7, 10

      encounters with, 328–29, 330, 346, 379–80

      escorts to, 384

    exploration of Arctic, 382

    historic period, 188–203

    and hunting, 199, 260, 268–69

    implements, 189–94

    industrial development, effects of, xxvi–xxvii, 402

    and land, 257, 360

      See also Land; Landscape

    language, 274–77

      See also Land; Landscape

    legends of polar bears, 113–14

      See also Legends

    maps by, *288*, 289

    mechanical ability of, 194

    "memory culture," 273

    and meteorites, 8

    narwhals, killing of, 133

    Nunamiut, 194–96

      writings about, 419

    oral tradition, 368n

      Pingok Island, 263–64

    obligations of, 189n, 199, 200

    philosophy of,

      acceptance of existing reality, 411

      depression (*perlerorneq*), 243

      cf. Europeans, 411

      fear, 7, 201

      knowledge of darkness in humans, 242–43

      and winter, 242–44

      See also Wisdom; Patience

    physical characteristics of, 418

    Polar Eskimos, 92, 188, 243, 346, 382

    and polar bears, 89, 108, 113–14

    pre-historic period, 178–88

    route-finding by, 290–92

    sacred relationships with animals, 199–203

    Sadlermiut, 188–89

    Shaman light (*quamaneq*), 243, 297

    sleds, 193

    stories, importance of, 270–73, 296, 297–98, *See also* Legends

    trade with whalers, 6–7, 73, 194–95

    tribes, *191*

    walrus ivory, use of, 193

Explorers in Arctic, 308–54

    Austrian, 368

    American, 366–71

    Chinese, 339

    comparison to astronauts, 308

contributions to arctic
knowledge, 354
cooperation between countries,
368
courage and determination of, 308
Danish, 375–76
Dutch, 324
encounters with Eskimos, 328–29,
330, 346, 379–80
English, 320, 330
excitement of first trip, 392–93
French, 321–23
Greeks, 314, 340
Irish, 315–16
motivations for, 309–12
motives and results examined,
358
mission and purpose of, 359
Norse, 317–18
Portuguese, 322
Russian, 323, 339
struggles against elements, 359–60
See also individual explorers'
names
Extinction of animals, 49–52
Pleistocene extinction, 51

Failures of British expeditions,
360–65
Fairbanks, 54, 80, 241–42
Fata morgana, 238–39
Fear in Eskimo experience, 7, 201
Field biology, limitations of, 62n, 94,
269
Finley, Kerry, 149
Flaherty, Robert, 197–98
Fox, arctic, 49, 266–67
Fox Island, 390
Fram (ship), 372–73
Franklin, Sir John, 261, 342, 373–74
fatal voyage, 359, 361–62, 379–80
search for, 363–65, 377–78
Franz Josef Land, 368

Frobisher, Martin, 326–27, 368
Fuca, Juan de. *See* Valerianos,
Apostolos
Fur trapping, 337, 338
Future of Arctic, xxviii

Gabriel (ship), 326
Gambell, 407
Geese, snow, 32, 33, 152–56, 313
migrations, Alaska to California,
152–54, *156*
Geist, Otto, 193
Geography of Arctic,
continuity of, 281
imprecision of, 282–83
distortion of on Mercator
projection, 280
early maps, 281–82
Geography of the mind, 294
Giddings, Louis, 179–80
Gilbert, Sir Humphrey, 325
Glaciers, xxii, 208–9
God, as light, 248
Godthåb, 328–29, 330
Gog and Magog, Gogmagog, 17–18
Gray, David, 63
Great Bear (Ursa Major), 16–17
Great Plain of the Koukdjuak, 156,
313
Greek conceptions of Arctic, 16–17
"Land of the Hyperboreans," 315
Greely, Adolphus, xxi, 368–70
failure of expedition, 370
Greenland, 236, 281, 286, 327–30,
370
Danish exploration of, 375–76
earliest maps of, 309–10
early explorations, 317
first settlements, 317
Godthåb, 328–29, 330
icebergs, ice cap, 208–9
lost colonies, 240

Greenland, (*cont.*)
  Mercator projection maps, 280
  polar bears, 93
Greenland right whales. *See*
    Bowhead whales
Griper, HMS, 347, 353
Gull, ivory, 149–50
Gunn, Anne, 60, 72

Haines, John, 170
Hansson, Rasmus, 91–92
Hare, arctic, 44–45
Harington, Richard, 55
Haycock, Maurice, 224–28
Hazen Strait, 15
Hearne, Samuel, 342, 373–74
Heat retention in animals,
  Allen's rule, 67
  Bergmann's rule, 67
  muskox, 67–68
  polar bears, 84, 87–90
Hecla, HMS, 347, 351, 353
Henrichsen, Poul, 54–55
Hibernation of animals, 24, 90
Hickey, Cliff, 75
Holocene, 38, 174n
Hudson, Henry, 335–38
Hudson's Bay Company, 73, 337,
    361, 365
Humboldt glacier, xxiii, 209
Hunting, 77–78
  methods of Eskimos, 108–9,
    260–61, 268–69
  obligations of, 199, 200
  understanding by Eskimos,
    199–203
  walrus, 407–15
Hyperborea, 17, 315

Ice, 165–66, 204–24
  appearance of, 210
  behavior of, 210
  dangers to ships from, 214–19,
    262, 304–5, 359, 371

edges, 79, 123, 132, 223, 282
effects of winds and currents on,
    212
as habitat, 221–22
freezing point of, 210
ice islands, 209
ivu (Eskimo), leaping ice, 176
open water, 213–14
pack ice, 211, 214–16
structure of, 209
tectonic activity of, 213
varieties and patterns of, 212–13
See also Icebergs
Icebergs, 204–10, 216n, 244–51
  cf. cathedrals, 204, 248–49
  colors of, 207
  composition of, 207–8
  descriptions of, 206
  cf. mountains, 245
  size of, 207–8
  tabular, 209
    Brendan encounter with, 316
    Davis encounter with, 329
Icebergs, The (painting), 245–47
Ice floes, dangers of, 120, 214–19,
    304–5
Ice Haven, 324
Ice islands, 209
Iceland, 236
  early explorations of, 316–17
  sagas, 307–8, 318
Icy Cape, 341, 352, 362
Ilingnorak Ridge, xix–xx, 203
Ilira (Eskimo), fearful awe, 7, 201
Imagination and landscape, xxvii, 13,
    272–73, 294
Industrial development in Arctic,
    xxvi, 397–99, 418
In Northern Mists (Nansen), 371
Insulae Fortunatae (Blessed Isles),
    283, 315, 319
International Polar Year, first, 369

International Union for the Conservation of Nature and Natural Resources (IUCN), 81, 87
Inuit Circumpolar Conference, 284n
Investigator, HMS, 45–47, 48, 261, 300, 375
Irish imramha, 307–8, 315–16
Israel, Edward, xxi, 370

Jahner, Elaine, 273–74
James Bay, 18n, 27, 81, 93, 335
Jeanette (ship), destruction of, 371
Jelinek, Arthur, 50–51
Jingfors, Kent, 68, 70
Jones Islands, 77, 253
Jonkel, Charles, 106
Journal of a Voyage for the Discovery of a Northwest Passage from the Atlantic to the Pacific (Parry), 355
Journals of arctic expeditions, 420
  comparison of several, 358–59, 373–75

Kaffeklubben Island, 282
Kane, Elisha Kent, 366–68
Kane Basin, 368
Kappia (Eskimo), fear of violence, 7, 201
Karluk (ship), 262
Kayak, 185, 229, 382
Kent, Rockwell, 390–92
Ki-lin of China
  compared to narwhal, 150–51
Killer whales. *See* Orcas
King William Island, 358, 365, 379
Kokogiag (Eskimo), many-legged bear, legends, 113–14
Kuptana Site (PjRa18), 45–49, 52, 74–75

Labrador Sea, 204
Lancaster Sound, 119–52, 346

Natural Site of World Heritage Quality, 121n
Land
  animal perception of, 268
  integration with, 200–201, 260, 264–66, 279
  and language, 277–78
  obligations toward, 228
  qualities of, xxiii, xxvii, 5, 228, 390, 392, 411
Landscape, 255–56
  and imagination, xxviii, 13–14, 257, 271–72, 294, 391, 414
  and language, 277–78
  and story, 272–73
  spiritual, 273–74, 295
Landscape painting, *See* Painting
Land-use and occupancy studies, 264–65
Language
  aboriginal, 274–75
    Hopi, studies by Whorf, 274, 277–78
  Eskimo
    characteristics of, 274, 276–77
    Inuktitut, studies of by Carpenter, 275–76
    loss of, 277
    "memory culture," 263
L'Anse aux Meadows, 318–19
Larsen, Thor, 102–3, 104
Legends, 308
  of narwhal tusks, 142–43
  of polar bears, 94–95, 113–14
  of unicorn and narwhal, 140–41
Lemmings, 35–37, 49, 160, 175, 240
Lévi-Strauss, Claude, 275
Light, 23, 248–49
Light in Arctic, 224–51
  contrast in, 240–41
  fluctuation of, 419
  ice, water, and light, 226
  light-fall, 29–30

Light in Arctic, (*cont.*)
  mirages and images, 23–24, 236–39
  northern lights (aurora borealis), 232–36
  and painting, 225–27
  qualities of, xx, 226, 227
  refraction, reflection on ice of, 231
  and skies, 229
Little Ice Age, 186, 382
Ljungblad, Don, 125–26
Longspur, Lapland, 72, 414
Lok, Michael, 325–27
Loons, 224
Lore of the Unicorn (Shepard), 141–42
Luminist tradition, 227

Mackenzie, Alexander, 342
Mackenzie King Island, 15
Mamen, Cape, 15
Make Prayers to the Raven (Nelson), 265
Mandeville, Sir John, *Travels*, 320
Maps, arctic
  early maps, 281–82, 333
  Eskimo, 286–89, *288*
  increased information for, 342, 344
  Mercator projection, distortion in, 280
  necessity of for travel, 279–80
  perspectives of, 280
  Ptolemaic cartography, 319–20
  of shorelines, waterways, 359
  sky maps, 319
  varieties of, 280–81
  Zeno maps, 333
  See also map section beginning on page 421 and maps on pages xxii, 19, 46, 82, 122, 156, 174, 191, 223, 231, 253, 288, 331, 341, 369 and 381
McGhee, Robert, 181, 184

M'Clintock, Francis, 363, 364, 365, 375
M'Clure, Captain Robert, 45–46, 261, 287, 375
  receives Admiralty prize for Northwest passage, 364
Melville Island, 13, 299, 301, 375
Mental maps, 295
  See also Land; Landscape; Route-finding
Mercy Bay, 47
Metabolism in arctic animals, 30–31
  of muskox, 66–67, 69
  of polar bears, 87–88
Meta Incognita, 405–6
Meteorites used by Eskimos, 8
Migration of animals, 152–78
  birds
    at Bering Sea, 162–63
    at Tule Lake, California, 152–57, *156*
  "breathing of the land," 162
  caribou, 168–71
  cycles
    annual, 160
    seasonal, 166, 382–83
  "familiar area," 158
  fish, 164
  "home range," 159
  large scale, 158
  numbers, 120–21, 164
  rhythms of life, 171
  seals, 166
  seasonal cycles, 166
  timing, 159–60
  whales, 164–65
  Y-K Delta, 163–64
Migration of humans
  America, 178–203
  archaeological findings, 179
  Arctic Small Tool tradition, 180–81
  Bering land bridge, 178–79

Dorset period, 182–83
Pre-Dorset period, 181
Thule cultural period, 180
waves of immigration, 179–80
Mining in Arctic, 397
Mirages and images in Arctic,
   236–41
  effect on travelers, 238–39
  fata morgana, 237–39
  inverted images, 237
  Novaya Zemlya images, 24
  resemblances, 240–41
  superior images, 236
Mooneshine (ship), 327–33
Movements of life in Arctic, 160
Muir, John, 79
Muskox (*Ovibos moschatus*), 42–75
  in Alaska, 56, 74
  and birds, 72
  in Canada, 56
  capture of, 74
  description of, 54, 57–60
  defensive formation, 61
  eyes, 59
  gait, 59–60
  in Greenland, 56
  habitat, 70–71
  hair, 57–58
  herd structure, 62–63
  hunting and butchering of, 48
  mating and reproduction of, 63–65
  metabolism, 66–67
  Oomingmag (Eskimo), muskox,
    57
  origins of, 55
  population, 49
  route-finding by, 66
  skeletal debris of, 45

Nanaskivik Mine, 397
Nansen, Fridtjof, 311, 370–73
  theory of polar drift, 371
  In Northern Mists, 371

Nares Strait, 212
niches, 25, 38
Narwhal (*Monodon monoceros*),
   119–51
  in Bering Strait, 126–27
  capture of, 143
  classification of, 133
  color, 131
  as "corpse whale," 129
  description of, 130–31, 135–36
  feeding behavior, 134–35
  future of, 148–49
  habitat of, 132
  and ice, 132–33
  and *ki-lin*, 150–51
  killing of by Eskimos, 133n
  mating and reproduction of, 133
  movements of, 134–35
  name of, 128–29
  and oil exploration, 128, 148
  origins of, 136
  physiology, 136–37
  as prey, 84, 132
  in savssats, 132–33
  senses, 138–39
  skin, uses of, 148
  tusks, 129, 142–48, 327
  and unicorn, 142
  "whale lice" on, 134
Nature and Culture (Novak), 245
Nelson, Richard, 94, 192, 270,
   275–76
  Make Prayers to the Raven, 265
Nettleship, David, 121n, 155–56
Newfoundland,
  early discoveries, 320–24
Nome, 164, 167
Northeast Passage, 324–25
Northern lights (aurora borealis),
   232–36
  causes, 233–35
  Eskimo descriptions of, 232
  scale, 233

Northernmost point of land, 282–83
North Georgia Gazette and Winter Chronicle, 349, 355, 406
   See also Parry, William
North Pole, 16–19
   Chandler Circle, 18
   Geographic, 16, 18
   Geomagnetic, 18
   Magnetic, 18, *19*
   Pole of Inaccessibility, 19–20
   quest for, 335, 342n, 365–66, 368
      Peary's, 370, 371, 377, 384–85
North Star (Polaris), 16
North Water, 3, 214
Northwest Passage, 205, 308–54, *341*
   Admiralty prize for discovery of, 341–42
   awarded M'Clure, 364
Norwegians,
   early arctic explorations, 317
   Greenland settlement, 317
   Newfoundland settlement, 318
Novak, Barbara, *Nature and Culture*, 245
Novaya Zemlya, 323, 324, 335
   Novaya Zemlya images, 24

Oases in Arctic (summer), 34
Oceanographer (ship), 77
Oil and gas in Arctic
   drilling for oil, 417
   effect of drilling in Alaska, 121, 128, 393–97
   search for, 290
Oodaaq, 21, 283
Oomingmaq (Eskimo), 57
Open polar seas, search for, 365–67
Open water in Arctic, 213, 22, *223*
Orcas, 167
Øritsland, Nils, 87–88, 116n
Oscillations of life in Arctic, 175–76

Outer Continental Shelf Environmental Assessment Program, 77n, 262
Owl, snowy, xx, 35, 44–45, 242, 272

Painting,
   in the Arctic, 225–26
   Icebergs, The, 245–47
   luminist tradition, 227
Parry, William, 10, 230, 346–54, 366
   at North Magnetic Pole, 348
   Journal of a Voyage for the Discovery of a Northwest Passage from the Atlantic to the Pacific, 355
Parry Channel, 184
Passage to Cathay, *See* Northwest Passage
Patience, 102, 176, 261
Peary, Robert, 283, 310, 370–73
   at North Pole, 384–85
   comparison to Stefansson, 386, 389
   journals, 385–86
   perils of journeys, 377
Peary Land, 70, 180, 184
Permafrost, 28–29, 210
Peter the Great, 324, 339
Pike, Warburton, 373–74
Pingok Island, 252–74, *253*, 302
   aboriginal history, 262–64
   animal life on, 254, 266–67
   birds on, 259
   derivation of name, 262–63
   early history, 261–62
   Eskimo oral history, 263–64
   excavation of early homes, 263
   landscape of, 255
   location of, 253
Place, sense of, from Tuan, 278–79
Plankton in Arctic Ocean, 77, 220
Pleistocene, 51, 85, 178

Polar bear (*Ursus maritimus*),
   76–118
  activities of, 79
  blubber and insulation, 84, 87–89
  color, 84, 85n
  cubs, 91–92
  denning behavior, 81–82, 89–92
  description of, 78–79, 86
  diet, 86
  cf. Eskimos, 89, 108
  fear of orcas, walrus by, 109
  feeding and social behavior, 104
  fur, 84–85
  gait, 83
  habitat, 18n
  heat retention in, 84, 87–90
  hunting behavior of, 84, 94–95,
    99–100, 102, 108
  as left-pawed, 94
  legends of, 113–14
  mating and reproduction of,
    90–92, 105
  metabolism of, 87
  nose, 94–95, 98–99
  population, 115
  predation on humans by, 109, 110–
    11, 114–15
  radio collaring of, 117–18
  route finding by, 98
  size, 82–83
  sleeping behavior, 88–89
  tracks of, 97–98
  as traveler (*pisugtooq*), *82*, 92–93
  and zoos, 85n, 112
Polar Bear Specialist Group of the
  IUCN, 81
Polar drift,
  discovery by Nansen, 371–73
Polaris Mine, 397
Pollution control, 417
Polynynas, 213, 214, 222, 368
  See also Open water

Pond's Bay, Pond Inlet, 1, 11, 49
"Pool of Corpses," 129
Pre-Dorset culture, 181–82
Prey/Predator studies, 99–100
Prince Patrick Island, 365
Prudhoe Bay, 253, 393

Qillarsuaq, 381–82
Quantum physics, 250

Radar stations, xxvii
Rapoport, Amos, 296
Rasmussen, Knud, 201, 380–81, 384
Rensselaer Harbor, 366
Resolute, 224
Resolute, HMS, 46, 300, 364
Resourcefulness in Arctic, 94–96,
    193, 194, 334, 367
Rhythms of life in Arctic, 171–76
  climatic change, 173–74
  indigenous rhythm, 176–77
  oscillations, 175–76
  sea-ice formation cycle, 174
Robin, 160n
Robus, Martha, 70, 72
Roosevelt (ship), 384
Ross, James, 18
Ross, Sir John, 10, 346
Ross, W. Gillies, 10
Route-finding, 66, 98, 100, 290–92
  See also Migration
Russia, 20, 80, 155, 220, 324, 335,
    339–40, 371n, 412–13

Sabine, Cape, xxi, 370, 382
Sadlerochit River, 68, 70–71
Saint Lawrence Island, 165, 407–15
Salmon, 164
Samis (Lapps), 20n, 186
Sanderson's Hope, 330
Savssats, 104, 132–33
Schledermann, Peter, 187

Schweinsburg, Ray, 93, 96, 108
Schweitzer, Albert, 411
Scoresby, William, 112, 145–46, 214,
    345
    Account of the Arctic Regions,
        10, 239–40, 343
Scott, Robert, 310–11
Scurvy, 334
Seals, 13, 122
    and ice, 124
    hunting of, 76–78
    as prey, 84, 100–101
The Seaman's Secrets (Davis), 332,
    334
Seasons, 27
Senses used by Eskimos, 260, 291
Seton, Ernest Thompson, 56, 373–74
Sevoukuk Mountain, 407, 412
Shamans, 107, 201, 241
    shaman light (*quamaneq*), 243,
        297
Shepard, Odell, *Lore of the
    Unicorn,* 141–42
Shipwrecks in Arctic, 214–19, 262,
    359–61, 371n
    See also Explorers in Arctic
Silverman, Helen, 135
Skies in Arctic, 229–30
    sky maps, 291–92
Sled, Eskimo, 193
Smith, Tom, 99
Snowblindness, 360
Snow, 68, 221
Soil, 25–27
Solar arcs and halos, *231*
Solar mirages, 23–24
Soodoc (ship), 204, 244–45
Sounds in ocean depth, 138–39
Southampton Island, 188, 189, 289
Space, concept of, from Tuan,
    278–79
Spiritual landscape, 273–74, 295
Stars, in Arctic, 16, 22

Starvation Cove, 380
Stefansson, Vilhjalmur, 48, 56,
    238–39, 262, 386–89
    lack of leadership, 387
    life after return from Arctic,
        387–89
    cf. Peary, 386, 389
    social Darwinist, 387
Steller, Georg Wilhelm, 339
Stirling, Ian, 99, 102
Story,
    importance of, 270–71
    interpreter of region, 272–73
    local landscapes revealed, 296
    "place fixing" by, 297–98
Sun in Arctic,
    arcs and halos, 230, *231*
    energy from, 29–30, 33, 234–35
    position of, 20, 419
        in summer, 21–22
        in winter, 22, 23
    sun dogs, 230
Sunneshine and *Mooneshine* (ships),
    327–33
Survival preparations, 302–3
Svalbard, 80, 81, 110, 281
Svavarsson, Gardar, 317
Sverdrup, Otto, 56, 372, 389
Swinton, George, 182

Taimyr Peninsula, 55
Takin, 56
Teal, John, 56
Temperate-zone attitudes, 11–12, 20,
    220
Terror, HMS, 361–63, 379
Thank God Harbor, 368n
Thesiger, Wilfred, 39
Thomassen, Jørn, 90, 91–92
Thompson, D'Arcy Wentworth, 147
Thomsen River, 42–44, 48
Thorne, Robert, 322
Thule (Uummannaq), 188, 286, 384

Thule culture, xxv, 180, 184–85, 285
Tides, 252
Time in Arctic, 171–73
Tolerance, 313–14
Tôrnârssuk (Eskimo), "the one who gives power," polar bear, 113–14
Trade between Eskimos and whalers, 6–7, 73, 194
Trade routes in Arctic, 47
Trade, 6–7, 73
Trans-Alaska pipeline, 393–97
Travels (Mandeville), 320
Trees of Arctic, 28, 29
    tree line, 27–28, 184
    in tundra, 29
Tropical ecosystems, 31
Tuan, Yi-Fu, 278–79
Tule Lake, 152–58
Tundra
    biological detail in, xxiv–xxv, 259–60
    birds on, xix–xx
    of Pingok island, 254
    soil of, 26
Turner, Frederick Jackson, 256
Tusks of narwhals, 129, 142–48
    description of, 143–44
    male display of, 146
    purpose, 145
    trading of, 142
    use of by Eskimos, 147–48
Twilight in Arctic, 22–23
Twin Otter, 299, 405

Uexküll, Jakob von, 268n
Umiak, 184, 185
Umwelt (German), self-world, 268–69, 313
Unicorn, 140–43
United Nations, 121
Uspenskii, Savva, 80
Utukok River, 197

Valerianos, Apostolos (Juan de Fuca), 340
Vancouver, George, 342
Verrazano, Giovanni da, 321
Vibe, Christian, 132–33, 173–75, 286
Victoria Island, 47, 48

Walrus, 164, 165, 347
    carnivorous (*angeyeghaq*), 124
    danger from, 124–45
    hunting of, 407–15
    ivory use, 193
Water bear, 172
Watson, J. Wreford, 294
Wealth, 10, 13–14, 311–13, 337
West Water, 2, 3, 10, 214
Weyprecht, Karl, 369
Whalebone Alley, 412–13
Whale-fisher's bight, 337, 367
"Whale lice," 134
Whales, 166. *See also* individual whale names; Whaling
Whaling, whalers, 1–10, 218, 262, 338, 343–44
    blubber, value of, 3
    crews and ice, 218
    Cumbrian (ship), 1–10
    daily life, 9–10
    trade with Eskimos, 6–7, 73, 194–95
Wheatear, 167–68
White-out, 239, 291
Whorf, Benjamin Lee, 274–75, 277–78
Willoughby, Hugh, 323
Willows, 28, 29, 71
Winter Harbor, 349–52, 364, 375
Winter in Arctic, 221, 241–44, 349–54
    by Parry expedition, 349–54
    darkness, 242
    depression, 243
    effect on life, 241–44

Winter in Arctic (*cont.*)
  fears magnified, 243
  preparations for, by animals, 34–35
Wisdom, xxvii, 38–40, 248
  of Eskimos, 38–41, 298–99, 411
Wolf, xix, 191, 268, 350, 393
  population wiped out, 49
Wrangel Island, 32, 33, 81, 155, *156*,
    157, 339, 371n, 388
Wright, John Kirtland, 367

Y-K (Yukon-Kuskokwim) Delta,
    163–64
Yttygran Island, 412
Yukon territory, 292–93

Zoos, capture of animals for,
  muskox, 74
  narwhals, 143
  polar bears, 112